DICTIONARY
of
BATTLES

DICTIONARY
of
BATTLES

The world's
key battles
from 405 BC
to today

General Editor
DAVID CHANDLER

HENRY HOLT AND COMPANY
NEW YORK

First published in the United States in 1988 by
Henry Holt and Company, 115 West 18th Street,
New York, New York 10011.

Published in Canada by Fitzhenry & Whiteside Limited,
195 Allstate Parkway, Markham, Ontario L3R 4T8

Library of Congress Cataloging in Publication Data

The Illustrated Dictionary of Battles.

1. Battles — Dictionaries. 2. Military history —
Dictionaries. 3. Military art and science — Dictionaries.
I. Chandler, David G.
D25. A2144 1988   904'7   87—12046
ISBN 0-8050-0441-6

This book was conceived, designed and produced by The
Paul Press Ltd, 41/42 Berners Street, London W1P 3AA

General Editor: D.G Chandler
Section Authors: Matthew Bennett, D.G. Chandler, J.L.
Collins, Nicholas Hooper, J.L. Pimlott, J.G. Warry, Peter
Young
Associate Authors: Royston Boss, Warren W. Hassler Jnr,
Nicholas Kingwell, John Patrick Scrivenor
Cartography: Map Consultants
Picture Research: John and Diana Moore (Military
Archive and Research Services)

Art Director: Stephen McCurdy
Editorial Director: Jeremy Harwood

*Producing a book of the complexity of The Dictionary of
Battles is never plain sailing, but the task has been made
easier by the whole-hearted enthusiasm of the section and
associate authors. The latter contributed the following to the
book. Royston Boss (Chapter Two) Taginae and Casilinum;
Nicholas Kingwell (Chapter Three) Bosworth, Sluys; Professor
Warren W. Hassler (Chapter Six) Railways, Communications
and Warfare, Antietam, Buena Vista, Chancellorsville,
Gettysburg, Hampton Roads, Manila Bay, Vicksburg; Patrick
Scrivenor (Chapter Seven) The Rise of Air Power, Great
Commanders of the Two World Wars, First World War
battles. In addition, David Chandler wrote Cambrai and
Colenso; Peter Young wrote Naseby. The Paul Press would
like to thank Rob Cowley of Henry Holt and Company for
his help and advice and, above all, David Chandler, for his
boundless enthusiasm and good humour during the creation of
this book.
Italics in the main text indicate a cross reference to a battle
entry.*

First American Edition

Printed in Great Britain

10 9 8 7 6 5 4 3 2 1

ISBN 0-8050-0441-6

Contents

Introduction

David G Chandler

Homo Sapiens has never been a pacifist by nature. Over the three and a half millenia of recorded history, it has been calculated that the human race has known barely 292 years of supposed freedom from the horrors of organized warfare — and that estimate only takes into account "civilized" peoples and societies whose activities are known from surviving records and writings. In very primitive societies the condition of what would now be called "guerrilla warfare" was almost certainly endemic. Alas, the 18th-century philosopher Jean-Jacques Rousseau's idealistic concept of a happy and almost tension-free "state of nature" is less likely to have been the case than Thomas Hobbes' grimmer 17th-century view of human life as having been ". . . nasty, brutish and short." In our own generation, the proud boast that Western Europe has enjoyed over four decades of so-called peace, since the end of the Second World War, that the American and Soviet super-powers have avoided direct collision and that there has been no recourse since 1945 to nuclear warfare cannot disguise the fact that this bedevilled planet has been the scene of well over 200 definable wars since 1945.

At the same time, the innate pugnacity and aggressiveness of man — linked, no doubt, to the creative and inquisitive drives that form his saving graces and distinguish him from other denizens of the animal kingdom — exert a compelling fascination. War can bring out the best in mankind as well as the worst. But, as General William Tecumseh Sherman stated after the US Civil War, "War is hell" — a fact of which he certainly should have been fully aware following the harsh treatment he meted out to large areas of the Confederacy during his celebrated "march to the sea" in 1864–5.

The aims behind this book

This book sets out to study the perennial subject of man at war, seeking to analyze the successive stages the art and science of warfare have passed through from the time of ancient Greece to the present day. What becomes clear is that, as Thomas Hardy described it all too accurately in *The Dynasts*, war makes ". . . rattling good history", while ". . . Peace is poor reading". The Prussian military philosopher, Carl von Clausewitz, confirms this in his description of warfare as a "passionate drama", and so it is to be sure. Few other subjects possess such tension or excitement: great armies and ideas triumphant or crushed, and whole nations and peoples, even philosophies, indelibly affected by the result of vast conflicts — the outcome of which are sometimes decided by a seemingly minute

issue — ". . . the single drop of water," as Napoleon wrote, "that causes the bucket to flow over". No person with a feeling for history can be wholly immune from the grim fascination of war, although naturally the degree of interest and commitment varies enormously even amongst declared historians. A few self-styled idealists occasionally try to connote such an interest with militarism. This is in no way the case, any more than the study of medicine may be deemed to conceal a secret desire to see the propagation of disease. As I wrote almost a quarter of a century ago in the Introduction to my first published book, ". . . no one would deny that all wars and battles are regrettable acts of human folly, causing unjustifiable agony and distress to combatants and non-combatants alike – but these considerations should not preclude their serious study, if only to avoid the mistakes of the past which made such tragedies inevitable. If battles can be described as the punctuation marks on the pages of history when the study of their causes, course and results must be vital to any understanding of our common European heritage." A quarter of a century later, I see no reason to change this statement — except that, with the acquisition of greater knowledge, I would expand the final phrase to encompass the entire human experience, heedless of geographical, religious, racial or political limitations. For such is the scope and canvas covered by this new book.

The causes of wars

Political philosophers, sociologists and psychologists have argued at length whether war springs from civilization, with which they claim it shares a common origin, or from the weaknesses of human nature. There is little doubt that warfare has become more intensified as civilization has progressed, but if this school of thought is correct, then war can surely be eliminated like a disease. On the other hand, if human nature is at fault — and organized warfare certainly pre-dated the emergence of nation-states — then it follows that the prosecution of modern war is a reversion to innate barbarism, which only an intensive and long process of education for peace can hope to eradicate. The argument continues to this day, but everyone has been forced to admit that war and historical change are closely associated. The verdict of war has continuously been the deciding factor in historical evolution — Greek victory in the Persian Wars saved Western Europe from an Asiatic dictatorship, for instance — and the rise and fall of almost all great empires has been associated with military success or failure. When all other forms of decision have failed, war has always been the final arbiter, the acid test; indeed, some would see in it the "hand of God" although in not a few cases "might" has triumphed over "right", at least in the short-term.

The effects of war

Practically everybody agrees that war is basically evil and wholly wasteful, but many great thinkers have differed on the totality of its wickedness. On the one hand, Professor Arnold Toynbee declared that "War is the proximate cause of the breakdown of every civilization", the solvent of moral and material ideas. Nations initially raise forces for self-defence, but, all too often, these justifiable aspirations develop by leaps and bounds until they propagate a resurgence of militaristic ideals — and these a desire to impose a *Pax Romana* on other countries, which in turn leads to war — the very object the original troops were recruited to avoid. On the other hand, Professor Nef and the German Werner Sombat believe that war has a genuine value as a stimulus to social and technical development: the American Munsford wrote that "the machine was propagated by war", claiming that the adoption of gunpowder led to the development of the iron industries of the world and thence to the age of the machine. Few would deny that many war-time inventions have inspired valuable peace-time developments; many surgical and medicinal techniques have been developed to repair the damage of war — the discovery of penicillin by Sir Alexander Fleming or the perfection of blood transfusion and plastic surgery are just three examples — while German rocket research during the Second World War helped open up space and led to the creation of an entirely new field of human knowledge. Thus, even war has had its uses, although all the benefits it has indirectly conferred could equally well have been developed in time of peace — at least eventually. The tragedy has always been that, as man's constructive powers have grown, so in proportion have his powers of destruction — but fortunately his awareness of his ability to destroy himself has never been so acute.

The study of war

How can the study of military history contribute towards the encouragement of peace? The value of any form of historical study has been variously assessed by different authorities. The Greek philosopher, Dionysius of Halicarnasus (40–8 BC) once described history as "philosophy teaching by example"; on the other hand, the great American industrialist, Henry Ford, once went on record as saying "History is bunk". Both assertions contain an element of truth as far as the study of military history is concerned. As applied to many other things in life, true value depends on correct application. A superficial study of the subject may easily lead to delusions involving glory and military aggrandisement in emulation of the great captains of the past, but a detailed study of casualty lists, of

atrocities, economic dislocation and the general misery and waste (both human and material) caused by war can only convince a sane man of its utter folly. The lessons of history are there for those able to read them, and although the old adage "history never repeats itself" is true in so far as exact conditions never recur twice, close resemblances between events separated in time can be traced, and a great deal can be learnt from a real knowledge of the past and the experience it reveals. To prove the point, let us mention three instances: Napoleon drew from his studies of classical antiquity to lead the Army of Reserve over the Alps into Italy in the spring of 1800; the experts declared that such a feat was impossible, but Napoleon was aware that Hannibal, plus a contingent of elephants, had safely accomplished it in 218 BC, and where such huge beasts could travel, French soldiers and guns could certainly follow. On the other hand, Hitler ignored the lessons of the past in June 1941 when he launched the Nazi invasion of Russia as Napoleon had done 129 years earlier; the dire experiences that befell Charles XII of Sweden when he undertook a similar enterprise in 1709 were disregarded by both men and in the end both ventures ended in similar catastrophe. The lesson would seem to be that the experience of the past should be treated with profound, but critical, respect by governments and soldiers alike.

The student of military affairs, must, however, avoid one dangerous pitfall. It is both insufficient and wholly deceptive to regard war as an isolated phenomenon. Clausewitz rightly stressed that "War is the continuation of policy by other means": it is impossible, he says, to understand the significance of any war or particular battle unless the political circumstances — the ambitions or fears that led to the collision between governments and then peoples — are kept clearly in mind. However, even this enlarged scope of study is not enough. Besides the study of the general situation and the policies of the states concerned, it is equally important to take into account the relationship between governments and their armies, the military theories currently in vogue (and their origins), the types of weapons in use and the general state of technological development and their effects on tactical organization and the actual methods of fighting, not forgetting the information, communication and supply systems available at the time. The implications of terrain, climate and weather are equally significant. Only when this awesome list of factors is kept in balanced perspective can the true lessons of military history be extricated and evaluated. Every separate major phase in the development of the art of war must therefore be studied in relation to its own particular environment, for each successive social system has produced its own adaptations and characteristics. The series of chapters that follow examine each broad period in turn in general terms, studying certain aspects in special sections, and adding a selection of examples to add illustration and understanding to precept.

CHAPTER ONE
The Classical World

The battles in this chapter of this book all belong to the period conventionally described by historians as "Classical Antiquity" – but the nature of military development means that the story must be taken further back to the even more ancient arts of war as developed in the Near East. The reason for this is simple, since the impact of events in Egypt and Western Asia on later developments in south-east Europe is inescapable.

Unfortunately, it is impossible to reconstruct the battles of the Egyptian pharoahs and the Assyrian kings with the same degree of detail as is possible when it comes to Greek and Roman military history, where there is manuscript reference from classical authors to provide a firm foundation of historical evidence. However, thanks to the discoveries of archaeologists and scholars during the last 150 years, it is now possible to describe the wars of the ancient Near East, even if it is still difficult to focus on specific battle tactics or campaign strategies. For this reason, the great military conflicts of ancient Egypt, the Middle East and south-west Asia Minor are covered here in general and prefatory terms before specific classical developments are scrutinised in closer detail.

THE AGE OF THE WARRIOR *A Scythian axeman of the early Classical period. Such warriors served as mercenaries in Greek armies.*

Sources of evidence
Over at least 2,000 years before the first Persian invasion of Greece in 290 BC, the Egyptian kings of Memphis had united the kingdoms of Upper and Lower Egypt under their control; when they did so, civilized arts had already been practised throughout several millennia in the Nile valley. Present-day knowledge of the events that took place during this period stems from several sources. There are the hiero-

CHARIOTEERS OF EGYPT *This drawing vividly captures the character of Egypt's two-man chariots, which were highly mobile.*

glyphs and the demotic script that was developed from them. In addition, ancient Greek historians wrote of Egypt, though what they wrote has often survived only in a garbled, summary and second-hand form, while Manetho (c.280 BC), an Egyptian priest, also composed a history of Egypt in Greek for the benefit of Ptolemy II (Manetho's chronological division of Egyptian history, according to the dynasties of kings, is still in use today as a guide to relative dating). The fact that Egyptian history was largely recorded in Greek also explains the Greek names by which ancient Egyptian personalities and sites are often still known today.

Similarly, the history of Assyria and Babylon, as revealed by cuneiform texts since their decipherment in the last century, tends to confirm the manuscript tradition of Biblical narratives. On the other hand, current knowledge of the Hittites comes almost entirely from archaeology and modern interpretation of inscriptions, monuments and clay tablets. In the Hittite empire, centered in Anatolia, more than one language and more than one form of writing were in use, though the Hittites themselves were apparently an Aryan people, speaking an Indo-

European tongue. References to them certainly exist in the annals of other civilizations, but what has been learnt about them in the last century adds a new dimension to our knowledge of the ancient Near East.

Egypt and its enemies

At different times, the Assyrians and Hittites both threatened Egypt, but they were not the only, or the earliest, enemies of the Egyptians. To the kings of Memphis and Thebes, the unity of the Nile valley must have seemed a question of obvious destiny. The rulers of the first two dynasties campaigned against the Nubians in the far south, while the pharaohs of the 12th and 18th dynasties pushed their Nubian frontier even further southwards, ultimately upriver almost as far as the Nile's fourth cataract. At a much later date (671 BC), when

THE WORLD OF HOMER *Hector and Achilles battle outside Troy. The depiction is accurate as far as weapons are concerned.*

lower Egypt was occupied by the Assyrians, Nubian leaders took the initiative in expelling the invaders, though these self-interested deliverers were in turn forced to retreat.

Like the Ethiopian mountains of the south, the Libyan desert in the west must have seemed to provide natural frontiers for the civilizations of the Nile valley. Yet, in the 13th and 12th centuries BC, Egypt's warrior pharaohs were obliged to conduct major campaigns against invading Libyans – Libya being the ancient name given to all Africa west of the Nile. There Libyan attacks were combined with those of other invaders, who apparently

came from north Mediterranean countries. The "Sea Peoples", to whom Egyptian inscriptions enigmatically refer in this context, were probably Aryan for the most part, but, like the Hittites, they may have included several ethnic groups, who either acted in collusion or saw in the wealth of the Nile valley a common prize.

The battle of Kadesh

Before the Libyans and their mysterious allies had been confronted and finally crushed, conflict between Egyptians and Hittites had culminated in the great battle of Kadesh (c.1290 BC). The fame of this battle rests, among other factors, on the fact that its details are inscribed with vivid illustrations on the walls of the temple at Thebes. Though the Egyptian account is framed so as to suggest an Egyptian victory, in reality it appears that the Hittites trapped Ramses II in the Orontes valley in Syria by persuading him that their army was encamped near Aleppo. Ramses accordingly deployed his army to assault or besiege the town of Kadesh; he had no intention of fighting a pitched battle, though one developed almost immediately. What saved him was his fortunate capture of some enemy scouts, who, under strenuous interrogation, corrected his misleading impression.

In this battle, mobility was one of the key factors. The Hittite chariots carried three-man crews (including the driver), while the Egyptian equivalents carried only two. This seems to indicate that the Hittites could concentrate more fighting men in less time than their foe. On the other hand, the Egyptian chariots may well have been lighter and more mobile. Certainly, the Egyptians seem to have rallied after a bad start and Ramses was lucky enough to force a draw.

The battle led to a treaty between the two powers, with a Hittite princess marrying the Pharaoh. The full terms of the agreement were recorded in hieroglyphics at Ramses' great temple of Abu Simbel in lower Nubia. The corresponding Hittite version appears in cuneiform characters on a clay tablet discovered at Bogaz Keui in Turkey, the site of the ancient Hittite capital of Hattusa.

The rise of Assyria

Although, under strong pharaohs, Egypt was still able to react against invasion and hostile encirclement, the war unquestionably weakened both the Egyptians and the Hittites, so clearing the way for the expansion of Assyrian power. Indeed, the eagerness with which both belligerents came to terms after Kadesh suggests that they were both aware of the threat that Assyria posed.

The Assyrian empire came into existence in very much the same way as many others – that is, as a defensive measure. The logic follows a simple pattern. An independent, but threatened, people attempts to secure itself by setting up a belt of buffer states and subject allies, until

THE MIGHT OF ASSYRIA *The mobility of Assyria's armies was a key factor in the carving out of a major Middle Eastern empire.*

this self-same expansion of imperial frontiers brings the central power into conflict with new enemies and so necessitates new wars of conquest. As far as the Assyrians – the Semitic people of Ashur, who had immigrated and mingled with Sumerian and other Mesopotamian populations in the third millennium BC – were concerned, the first menace came from alliances forged by the Babylonian cities to the south, including Chaldean Ur. To the north-west, the Aryan Hittite and Mitanni peoples would also have been glad to overrun Mesopotamia.

In the event, however, the warlike kings of Assyria triumphed, and both sets of their enemies were subjugated to the Assyrian yoke. This term is

not chosen lightly. Assyrian expansion relied upon ruthless methods; rebel populations were deported *en masse*. The policy of expansion continued in the 8th century BC, when Assyrian armies reached Syria and Palestine, thus coming within striking distance of Egypt. In the face of Israelite resistance, the Assyrian king Sargon II invaded Samaria, following his conquest with the accepted policy of mass deportations and also planting Assyrian colonists, who later merged with the Jews to form the religiously schismatic Samaritan sect. In the same period, the Assyrians came to dominate the Phoenician cities of the coast, recruiting ships and crews from this source. This was a timely move, since a navy was essential if the Assyrian kings were to counter any Egyptian operations in this area. Assyrian power now reached its zenith. Not only did the Assyrian king Essarhaddon invade and occupy

Egypt, but, nearer home, Babylonia was subjugated.

However, Assyrian imperial history then followed a course, which, in many ways, was typical of other empires of this kind. Expansion meant extended lines of communication, which became increasingly difficult to maintain – especially when confronted with Egyptian resurgence. In the second half of the 7th century, Psamtec I, founder of the 26th dynasty – who incidentally employed Ionian Greek mercenaries – was able to drive the Assyrians from the Nile Delta. Meanwhile, Assyria's subjects in Mesopotamia also revolted, and, in 612 BC, the Assyrian capital of Nineveh was destroyed by an attack launched by a coalition of Assyria's enemies. Among these, the Babylonians were the predominant force. They inherited the Assyrian empire, together with a great deal of Assyrian policy and method.

The riddle of Troy

Whether we consult Biblical narratives or the inscriptions and monuments of the Egyptians, Hittites or Assyrians, the way in which war was waged in the ancient Near East seems to exhibit a remarkable uniformity over a period of many centuries. The war chariot had been adopted in Egypt about 1600 BC, under the influence of the foreign Hyksos kings. These rulers, whose power endured for some 250 years, had led Semitic invaders into the Nile delta and extended their dominion southward. Both Egyptian and Asiatic pictorial representations testify to the combined use of the chariot and the bow. The practice was for the chariots to carry an archer into battle, a quiver of arrows being slung on the chariots side rail.

A completely different picture emerges, however, when we read the Homeric poems, which were probably composed – though not necessarily written down – in the Greek settlements of Asia Minor in the 8th century BC at a time when Assyrian expansion was reaching its apogee. In the battles of the *Iliad*, the bow, though employed on occasion, is not a universal weapon, while the way in which the chariot was used is totally different. Though warriors are carried into battle in chariots, they dismount to fight with spear, shield and sword.

Homer's world, therefore, clearly does not belong to the great bow-and-chariot epoch of the Near East. Nor does it reflect the warfare of classical Greece, in which chariots played no part at all. It is natural to suppose that the poet of the *Iliad* attributed to a past age the arms, armor and battle tactics of times nearer to his own and so produced a pastiche. Anachronism of this kind is common enough in poetry, and from a literary point of view it gives no grounds for complaint.

What it comes down to is that "Homeric civilization" is a fictional hybrid concoction, a poet's world, comparable in kind with romantic medieval evocations of King Arthur and Roncesvalles. Homer and archaeology are as often in conflict as in agreement. The Cretan Bronze-Age despots of whom glimpses can be caught through Linear B are the true-to-life contemporaries of Pharaonic, Hittite and Mesopotamian dynasts. Whatever the truth about Troy, Homer's heroes, though alive for ever in the imagination of readers, are not contemporary with anybody.

The empire of Cyrus the Great

Tales of Troy apart, Asiatic wars cannot be confidently related to Greek history until the rise of Cyrus the Great, the ruler of Persia, and the conflict that subsequently developed between Persia and the city-states of classical Greece. In 490 BC Darius despatched a punitive armada across the Aegean to punish the Greeks for their support of rebel Ionians in the empire. However, the Athenians with a few allies overcame the Persians when they landed at Marathon, and the project of conquering Greece was left to Darius'

THE TROJAN HORSE *A modern replica of the wooden horse that, according to Homer, the Greeks are said to have used to infiltrate Troy and bring an end to their 10-year siege.*

son Xerxes. A succession of famous battles was the result. A small Spartan force perished heroically at Thermopylae in northern Greece, but Xerxes' fleet was defeated heavily by the Greeks at *Salamis*, and Mardonius, his son-in-law, whom he left to winter with an army in Boeotia, was vanquished and killed by the Greeks in the following year.

Rome and Greece

Roman civilization was contemporary with that of Greece, not susequent to it. As Roman military methods evolved, so did the use of the Macedonian phalanx by Alexander the Great's successors in the east. However, it was the Roman legionaries who eventually triumphed over the phalangists.

Roman military history can barely be distinguished from legend until the 3rd century, except in general terms. By an arrangement attributed to King Servius Tullius (c.578-535 BC), the five classes of citizen soldiers were equipped according to their means, the richest providing the cavalry and the poorest the lightly-armed elements. In action, the infantry probably fought in an unbroken front line, like that of a Greek hoplite force.

After reforms by the revered, but semi-legendary, dictator Camillus in the early 4th century, the Roman legion was increased in strength from an original 3,000 by another thousand or more, now being split into units of 30 maniples (*manipuli*) each consisting of two centuries of 60 to 100 men per century. In battle, lightly-armed skirmishers (*velites*) led three ten-maniple lines of heavier troops ranged one behind the other, with regular intervals to left and right of each maniple. The front line (*hastati*) was followed by a second (*principes*) and a third (*triarii*); the maniples to the rear covered the intervals between those immediately ahead of them. The system helped battlefield flexibility, since a rear line could promptly advance to fill the gaps in a front line, or a front line fall back into the gaps left deliberately open behind it, as the situation dictated.

The adoption of these tactics was associated with the introduction of the javelin to take the place of the thrusting spear, on which the unbroken line of a Greek hoplite army had relied. The Greek historian Polybius (born c.200 BC), gives a good account of this, while Livy, though providing a picture of even earlier maniplular tactics, does not provide a very clear record of their application in action. In general, early Roman victories over other Italian peoples are hardly better documented than the Pharaonic conquest of the Nile valley, or the Hebrew penetration of Canaan.

Origins of the legion

More is known of the Roman army in the period after the reforms associated with the name of Gaius Marius at the end of the 2nd century BC were introduced. The maniple now virtually disappeared and the legion, now 6,000 at full strength, was divided for tactical purposes into ten cohorts. Legionary cavalry, originally 300 strong (in ten *turmae* of three *decuriae* each), had already been supplemented by horsemen drawn from Rome's Italian allies. From the beginning of the 2nd century, it was largely replaced by auxiliary contingents drawn from provinces outside Italy.

Legions were by no means always at establishment strength; those of Julius Caesar and Pompey, for instance, contained about 3,500 men. In the days of the early republic, the two consuls had each commanded two legions, but political expansion entailed giving the command of additional legions to proconsuls. After the disastrous loss of three legions by Varus in Germany in 9 AD, the number of legions serving the empire was reduced to 25, and remained so until the mid-2nd-century, when the strength was raised by five. Three more were added about 197 AD, while, in the 4th century, the number rose to about 175. At the same time, however, the strength of each individual legion diminished, being reduced to 1,000 men under Constantine.

Of prime importance in the

Roman legion at all times were the commanders of centuries. These were the centurions, men promoted from the ranks, who can be contrasted with the six military tribunes serving on the legion's general staff, to whom military service was often a step in a political career. Also political in origin were the *legati*, initially

ROME'S MIGHTY LEGIONS
Rome's hard-fighting infantry was the backbone of the thrust that carved out the ancient world's greatest empire.

deputies of provincial governors. Julius Caesar often appointed them as legionary commanders, and as such they persisted in imperial times.

After the reforms of Gaius Marius, cohorts, like the old maniples of the early republic, fought in a three-line formation, though, as the records of actual battles show, such standard tactics were obviously adaptable. There can be no better example than the brilliant improvization of Julius Caesar at *Pharsalus*, when he created an oblique fourth line of

single cohorts withdrawn severally from each of his eight legions to offset his shortage of cavalry.

Into the Dark Ages

From the 3rd century onward, however, the military usage of the Graeco-Roman world was really neither Roman nor Greek. Barbarian auxiliaries, absorbed into the citizen body of the empire, fought in their own way with their own weapons under their own leaders. On Trajan's column, the mailed horsemen (cata-

CAVALRY IN ACTION *A Roman cavalryman. In the hey-day of the empire, the cavalry was mainly recruited from provinces outside Italy.*

phracti) figuring among Rome's Danubian foes, not to mention the Oriental archers in flowing robes, are just as representative of the armies that defended the imperial frontiers in the 3rd and 4th centuries as of those which assailed them. If the Graeco-Roman tradition surviv-

ed at all, it found its new center in the eastern empire, where it was to survive until the rise of the Turks and the eventual fall of Byzantium towards the end of the Middle Ages. Despite romantic links with the past – the legend of King Arthur in Britain as the leader of a Romano-British army fighting to preserve the legacy of imperial civilization is one example – the successive centuries saw the birth of a new fighting force in which cavalry was to play the predominant role.

13

Warships of the ancient world

In the second millennuim BC, Cretan navies dominated the Aegean area, but little is known of the actual details of naval warfare during this period. In the world described by Homer, the function of a warfleet was to transport an army, with fighters doubling as rowers. Similarly, commerce and piracy were hardly separate vocations. A crew that was strong enough to defend itself and its own cargo was strong enough to rob others, and there was no power to prevent it from doing so. In the 7th and 6th centuries BC, recognizable navies developed – whether for the protection of trade or the extension of piracy – their fighting ships being mainly oared galleys. This remained the case throughout classical times.

Triremes and their tactics

Early Greek references are to ships of 20 or 50 oars, and representations of such ships have survived. However, galleys of two and three superimposed oar banks were in use among the Phoenicians before this, the navies of both Egypt and Assyria making use of these biremes and triremes. At the end of the 5th century BC, the normal complement of an Athenian trireme was about 200 men. Most of these were rowers, though a score of seamen were also carried to manage rigging and tackle, plus a fighting party of marines of about the same strength.

Boarding, ramming and missile attacks were the tactics used. The Athenians excelled in the use of the ram. This was a forward extension of the keel, so carrying the whole weight of the ship behind it. The stem post was built up above the ram, with a toothed projection at deck level to protect it against the shock of impact when ships clashed in battle.

Ramming was usually aimed at the enemy's broadside. The manoeuvre known to the Greeks as *diekplous* (sailing through) involved breaking the enemy's oars by rowing past the opposing vessel and then swinging round to strike at the most vulnerable point of the hull. This led to the practice of stationing a rear line of ships in battle to cover any gaps that might occur in the front line, so preventing the enemy "sailing through" to carry out this destructive manoeuvre.

Triremes, which were the typical war galleys of the 5th century, were not all built to one pattern by any means. The Phoenician triremes that fought at *Salamis* were higher than the Greek galleys, and it was expected that this would give them an advantage in boarding and missile combat. In the event, however, the lower, more manoeuvrable vessels of the Greeks proved their superiority. The situation differed in the Peloponnesian War, when Corinthian triremes were made with heavily reinforced prows, which assured them of victory in head-on ramming tactics, much to the discomfort of their Athenian enemies.

Deck structures also varied in the course of the classical period. A foredeck and quarter deck were probably normal, with the intervening rowers' benches either left open to the elements, or protected by an awning. It has, however, been argued that there were side decks facilitating communication and access between poop and forecastle.

Heavier galleys

In early galleys, one oar was generally pulled by one man. In a trireme, there were therefore three oars and three rowers in any section on either side. Later, heavier galleys were introduced, with more than one rower to an oar. The quinqueremes, septiremes, and decaremes of the period were evidently classified according to the number of rowers on one side in each section, though the number of oar banks is not likely ever to have increased above three. The actual deployment of oars and rowers has been the subject of much controversy, but it is probable that there were as many ways of constructing and equipping triremes as there are modern theories about them. Large single square sails were used when long voyages were expected, most commonly with a single mast, but it was the preferred practice to leave sails behind if fighting seemed imminent. Steering was by means of two stern paddles, one on each side.

The need for larger and heavier galleys made itself felt in wars that were undertaken further from home; on distant expeditions, stronger and sturdier craft were required in order to withstand the elements. The

LIVING RECORD *These frescos at Thera (Santorini) date from the 16th century BC and depict a "naval expedition".*

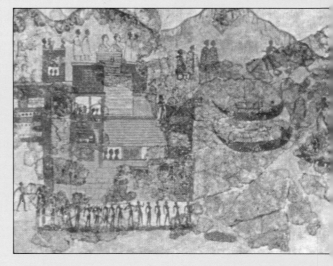

MASTERS OF THE MEDITERRANEAN *It took time for the Romans to realize the need for naval power, but, by 70BC, they were masters of the Mediterranean. this sculpture depicts a typical galley; note the forecastle and the forward extension of the keel for ramming.*

Carthaginian fleets and those of the Sicilian Greeks, were menaced at least as much by storms as by enemy action in their attacks upon each others' coastlines. In the same period that saw the evolution of heavier ships, formidable marine catapults were also developed to be mounted in the prows of fighting vessels.

Grappling and boarding
By inclination the Romans were landsmen; until the Punic Wars, they depended mainly on the fleets of the Greek maritime cities to which they were allied for naval support. However, the naval battles of Mylae, Ecnomus and the Aegatian Islands (260–241 BC) between Romans and Carthaginians saw the development of boarding tactics in which the Romans literally grappled their enemies, fighting what were virtually land battles at sea. The Roman grappling gear was termed a *corvus* (raven). Claws were fitted at the end of a swivelling derrick-like gangway designed for use by a boarding party. Roman warships also featured wooden castles at prow and stern which allowed missiles to be launched from an advantageous height, while at the same time providing cover against enemy missiles.

Lighter ships again
After the final defeat and destruction of Carthage in 149 BC, the Romans were slow to recognize that they were now solely responsible for protecting trade routes and coasts; but in 70 BC, special legislation gave Pompey (Gnaeus Pompeius) the means and the authority to rid the sea of pirates. With 500 ships at his disposal, he divided the Mediterranean into 13 action zones and made each of his subordinate commanders responsible for clearing one of them.

Total success was achieved in three months; to have accomplished this, Pompey must have relied on heavy galleys capable of surviving what were long continuous periods at sea for ships of this type. But the advantage did not always lie with the heavy vessel and, for one reason or another, the trend towards heavier galleys was reversed in later antiquity. Ancient fleets in general could be quickly constructed, and this was particularly true where lighter galleys – always easier to man – sufficed. In 49 BC, for instance, Julius Caesar had 12 ships built from freshly-cut local timber in the space of 30 days for the purpose of blockading his enemies in Marseilles (Massilia). At the battle of *Actium* in 31 BC, between Octavian and Mark Antony the greater manoeuvrability of lighter ships also proved its worth.

ACTIUM
ROMAN CIVIL WARS OF THE SECOND TRIUMVIRATE
31 BC

A sea battle off the eastern Adriatic coast, in which Octavian (Caesar Octavianus, later the Roman Emperor Augustus) defeated his rival Mark Antony (Marcus Antonius), so making himself undisputed master of the Roman world. Though Mark Antony's fleet outnumbered Octavian's by 500 ships to 400, the Romans had a decisive margin of naval superiority, since rowers were not available to crew many of Antony's galleys.

The struggle for power between Antony and Octavian, the two most influential of the three *triumvirs* who ruled the Roman republic after the murder of Julius Caesar and suppression of the revolution led by Brutus, had personal as well as political origins.

The conflict began in 32 BC, when Octavian declared war on Cleopatra and deprived Antony formally of his political status. Antony, together with Cleopatra, was by this time in Greece. Here, rallying troops and ships at Ephesus, he set up his headquarters at Patrae, setting up an advanced military and naval base at Actium, near the mouth of the Ambracian Gulf on the coast of Epirus. It seemed to many contemporaries that Antony was poised to strike against Italy – in fact, as Antony realized, his alliance with Cleopatra, his use of her money and her presence in his camp would have made any such move politically inopportune. If he had taken this course, he would have appeared to threaten Rome as the ally of a foreign invader, so he decided to play a waiting game, expecting Octavian to cross the Adriatic to confront him.

Prelude to battle
It was Antony's intention, no doubt, to fight on land, for he could rely on a force of 100,000 foot and 12,000 cavalry. However, the confrontation he awaited came about more suddenly than he had planned, for Octavian, with 400 ships, 80,000 infantry and 12,000 cavalry, made the crossing soon after midsummer (31 BC) and fortified a camp some ten miles north of Antony's own position near Actium.

In the two months of manoeuvre and skirmishing that followed, Antony's situation deteriorated. Octavian did not attempt to force a pitched battle on

land, while Antony could not dislodge the Romans from their entrenched positions around his camp. Meanwhile, Agrippa, Octavian's brilliant admiral, had won control of the Ionian islands, so cutting off Antony and Cleopatra from their supply bases in the Peloponnese. Sickness and discontent increased among Antony's troops and desertion became a problem – one of the most influential deserters was Domitius Ahenobarbus, his long trusted subordinate and supporter. A decision was needed, as the position was obviously untenable. An escape route by land, through Macedonia, was open, but Cleopatra was not in favor of this. She wished to reach Egypt the quickest way – and this was by sea.

Antony's ships were heavy war galleys – many of them being decaremes and octoremes, which required three times the number of rowers that were needed to work Octavian's light *libumae* (probably simple triremes). These light ships were not noted for their seaworthiness on long voyages, so Octavian had been lucky to cross the Adriatic without loss. In the coming battle, however, they were to prove their value. Antony, by contrast, had difficulty in manning his large ships and had no other recourse but to press local peasant levies into service for this purpose, with the result that many of his crew were unskilled. Even given this, he could not fill his vessels to their full complement; finally all the Egyptian galleys – save 60 – were burnt on the beach by his orders. The fleet with which Antony eventually engaged Octavian therefore numbered around 360 ships.

Action at Actium
The decisive engagement was delayed for several days by rough weather and when it came, it was untypical of other sea actions of the period. Instead of using the customary ramming and boarding tactics, both fleets relied on missile attacks – the missiles being launched both by hand and by catapult – to bring them success. In this kind of battle, Octavian's lighter, more manoeuvrable craft had an obvious advantage, circling round Antony's cumbersome galleys – sometimes three or four to one – and pouring in fire darts and incendiary projectiles from whatever direction they chose, and always being swift enough to dodge any clumsy ramming attempt by their opponents.

Before battle was joined, Antony's fleet was drawn up in front of the narrow strait leading to the Ambracian Gulf. Antony himself commanded the right wing, where he faced Agrippa's squadron. Before action was joined, he visited the captains of the individual vessels under his command in a small boat to give his last-minute orders. His instructions were that they should stay inshore, as if at anchor, fighting a defensive action. Behind the main battle line, Cleopatra with the surviving 60 ships of the Egyptian contingent, guarded the treasure chest on which payment of both army and navy depended.

Despite Antony's orders, Sosius and Marcus

16

Octavius, commanding his left and center respectively, allowed their galleys to be lured seaward by the enemy, who attacked first but soon, following Octavian's instructions, then staged a feigned withdrawal as if in defeat. This gave the lighter Roman vessels sufficient searoom in which to exploit their superior powers of manoeuvre. What turned the tide of the battle, however, was the sudden break-out of Cleopatra's ships in full flight for the Peloponnese. This move threw the fighting vessels that had screened the Egyptian queen into confusion, while it led Antony to board one of his quinqueremes, abandon his command, and follow her. When she realized that Antony was behind her, Cleopatra signalled for him to come aboard her own galley. Here, he sat alone in the prow, and three days of sullen silence ensued before he could be persuaded to approach her – at least, so Plutarch writes, probably on the testimony of Olympus, Cleopatra's physician.

Meanwhile, Antony's crews, at first ignorant of his flight, continued the battle until around 4.00 pm. A heavy sea then set in, and wind must have fanned the flames in the blazing hulks. Eventually, 300 vessels surrendered to Octavian, 5,000 men having been killed. Antony's land forces, at first unable to believe that their commander had deserted them, did not capitulate for a further seven days. What made one of the legendary soldiers of his day behave in such an uncharacteristic manner? Poets have ascribed his motives to blind infatuation and scholars have not succeeded in explaining otherwise. What is clear is that Antony had certainly been prepared for flight, for he had stowed sails in his ships – an unusual measure if fighting was expected. The escape southward was probably his contingency plan in case of defeat.

The fall of Antony

From Greece, the fugitives ultimately reached the Egyptian port of Alexandria, where Antony was able to raise new military and naval forces, but eventually these, too, deserted him. All Cleopatra's wealth could not keep them loyal to a leader who had betrayed his own men. When Octavian, after returning briefly to Italy, attacked Egypt the following year, Antony's position became hopeless, but scarcely deserving of pity. At Actium, he had left his followers in the lurch, and as a would-be leader he was now without a following. Falling on his own sword, he bungled an attempt at suicide, but died in Cleopatra's arms. Cleopatra became Octavian's prisoner. He treated her courteously, but she killed herself with poisonous asps, which she had kept in reserve for just such an occasion.

The political consequences of Antony's defeat were profound. Victory at Actium secured Octavian mastery of the Roman world by discrediting the one man who might have overthrown him. Thus, it marked a decisive moment in Rome's transition to empire. It also taught Rome the importance of ensuring that the control of Egypt remained firmly in Roman hands to ensure the smooth supply of grain on which the city depended.

AEGOSPOTAMI AND ITS SEQUEL
PELOPONNESIAN WAR
405 BC

The battle that marked the climax of the Peloponnesian war between rival alliances of Greek city states, when an Athenian fleet of 180 ships, commanded by Conon, Philocles and Adeimantus, confronted an opposing allied fleet of some 200 vessels under the Spartan admiral Lysander in the Hellespont (Dardanelles).

In the last decade of the 5th century BC, the struggle between Athens, the cultural center of the Hellenic world, and the warrior state of Sparta for supremacy had become focused on the eastern Aegean and eventually in the Hellespont. The control of the narrow seas here was essential to the Athenians if they were to keep the city supplied with grain, for persistent enemy occupation had deprived them of their own farmland in Attica. On land, the corridor between the Long Walls, which connected the city of Athens with its port at Piraeus, was an essential link in the chain of communications by which Black Sea corn reached the city – but the route depended essentially on the Athenian navy maintaining control of the sea.

Athens versus Sparta

In August 405 BC, the Athenian fleet of 180 ships was stationed on an open coast on the Thracian Chersonese (Gallipoli Peninsula), near a rivermouth called Aegospotami ("Goat Rivers"). Across the Hellespont, less than five miles away, Lysander, the Spartan admiral, commanded a fleet which he had recruited from Greek maritime cities with the help of Persian subsidies. He was assisted by a troops from neighboring Abydos, and had occupied the city of Lampsacus.

For four successive days, the Athenian ships deployed outside Lampsacus harbour, offering Lysander battle, but, when Lysander failed to confront them, they returned each evening to their anchorage at Aegospotami. This was extremely exposed. The Athenian commanders were warned of the dangers of their position by Alcibiades, an exiled Athenian general and politician now living in retirement in the locality. He advised them to withdraw a few miles along the shore to Sestos, which would have provided them with a secure harbor and an adequate supply port. Alcibiades' advice, however, was contemptuously rejected.

The trap is sprung

On the fifth day of the confrontation, as the Athenian ships again returned to the beach at Aegospotami having once more challenged the enemy unsuccessfully, swift Spartan patrol vessels followed them at a distance. This had been the case on the previous evenings, but, on this occasion, a shield flashed in mid-channel – a signal to the main Spartan fleet at Lampsacus. Lysander had been studying the Athenian routine and now saw the opportunity for a surprise attack. By this time, the Athenian triremes were only half-manned, most of the crews having made their way inland to forage for food. The Spartan ships carried armed soldiers, ready for action on shore, who, under the command of Lysander's subordinate Thorax, landed and easily dealt with the scattered Athenian oarsmen, some of whom were killed and others captured. A few were lucky enough to escape and take refuge in the local walled river compounds.

The Athenians were taken totally by surprise, with the exception of Conon, the one Athenian commander on whom Alcibiades' warnings had perhaps made some impression. He had been on the alert, so, when he saw Lysander's galleys approaching, he made desperate efforts to rally the Athenian crews, but, dispersed as they were, there was no way of saving them. Conon put to sea and made his escape with the nine ships whose crews he had managed to muster before the Spartans moved in for the kill.

In accordance with the naval practice of the time, the sails of these nine ships had been put ashore at Aegospotami when battle was intended, and therefore were now in the hands of Lysander's men. With typical Athenian audacity, Conon rowed across the Hellespont to Lampsacus, the base from which Lysander's onslaught had been launched, and plundered the necessary sails from the Spartan stores. This bold move enabled the surviving flotilla to set sail westward and race for safety, soon leaving the Hellespont behind it.

The Spartan revenge

Meanwhile, Lysander returned to Lampsacus in triumph with the vessels which he had captured and as many of their crews as had fallen into his hands alive. A trial for war crimes and atrocities soon followed. Philocles, one of the Athenian commanders who had fallen into Spartan hands, had himself been personally responsible for throwing the crews of captured Spartan galleys into the sea, while the Athenian ruling assembly had added to an already substantial record of war crimes by recently voting to cut off the right hands of all captured enemy oarsmen. Now was the time for reprisal. Mainly at the instance of Lysander's allies, 3,000 accused Athenians were put to death. An exception was made in the case of one of their commanders, Adeimantus, who had opposed the assembly's decision.

Conon, for his part, at last reached Cyprus, where he found asylum with the pro-Athenian Greek ruler Evagoras, with eight of the ships with which he had fled from the Hellespont. The nineth ship, the *Paralus*, the official galley of Athens, used for the despatch of state missions and communications, made for Piraeus. When it arrived at night with news of the disaster, the implications of the defeat were only too quickly understood. The immediate response was almost hysterical; the citizens, in a mood of desperation, prepared themselves for a bitter siege.

Starved into surrender

Lysander, for his part, did not hurry. Having sent news of his victory to Sparta, he sailed to the Bosphorus. Byzantium and Chalcedon, the two cities on either side of the strait, which had been previously allied to Athens, surrendered to him, and he left a Spartan military administrator in charge of the area. This gave Sparta complete control of the grain supply route, Lysander now sailed southward from the Hellespont with 200 ships and made his way slowly towards Athens, receiving on his way the submission of the Aegean cities that had supported the Athenians. To all captured Athenian citizens, as in his Bosphorus operation, he granted safe conduct back to Athens – this move was not as magnanimous as it might have seemed, for Lysander knew full well that they would swell the number of the starving in the forthcoming blockade and siege. When at length he anchored off Piraeus and blockaded the port, the Athenians were already beleagured by Spartan-led armies. After four months of protracted negotiations during which many Athenians starved to death, Athens finally surrendered in the spring of 404 BC.

AQUAE SEXTIAE AND VERCELLAE
INVASION OF GAUL BY THE CIMBRI AND TEUTONES
102 and 101 BC

The Roman consul Gaius Marius defeated the Teutones and their allies the Ambrones at Aquae Sextiae (Aix-en-Provence); together with his consular colleague Lutatius Catulus, he annihilated the Cimbri near Vercellae the following year. The strength of the barbarian forces was reported to be a minimum of 300,000 (excluding women and children). The combined Roman consular armies numbered 52,000 men. The twin victories secured Gaul for the Mascent Roman empire and removed the threat the barbarians had been posing to the security of Italy itself.

Thanks to the indecisive movements of the migrant northern barbarians, the emergency that had prompted the re-election of Marius, one of Rome's greatest generals of the republican era, as consul in 104 BC did not become acute until two years later. Then, having reached the Pyrenees, the Cimbri and their Celtic allies the Tigurini turned about and trekked eastward, intent upon an Alpine crossing into Italy; the Teutones and the Ambrones marched along the Mediterranean coast, threatening a simultaneous invasion from the northwest. Marius, encamped near the mouth of the Rhône, did not immediately offer battle, but when the barbarians by-passed him, he followed and overtook them.

Fighting the barbarian threat
The Romans clashed with the Ambrones first over possession of a watering place near Aquae Sextiae. Skirmishing led to a general engagement, and the Ambrones, over 30,000 strong, were routed. The Romans sent an uneasy night, having had no time to fortify a camp, but the barbarians were not in a mood to counter-attack.

Two days apparently elapsed before the Teutones could concentrate their forces. By this time, Marius had taken up a strong position on high ground and posted 3,000 men under Claudius Marcellus in hiding in the woods of the surrounding hills. The barbarians, drawing confidence from Marius' previous refusal to fight, attacked the Romans uphill. They were, however, firmly resisted and eventually repelled. As their line wavered, Marcellus' men fell on them from the rear, and they were utterly destroyed. Contemporary reports chronicled 100,000 barbarians killed or captured.

Slaughter of the Cimbri
Meanwhile, the Cimbri and Tigurini, in their circuitous march eastward, did not reach and cross the Alps until the following year. Catulus tried to hold the line of the river Adige against them, but was obliged to fall back with his 20,300 men towards the Po. Here, the Cimbri, still ignorant of events at Aquae Sextiae, waited to be joined by their Teutonic brethren. But Marius, ever ready to take advantage of any respite offered him, reinforced Catulus with his own 32,000-strong army from Gaul, and by exhibiting his captives to the barbarians, brought them face to face with defeat.

In the battle of Campi Raudii (east of Vercellae) which followed, the leaders of the Cimbri showed that they were by no means unsophisticated tacticians, and tried to isolate the Roman infantry by decoying its left-wing cavalry to one side. The battle was fought in mid-summer – a fact that possibly favored the Romans, who were used to the heat. However, the fighting was confused and there was no obvious tactical plan. Marius, whose troops formed the wings of the Roman army, at one stage lost contact with the enemy amid the swirling dust, while Catulus' forces in the center collied with them almost by chance.

The eventual Roman victory can best be accounted for by the preparatory programmes of intensive training and military reorganization with which Marius' name is associated. The Cimbri were slaughtered as the Teutones had been before them. Many of them, both men and women, committed suicide, but 60,000 prisoners were nevertheless reported as being taken. Yet, despite the scale and importance of these victories, many Roman historians played down Marius' role. The reason for this is not surprising, since Sulla, Marius' former quartermaster – with whom his relations had become much strained – served in the campaign against the Cimbri under Catulus – and it is on Sulla's account that most subsequent histories are based.

CHAERONEA
THE AMPHISSAN WAR
338 BC

In late autumn of 339 BC Philip of Macedon, having marched into Phocis and threatened Boeotia with a force of some 30,000 Macedonians and Thessalians, defeated an allied army at Chaeronea, so establishing Macedonian domination of Greece. The entire Greek army was probably 35,000 strong.

On the pretext of redressing what he claimed was a sacrilegious encroachment by the citizens of Amphissa on temple territory near Delphi, Philip led his army southward over Mount Oeta into Doris in 338 BC. He then turned aside through Phocis to settle his outstanding differences with the Thebans. Under the influence of the orator Demosthenes, Athens had come to regard the Macedonians as a menace to Greek freedom and uncharacteristically allied itself with Thebes.

During the winter of 339–338 BC, the Macedonians

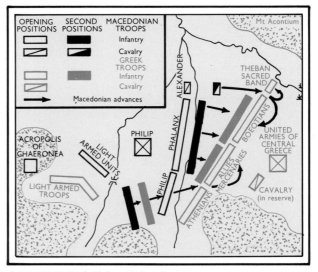

CHAERONEA *Philip of Macedon's tactics were a variation on the well-tried classical ruse of the feigned withdrawal.*

held the passes over Mount Oeta at Cytinium and Elatea, so cutting the Thebans off from their garrison at Nicaea near Thermopylae – a frontier post whose possession by Thebes was disputed by Philip. Athens had sent 10,000 mercenaries to Amphissa to defend the pass over the Parnassus range on this sector, while the main Greek force, two days march eastward, blocked another important pass at Parapotamii. The Greeks and Macedonians in Phocis thus confronted each other over the plain through which the river Cephissus flowed, an average distance of ten miles separating the two armies.

The following midsummer, Philip led the Greek mercenary garrison at Amphissa to believe that he intended to withdraw northward. He waited until their vigilance was relaxed and then slipped through the pass, over Parnassus, and destroyed the town, annihilating the garrison in the process. He was now able to threaten the Greeks at Parapotamii from the south, and they consequently withdrew eastward towards the walled citadel of Chaeronea. There, they took up a strong position where the plain narrowed to some two miles between the mountains and the river. In the second half of the summer Philip made one final offer of peace terms. When these were refused, he concentrated his forces for a pitched battle.

The triumph of Macedon

In the Greek army, the federal Boeotian troops under Theban leadership were drawn up on the right. The comparatively raw and inexperienced Athenians were on the left. On the extreme right wing, the Theban *corps d' élite* – the 300-strong "Sacred Band" – were stationed on a hillock close to the River Cephissus. In the center of Philip's opposing battle line was the Macedonian phalanx, with its long pikes and light shields. The king's son, Alexander (afterwards "the Great"), then only aged 17, commanded the heavily-armed cavalry on the left with an entourage of experienced officers.

Philip himself, with the Hypaspists, an élite guards regiment, took the right wing. His tactics were a variation on the well-tried ruse of feigned retreat. The Hypaspists, the first to engage the enemy, withdrew gradually, luring the unwary Athenians into a pursuit. The center of the Greek line was forced to extend to the left in order to maintain contact with the Athenians, but in doing so, it lost contact with the Thebans on the right. Alexander charged with his cavalry into the gap that was thus created. The Macedonian phalanx followed.

The "Sacred Band" were isolated and annihilated, every man dying heroically at his post. Philip then counter-attacked against the over-extended Athenians, who were now outflanked on their right by the Macedonian phalanx. Some 1,000 Athenians were killed and 2,000 captured, but Philip did not pursue the fugitives. His purpose was to control Greece – not to destroy it – and by his victory he achieved it.

CUNAXA
REVOLT OF CYRUS AGAINST ARTAXERXES II OF PERSIA
401 BC

At Cunaxa, a village about 60 miles north of Babylon, armies led by the pretender Cyrus and his brother Artaxerxes II clashed in a dispute over the succession to the Persian throne. Apart from his reported 100,000 Asiatic followers and 20 scythe-wheeled chariots, Cyrus led 14,000 Greek mercenaries. Artaxerxes' army was reputedly 400,000 strong, with 150 scythe-wheeled chariots.

Following the course of the Euphrates, Cyrus had advanced southwards into Babylonia. Between the ancient fortification known as the Median Wall and the east bank of the Euphrates, an apparently defensive ditch had been dug, but no enemy was there to man it, and Cyrus continued his march. Lack of opposition at this stage suggested to Cyrus that Artaxerxes had abandoned any immediate intention of offering battle; the king, in fact, had been long mustering his forces, and even now a numerous contingent under his general Abrocomes had not arrived.

News of the enemy's eventual approach took Cyrus by surprise, but the locality favoured his smaller force well enough. To the west, he was protected by the Euphrates, while a line of hills barred any hostile encircling move from the east. The Greeks were drawn up on Cyrus' right, with a supporting force of 1,000 Paphlagonian cavalry. The royal troops advanced slowly, but when the two armies were only a short distance apart, the Greek heavy infantry launched a fierce attack that swept away all resistance. Despite Cyrus' last-minute orders to converge on Artaxerxes himself, the whole Greek force, under command of the Spartan Clearchus, then pursued the enemy with a recklessness that did little credit to their professional expertise Tissaphernes, Artaxerxes' viceroy and marshal, probably posted with Artaxerxes himself in the

CUNAXA *Greek success on the right wing was offset by disaster in the center, where Cyrus himself was killed.*

center, ordered a counter-attack by the scythe-wheeled chariots, but the chariots were unmanoeuvrable and so easy to dodge.

This apparent success brought danger in its train, however, as Cyrus was quick to realize. The advance of the Greek wing of his army exposed its left flank to a fresh attack from Artaxerxes' centre, so Cyrus led his mounted 600-strong bodyguard in a ferocious charge against the enemy lines opposite him to counter this threat. He broke through and, in what amounted briefly to single combat, wounded his brother in the chest. At the same moment, however, one of Artaxerxes' guards dealt Cyrus a mortal blow under the eye, and, with the death of the pretender, the war was decided.

Tissaphernes, in charge of Artaxerxes' troops on the battlefield while the king's wound was being tended, did not renew his attack upon the triumphant Greeks, but instead concentrated on sacking the enemy baggage camp. This was a simple operation, since the Asiatic troops on Cyrus' left wing, under command of his Persian supporter Ariaeus, had fled from the field on learning of the prince's death. A body of Greek guards in the camp, though sustaining casualties, succeeded in extricating their baggage, their slaves and one of Cyrus' concubines. The Greek victors on the right wing, now three miles away, knew nothing of Cyrus' death until the next day.

The Greek withdrawal
After a hesitant period of sparring and manoeuvre, the Greek commanders were invited by Tissaphernes to a parley, at which they were treacherously seized and put to death. The surviving Greek force, about 10,000 strong, refused to trust the enemy further, and spent the next year marching home – at first harassed by Tissaphernes' forces, then fighting their way through the inhospitable tribesmen to the north and eventually marching along the southern shore of the Black Sea. Xenophon, the Athenian leader, played a major part in planning and leading the march at least according to his own accounts.

GAUGAMELA (ARBELA)
INVASION OF THE PERSIAN EMPIRE BY ALEXANDER THE GREAT
331 BC

This famous battle that completed the overthrow of the Achaemenid dynasty, which had ruled the Persian empire for over two centuries. Alexander commanded 40,000 infantry and 7,000 cavalry, drawn mainly from Macedonia, Greece and Thrace. The Persian ruler

Darius III deployed 16,000 heavy infantry, including Greek mercenary hoplites, 40,000 cavalry and 200 scythe chariots, plus hosts of tribesmen from all quarters of his dominions.

Alexander the Great's attack on the mighty Persian empire was one of the most decisive campaigns of all military history. Before advancing inland across Mesopotamia, his first move was to secure the Mediterranean coastline in his rear. He had already defeated Darius' generals at Granicus on the Hellespont (334 BC) and Darius himself at Issus in Syria (333). The confrontation at Gaugamela, in the neighbourhood of Arbela, was to decide the future of the empire.

A field prepared for action
In a plain seven miles wide, Darius had prepared a battlefield rather as if it had been a sports stadium, levelling it to favor his chariots and planting spikes to deter enemy cavalry. On the eve of the battle, Alexander thoroughly reconnoitred the area and took these preparations into account. He drew up his central Macedonian phalanx and two cavalry wings in such a way that all three could act as independent units – if necessary in isolation.

On the morning of the battle, Alexander led his élite "Companion" cavalry towards the extreme right of the plain. This meant that Bessus, the commander of Darius' left wing was obliged, as he advanced, to move correspondingly outwards to preserve the outflanking advantage which his superior numbers gave him. The Persian center now could not maintain contact with its left without being drawn sideways to avoid this, Bessus made an enveloping movement and poised himself for immediate attack.

However, Alexander struck first with his vanguard of light cavalry, and, after surviving fierce counter-attacks, triumphed over the massed Scythian and Bactrian horsemen opposed to him. While battle still raged, his phalanx, which had been provided with flank guards and a rear formation capable of turning about and fighting an attack from behind, drove off a Persian raiding force, which was attacking Alexander's camp.

By this time, Alexander had completely broken up the Persian left and swung inwards. The Persian center was already crumbling under his attacks when he received an urgent appeal for help from his second-in-command Parmenio, whose cavalry on the left wing were still under heavy attack from Darius' general Mazaeus. Alexander abandoned his pursuit of the routed enemy in front of him to support Parmenio, but, as he crossed the battlefield, collided with the fleeing raiders the phalanx driven from the camp. Confusion reigned, for blinding dust clouds had here been raised by the Persians' scythed chariots.

However, at the cost of 60 Macedonian lives, Alexander brought relief in time, and Parmenio went on to capture the Persian camp. Alexander himself led a nightlong pursuit of the enemy.

LEUCTRA
SPARTAN INVASION OF BOEOTIA
371 BC

Battle that ended Spartan domination of Greece. In it, the Theban general Epaminondas, commanding an army of Thebans and other Boeotian troops (around 6,000 infantry and 600 cavalry), defeated and killed the Spartan king Cleombrotus and routed his Spartan army, which, with its allies, numbered some 11,000 (10,000 infantry and 1,000 cavalry).

Attempts to draft a plan for peaceful co-existence among the Greek states having recently failed, Cleombrotus, who had been garrisoning Spartan outposts in Phocis, marched into Boeotia soon after the midsummer of 371 BC. He was bent on compelling Trebes to recognize the autonomy of the Boeotian towns it normally controlled.

Sparta was the most feared state in Greece, its military supremacy being based on its warrior class. With the exception of the *helots* (slaves), all Spartans were soldiers.

No Spartan army had previously been beaten in a full-scale pitched battle by the forces of another Greek state, although ambushed or isolated Spartan detachments had on occasion been overwhelmed and destroyed. The normal method of defence adopted by Sparta's enemies was to seek shelter behind strong fortifications, for the Spartans were not expert in siege warfare. This, however, was not the course now taken by Epaminondas. He and his loyal collaborator Pelopidas had devoted years to the training of a Theban *corps d'élite* – the "Sacred Band" – and they now felt capable of meeting the Spartans with an equal professionalism.

Theban battle tactics
Even before the time of Epaminondas, Thebes had developed new battle tactics, which relied on the use of a dense concentrated formation for success. At Delium in 423 BC, for instance, the Thebans had won victory by launching a right wing that was 25 ranks deep against the Athenians, who were drawn up in the more normal eight ranks. At Leuctra, the Theban hoplites who barred Cleombrotus' way ranged themselves 50 deep against a Spartan line of 12 ranks.

In a hoplite battle, it was important that the continuous front line of shields and spears should not be breached, for every man's shield protected his left-hand neighbour. Rear ranks were necessary in order to replace exhausted, wounded or fallen men – yet they were not merely a reserve, since the shield had an offensive, as well as defensive, use. The enemy line could be broken by pushing with the shield, not merely by striking with the spear; at Leuctra, sheer weight of numbers, thrown behind the front rank and concentrated on a narrow sector of the enemy's right wing, forced the Spartans to give way. Cleombrotus himself fell mortally wounded in the action, though his bodyguard carried him still breathing from the battlefield and the Spartans retreated in comparatively good order to their camp.

The spearhead of the Theban attack was led by the "Sacred Band" under Pelopidas. It took place on the strongest enemy sector – the Spartan right wing – with the Thebans advancing in a slanted formation and the results were such that the battle was really decided before the Boeotians' own right wing could even make contact with the Spartans' Peloponnesian, Phocian and other allies, who constituted the left and center of Cleombrotus' army. In the circumstances, the more numerous Spartans would not have expected to be outflanked. Rather, they would have hoped to outflank the Thebans, had not Epaminondas' manoeuvre taken them by surprise. The move was all the more astonishing, since the left wing of a Greek army usually rested on the defensive – a natural physical consequence of shielding oneself with the left arm against an opponent's right. The slanted formation (or "phalanx") probably moved at speed in a slanted direction, and Cleombrotus may have belatedly seen a danger that his right wing would be enveloped. Certainly, he tried to extend his line to meet the threat, but the Thebans caught him awkwardly, with this manoeuvre still uncompleted.

The battle had begun with a cavalry engagement, for Cleombrotus had stationed his cavalry in front of his main battle line as a screen. The Spartan force was attacked by Epaminondas' Boeotian cavalry, which was

LEUCTRA *Sparta's thrusts were decisively checked by Epaminodas with the total defeat of the Spartan army.*

very much superior to them. The Spartan cavalry was thrown back on to the hoplite line behind them, causing confusion and perhaps impeding any attempt to advance. The importance of this must not be overlooked, for it removed any threat to the right flank of the Theban hoplites as they made their diagonal attack – a threat to which their staggered formation otherwise would have exposed them. At Amphipolis in 422 BC, for instance, an Athenian commander had incurred disaster by exposing the unshielded right flank of his troops to the enemy front.

The Spartans seek terms

By retreating to their camp, which occupied a naturally strong position on a scarp behind a ditch, the Spartans gained a much-needed respite, and some of them were in favor of renewing the battle. But they had as little confidence in their allies as the Thebans had in theirs, and finally accepted terms that allowed them to bury their dead and march out of Boeotia with a show of dignity. Apart from their doubts as to the loyalty of their allies and satellite forces, the number of casualties they had suffered was a crucial factor in their decision to accept defeat. Sparta was dominated by a military caste of "Spartiates", who probably provided about one third (1,200 men) of the total Spartan military establishment; and one third of these fell at Leuctra. Xenophon says that 700 Spartiates were engaged in the battle. Either from a military or political point of view, it would have in any case been rash to invite further loss. Diodorus reports 300 Theban dead. This seems a reasonable figure if Xenophon's estimate of an overall 1,000 casualties on the Spartan side is accepted.

The Theban supremacy in Greece, for which the battle of Leuctra paved the way, lasted for only nine years. Greek politics being as they were, it was predictable that the shifting patterns of alliance would sooner or later operate against Thebes and that diplomatic manoeuvre would deprive the Thebans of their brief military advantage. But from a purely military standpoint, the victory at Leuctra was not the result simply of a tactical formula to which a Spartan hoplite army had at last proved vulnerable. Its lessons seem to have been well learned by Philip II of Macedon, who had been a hostage in Thebes.

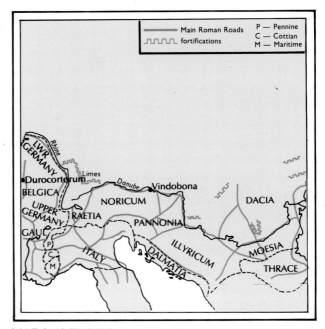

MARCUS EMPIRE *Marcus Aurelius' principal task was to stabilize the eastern frontiers against barbarian pressure.*

commanders brought a much needed stability to the empire. In the east, the Parthians were repelled and Mesopotamia occupied by Roman forces, while, on the Danube, Germanic and Sarmatian tribes were defeated. The war potential of the empire at this time was 30 legion supported by approximately 225,000 local auxiliaries.

In 161, when Marcus Aurelius inherited the imperial throne from his father-in-law Antoninus Pius, the world had seemed peaceful. Even the pressure on Rome's Danubian frontier, resulting from westward barbarian migrations, had not yet mounted sufficiently to pose any real threat. However, the ever-hostile Parthians, under Vologeses III, now occupied Armenia and, after the defeat of two Roman provincial armies, invaded the province of Syria.

The Roman response was swift. In 162, Lucius Verus, whom Marcus had, apparently in conformity with his predecessor's intention, accepted as an imperial colleague, campaigned in the east and, through the agency of excellent deputising officers, drove the Parthians from Armenia and occupied Mesopotamia. Unfortunately, Verus' troops, returning from the east, brought a virulent plague with them; the epidemic, at a time when the numerical strength of the military establishment was all-important, must have been strategically debilitating for the Roman war machine.

In 166, Germanic tribes, no doubt realizing the opportunity that Roman pre-occupation with the east presented, crossed the Danube and penetrated into northern Italy itself, threatening Aquileia at the head of the Adriatic Sea (167). Marcus Aurelius, recruiting two new legions and marching, together with Verus,

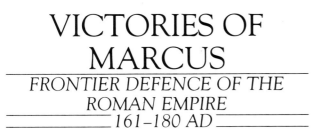

VICTORIES OF MARCUS
FRONTIER DEFENCE OF THE ROMAN EMPIRE
161–180 AD

The successful defence of the imperial frontiers by the Emperor Marcus Aurelius and his subordinate

through north Italy, forced the barbarians to withdraw. Meanwhile, able Roman commanders had secured the Danube provinces against Germanic inroads.

An empire in conflict

Lucius Verus was not a colleague worthy of Marcus either in terms of character or ability, so his death in 169 was not greatly mourned. At that time, however, the German peoples of central Europe – notably the Marcomanni and the Quadi – probably acting in collusion with the Sarmatian tribe of the Iazyges – threatened the imperial frontiers once more. The barbarians again invaded Italy and besieged Aquileia, but were again repelled. Marcus Aurelius waged war successfully against the Iazyges, and eventually found himself in a position to impose a durable settlement on the Germans beyond the Danube, but his plans were foiled by the news that Avidius Cassius, who had been Verus' distinguished subordinate in the east and was now provincial governor of Syria and Egypt, had raised a rebellion and been proclaimed emperor by the troops under his command.

Marcus hastily marched eastwards, but, even before he could arrive to quell the revolt, Cassius was murdered by one of his own centurions. The emperor, however, did visit Egypt and Syria in order to stabilize the situation. He returned to Rome to celebrate his triumph over his Danubian enemies, but in 177 the Marcomanni and their allies renewed hostilities, harassing the Roman province of Pannonia (in the region of Hungary).

Marcus Aurelius again defeated the Marcomanni, the Quadi and the Iazyges, but, when he was about to achieve a political settlement, he was once more cheated – this time by a peaceful death at Vindebona (Vienna) in 180. Before dying, he had enrolled entire frontier tribes and settled them on land which they were allowed to possess in return for military service as imperial contingents. This was certainly an answer to the ever increasing problem of barbarian numbers, but it was a far from perfect one. The "friendly" barbarians who served Rome against their hostile counterparts could very easily raise the price of their allegiance, or themselves become a direct threat.

METAURUS, THE
SECOND PUNIC WAR
207 BC

Key battle of the Second Punic War between Rome and Carthage, in which combined Roman armies under the consuls Marcus Livius and Claudius Nero annihilated the Carthaginian reinforcements that Hasdrubal Barca had led across the Alps to join his brother Hannibal in Italy. The Roman forces numbered upwards of 20,000, while the Carthaginians numbered 11,000, plus ten

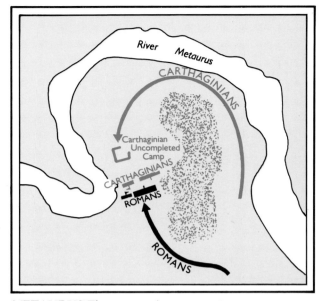

METAURUS *The unexpected emergence of Nero's forces on the Carthaginian right led to Hasdrubal's defeat and death.*

elephants; the victory, won at a cost of 2,000 Roman casualties, was the turning point of the Second Punic War, since it led to the collapse of the Carthaginian position in Italy.

In 207 BC, the conflict between Rome and Carthage was evenly balanced. Though Hannibal, Carthage's supreme military genius, had inflicted crushing defeats upon the Roman armies at Lake Trasimene in northern Italy (217 BC) and at Cannae in the south (216 BC), his army was not strong enough to take Rome either by storm or siege, so, for the next nine years, he was reduced to fighting a war of attrition – the type of war that, in the long term, Carthage was least equipped to win.

In that year, therefore, Hannibal, who was still trying to persuade Rome's allies in southern Italy to join him, was confronted by a Roman army under Claudius Nero, who had been sent south to contain Hannibal's movements. The great Cathaginian general was also awaiting reinforcements led by his brother Hasdrubal, but here Hannibal was to make a costly mistake. Remembering his own difficulties in crossing the Alps ten years earlier, he did not expect the relieving force to arrive in Italy as quickly as it did.

The intercepted despatch

From the Carthaginian viewpoint, it was obviously important that the two brothers should get into contact as soon as possible, so that they could combine their forces. Though Hasdrubal wasted precious time in a futile siege of Placentia, he did send a party of six horseman – four Gauls and two Numidians – south to Hannibal with a despatch outlining his plans. But, here fate took a hand.

With incredible skill and daring, Hasdrubal's

messengers made their way south through the whole length of Roman-occupied Italy and almost reached Hannibal's camp. By chance, Hannibal was on the move and, in trying to follow him, they lost their way and were intercepted by a Roman foraging party. Hasdrubal's letter, proposing a union of the two Carthaginian armies in Umbria in central Italy, was thus intercepted.

The Roman response
Determined to prevent any such combination, Claudius Nero moved suddenly and secretly at night to join Marcus Livius, the consul in command of Rome's northern army, who was facing Hasdrubal near Sena, south of the Metaurus river. According to tradition, Nero covered the 240 miles involved in six days. This would be easily credible if his force had consisted entirely of cavalry, but this was not the case. Perhaps some way of sharing horses was devised.

In any event, Nero's cavalry and infantry reached Sena simultaneously – and, even more importantly, without either of the Carthaginian commanders being aware of their move. At the start of their northern march, even Nero's own men were kept ignorant of their destination and their march into Livius' camp was carefully timed to take place after dark. Even the billeting was arranged so as not to increase the camp's size – an increase that could have been detected by Hasdrubal's scouts.

Taken by surprise
The Romans held an immediate council of war. It was argued by some that Claudius Nero's men should rest after their gruelling march, but Nero himself insisted on immediate action. If they waited, he argued, the advantage of surprise might be lost; at all cost, Hannibal could not be allowed to find out what was happening before his brother was defeated.

Meanwhile, Hasdrubal was encamped 500 yards away. Suddenly, he heard not one, but two, trumpet calls echoing in Livius' camp, and his knowledge of Roman military procedure told him that he faced two consular armies. Dismayed by this totally unforeseen situation, he struck camp that night. All the next day, pursued by the Romans and deserted by his guides, he retreated up the southern bank of the Metaurus, hoping to find a place where he could safely cross the river. But up-stream, where the channel was narrower, the banks were correspondingly steeper, while the Roman cavalry, under Nero, and lightly-armed auxilliaries, under the praetor Porcius Licinus, were already harassing the Carthaginian rear. He tried to set up a fortified camp, but, before he could do so, the Roman main body, commanded by Livius, came into sight.

The battle begins
In the circumstances, Hasdrubal chose his ground well, taking up position between a sharp hill spur and the river bank, so that there was no danger of his smaller force being outflanked by the enemy. He stationed his Gauls, whose general lack of battle stamina inspired him with little confidence, on the left, where they were protected by the hill. In the center were the Ligurians, who had joined Hasdrubal recently in north Italy, with the elephants he had brought from Spain in front of them. Hasdrubal himself led the Spaniards, who were extended across the valley on his right. Only a nucleus of Carthaginian troops was involved; at Metaurus, as was their common practice, the Carthaginians relied mainly on mercenaries and allies. On the Roman right, Claudius Nero found his advance obstructed by the jutting hill spur, while, further to the left, Livius faced Hasdrubal himself.

The battle opened with a Carthaginian elephant charge. This drove the Romans back temporarily, but the unwieldy beasts soon became terrified by the growing commotion of the battle, while some were driven into a state of fury by the wounds they received. The maddened elephants therefore rapidly became a menace to their own troops and in many cases their drivers, following standard orders, killed them by hammering chisels into the base of their skulls.

The decisive blow
Nero quickly discovered that, though the nature of the terrain meant he could not get to grips with the enemy, the Carthaginians were equally unable to attack him. He therefore decided on a tactic he had previously used successfully; withdrawing abruptly from a position it seemed unnecessary to defend, he led a mixed force of cavalry and infantry behind the Roman lines to emerge unexpectedly on the enemy right. The weight of his added numbers here tipped the scales of battle decisively – Hasdrubal's flank was turned and his battle line encircled. He himself, after desperately attempting to rally his men, made a suicidal charge on a Roman cohort and fell, fighting to the last.

The Roman triumph
Hasdrubal's foreboding about the quality of his Gallic troops proved correct. Many of the Gauls in his army simply had not mustered in time for the battle. Stragglers among them were killed or captured by the Romans, while others were found lying drunk in the half-completed camp and butchered where they lay. Some escaped, but Livius, even when told that a detachment of cavalry would be enough to mop up the fugitives, judged the operation not to be worthwhile. Of the Carthaginian elephants, six, according to the historian Polybius, were left dead on the field and four, having been abandoned by their drivers, were captured. The victory was overwhelming and complete.

Claudius Nero, however, was not content to rest upon his laurels. He and his army immediately marched back to their base in southern Italy as quickly as they had come, to confront Hannibal once more. Nero added a touch of the macabre to his arrival; he had had Hasdrubal's head preserved carefully and, on his arrival at his old positions, ordered it to be hurled into Hannibal's camp. He also exhibited some of the African prisoners he held captive, releasing one of them to report events in detail to Hannibal.

Hannibal is said from this moment to have recognized that Carthage was doomed to defeat. In this, he was correct. The battle of the Metaurus was in every way decisive. It was not only an overwhelming local victory – it determined the future course of the war, the peace Rome imposed that followed it and subsequent world history.

THE MILVIAN BRIDGE
WAR BETWEEN CONSTANTINE AND MAXENTIUS
312 AD

A struggle between two rivals for the imperial power that terminated in the defeat of Maxentius in battle on the banks of the Tiber. Constantine led an army from Gaul of less than 40,000 men. Maxentius' large war establishment, recorded as being 170,000 strong, was deployed throughout Italy in various garrisons; it was particularly strong in the neighbourhood of Rome.

Both Constantine and Maxentius, flouting Diocletian's precedent of appointing emperors by nomination, claimed imperial power as a hereditary right. Based in Rome and garrisoning Italy, Maxentius had hitherto defied all attempts by his imperial rivals to dislodge him; in 306–7, Severus and Galerius had both failed. Revolt in Rome's African province had threatened to deprive the city of its essential overseas food supplies, but the rebellion had been overcome by Maxentius' officers in Africa, so averting this danger. Now, however, Maxentius faced a new challenge from Constantine and his legions. Descending from the Alps near Segusio (Susa), with a force already battle-hardened in campaigns against the German tribes on the Rhine, Constantine quickly demonstrated his ability both to storm towns and win pitched battles. He rapidly captured Maxentius' strongholds of Augusta Taurinorum (Turin), Mediolanum (Milan) and Verona, and marched southward towards Rome, taking Mutina (Modena) on his way.

Constantine's advance
Realizing that the key to Constantine's success lay in mobility, Maxentius abandoned his static strategy. If he was to take advantage of his superior numbers, it was essential that he should concentrate his scattered forces, and, with this purpose in mind, he despatched troops along the Flaminian Way, eventually following in

person. To expedite military movements across the Tiber, he had recently constructed beside the Milvian bridge a wooden one, resting on pontoons and incorporating a collapsible middle drawbridge section as a precaution against attack. However, he was not quick enough. Constantine's resolute cohorts, with Christian emblems blazoned on their shields, set upon him while his army was still extended in a straggling column along the Flaminian Way towards the village of Saxa Rubra, nine miles north of Rome.

Christian historians, applauding Constantine's religious sympathies, have seen faith, providence and miracle in his successful challenge in the face of vastly superior numbers, but the future emperor's military calculations are more likely to have been based upon the strategy and tactics that he had used on other occasions. It seems that at Saxa Rubra he had given ground in the first onset, but a flying column, launched southwestward on the Via Cassia, probably took Maxentius' army in the rear. Maxentius, faced with the danger of encirclement and isolation from his base, hastily ordered a retreat, seeking safety once more behind the walls of Rome. However, as his now panic-stricken troops converged on the pontoon bridge, the collapsible section collapsed and Maxentius, with many others, was drowned in the Tiber, then swollen with October rains.

Victory at the Milvian Bridge did not leave Constantine supreme ruler of the Empire. The presence in Illyricum of Valerius Licinius, another imperial pretender, called at first for diplomacy and then for further war. But the campaign against Maxentius was of considerable military significance. Constantine seems at Saxa Rubra, no less than at Turin, deliberately to have yielded ground on his main front in order that the advancing enemy might more easily be enveloped by his flanking contingents. More important still, the speed of his movements, which everywhere took his enemies by surprise, exploited principles that he was later to apply in defence of the imperial frontiers, where fixed garrisons were able to rely for support on a highly mobile striking force, ready in emergency for despatch to any danger point.

FALL OF PALMYRA
AURELIAN'S EASTERN CAMPAIGN
273 AD

After a battle at Emesa (Homs), in which he shattered the 70,000-strong Palmyrene forces, the Emperor Aurelian laid siege to Palmyra, where Queen Zenobia Septimia had previously sought to establish herself as Empress of the East. With an army that probably numbered no more than 50,000 men, he captured both city and queen. When Palmyra rebelled against him some months later, he destroyed it.

Having been made Emperor of Rome in 270 by the troops he commanded, Aurelian (Lucius Domitius Aurelianus) successfully repelled invading Danubian barbarians, as well as dealing with three rival pretenders to the imperial purple. He had also to face political dissidents in Rome – the result of his drastic attempts to reform the debased Roman coinage. While he was occupied with these tasks, Zenobia, queen of the powerful Syrian oasis city of Palmyra (Tadmor), saw the opportunity to claim the imperial title, first in her young son's name and then in her own.

Aurelian, marching eastwards (272), found time to subdue the invading Dacian tribes, but he withdrew Roman troops from the further side of the Danube, so making the river the eastern European frontier of the empire. As he led his army through Asia Minor, the Palmyrene forces offered no resistance – in any case, the mountainous terrain was unsuitable for the cavalry on which they largely relied. The Romans gained their first victory in this campaign in an action on the Orontes in Syria. Zenobia's general, Zabdas, retreated from his base at Antioch as a consequence, with what survivors he could rally, and fell back on Emesa, where he concentrated his full strength. In the battle that followed, Zabdas' cavalry put Aurelian's horsemen on the wings to flight – though the flight may initially have been feigned. However, the Roman legions in the centre won the day and defeated the Palmyrene cavalry in detail when it returned from its reckless pursuit.

A city under siege
Zenobia now withdrew the remnants of her forces behind the strong walls of Palmyra, so, in the heat of summer, Aurelian marched his army across 80 miles of desert to lay siege to the city. He bought off the hostile desert tribes and when Zenobia's Persian allies sent a relief force, he defeated it. Persian help had been the queen's best hope and she at last sought refuge with her Persian friends. Fleeing from the city by night and slipping through the Roman lines, she and her bodyguard, mounted on swift dromedaries, rode eastward towards the Euphrates. But she was pursued and captured at the river crossing by Roman cavalry, who brought her back a prisoner to Aurelian.

The emperor at first dealt leniently with the city, but executed those counsellors on whom the queen seemed glad enough to lay the blame. He himself was recalled westward by a further outbreak of Danubian warfare, but when Palmyra rebelled and massacred its Roman garrison (273), he swiftly returned and reduced the city to ruins, some of which still stand. Zenobia herself, was exhibited in Rome as a captive when Aurelian celebrated his triumph in the following year (274). But not only was her life still spared; she received a pension, was established in a comfortable country villa, and married a Roman senator.

Zenobia has survived in history as a romantic character, but the personality of Aurelian is the one worthy of detailed study. The dauntless vigor and

integrity that marked his career restored cohesion to what had been a chaotic and crumbling empire. Such men are not readily replaceable. This was amply demonstrated after 275, when Aurelian was murdered as the result of a petty conspiracy among his staff. The Roman world had to wait almost another decade for Diocletian, its next comparably strong emperor.

THE PYRRHIC VICTORIES
INVASION OF ITALY AND SICILY BY PYRRHUS OF EPIRUS
280–275 BC

Bent on western conquest, Pyrrhus, the Greek king of Epirus, supported the Greek city of Tarentum (Taranto) in its war against republican Rome. He crossed the Adriatic with 20,000 infantry, 3,000 cavalry, 2,000 archers, 500 slingers and 20 elephants. The Romans and their Italian allies could probably count on a war potential of about 50,000 men.

The victories of Pyrrhus have become proverbial for their inconclusive results and have added a phrase to military terminology. His Italian expedition started badly, since he suffered heavily from a storm in his Adriatic crossing, while the support he received from his allies in Italy was disappointing. At Heraclea in Lucania, his first battle with the Romans (280 BC), he

PYRRHUS IN ITALY *Hannibal rated Pyrrhus second only to Alexander the Great in the hierarchy of classical generals.*

commanded a force of some 25,000 men, with 20 elephants. The Roman army with its Italian allies was probably about equal to his in numbers. Casualties are variously reported, but Pyrrhus had the best of the battle. The following year, a two-day battle was fought at Asculum (279 BC) in Apulia, in which Pyrrhus was still just about the victor.

Unable to capture Rome or shake the loyalty of Rome's allies, Pyrrhus temporarily shelved the war in Italy and, leaving garrisons behind him, transferred most of his forces to Sicily, where he supported Greek cities against the Carthaginians, who were then allied with Rome. He almost ousted the Carthaginians from the island, successfully storming their stronghold at Eryx (227 BC). His Greek allies, however, quarrelled among themselves and with him, some of them taking sides with the Carthaginians.

In the circumstances, Pyrrhus decided to return to Italy. Here, in 275 BC, he fought the Romans again at Malventum. On this occasion, the battle was drawn, and Pyrrhus again characteristically looked for new wars in Macedonia and Greece. He left Italy with an army one third the strength of that which he had brought with him. The garrison he left in Tarentum held out until 272 BC, and then surrendered to the Romans. In the same year, Pyrrhus, now involved in Peloponnesian politics, was killed in a street fight in Argos.

Lessons of the wars

In Sicily, Pyrrhus' failure was a determinant of history. As he himself prophesied, Rome was destined to inherit the Carthaginians as enemies. His campaign in Italy has passed into legend, as stated above, but it was not so much the costliness of his victories that rendered them barren. Just 75 years later, Hannibal, after defeating the Romans resoundingly at Trebia, Trasimene and Cannae, failed for the same reasons. Neither man was able to capture Rome, or win enough support from the peoples of Italy to achieve a decisive success. On both occasions, the political genius of the Romans really won their wars for them; in the 3rd century BC, the cities allied to them were fully conscious of the advantages they enjoyed.

Secondly, at a purely strategic level, the Romans gained confidence and experience from Pyrrhus' wars. Their weapons and tactics proved quite capable of coping with the Macedonian phalanx, which was probably more heavy and cumbersome than the version used by Alexander the Great. Certainly, it ran into difficulties at Asculum, where it was required to manoeuvre on broken ground.

Again, Pyrrhus' elephants, which struck terror into horses and so had thrown the Roman cavalry into confusion at Heraclea, proved not to be as effective at Beneventum, since, by this time, the Romans had learnt how to deal with them. The elephants themselves could be easily frightened, and so driven to run riot among their own troops. The Romans never forgot this valuable lesson.

PHARSALUS
THE CIVIL WAR BETWEEN CAESAR AND POMPEY
48 BC

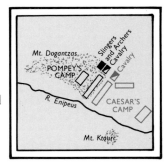

At Pharsalus in Thessaly (North Greece) Julius Caesar and Pompey (Gnaeus Pompeius) clashed in their struggle for control of the Roman world. Caesar commanded 22,000 men and Pompey about double that number. Caesar's victory in the battle was complete, but he still had to fight Pompey's confederates – notably in Africa and Spain – before he emerged as supreme ruler of Rome.

In the summer of 48 BC, Caesar abandoned his difficult and dangerous position at Dyrrhacium on the east Adriatic coast, where he had been attempting to besiege Pompey's numerically superior force. He now marched eastward through Thessaly. His main object in making this move was either to find much needed supplies of food for his troops, or to threaten Pompey's subsidiary bases in Greece. The superior fighting qualities of Caesar's legions effectively offset Pompey's larger numbers – a fact that was understood on both sides, at least by the two supreme commanders.

When Caesar struck camp at Dyrrhacium, Pompey's best course would probably have been to invade Italy, where the former's supporters would have found it extremely difficult to muster a defence. However, divided counsels prevailed in Pompey's camp, and he was pressed by the wealthy, noble and politically influential men on his staff to follow the enemy eastward and bring Caesar to battle. Accordingly, in early August, the opposing armies were encamped opposite each other near Pharsalus in Thessaly on the north bank of the Enipeus river. Pompey, without full confidence in his troops, still apparently favored a war of attrition, but, again under pressure from his own subordinates, led his men out to battle on the very day that Caesar was preparing for another march.

Indecision and decision

Hesitant to the last in pursuit of a strategy which had been forced upon him, Pompey ordered his troops to await the enemy attack. He feared that his comparatively inexperienced levies might lose cohesion in the course of an advance, and was anxious that they should not sacrifice the advantage they held of the higher ground. Caesar, however, was glad that the initiative had thus been left to him and welcomed the opportunity of striking the first blow.

Pompey's cavalry, massed on his left, though consisting mainly of young and raw troops drawn from Rome's eastern provinces, outnumbered Caesar's 1,000 horsemen by five to one and posed an obvious outflanking threat. To meet the danger, Caesar, leading his élite 10th legion on the right wing, positioned eight infantry cohorts obliquely behind him (these totalled only 3,000 men and were combined by Caesar to form six cohorts of full strength). These had orders to use their heavy javelins (*pila*) as lances to strike at the faces of the enemy cavalrymen. The tactics were successful, the Pompeian cavalry being thrown into confusion. As they fled, Caesar, calling up his third line of reserves, converged on Pompey's unprotected center and encircled it.

Pompey, stationed on the right wing of his own army, had not joined battle, waiting to see the effect of the cavalry charge on the other side of the plain. As soon as he realized the catastrophe that had enveloped his left and center, he rode away in despair from the battlefield to his camp. But even here, the victorious Caesarians pursued him, soon assaulting the camp's ramparts. He eventually escaped, to the Thessalian coast, and made his way by ship first to Mytilene, then to Egypt, where he possibly hoped to raise fresh troops. The clique of courtiers who ruled in Alexandria, in the name of the boy king Ptolemy XIII, were not prepared to back a loser, however, and Pompey was murdered as he stepped ashore.

As for Caesar, luck played an important part in his victory, as it did throughout his career. However, he was also supremely resourceful. In this battle; his ingenious use of seasoned infantry against numerous, but ill-trained, cavalry was a stroke of inspiration.

ROME'S CAPTURE BY THE GOTHS
ALARIC'S INVASION OF ITALY
410 AD

Alaric, the ruler of the Western Gothic settlers in Rome's Danubian province of Moesia, was himself a senior Roman officer, but hoped to extort further subsidies and concessions from the Emperor Honorius and so invaded Italy. Sheltered by the walls of Ravenna and supplied from the sea, Honorius refused to submit, even though Alaric's Gothic army, swollen by runaway slaves to around 40,000 men, besieged and ultimately plundered Rome (408-410).

Honorius had reigned over the western provinces of the empire since 395, sharing power with Arcadius, the Emperor of the East. Being no soldier himself, he

needed to employ an able general, but had unwisely put to death his commander-in-chief Stilicho, who alone had been able to check the depredations of Alaric in Italy and Greece.

The western Gothic community, to which Stillicho had granted land in Illyricum, had established itself north of the Alps in Noricum as a result of further migration in 408. After sending an ultimatum to Honorius at Ravenna, Alaric marched south through Italy and laid siege to Rome. His army laced the skill or equipment to storm fortifications, but Rome was vulnerable to blockade. Controlling the mouth of the Tiber, Alaric starved the city of all seaborne supplies. After suffering severe privations, during which help from Honorius at Ravenna was vainly expected, the Roman population and its prefect surrendered, agreeing to an alliance with Alaric and paying him an indemnity.

Negotiations and sieges

Honorius, still based at Ravenna and harassed by continual reports of rebellion in Britain and Gaul, at first confirmed these terms, but afterwards went back on his word – whereupon Alaric again laid siege to Rome. Still temporizing, Honorius invited Alaric to negotiate with him at Ariminium (Rimini), and abandoning his siege, Alaric embarked on further diplomacy. When his terms were rejected, however, he returned to Rome, which he could now control without occupying. He ordered the citizens to renounce their allegiance to Honorius and install their prefect Attalus as their ruler. They soon obeyed.

Alaric then campaigned in north Italy, but was powerless to take Ravenna, which had been reinforced unexpectedly by 4,000 troops from the eastern empire. Meanwhile, Attalus at Rome failed to despatch an effective force against the Ravenna government's supporters in Africa, on whom Rome's food supplies depended. Alaric deposed him, and re-opened negotiations with Honorius. For the third time these proved fruitless, and, for the third time, Alaric laid siege to Rome. In August 410, the city fell into his hands by treachery, a handful of Gothic slaves within the walls contriving to admit the besiegers. The Goths pillaged Rome for three days.

Since Honorius' governor in Africa still controlled food supplies to Italy, Alaric planned the invasion of Africa, and for this purpose assembled a fleet at Rhegium. A storm destroyed his ships, however, and he himself died suddenly at Consentia in late 410.

The capture of Rome was little more than a symbolic event, but it focuses attention on the changes which had almost imperceptibly affected the empire. Roman citizenship had been widely granted to barbarian peoples, and the political distinction between the two was disappearing. High-ranking officers in the Roman army were frequently of barbarian origin; Stilicho, Alaric's great rival, himself was a Vandal by origin. Similarly, Alaric himself may be seen equally as an invading Goth, or a dissident Roman general.

SALAMIS
PERSIAN INVASION OF GREECE
480 BC

Naval battle during the Persian invasion of Greece, in which the combined Greek fleet of 380 vessels defeated the 1200-strong Persian fleet, at a cost to the Persians of 200 ships. The Greeks lost about 40. The victory was a key factor in Greek survival.

During the summer of 480 BC, Xerxes's navy was playing a crucial role in the Persian ruler's overall strategy for his invasion of Greece. Its task was to keep pace with his coastal march through Thrace and northern Greece, so posing a continuous threat of seaborne landings in the rear of any Greek resistance. The battle of Salamis, that autumn, was to over-turn Xerxes' master plan and so marked a crucial switch in Greek fortune.

Greek strategy was based on one main premise. In the face of the Persian invasion, the Greeks determined to remain on the defensive and to fight in places where the Persians could not take advantage of their numerical superiority. The battle of Salamis was no exception. The Greek fleet of 380 ships, mainly made up of Athenian, Peloponnesian, Isthmian, Euboean and Aeginetan vessels, was based on Salamis. Though the Persian fleet had suffered losses due to storms and Greek action off Euboea, it had compensated for this by recruiting reinforcements from the maritime cities that Xerxes had already occupied in northern Greece, so its final strength was approximately 1200 vessels.

The Persians were themselves an inland nation, so Xerxes' navy was manned by Phoenicians, Egyptians and Ionian Greeks from Asia Minor. These last obviously could not be regarded as totally reliable in a war against their own kindred, so Xerxes established

himself on a golden throne at a high point overlooking the island and intervening strait, to enable him to observe personally how all the various contingents of his navy conducted themselves in battle.

Deceived by the enemy
On the eve of the battle, the final Persian dispositions were as follows. Xerxes had already sent his Egyptian squadron around Salamis to seal the strait at its westward mouth, so forestalling any Greek withdrawal. The main body of the fleet was strung out in a long line against the Attic shore, extending from Munychia, the fort of Piraeus, into the Salamis strait, where it faced the opposing Greek ships based on the island. After dark, the eastward division of the Persian fleet moved out to sea and blocked the eastward mouth of the strait. A detachment of Persian troops was posted on the mid-channel islet of Psyttaleia to deal with any survivors from the battle who might swim ashore there.

So far, all seemed as if it was going to plan, but there was one crucial miscalculation. In sending his Egyptian squadron to seal off the west of the strait, Xerxes had acted on false information deliberately supplied to him by Themistocles, the wily Athenian commander, who was anxious at all costs not to give his quarrelsome allies in the combined Greek fleet an excuse to disperse. Thus, by blocking this potential escape route, the Persians were playing into Themistocles' hands.

The battle and its aftermath
The Greek leaders on Salamis learned of their encirclement belatedly after dawn and most of them – though not, of course, Themistocles – were thrown into panic. The confusion that followed may have delayed them putting to sea, for Xerxes' ships moved in and attacked them before they could get under way. However, the Greeks rallied and a general engagement developed in the narrow waters where the Persians could not exploit their numerical superiority, just as Themistocles had always intended. Indeed, the Greeks' brief hesitation may have worked in their favor, since it may well have looked to the Persians like an attempt at withdrawal and so induced the attackers to break their disciplined order.

Superior skill and discipline, as well as faster and lower ships that were more manageable in the choppy sea, enabled the Athenians on the west wing to overwhelm the Phoenician vessels opposed to them, many of which were driven on to the Attic coast. The triumphant Athenians were then able to turn eastwards, taking the Ionians, who were already locked in battle with the Peloponnesians and Aeginetans, in the flank and rear. Driven headlong by the Athenians, the Ionians collided with their own incoming ships and the consequent wreck and confusion made them an easy prey, their flight becoming a rout. Greek *hoplites* landed on Psyttaleia and slaughtered its Persian garrison to a man.

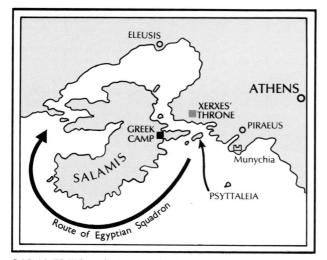

SALAMIS *When the Persians broke order in the narrows, the Athenians on the west were able to turn the tide of battle.*

According to contemporary accounts, 200 Persian ships were sunk at a cost to the victorious Greeks of about 40 vessels, though their crews mostly swam ashore. Though the Persians were still numerically superior, Xerxes, despairing of a naval victory, withdrew his fleet from the waters of mainland Greece. Of even more significance for the future was the emergence of Athens, with its 200-ship navy, as a naval power – a crucial development in Greek history.

VICTORIES OF TRAJAN
DACIAN AND PARTHIAN WARS
101/2, 105/6, 113/7 AD

A series of victories won by the Emperor Trajan in Dacia, north of the Danube, and in Mesopotamia, which marked the expansion of the Roman Empire to its greatest extent. As a result of his defeats, Decablus, the Dacian king, committed suicide in 102 AD; in 115, Trajan reasserted Roman power in the east against Parthia and conquered Mesopotamia before his death. Faced with superior enemy numbers on its long perimeter, the Roman Empire in the 2nd century deployed no more than 30 legions of about 5,000 men each. Auxilliaries, perhaps totalling 200,000, were recruited locally.

Though the Roman Emperor Domitian had won an ostensible victory against Decebalus in 89 AD, he nevertheless found it necessary to buy him off with

TRAJAN'S EMPIRE *Trajan brought Rome temporary military triumph over Parthia and expanded her Danubian frontiers.*

handsome subsidies and negotiating favorable treaty terms to counter the Dacian threat to Rome's Danubian frontier. One of Trajan's first military tasks, therefore, was to deal with the Dacian menace. Accordingly in 101 AD, the emperor, taking with him part of the Praetorian Guard, reached Viminiacum on the Danube, where a Roman garrison was already established. He crossed the river, leading his troops northward probably in two columns, but could not overcome the natural defences of the Dacian capital at Sarmizegetusae before winter set in.

Trajan wintered with his army on the Danube, his garrisons along the line of the river protecting the Roman province of Moesia to the south from Dacian attack. In the spring (102), he renewed his offensive successfully and imposed a treaty on Decebalus, the terms of which were not unduly severe. War broke out again in 105, however; this time, Trajan's armies converged on Sarmizegetusae and took it. In 106, Decebalus, forced to seek refuge in the forests and mountains in the north of the region, was pursued relentlessly by the Romans and eventually committed suicide to avoid capture. Dacia was incorporated into the Empire as a Roman province.

A period of peace followed the Dacian wars, but in the east the territory of Armenia was a permanent bone of contention between the Romans and the Parthians, since it was in this area that the spheres of influence of both powers intersected. Trajan was determined to settle the question once and for all in Rome's favour, and in 113 he launched a great eastern campaign, in which he relied not only on the Roman legions already posted along the frontier and their supporting local auxiliaries, but on the seasoned troops who had served him on the Danube. He was still ably supported by his brilliant lieutenant of the Dacian campaign, the Moorish cavalry commander Lucius Quietus. The conquest of Armenia (114), which was swiftly achieved could only be secured by a further expedition into Mesopotamia; accordingly, Mesopotamia was occupied in 115.

After wintering in Antioch (115-6) – where his life was endangered by an earthquake – Trajan led his army southward into Babylonia and drove the Parthian monarch Osroes from his capital at Ctesiphon. Having built a rivergoing fleet, Trajan eventually reached the mouth of the Tigris, but, at this stage, revolts in Mesopotamia and unrest in the Mediterranean provinces forced him to retreat. He subdued the Mesopotamian rebels, but was still marching westward when he fell ill and died (117) at Selinus in Cilicia (southern Turkey).

The Roman Empire under Trajan reached its greatest extent. His enlightened rule was the object of nostalgia among later generations of Roman citizens; although he kept imperial defence and administration firmly under his control, he was skilled in selecting and using deputies. It is doubtful, though, if his eastern campaign justified the effort it entailed.

CHAPTER TWO
The Dark Ages

The "Dark Ages" is one of those popular terms with little true historical meaning. It is held to have begun with the end of the Roman Empire in 476 and, in the best traditions of school-room history, as having ended in 1066 with the Norman Conquest of England. The first date is irrelevant as far as Britain is concerned, since the country ceased to be a province of the western empire almost 70 years before the fall of Rome; the second is relevant only to England. What is clear is that there was no sudden transition from a "dark" to an "enlightened" age. The evidence, insofar as it exists, serves to support the twin contentions that historical periods are largely a matter of convenience, and that, however useful they are as broad definitions, it is dangerous to base too many assumptions on such inevitable generalizations.

In what way was this period "dark"? Life was frequently short and brutish, but these are characteristics that could be applied to most of human history. Again, belief that this was a "dark age" often relies on the absence of source material, though it is worth remembering; that, as far as parts of Europe – Britain and Gaul for instance, – are concerned, rather more is known about this period than about the entire period of Roman dominance. Accordingly, many scholars now think it is more useful to define this period as "early mediaeval," rather than use the perjorative term of the "Dark Ages".

The absence of sources

When it comes to military history, however, the absence of sources is particularly acute. Even as far as the later Roman Empire is concerned, there are many areas of military organization that are unclear, but

GERMAN WARRIOR *A German foot soldier of the 9th century. He carries a spear, which could either be thrown or used as a pike for thrusting.*

the problems are multiplied in the period under discussion here, little information surviving on organization, equipment, strategy and tactics. Also, as will be seen, there are few accurate blow-by-blow battle descriptions. This, however, is not an unmixed blessing. Lack of specific detail forces historians to examine the campaigns and the nature of warfare – both of which are more important reflections of society than the individual battles themselves. The temptation to concentrate on the latter is obvious; battles, like football games, are exciting, over quickly, and normlly have clear-cut winners.

It was an over-reliance on battle-oriented studies and a distorted view of the "Dark Ages" that led to the

birth of what has been termed the "myth of medieval warfare", at the heart of which lies the notion that "arrogance and stupidity" combined with other "unsoldierlike qualities" to produce a form of warfare that was near chaotic at worst and disorganized at best. The classic statement of this myth in English is Sir Charles Oman's *A History of the Art of War in the Middle Ages*, first published in 1884. Despite the appearance of works of much weightier scholarship, Oman's work continues to be taken seriously. Modern scholars, however, have demonstrated, that when evidence is copious or at least detailed, early mediaeval warfare could be both sophisticated and well-organized.

From empire to barbarianism

As a political structure, the western Roman empire took a long time to die, and the eastern empire took even longer. The customary date for the fall of the west is 476, when the barbarian general Odovacar began to rule in Italy directly, without the customary puppet emperor, but nothing else really changed. By that time, too, the other western provinces were already ruled by different barbarian peoples, and a great deal that was "Roman" in terms of culture, administration and religion survived in them. To the east, the Byzantine Empire survived until the 15th century, although its power was on the decline after the sack of Constantinople in 1204.

In place of the western empire, a number of successor states were established. The most successful barbarian race was the Franks. In the late 4th century, they were only one of many such groups who had settled in Gaul; the great king and warrior Clovis (471–511), however, unified the Frankish tribes and brought the bulk of the province

EMPIRE IN THE EAST *A medal struck to commemorate a victory of Justinian's general, Belisarius, who fought successfully in Italy.*

under his rule. His sons and grandsons subdued the remainder, going on to establish a fluctuating protectorate over many peoples east of the Rhine, reaching as far as Hungary on one occasion. However, by the end of the 5th century, royal power had been succeeded by a plethora of local potentates.

Elsewhere in Europe other peoples established states. In Britain, the Germanic invaders (called Anglo-

Saxons to distinguish them from their continental cousins) conquered the lowlands and established several competing kingdoms. In Spain and around Narbonne, the Visigothic kingdom endured until it was over-

turned by the Muslim advance in 711–15. The north of the peninsula remained in Christian hands, however; when Muslim power began to weaken in the 11th century, the scene was set for the *Reconquista* (reconquest) that was to drive the Moors out of the peninsula. Italy was conquered by the Ostrogoths, who sought to preserve Roman civilization and government in full. The achievement of their king Theodoric (490–

526) was undone by the destructive Byzantine conquest (535–552), and a new barbarian people, the Lombards, quickly overran much of the peninsula after 568. The Lombard kingdom dominated Italy until the Frankish conquest of 774.

The reunification of Gaul

It was the achievement of the Carolingian dynasty (kings from 751) to reunify Gaul. This was the work of Charles Martel (714–41), whose defeat of the invading Moors at Tours put an end to their attempt is expand from Spain, and his son Pepin III (741–68). The Carolingian achievement, however, reached its apogee with Charlemagne (768–814), who created a vast empire, stretching from the Elbe to the Atlantic, and

UNITING GAUL *Clodovingian, 6th-century king of the Franks, was a member of the dynasty that succeeded in reuniting Gaul under a single ruler.*

from Denmark nearly to the Ebro and south of Rome. This achievement was recognized on Christmas Day 800, when he was crowned as the first Holy Roman Emperor. Unfortunately, the problems involved in holding such a vast state together, under pressure from natural centrifugal tendencies and external attack from the Vikings, Saracens and Magyars (a Hunnic race) could not be overcome, and disintegration set in from the later 9th century. However, it was out of the ruins of the Carolingian empire that the political geography of modern Europe ultimately evolved, although there was nothing inevitable about the form it would take. In what would become France, royal power again waned and the future seemed to lie with a number of regional forces – Anjou, Flanders, Aquitaine and Normandy, for example. Between the Moselle and Elbe rivers the Ottonian dynasty of kings from Saxony succeeded in arresting the

MAN OF WAR *Charlemagne's campaigns were carefully organized, as the elaborate preparations he made to subdue the Hungarian Avars in 791 demonstrated.*

process of political fragmentation and reversing it for a while in the 10th century, welding together the different nations into a powerful kingdom. Under this dynasty, the advance to the east began at the expense of the Slavs, while Otto I also succeeded in conquering the Italian kingdom (the northern two-thirds of Italy) in 962. The south, a patchwork of Lombard states, Byzantine possessions, and Muslim Sicily, were conquered by Norman adventurers in the 11th century (the battle of *Civitate* marks one stage in this process).

Further east there were important developments as well. The spread of militant Islam sheared off the richest provinces of the Byzantine empire. At the same time, in the 7th century, the Balkan peninsula was overrun by Slavs, Avars, and then Bulgars, whose empire threatened the Byzantine capital of Constantinople itself, until Basil II destroyed the Bulgars at the end of the 10th century. The 11th century saw the Byzantine empire reach a new peak of power, but decline set in after its defeat by the Ottoman Turks at *Manzikert* in 1071.

Elsewhere in the continent, new states continued to emerge in the 10th century. North of the Danube lay the kingdoms of Bohemia, Poland and Hungary, while, in Russia, the *Rus* (Viking) kingdom of Kiev became the dominant power in the 10th and 11th centuries. At the other end of Europe, the legacy of the Viking invasions in Britain was the establishment of a united English kingdom under the West Saxon dynasty.

Wars and warfare

It is clear from this, that, in many places, warfare was almost constant during this period as political fortunes shifted, particularly in border regions. Frankish chroniclers in the 8th century, for instance, thought it worthwhile to record the lack of an expedition in 790: the Royal Frankish Annals for that year state simply that Charlemagne "did not undertake a campaign but again celebrated Christmas and also Easter at the city of Worms. And the date changed to 791 . . ." In these circumstances, it is practically impossible to talk of wars in the modern sense. Frequently, war was almost endemic, with a few interludes of peace, although most wars were relatively brief, being confined to a short summer campaigning season.

The causes of war were complex, several motives being given for them in the contemporary sources. The punishment of a rebellious subject, the avenging of a slight or the pursuit of a blood-feud, the desire for territorial gain or for glory, and even the desire to spread the Gospel all feature. But, above all, stands the economic motive. War provided a means of making profit. The mark of a successful king was the ability to be generous to his followers, so ensuring their loyalty. As few rulers had access to sources of gold and silver, and as trade was relatively restricted, the easiest way to acquire wealth was to attack suitably weaker neighbors. Thus, most campaigning involved the ravaging of enemy territory, both in order to extract wealth

and to emphasize the futility of continued resistance. Occasionally, however, it is possible to identify a policy intended to win the "hearts and minds" of the enemy population. In 1013, for example, Swein of Denmark deliberately restricted his plundering in the north of England after its submission, resuming it only as he crossed Watling Street.

PEAK OF POWER *Byzantine 10th-century warriors. Campaigns of conquest, brought the empire to the peak of its power during this period.*

Plundering in this way served several purposes. The king could use his share of the loot – or any tribute paid to secure peace – to reinforce the loyalty of his nobles. Armies were able to augment their supplies from the food they seized – indeed, this was often essential, since few ever relied entirely on what they could take with them on campaign. There could be great pressure on kings to undertake such profitable raids; the Franks, for instance, are supposed to have told King Theuderic (511–34) that they would desert him for his brothers if he refused to lead them against the Burgundians. He satisfied their plunder-lust by turning them loose on a rebellious province instead.

Harnessing the war-like energies of the aristocracy and their followers to external wars could thus ensure internal peace. Successful wars were also vital for the financial well-being of a monarchy that had to provide generously for the aristocracy notionally subject to it. Without plunder, the resources of each dynasty were soon exhausted, and it either lost control – as the Merovingians did in 7th century Gaul – or found itself supplanted, as the Merovingians found in 751. Even in the Byzantine Empire, where the existence of a strong centralised administration meant that taxes continued to be levied, military success was vital to political stability.

The economy and recruitment

Accompanying and underlying the disintegration of the Roman Empire was an economic change that affected the way in which armies were organized. In its heyday, the Roman state raised money through taxation, the bulk of which went to pay for the maintenance of an army, several hundred thousand strong, for the defence of the empire's borders. In the 3rd and 4th centuries, however, when an increasingly high proportion of this army was recruited from barbarians (from outside the empire, or prisoners of war settled on lands within the empire), the system changed, with part of the army relying on land for some of its income.

The process culminated in the 5th century. As the empire in the west became incapable of solving its military problems, whole barbarian nations under their own rulers were allotted land to live on in return for the military assistance they agreed to provide the emperors. The first such settlement was of the Visigoths in part of Aquitaine in 418. Though the system was not entirely a bad one, the end result was the takeover of the empire from within (although this happened only because it was already perilously weak).

The process continued further in the eastern empire. In Byzantine Italy, the army literally replaced the local land-owning aristocracy. In the

7th century, much of the burden of recruitment and support that the Byzantine forces in Italy required was met from grants of land.

Thus, the transition from a state based on tax revenues to one based on possession of land preceded the so-called "fall of the Roman empire", but the process was not yet complete. The barbarian kings who succeeded the emperors continued to raise some money by taxation, but land increasingly became the basis of power. The key to the raising of military forces during this period is the deliberate use of land to secure the services of warriors – a principle enshrined in the Feudal System of the Middle Ages. Put at its simplest, this meant that, when kings gave land to aristocrats, they expected it to be used to support the bands of warriors the state required.

Although it is probably true that, in the German kingdoms, there was an obligation for all free men to serve in the ranks when occasion demanded, the brunt of fighting was borne by the better-off landowners and their followers. The central institution of warfare in this period, outside the Byzantine Empire, thus was the retinue, or military following, of kings and aristocrats. They were bound by special ties of loyalty, reinforced by lordly generosity – the Anglo-Saxon poems *Beowulf* and *The Battle of Maldon* provide us with a detailed insight into this world, where the "ring-giver," or "lord of the rings," expected – and was given – devoted service by his followers. These military households were the professional armies of the time, their major obligation being their readiness to fight in defence of their lord's person and land, though preferably in aggressive wars of loot.

Numbers and organization

There is widespread agreement among historians that the armies of this period were small in number; a force of 10,000 warriors was exceptional. This contradicts the figures given in the chronicles of the period, but it is generally agreed that these rarely provide an acceptable basis on which to calculate. When we look at

the size of the Viking bands active in the west, for instance, the conclusion is that most of them were numbered in hundreds.

The exception is the "Great Host," which operated from 865 to 896. This in all likelihood consisted of a few thousand men, at least as witnessed by the amount of damage it was able to inflict. However, the obvious fact is that Europe as a whole was technologically backward, the natural consequence being that the pool of men free from agricultural duties and so able to devote themselves to the pursuit of arms was necessarily limited. In such a society, therefore, it also follows that a small number of determined, well-equipped men could achieve a great deal, as the Normans did in southern Italy. These considerations also apply to the figures contemporaries give for Byzantine and Arab armies, even though greater faith is often shown in them.

Battlefield tactics

Contemporary western accounts give only the slightest insight into battle tactics, although the military manuals of the east make things clearer. Many records give the impression that, in the west, battles rapidly degenerated into single combats – another part-myth of early mediaeval and mediaeval warfare. History, however, shows that western armies not infrequently inflicted defeats on Byzantine and Arab armies; indeed, soldiers from the west were considered skilled enough to be employed as mercenaries by Byzantines. The chroniclers, it is clear, were writing for aristocratic audiences, and so their accounts concentrate on the heroic deeds of the few, rather than providing an objective report.

Some battle descriptions do, however, provide us with an indication of some of the tactics employed. Infantry generally formed line, even if, like the English and some of the Germans (like the Swabians at *Civitate*), they rode to battle. On foot, the infantry could either stand firm, acting as missile troops, or, fighting with swords, axes and spears, they could engage opposing infantry.

Manoeuvrability was limited, although Germanic infantry used a formation Latin writers described as a "wedge" when they charged.

The tactics light cavalry employed depended on their weapons. The Hunnic and Turkish cavalry consisted of mounted archers, who relied on fast movement and shooting a cloud of arrows to demoralize and disorganize the enemy before closing in to finish them off when their formation was broken. Other races fought on horseback with sword and spear – examples of these are the Arabs, Saxons, Bretons and Gascons. The Franks, from the 8th century at

HASTINGS *The Bayeux Tapestry provides an invaluable record of how Saxons and Normans fought.*

least, depended on the disciplined charge of their heavy cavalry, a technique which the German kings imitated two centuries later. Both found that a well-organized and co-ordinated charge was sufficient to sweep away the opposing horse archers, whose arrows could inflict little injury on armored men (see *Lechfeld*. In Byzantine armies, all these troop types were employed, but cavalry had the crucial role.

There, the cavalry were trained and equipped to fight both as shock troops and archers.

Battles and campaigns

The great majority of campaigns did not involve a pitched battle. This was not because, as Oman thought, mediaeval commanders in the west were rarely capable even of finding each other. Rather, they were men of common sense – at least, on the whole. War was taken seriously, but a number of factors combined to make it best to avoid a decisive clash. Armies were expensive to raise and battle was usually risky. If

the objectives of a campaign could be achieved without it, naturally the sensible thing to do was to avoid it. Thus sieges and plundering are the commonest features of warfare in this period, while the payment of tribute to secure peace was not uncommon. Generally, a policy of sensible calculation and caution prevailed. Warfare in both east and west was not without its hotheads, but they tended not to survive for very long in a hard world. The exception to this rule was civil war. Here, it was often necessary to risk battle in order to secure support, or to die trying to win it.

The Rise of Heavy Cavalry

By the end of the 11th century, warfare in western Europe was dominated by heavy cavalry, which was made up of either landowners or their retainers. They were men whose exploits included the conquest of southern Italy and England, the establishment of Europe's first colony – this was Syria – as a result of the First Crusade (1095–9) and who were advancing the frontiers of Christendom against pagans and unbelievers in Spain and central Europe. They were the warriors who so impressed the Byzantine princess and historian Anna Comnena that she commented "a mounted Kelt is irresistible; he would bore his way through the walls of Babylon. . . ." How this dominance was established has not been entirely explained, but the main stages of the process can be clearly defined.

The battle of Adrianople

In 378, an imperial army was crushed by a force of Goths and Huns at Adrianople, the eastern emperor Valens being among the dead. There has been a tendency to exaggerate the role played by the Gothic cavalry in the conflict – Adrianople was essentially an infantry battle – and so to mistakenly class it as a turning point in military history. In fact, the Romans had already been experimenting with armored cavalry in the later part of the 3rd century, while the Germans did not rely on cavalry alone in their wars. Among most barbarian peoples, only the wealthy fought as cavalry and men of lesser economic and social status fought on foot as spearmen and archers.

What is clear is that it seems as if the Anglo-Saxons were the only barbarian peoples not to have used the horse to fight from, although the evidence is sparse. In the armies of the east Romans, though cavalry was playing an important role by the 6th century, it is equally clear that the infantry were not a neglected fighting arm.

The Carolingians and the stirrup

According to many historians another turning point in the rise of heavy cavalry came in the 8th century. At first, it was held that the Frankish ruler Charles Martel realized the need to raise large forces of heavy cavalry after his clash with the Arabs at the battle of Poitiers in 732. He provided the necessary economic base for this through massive seizures of church property, which was then granted to warriors in return for mounted military service. When this theory was discredited, Lynn White put forward a modified version of it, claiming that it was knowledge of the stirrup that permitted the development of true heavy cavalry, since it was this that gave the rider a firm enough seat from which

sword and lance could be used in "mounted shock combat". It was this advance, so White claimed, that made the cavalry the master of the battlefield from the first half of the 8th century onwards.

Many objections have been raised to this interpretation, however. While the benefits conferred by the stirrup are indisputable, there is no evidence that knowledge of it reached western Europe at this time – nor that cavalry became a major element in Frankish armies before the end of the 8th century. The success of the Carolingian dynasty in its wars of conquest, which continued for almost a century, lay in its methods. Its command of the art of siege warfare allowed it to conquer Aquitaine and north Italy; its

BYZANTINE AND ACTION *A Byzantine horseback warrior of the 11th century. Cavalry played an important role in the armies of the eastern empire from the 6th century AD onwards.*

mastery of logistics made it possible for the monarchy to field armies far larger in number than those of its foes, who consequently were reluctant to face the Carolingians in battle; its armies also fought with a destructiveness and sheer savagery that destroyed the ability and will of most opponents to resist. The Carolingians ground down their enemies between fire and sword.

This is not to belittle the role of heavy cavalry in the armies of Charlemagne. Though estimates of the numbers available around the year 800 vary from between 5,000 and 35,000, what is certain is that the Franks possessed a truly formidable cavalry arm. The key lay in their ability to equip large numbers of these

If they maintained their discipline, they were irresistible, while their superior equipment also gave them an advantage should they need to fight on foot. There is no reason to suppose that this was unusual.

Germany in the 10th century

The division of Charlemagne's lands by his grandsons left the East Frankish (German) kingdom with relatively few Franks from which to recruit. When Henry the Fowler, the ruler of Saxony, became king (918–36), he created his own body of armored cavalry in what amounted to a military revolution. They gave his dynasty (the Ottonians) an advantage over its enemies in Germany, Slavonia and Italy for several generations, and were, though always a minority element (perhaps 6,000 in the 980s), the dominant element of German armies from this time.

The Saxon nobility had hitherto been used to fighting on horseback as light skirmishers, incapable of engaging the Franks on equal terms. Henry turned them into disciplined, professional soldiers able to fight in the Frankish manner, living in retinues, or off money grants. Before the battle of Riade (933), he reminded them of their training; they were to maintain their line, using their shields to deflect the first volley of arrows, and only then to spur their horses to close with the Magyars before they could discharge a second volley. It was on these men that the success of the German empire was founded in the 10th and 11th centuries.

The "couched" lance

The Frankish and German heavy cavalry used the lance as a thrusting or throwing weapon, the crucial stages of a battle being decided by sword-play. However, at the end of this period, a significant development took place in cavalry warfare – this was the "couching" of the lance under the arm, so realizing the full potential that the stirrup and a high saddle gave a rider in mounted shock combat.

This "jousting" technique united the momentum of horse and rider into one irresistible projectile. It was developed to unseat a mounted opponent, as the Bayeux Tapestry depicts – albeit at an early stage of development at the time of the battle of *Hastings*. In the tapestry, some Norman knights are shown fighting in this way, though the majority are still seen thrusting with their spears, overarm or underarm. This may have been a response to the type of formation the English took up and its position on the battlefield, both of which made jousting unsuitable.

A combination of factors was therefore required for the flowering of heavy cavalry as the dominant battlefield force in the 10th and 11th centuries, chief amongst them being the necessary military and social elite, which was expensive to equip, train and support. Even while this dominance was being established, however, the importance of infantry was never forgotten, as shown by the battle of Hastings and the events of the First Crusade.

ANGLO-SAXON AND NORMANS
Though for the early part of this period, the Anglo-Saxons did not fight from horses, they had joined the other barbarian peoples in organizing cavalry forces by the time of the 8th century, as this set of ivory chess pieces (left) shows. From that time on, cavalry gradually became a formidable battlefield force, particularly in the hands of the Carolingians and, later, the Normans in their campaigns in Italy and at Hastings (above).

expensive warriors with mail-coats, helmets, swords and lances, and suitable horses, and the explanation of how they were able to afford to do this is an economic one – the ability to raise taxes. Charlemagne paid careful attention to the equipment of his armies – including infantry and light cavalry – and to supplying them on campaign.

Pitched battles were rare in these wars. When they did occur, the Frankish armored cavalry possessed a distinct advantage over their less-armored enemies – so long, that is, as they remembered their training (see *Süntel Mountains* and the *Dyle*). Their tactic was to charge in close formation, so as to hit the enemy line in a single mass, and to fight at close-quarters with swords.

ASHDOWN, SAUCOURT, PARIS AND THE DYLE

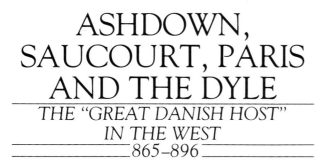

THE "GREAT DANISH HOST" IN THE WEST
865–896

During its long career the "Great Danish Host" fought many battles, but, because Christian chroniclers had no interest in recording Christian defeats, details of only three battles survive, and those are sparse. At Ashdown (871), Ethelred of Wessex and his brother Alfred won a victory, which was of no long-term importance. At Saucourt (881) Louis III of West Francia ("France") defeated a small foraging band, while in 891 the "Great Host" met defeat at the hands of Arnulf, ruler of the East Franks, on the Dyle near Louvain. There are also details of the siege of Paris (885–6). Here, a bridge prevented progress up the Seine. It was successfully defended, but the passage of the river was later conceded by Emperor Charles the Fat.

The "Host" in England
Late in 870 the "Great Host" fortified a winter camp in Wessex at Reading, on the River Thames. Saxon reaction was prompt, but, though the ealdorman of Berkshire drove off a foraging party at Englefield, an assault on Reading itself by King Ethelred of Wessex and his brother Alfred was repulsed. Four days later, however, the armies met again on the Berkshire downs at Ashdown.

The battle took place on the hillside – at a place where a single thorn-tree grew, around which the fighting took place. The Vikings drew up in two divisions on the higher ground; Kings Bagsecg and Halfdan, with their followers, formed one, while their earls and their warbands formed the other. Each division organized itself in standard shieldwall formation. The English followed suit, but, because Ethelred was slow to leave Mass, Alfred was forced to bear the initial brunt of battle with his own wing alone.

It is not clear whether the commitment of the remaining West Saxon contingent tipped the scale, but the Vikings broke and fled back to Reading. Their losses included one king and five earls, but not the thousands the chroniclers reported. Indeed, they were able to recover quickly enough to inflict several defeats on the West Saxons in the following months – at least nine battles were fought, including Wilton (871), at which they won victory through use of the tactic of the feigned flight. By the end of the year, Alfred (now king) was forced to buy peace, but, by refusing to surrender completely, he was able to make it difficult for the Vikings to plunder in their accustomed fashion.

The battle of Saucourt
In 878, however, Alfred fought the "Great Host" to a standstill. As a consequence, those of its number who did not wish to settle in occupied England crossed to Francia to exploit the discord that had arisen between the great-grandsons of Charlemagne. The Franks' internal problems enabled them to establish their position, and it was not until July that Louis III, king of the west Franks (the region between the Loire and Meuserivers), took the field with a cavalry force and rode against the Danes based at Courtrai. Louis's scouts

THE "DANISH HOST" *Viking penetration of north-west Europe and Britain saw many raids and battles. Peak activity*

was between 865 and 896; permanent Viking success, however, only came with Cnut's accession to the English throne in 1016.

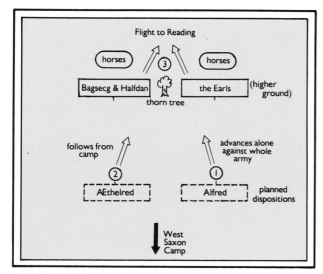
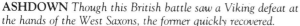

ASHDOWN *Though this British battle saw a Viking defeat at the hands of the West Saxons, the former quickly recovered.*

helped him to run a Viking band to ground in the *villa* (fortified manor house) of Saucourt, but the Franks force lacked the confidence to attack them. The issue was forced, however, when "a few" Danes launched a sally, killing about 100 of the Franks. Louis' forces wavered, and it was only the sight of their young king leaping from his horse to stand his ground that rallied them to turn and slaughter the Vikings. Louis followed up his victory by building a fort to discourage further raids south towards Cambrai, and the host moved its base further away, into the kingdom of the East Franks.

So much can be accepted, but it is here that contemporary sources and historical probability contradict one another. Danish casualties were put at between 8,000 and 9,000, but it is unlikely that the entire host contained such a number. The battle was lauded as a brilliant victory and aroused much contemporary interest, yet only a single band of Danes was involved, and the activity of the remainder was hardly impeded. Although Saucourt showed that the "Great Host" was not invincible, it still was difficult to drive the Danes off completely. Louis's own defiance was short-lived – he died in a fit of drunken lust in 882 and the Vikings soon returned to exploit the discord that ensued in the kingdom.

The siege of Paris

By the mid–880s, the defences of the Seine-Rhine area were beginning to harden, as towns and churches were fortified. In 885 the "Great Host" accordingly changed its base, moving to the Seine basin, a region that had enjoyed freedom from Danish attack for several years. The way to Burgundy, however, was blocked by the defenders of Paris - at this time, a fortified island in the Seine whose two bridges, each with a fort on the bank, prevented the passage of the Viking fleet.

The broader northern channel was the focus of the Viking efforts at first, an eye-witness account of their

forces estimating them at 700 vessels and 40,000 men (a grossly exaggerated total). On November 26, they launched a two-day assault on the northern tower, which, although it was not fully built of stone, managed to resist their attempts to storm, undermine and burn it. The Danes accordingly set up their own fortified camp, and foraged for supplies for the winter.

The next assault was launched at the beginning of February 886, and lasted for three days. The Vikings had made elaborate preparations for it in the form of battering rams and mantlets, but because it proved impossible to fill the ditch protecting the fort, these could not be brought into action. An attempt to float a fireship down river on to the bridge was frustrated by its stone piers. Nature came to the Vikings' aid on 6 February, when the southern bridge was washed away, which meant that its isolated tower could be taken, but the channel was found to be too narrow to be of use.

The Vikings now returned to their plundering, north into Francia and south into Neustria before transferring their camp from the north to the south bank of the Seine. From there, they could attack the walls of the island stronghold. Preparations were slowly being made to relieve Paris, however. Supplies were brought in March, while in June Odo, the city's commander, fought his way back in with reinforcements. By the end of the summer, the emperor Charles the Fat was on his way, and the Danes launched another furious and unsuccessful assault.

Despite this heroic resistance, the youthful emperor paid tribute to the Vikings and opened the river into Burgundy in mid-October. What the siege demonstrated was that stout walls could be defended against the Danes, who, at the same time, were capable of using sophisticated siege techniques.

Battle on the Dyle

In the summer of 891, part of the host again established a winter camp in Louvain. The first army sent against it was defeated on 26 June, near the river Geule; the Franks made a headlong and undisciplined charge

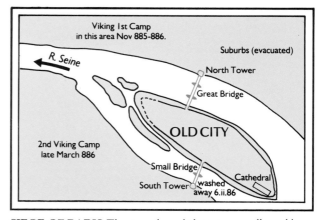

SIEGE OF PARIS *The siege showed that strong walls could defeat the Danes, despite their skill in siege warfare.*

against the awaiting Danes, who were drawn up on foot in a circle. Their mounted foraging parties then returned and fell on the Franks, killing many and seizing their baggage train. The action shows that the Danes could fight on horseback.

Arnulf, the ruler of the East Franks, now advanced against the Danes in person, who were by now based in a fortified camp in a loop of the river Dyle, protected by marshes. The East Frankish army crossed the river to get to grips with their foes, but, finding the ground unsuitable for a cavalry charge, dismounted. The *Annals of Fulda* say that grave doubts were expressed about this, because "it was unusual for the Franks to fight *pedetemptim*" – the theory that the Franks could no longer fight on foot is due to a misinterpretation of *pedetemptim*, which means "step by step". What actually happened was that the Franks launched a disciplined infantry assault and successfully stormed the Viking camp. Seventeen banners were captured, while the "Great Host" itself returned to England.

Battles of 1016

Some details also survive about two more battles from the so called "second Viking age" – those fought at Sherston and at the hill of Ashingdon in 1016. At Sherston, in Dorset, King Edmund II "Ironside" fought a drawn battle against Cnut and his English ally, Eadric "Streona", Ealdorman of Mercia. Edmund again arrayed his army in the traditional shieldwall formation with the "best men" in the front rank, and advanced to engage the Scandinavian-English army. After heavy slaughter, the two sides separated, and, on the following morning, the Danes left the field. On 18 October, after several victories over Cnut, Edmund met him again at Ashingdon in Essex. On this occasion, he drew up his forces in three divisions and advanced in echelon. Eadric, who had deserted Cnut, is blamed by the chroniclers for initiating the fight, which led to a heavy English defeat. Casualties among the English leaders and nobility were so heavy that they could no longer resist the invaders and England was partitioned between the two sides. This compromise lasted only until Edmund's death in November, however, after which Cnut brought the whole kingdom under his rule.

CATTERICK
THE ENGLISH SETTLEMENT OF BRITAIN
c.600

To counter the growing threat of the Anglian settlement around Bamburgh, King Mynyddog of the Gododdin sent an army south from his fortress at Din Eidyn (Edinburgh). Its destruction at Catraeth (Catterick) opened the way for English expansion north to the Forth. The poem *Gododdin*, though it does

not give a clear account of the fighting, is the only record of a Dark-Age battle in Britain, and so is the only authentic source of information on the general way in which battles were fought in this period.

Around 600, three attempts were launched to destroy the English kingdom of Bernicia, an outpost north of the River Tees based on the promontory fortress at Bamburgh. In the first, a coalition of Celtic kings from across the Pennines unsuccessfully besieged Bernicians on the island of Lindisfarne (c. 580s–90s). The second came from Gododdin, a kingdom that stretched from the Firth of Forth to the Tees and now was threatened by the Bernician presence.

The muster and its record

Catterick is the only battle in Dark Age Britain that has survived as more than a name – the battle of Mount Badon is a name alone. The reason for this is the survival of a poem by the contemporary Aneirin, describing the army that set out for Catterick from the north. Mynyddog recruited it from his own lands, and from other British kingdoms, men rallying to his banner from Elmet (the Leeds district of Yorkshire), Gwynedd (north Wales), Strathclyde (Cumbria and Galloway), and from among the Picts. According to the poet the army consisted of 300 cavalry when it set out, but, as infantry are also referred to, it is quite likely that each of the 300 hundred "heroes" led a retinue of followers.

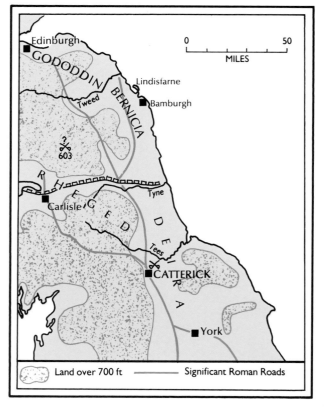

CATTERICK *A battle celebrated in a poem that raises more questions than it answers about warfare in the Dark Ages.*

However, it is a mistake to build on these bare facts to assume that this Celtic cavalry were organized like Roman cataphracts. If this had been so, it would imply that the romantic Arthurian legends have some bearing on Dark Age reality, which they do not; it would also mean Roman military organization survived Rome's withdrawal from Britain in the early 5th century, which is equally mistaken. Mynyddog remained in his fastness at Edinburgh to await the outcome of the battle, although the objective of the campaign is not clear.

There were two possible routes the army could take from Din Eidyn – along the east coast road, or south to Carlisle and across Stainmoor. Both led to Scotch Corner and Catterick, the latter being a strategic point in the north. It was a royal *vill*, the name used to describe an important administrative center; it was the site of a small Roman town that controlled the entrance to the fertile lowland of the vale of York; and it was close to the border between Deira and Bernicia. So much, at least, is known. The purpose of the expedition, however, can only be guessed at, since it has passed unrecorded, as has the exact details of the clash that ensued. It was probably not the intention to seize Catterick and drive a wedge between the two fledgling kingdoms, as such a notion was alien to the warfare of the time. It is more likely that it was intended as a *chevauchée* (raid) designed to cause as much damage as possible, and so to weaken the power of the Bernicians.

The fight at Catterick
The poem gives only a confused account of the battle that occurred around Catterick – its purpose was to praise the deeds of the dead heroes, and not to provide its readers with an accurate report of the fighting. What it reveals is that this was neither a surprise dawn attack, nor a fight for a river-crossing. It refers to plans and designs, to hundreds, wings and a van, to the 'battle-pen' (shield-wall), the throwing of spears and close-quarter fighting with swords. What it does not give is a coherent picture of the battle, and no reference to the tactics of the English. The only firm conclusion is the fact of Gododdin's defeat and the death of the 300 heroes.

CIVITATE
NORMAN CONQUEST OF SOUTHERN ITALY
18 June 1053

By 1052, Pope Leo IX had taken the unprecedented step of organizing a military coalition to fight against the Norman immigrants in southern Italy. However, the papal army was intercepted on the bank of the River Fortore by the combined forces of the Norman colonists in south Italy, before it could effect a junction with its Byzantine allies in Apulia. Leo's forces were completely defeated, while he himself was taken prisoner. By the 1070s, the Normans had established their mastery over the south.

A secular as well as a religious leader, Pope Leo IX regarded the Norman expansion into southern Italy as a threat to his power and prestige, and was determined to check it. However, his first expedition in 1052, when he relied on an army drawn from the Italian and Lombard nobility, plus Byzantine remnants from the south of Italy, came to nothing. In 1053, unable to obtain support from the German emperor, he decided to hire a troop of 700 Swabian infantry, and set out for the south again. As the army marched, its ranks were swollen by adventurers seeking pay and plunder, plus most of the non-Norman barons and the city militias of southern and central Italy.

Leo's plan was to join with the Byzantine forces, concentrated on Siponto in northern Apulia, and form a unified army, but this was foiled. The Normans assembled a force of some 3,000 cavalry, but "few" infantry (a recognized weakness), on the main road from Benevento; in mid-June they marched northwards from the fortress of Troia to intercept Leo, and on 17 June confronted him on the small plain where the Staina flows into the River Fortore. Although the strength of the former is unknown, it outnumbered the Normans.

Neither side was eager to put their fortunes to the test in the hazard of battle. Norman sources say that their offer to submit to papal authority was rejected, but, according to Leo, fighting commenced on the next morning, while negotiations were still in progress.

A surprise attack
On the morning of 18 June, the Normans, under Humphrey d'Hauteville, marched up the hill separating the armies, ready for battle. On the right, Richard

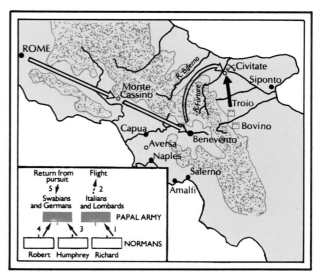

CIVITATE *In this clash between Pope and Normans, it was the Norman heavy cavalry that proved to be the decisive factor.*

d'Aversa, with a squadron of picked knights, faced the Italian contingents, who were viewed with near contempt. The Italians were grouped together on masse and were ignorant of good battle order – at the first impact of the Norman charge, they fled the field. In the center, Humphrey faced the Swabians, tall men who fought dismounted with long, two-handed swords that could cause terrible injuries to both men and horses. The archers on both sides exchanged fire and the Norman cavalry charged, but they were unable to break the tight formation of the Swabians.

The third Norman division – this consisted of Humphrey's half-brother Robert Guiscard and his followers from Calabria – was in reserve on the left with orders to charge at discretion. This Robert did, but the charge also made little impression, and it was the return of Richard with the triumphant right wing that proved the deciding factor. The Swabians were assailed from all sides, and cut down to a man. Leo was captured as he attempted to escape from the field; the wily pope soon concluded an alliance with the Normans, however.

Many details of the battle are confused. The papal center cannot have consisted of the 700 Swabians alone, given that they resisted two divisions of the Norman host, and included archers in their ranks. What is probably the case is that Leo's plan to confront the Normans with a vastly superior force miscarried, owing to the obstinacy of the Swabians, who, having joined the expedition to make a profit, forced him to fight when the Normans had the twin advantages of the better ground and surprise. The later realized the seriousness of their position and that they had to force an action before the numerical balance turned against them completely.

BATTLE OF HASTINGS
NORMAN CONQUEST OF ENGLAND
14th October 1066

The last of three major engagements fought in England in 1066, the battle of Hastings was the deciding conflict in the contest between the English ruler Harold and Duke William of Normandy, his rival for the throne. The strengths of the two armies are unknown, though modern historians have suggested that each army consisted of 6,000 to 7,000 men. The battle ended in Norman victory, but it was not until 1070 that William was firmly established in England. Hastings is unique in that there is a contemporary visual record of its course in the Bayeux Tapestry, completed only a few years after the battle.

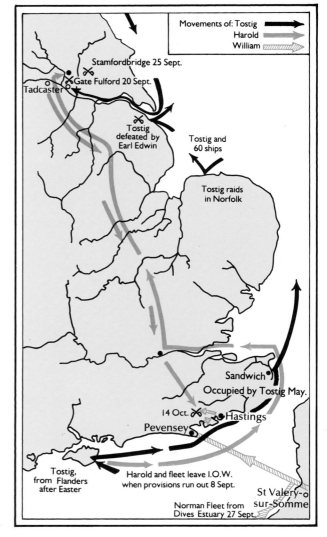

FROM NORTH TO SOUTH *After defeating the Norwegians at Stamford Bridge, Harold hurried south by forced marches.*

At the start of 1066, there were three men who possessed the military muscle to back up their claims to the English throne. The first of these was an Englishman – Earl Harold Godwinson of Wessex, and it was he who was crowned king. After Easter, he mustered a fleet and army to guard the south coast eastwards from the Isle of Wight against the threat of Norman invasion but, after four months, their provisions exhausted and term of service expired, he had to send his troops home. Meanwhile in Norway, King Harald Hardrada prepared to invade, while, in Normany, Duke William began to raise an army from among his subjects, plus the volunteers who rallied to his banner from much of France and even southern Italy, and started to build an invasion fleet.

Defeat of the Norwegians
The Norwegians were the first to make their move,

sailing into the Humber estuary in the north of England in mid-September. The two northern earls, Edwin and Morcar, mustered an army to meet the threat, but were heavily defeated at Gate Fulford on 20 September. For his part, Harold reacted as soon as he heard of the landing; in a fortnight, he organized an army and marched the 190 miles from London to York. At Stamford Bridge on 25 September, he and his troops achieved complete surprise and utterly defeated the invaders. Both armies fought on foot (the tradition that the English fought mounted in this battle stems from 13th-century Scandinavian misunderstanding).

The Norman invasion

The Norman fleet sailed on the evening of 27 September, making its landfall the next day. Harold who heard the news while still in the north, again decided on a rapid response. In under 14 days, he recruited a new army, sent a fleet to blockade the English Channel, and led his men in a 250-mile forced march south to a point just short of Hastings. To an outsider, there can be little doubt that what the chronicles termed this "reckless and impulsive haste" was an error, though, in Harold's eyes the desire to take William by surprise – a tactic he had used with success against the Norwegians – outweighed the disadvantages. These were plain. His men were exhausted, his army was smaller than it need have been, and time was on his side, rather than on William's.

At Hastings, William kept his men in a state of readiness. His scouts informed him of the English approach on the evening of 13 October, and early on the following morning he marched out to give battle. Thus, it was Harold, rather than the Normans, who was taken by surprise on this momentous occasion. The English army dismounted to form its shieldwall along the crest of a sharp ridge, with its flanks well protected.

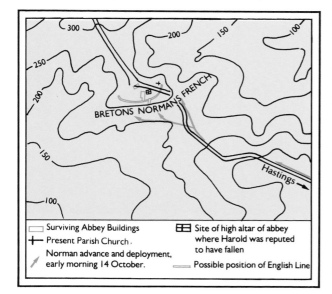

Surviving Abbey Buildings
— Present Parish Church.
Norman advance and deployment, early morning 14 October.
⊞ Site of high altar of abbey where Harold was reputed to have fallen
═ Possible position of English Line

HASTINGS *The battle's turning point was the feigned flights that lured the English from their strong ridge-top position.*

Harold stood on the highest point of the ridge with his *housecarls* (household warriors). Before him, were arrayed the men who had answered his call to arms; in the main, these were well-equipped landowners since, although the Bayeux Tapestry indicates armed men were also present, the English army was deficient in archers.

Battle to the death

Harold's forces occupied a strong position, but it was too constricted to take the whole of his army. He had also been forced to fight at a time and place not of his choosing. Below him in the valley, William's army formed up in three lines. The front rank consisted of archers, the next of heavy infantry, and the last of heavy cavalry – the Norman knights. William was in the center with the Normans, his Breton allies were on the left, and his remaining contingents on the right. The circumstances of the battle committed the English to defence, and the Normans to attack.

Action started around 9 am, when the first two Norman lines advanced – only to be repulsed with heavy losses by the great axes wielded by Harold's *housecarls*. The knights advanced in their turn, but they, too, failed to make any impression on the English ranks, whose weapons and height advantage helped keep the Normans at bay. The Bayeux Tapestry shows most knights thrusting with their lances, over and under arm – their newly-developed technique of using the lance "couched" was not well suited to charging a solid mass of infantry on a hill, since it had been devised to unseat mounted opponents.

On the left, the Bretons now began to fall back. The movement spread along the line, and threatened to turn into a rout, as the rumor spread that William was dead. Some of the English followed in pursuit. For the Normans, this was the crisis of the battle, but William halted the potential rout by his personal intervention, and the cavalry returned to the attack, cutting down the pursuing English.

With the main part of the English army still standing firm against renewed Norman attacks, it was clear that they could not be defeated by direct assault, and that another tactic would have to be employed. This was the feigned flight, the retreat of the knights tempting more of the English down from the ridge to be slaughtered. The units used for this ploy were the *conrois*, the name given to the contingents of individual lords that had trained together, so there is no dispute about the Norman cavalry discipline and ability to carry out this manoeuvre. Still the English army resisted, although diminished in numbers. The Norman knights and infantry together returned to the assault and finally began to make inroads into the shieldwall. The tradition that William ordered his archers to shoot at a high trajectory into the English ranks at this point is a 12th-century legend, and not well-founded, although there is no doubt that, in the final stages of the battle, his cavalry attacks were coordinated with archery fire.

Dusk was falling and, in spite of their losses, the English army might have survived until the safety of nightfall. At this moment, however, Harold fell, shot in the face by an arrow and then cut down by a party of knights (the tapestry shows this in an "animated" scene). His brothers Gyrth and Leofwine had fallen some hours earlier, so, after their king's banner fell, the survivors melted away into the Weald. Some of the English fought on to cover the retreat, but the battle was won and William's sole surviving rival for the English throne was now dead.

BATTLE OF THE LECH
MAGYAR INVASIONS 893–955
10 August 955

In the late summer of 955, a strong army of Magyar horse archers invaded Bavaria, intending to force Otto, the German king, into a pitched battle. This took place near Augsburg, where the outnumbered German heavy cavalry inflicted an overwhelming defeat on the Magyars. Their command structure was disrupted for decades, and the destructive raids they had been launching into the west were brought to an end.

By 955, the Magyars, a group of nomadic peoples living around the middle Danube, had been conducting

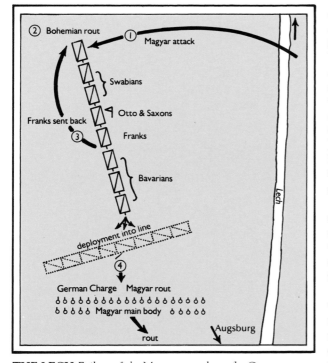

THE LECH *Failure of the Magyar attack on the German rear led to their defeat at the hands of the Moravian heavy cavalry.*

destructive raids far into western Europe for 60 years. They were a fast-moving race of horse-archers, who came to plunder rather than conquer, and consequently were difficult to bring to battle and defeat convincingly. Their normal tactics were to avoid pitched battle – at Riade (933), for instance, a trap had to be set to draw them into combat with King Henry's heavy cavalry. By the middle of the 10th century, however, the defences of Germany – based on a network of strong fortresses and increasing numbers of armored cavalry – were making Magyar raids less profitable. In that year, therefore, they reversed their tactics, setting out in the intention of inflicting a decisive defeat on their German foes. To this end, they invaded Bavaria and awaited Otto's approach.

On 8 August, the Magyars laid siege to Augsburg, but raised it the following day, when a rebel Bavarian noble warned them that Otto was nearby. The German ruler had set out from Saxony in late July and, on his march to Bavaria, had collected a small army of perhaps 4,000 men from the warbands of the various German duchies. His force thus consisted of seven "legions" of cavalry – "all iron-clad" in strong hauberks and helmets – who were trained to fight at close-quarters with swords, plus a contingent of Bohemian light cavalry. The lighter arms and equipment of the Magyars would be no match for them if they could get to close quarters.

Battle with the Magyars
The German army approached Augsburg on the morning of 10 August in a loose column. Three "legions" of Bavarians were in the van, followed by the Franks, Otto with the Saxons, picked warriors from the other German duchies marching under a standard decorated with an effigy of St Michael, two units of Swabians and, in the rear, the Bohemians with the baggage train. The route the army followed was deliberately chosen to pass through broken terrain, so as to frustrate any attack by the Magyars but, in fact, they seized the advantage by sending a force along the opposite bank of the Lech to attack the rear of the German column. This raiding force soon put the Bohemians to flight, but threw away the advantage it had gained by stopping to plunder the German baggage. Otto responded quickly by sending back his fourth division to see off the danger.

The remainder of the battle was something of an anti-climax. The Germans deployed into line and charged in good order. The bulk of the Magyars fled, while the bravest and best-armed – the Magyar chieftains – were isolated and cut down. Many of the fleeing Magyars were killed in the pursuit that followed.

Historians of the period assume the Magyar plan was to throw the German host into disorder and then to fall on it, but that, when the ruse failed, they left themselves open to the crushing German cavalry charge. This was one of the few battles in this period to which the epithet "decisive" can be applied – the death of so many Magyar leaders paralyzed the leadership.

MALDON
THE SECOND VIKING AGE
10 August 991–11 August 991

Maldon belongs to what historians term the "second Viking age" at the end of the 10th century. Some 93 Viking ships, and perhaps some 5,000 men, raided the east coast of England under the command of the Norwegian Olaf Tryggvason. They were brought to battle near Maldon in East Anglia, where Brihtnoth, Ealdorman of Essex, was defeated and killed. Peace had eventually to be bought by payment of the first *danegeld* (tribute) of Aethelred the Unready's reign.

Historians date the "second Viking age" as starting in 980, after which the tempo and forces involved in the Viking campaigns gradually increased until Swein and Cnut, successive kings of Denmark, were in a position to conduct extended campaigns in England, finally conquering the country in 1016. During this period, many battles were fought – in 1016 alone there were four major clashes and two sieges of London – but only Maldon has been satisfactorily described. The battle itself was not of primary importance in the context of Aethelred's reign – its significance lies in the fact that it was described in some detail in an unparalleled contemporary poem. The poet may not have been an eye-witness to the action, but his account is nevertheless the only contemporary record of an Anglo-Saxon army at war.

The Viking resurgence
The build-up to the battle started with the Viking fleet moving south from Ipswich to the estuary of the Blackwater, where a camp was established on Northey Island. In response, Ealdorman Brihtnoth raised an army from the men of his shire, plus retainers, and drew up opposite the island. The English dismounted to form

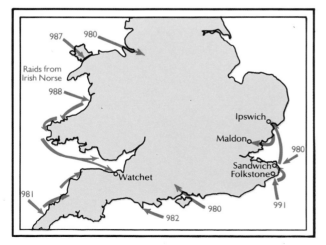

SECOND WAVE *The second Viking Age culminated in a Danish dynasty establishing itself on the English throne in 1016.*

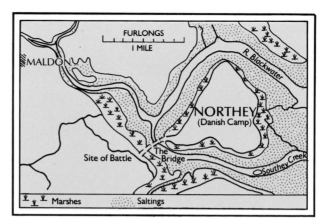

MALDON *Miscalculation by the over-confident Brihtnoth allowed the Danes to cross the causeway and give battle.*

the traditional shieldwall, and the horses were taken to the rear, while Brihtnoth and his enemy exchanged heroic speeches (these are the least reliable part of the poem). At first, three Englishmen apparently held the causeway, but, subsequently, Brihtnoth allowed the raiders to cross it and form up in battle order.

The battle opened with an exchange of hurled spears and archery fire, before the two shieldwalls came to close quarters with spears and swords. Before long, Brihtnoth himself was wounded and then cut down. A panic set in, many of the English running to the horses to flee. Since the conclusion to the poem, in common with its start, is missing, what happened at the end of the battle is unknown. The surviving portion concludes with the heroic resistance of some of Brihtnoth's retainers, until they, too, were cut down.

The aftermath of the defeat saw the first payment of *danegeld* to the Vikings, and, over the further 25 years the wars lasted, English resistance seems to have been ineffective. Aethelred's provisions for defence were dogged by ill-luck, treachery and poor planning (the *unræd* of his epithet means "ill-counsel"), but, the fact that England did not succumb until 1016 reveals that resistance was tenacious. The ability of the English government to raise, alternatively, fleets and armies, or large sums in taxation to pay the raiders and hire some of them as mercenaries, reveals that it was sophisticated, and far from paralyzed.

MAURIAC PLAIN
HUN INVASION OF EUROPE
Late June 451

In 451 the Huns under Attila ceased plundering the Balkan provinces of the eastern Roman empire and invaded Gaul. Many cities fell to them but, having been repulsed at Orleans, they were finally brought to battle on the "Mauriac Plain" near Troyes, by Aëtius, the *de*

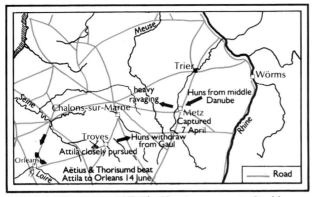

ATTILA IN THE WEST *The Huns' campaign in Gaul began with a thrust across the Rhine at Metz and a march on Orleans.*

facto master of the western empire, with an army in the main consisting of Germans settled in Gaul. The conflict was inconclusive.

The Huns' campaign in Gaul began when, after crossing the Rhine at Metz and taking the city, they made for Orleans. The reason for this was simple, since Sangiban, the king of the Alans, had secretly promised to desert the imperial authorities and betray the city to Attila. Prompt action by Aëtius, the Roman commander in Gaul and virtual ruler of the west, together with Theodoric, king of the Visigoths of Toulouse, prevented this, so Attila withdrew to a point on the "Mauriac Plain", five miles from the city of Troyes. Here the two armies drew up ready to do battle.

"Romans" and Huns

The number of Huns involved in the campaign was quoted as 500,000 by contemporaries, but, in fact, their strength is not likely to have been more than about

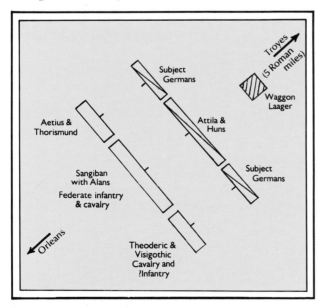

MAURIAC PLAIN *Charge and counter-charge led to a stalemate with the Huns retreating into a fortified waggon laager.*

10,000. They were mounted archers, horsemen of consummate skill and devastating mobility, the latter of which qualities made their victims exaggerate their numbers. They took the center, the wings of the army consisting of contingents from their German vassals.

The "Roman" army was even more motley in make-up, with true imperial forces playing only a minor role. Aëtius brought just a handful of regiments from Italy, and relied for the bulk of his troops on barbarian nations settled in Gaul. The largest contingent consisted of Visigothic cavalry and infantry – they formed the right wing and part of the left. The latter was completed by troops of Frankish cavalry and axe-throwing infantry, Saxons, Burgundians, Sarmatians, contingents of Gallo-Roman magnates and their retainers and the *Olibriones*. This last appears to have been a former imperial regiment no longer on the Roman payroll. Sangiban's untrustworthy Alans, heavy cavalry of Hunnic type, were in the center.

Attila in action

The battle opened with a contest for the high ground on the Huns' right, which Aëtius and the Visigoths won. Following this, Attila launched his whole army into an attack on the imperial line. The subsequent course of the battle is confused, the fighting continued until after nightfall. In one charge by the Visigoths, their king was killed, but the panic that should have followed such an event was avoided as, in the general confusion, his followers learned of his death only at the end of the day. Another Visigothic charge came close to killing Attila himself, an event that woud have led to the disintegration of his army and his empire. Eventually, Attila withdrew into his camp, a sort of waggon *laager*. To exact vengeance for the death of their king, the Visigoths prepared to renew the conflict the following morning, but Aëtius persuaded them to return home. He was anxious to save Attila and revert to his former policy of hiring Huns to use against the Visigoths and other German peoples.

The defeat did not weaken Attila's sway over central Europe; indeed, he invaded Italy the following year. However, it did demonstrate that the Huns were not invincible and saved many Gallic cities from sack.

RONCESVALLES AND THE SUNTEL MOUNTAINS
CHARLEMAGNE'S WARS
15 August 778 and 782

Although Charlemagne's reign was a period of incessant military activity, only two battles in it have been described. At Roncesvalles, Basques ambushed the rearguard of Charlemagne's army in the Pyrenees, while, in the battle of the Süntelberger, a Frankish army under three high palace officials was defeated by rebel Saxons under Widukind. In neither case is any indication given of the numbers involved.

Charlemagne on campaign

In 778 Charlemagne led what was probably the greatest host he raised during his reign into Muslim Spain, and, after a profitable campaign, the army withdrew across the western Pyrenees, through the land of the Basques. The slow-moving baggage train, heavily laden with loot of diverse kinds, was at the rear under Eggihard and Anselm, important palace officials, and Roland, the commander of the Breton contingent. All three were high-ranking and experienced officers.

Roncesvalles was a heavily-wooded pass. The lightly-armed Basques hid among the trees, waiting until the main force had marched by before charging down the flanks of the mountains to pounce on the baggage train. Although one account claims that the whole army was attacked, it is clear that the rear bore the brunt of the fighting. The struggle was brief, and, by the time reinforcements had reached the scene, the Basques had dispersed. The excuse preferred for the failure of the Franks to avenge their defeat was that, though they were both better armed and more valorous, their heavy equipment and ignorance of the difficult terrain made it impossible to pursue the audacious Basques. Charlemagne continued a chastened – and a poorer – man, yet it is difficult to see what further precautions he could have taken. The baggage had been entrusted to a strong guard and senior and tried commanders, all of whom perished.

Across the Elbe

In 782, Charlemagne did not himself campaign; instead, he sent a force of East Franks and recently subdued Saxons on a punitive expedition against the Slav tribes across the River Elbe, under the command of Adalgis, Gailo and Worad, three senior members of his household. On their march, they met with Count Theodoric, another active commander and kinsman of the king, leading a force hastily raised from *Ripuaria* (the Rhineland) to put down a Saxon revolt.

The two armies marched together to the Süntel mountains, where they set up separate camps on opposite banks of a river. Patrols established the location of the Saxon camp north of the mountains, but now dissension and rivalry took a hand. Adalgis and the others feared that Theodoric, as senior officer, would take the credit (and the greater share of plunder and captives) for a victory over the rebels. They decided to launch an assault on their own.

The decision itself was not at fault. The three men led a large army and were confident of victory, while the poorly-equipped Saxon light cavalry and infantry had a poor battle reputation. The trap the Franks fell into was over-confidence, which led them to dash pell-mell on the Saxon camp as if they had already routed the enemy. The Frankish charge, in loose order, was easily surrounded and heavily defeated. The casualties included two of the commanders, four counts and 20 other major nobles, with their retinues.

Both defeats were felt to be infamous, and so were not included in the court history in Charlemagne's lifetime. It was only after his death that they were recorded, the latter at least to serve as a lesson to the unwary.

TAGINAE AND CASILINUM
JUSTINIAN'S WARS IN THE WEST
552 and 554

Justinian's extended wars against the Persians, Vandals and Goths witnessed few decisive battles. Outstanding accounts were set down by Procopius, an eye-witness of much of what he described, and Agathias. At Taginae, the eunuch Narses with some 20,000 men – among them a high proportion of foreigners – brought the long war against the Goths, under Totila, to a rapid conclusion. Two years later, he cleared Italy of a Frankish horde put at the unlikely number of 75,000, defeating half of it under the Alaman Buccelin at Casilinum.

In his Italian wars, the Byzantine ruler Justinian was fortunate in being able to rely on two exceptional generals – Belisarius and Narses. The chief talent of the

TAGINAE *Halting the Goths' charge and trapping them between the wings of his army, Narses scored his greatest victory*

former was his ability to use his very limited military resources to greatest effect. He came to prominence by his successful defence of Daras against a superior Persian army through the inventive use of field defences to counter Persian cavalry superiority. In 533–534, he quickly overcame the once-powerful Vandal kingdom of North Africa with a small, but experienced, army of 10,000 men in two encounter battles at Ad Decimum and Tricameron. In each clash, the Vandals squandered their chances, and Belisarius's personal cavalry played a significant role. In 535 he took Sicily from the Ostrogothic kingdom of Italy with an even smaller army, and then conquered Naples and Rome through exploitation of his naval superiority. Outside the latter city, his mounted archers destroyed a Gothic army, whose spear- and javelin-armed cavalry simply could not get close enough to the Byzantine ranks to use their weapons. Belisarius then withdrew into the city, before whose fortifications the Goths were impotent.

Setbacks in Italy

Though the conquest of Italy was rapid, it was also ill-founded. A severe military crisis in the 540s threatened the core of the empire, and, to solve it, the Italian armies were starved of men and money, and so paralyzed. The Goths took the opportunity to rebel and reconquer the country against a divided Byzantine command and ill-paid soldiery. Under their capable king Totila, they combatted Byzantine strategic mobility by developing a fleet and overcame their weakness in siegecraft by demolishing the walls of many cities. The Byzantines were slow to react, though they regained control of the sea by defeating the Gothic fleet off Ancona in 551.

Justinian at last gave Narses sole command, but he refused to take an expedition to Italy without the assurance of sufficient material and financial support to overwhelm the Goths. With huge financial backing, Narses recruited an army of 20,000 or more – the greatest army Byzantium ever sent westwards, though it had a high proportion of Huns and Germans in tribal groups in its ranks. Totila's strategy was to garrison the key north Italian fortresses that controlled the bridges along the traditional invasion routes, but Narses countered this by using his fleet and pontoon bridges to cross rivers near the coast, so outflanking the Goths. His first objectives were the former imperial capitals of Ravenna and Rome.

Narses at Taginae

Gothic policy was to seek battle in the open field, so Totila, who had been covering Rome, broke camp and advanced along the *Via Flaminia* to meet Narses in the Appenines. Narses, confident of his superior numbers awaited the Goths in a defensive position at Taginae (Gualdo Tadino). Totila first tried to outflank Narses, a tactic he had been successful with previously. Narses prevented this by stationing 50 archers on a hill

commanding the only defile that an outflanking force could take. Baulked in a sharp initial action, the Goths resolved on a frontal attack in two stages. First they would await the arrival of 2,000 cavalry under Teias; secondly, the Byzantines were to be caught off balance by a rapid assault on their center. The Gothic force was arrayed conventionally, with infantry in the center and cavalry on the wings. Narses formed up similarly with an infantry center, reinforced with élite dismounted cavalry. His wings were composed of cavalry, each supported by 4,000 foot archers.

We are told that, to buy time while awaiting reinforcements, Totila's men performed equestrian exercises in the No Man's Land between the armies, and a duel was fought between rival champions. When Teias arrived, Totila seized the opportunity to attack, while the Byzantines were eating their midday meal. Putting the newly-arrived cavalry in front of his weak infantry, he shortened his frontage and launched his assault. To ensure an aggressive advance, the Goths were to fight only at close quarters with spear and sword. He himself led the charge, dressed as a common soldier.

Narses was well-prepared. His strengthened center was designed to halt the Gothic charge, and, to prevent disorder, his men had eaten in their ranks. When the Goths altered their formation, Narses reacted by pushing his wings forward and inwards to bring the 8,000 archers to bear on the advancing cavalry. The Goths had failed to take the Byzantines by surprise – instead, they rode into a trap.

Once the initial assault had failed, the Goths lost impetus and became disordered. Missiles rained in from the flanks, saddles were emptied and Totila was killed, or seriously wounded. The cavalry fled, carrying away the supporting infantry. In the gathering dusk, Narses mounted an all-out pursuit, killing or capturing most of the Gothic army.

Narses and the Franks

The same scheme of a tactical defensive to absorb enemy assaults, followed by a mounted counterstroke and pursuit, was used by Narses in 554 against the Frankish invaders of Italy. It took a year for him to risk bringing them to battle, at Casilinum near Capua, due to his constant desire to fight only when he could bring an overwhelmingly superior force to bear – he rated the Franks as the most successful of the German warrior nations.

Once again, a solid infantry center was formed, with specialist heavy infantry in front bolstered by dismounted cavalry. To the rear, foot archers and javelinmen were placed to shoot overhead, while the flanks were composed of mounted archers and lancers. The Frankish forces are described as consisting of mainly unarmored infantry, armed with shield, barbed spear and throwing axe, although there is some doubt as to whether the Byzantine accounts of the Franks' military methods are accurate. What is clear is that the

Franks formed a massive wedge and advanced with their shields interlocked. Their impetus almost carried them through the center of Narses' army, but, once the Franks were halted, the mounted wings closed in and destroyed them with a missile attack.

Narses won an impressive string of victories, turning the determination of the Goths to fight pitched battles to his advantage, but also benefiting from the greater resources at his disposal. The strain of the Gothic war told on the strength of Byzantium: Slav and Bulgar invaders pushed almost to the gates of Constantinople, while Italy was soon overrun by new invaders, the Lombards. The economic strength of the empire, however, ensured that it could always replace losses by recruiting experienced soldiers, increasingly raised from outside the empire. Such "checkbook generalship", had its disadvantages, however. As the Byzantinis were to discover, though it worked well in wars of conquest, it was less well-suited to defence of settled lands.

YARMUK
EXPANSION OF ISLAM
August 636

The most significant of several battles in the Muslim conquest of Syria, although its chronology is extremely confused in the absence of contemporary accounts. A strong Byzantine army (size uncertain), sent to the province by Emperor Heraclius, was repulsed by a concentration of Muslim armies of between 25,000 to 40,000 men. The Christian force was repulsed with heavy casualties and Syria and Palestine were lost to the empire.

Alarmed by the Muslim advance from Arabia into Syria, Heraclius (610–41) gathered a large army at his base in Antioch and sent it to secure the province. Islamic historians estimated its strength at being between 100,000 and 400,000 men, but neither figure is feasible. The effects of the long wars against the Sassanian (Persian) empire and the Avars in Europe had exhausted the empire's resources, and, in any case the Romans had been unable to field forces of this size for centuries, if ever. A Byzantine account suggests a more reasonable 40,000, although there is no other evidence to support this. However many men were actually involved, it was probably a balanced force of battle-hardened mounted and infantry spearmen and archers, as well as containing contingents of Christian Arabs and Armenians. Heraclius himself was now too ill to command in person. In contrast, the Muslim army was deficient in men and equipment. Its strength of between 20,000 and 40,000 was achieved by uniting the several Islamic armies in Syria; the resulting force consisted of substantial number of infantry, as well as highly-mobile Bedouin cavalry. Reinforcements

numbering between 500 and 800 marched across the desert from Iraq under Khalid ibn al-Walid, the chief general of the Muslim leader Abu-Bakr, the first caliph of Islam after the death of his son-in-law Muhammad.

The two camps
In the face of the Byzantine advance, the Muslims withdrew from Damascus and combined on the south side of the Yarmuk valley, where they decided whether to stand and fight, or withdraw into the desert to await reinforcements from Arabia. The Byzantine army established a base in the Golan, to the west of Lake Tiberias and close to the Wadi-Ruqqad, opposite the Arab host. The two armies faced each other for some weeks in July-August, each launching several attempts to draw the other out of position, before the decisive battle took place. Contemporary sources contradict each other on matters such as the names of commanders, the course of the battle, and even its date – the traditionally accepted one is 17–20 August 636. The Arab commander was probably Khalid ibn Walid, while the Byzantines split the command of their army between several generals, a fact that may have proved decisive in their defeat.

The decisive clash
The high ground of the Golan is deeply dissected by ravines, and so was ideally suited to an army of the Arab type – largely infantry spearmen and archers – while the nature of the terrain cancelled out the Byzantine advantage in cavalry. For three days the Arabs assaulted the Byzantine positions on the Wadi-Ruqqad without much success, until on the evening of 19 August a hot southern wind came to their aid, blowing sand in the faces of the Byzantine troops. The cavalry had to withdraw, and the Christian Arabs serving in the Byzantine ranks began to waver. Many men were lost in the ravines, as they attempted to withdraw by night. The final assault began the next day. It was a fierce action, and, according to Islamic tradition, the women with the army played an important role in rallying waverers. The Byzantine infantry resisted bravely, but were eventually decimated. The cavalry escaped the defeat, but were unable to impede the Arab pursuit, which destroyed the Byzantine army as an effective fighting force and prevented the possibility of a rally.

In Antioch, Heraclius was devastated by the news of the disaster. He had saved the empire from the threat of conquest by Persians and Avars – a brilliant soldier in his younger days, he had launched raids deep into Persian territory and annihilated the Persian army at Ninereh in 627 – but it was now too weak to mount another effort against the Muslims. Over the next five years, the cities of Palestine and Syria were reduced by Muslim columns who went on to conquer Egypt, one of the richest provinces of the empire. It took the Byzantines some considerable time to recover from the extent of these devastating blows.

CHAPTER THREE
Mediaeval Warfare

Certain forms of warfare dominate the period – the far-flung Crusades in Palestine; the raids and counter-raids of the Hundred Years War between England and France; the impact of the Mongol hordes and similar horse-archer formations on the less flexible armies of the west; the internecine city-state, conflicts of Italy; and, above all, the long, slow campaigns involving the construction and reduction of castles, where disease took a far greater toll of defenders and attackers alike, inflicting more casualties on them than they ever suffered in physical combat.

Medieval cavalry

What sort of soldiers were engaged in the many conflicts? This survey begins with a review of the varieties of troops involved.

Mounted men played an important part in medieval battles. In the west, the armored knight could deliver a devastating charge with lance and swords, invulnerable to most missiles. In the east, however, things were different, the emphasis being on fluid, skirmishing tactics, with the bow as the main weapon. When these two very different styles of warfare clashed, some fascinating encounters resulted. Of course, the division was not quite as clear as this; since medieval armies contained many troop types, but the knight was undoubtedly of key importance as far as the feudal armies of Christendom were concerned, though other men fought on horseback.

All these warriors were capable of fighting mounted, with the lance as their chief weapon. When desperate, or really determined, however, the knight shortened his stirrups, drew his sword, and laid about him with murderous élan.

Contrary to popular belief, however, knights were not exclusively mounted warriors. They could, and did, fight on foot.

MEDIAEVAL ARMIES *Throughout the period, armies were a balanced force. Knights often fought dismounted while archers and infantry had key roles.*

Horse archers and armored horses

As we move eastwards across the map of Europe, the nature of cavalry changes. The horse-soldiers of the east were true light cavalry, and more concerned with missile than melée weapons. Once on the Eurasian steppe and beyond the Caucasus, the horse archer held undisputed sway. Throughout the medieval period, the areas to the east of Hungary and Egypt were subject to periodic waves of invasion by these formidable warriors. The horse archers of the Seljuk Turks routed the Byzantines at *Manzikert* in 1071 and again at Myriocephalon in 1176. They swarmed over Asia Minor, ruling the area until they themselves were conquered by the Mongol bowmen. As the power of the Mongol Khans waned in its turn, the Ottomans rose to dominance through the use of light skirmishing cavalry, who pinned the Byzantines behind their city walls and eventually, when *Constantinople* fell to them in 1453, took over their empire.

Not all Oriental cavalry were of this type, however. As the Crusaders observed with astonishment at *Antioch* in 1098, some were armored from head-to-toe in small metal plates, while their horses were

similarly caparisoned to the knees. This type of armor is termed lamellar; it was worn by men known as *cataphracts*, in a style dating back to 700 BC. In the Middle Ages, the *cataphracts* formed the retinues of rulers or great nobles, not unlike the knights of the west, the difference being that they were *ghulams* (slave soldiers). Such servitude was not a badge of disgrace, however; rather it was recognized as a way of rising to great power through a display of military merit. The Mamluk sultans of Egypt (1250–1517) took their name from this type of soldier. Again unlike the knights, their role, although shock tactics were involved, still placed more emphasis upon the bow than upon the lance.

In addition to these dominant troop types, many areas provided tough light cavalry. In the East, the Crusaders employed *Turcopòles*, mostly horse archers, as scouts and skirmishers. In Hungary and Poland, men armed with light lances, maces and bows were also used in close combat – the originals of the later Hussars. In the north, near the Baltic, Lithuanians, and in the south, in Spain, there were the *genitors*. Both were light javelineers, who provided valuable support for the Teutonic and Aragonese knights respectively.

European infantry

Many military historians of the Middle Ages face a self-imposed problem. Because they have stressed the dominance of the mounted man-at-arms, they have been forced to explain each occasion when footmen overcame cavalry as an "infantry revolution". The truth is far simpler – foot-soldiers were always an important factor on the medieval battlefield. Of course, to the contemporary chroniclers – the people who wrote the histories of the time – the footsloggers came

KNIGHTS IN BATTLE Ucello's "Rout at San Romano" epitomizes mediaeval warfare. Note the lances, which were "couched" under the armpit in the charge.

from the despised lower orders, so their achievements were not worthy of record. While the deaths of knights and nobles were carefully noted, the massacre of these *pedites* (footmen) was a matter of no account. Class prejudice meant that their role was played down and ignored. There was also a fear of such men becoming powerful, and meddling in the affairs of their betters.

It is true that the feudal system was not designed to produce foot-soldiers, but there were other ways in which such forces could be raised. No state ever abandoned the policy of raising a general levy, if the occasion demanded it. In England, the Anglo-Saxon *fyrd* (host) survived for perhaps a century after the Norman Conquest, although in a reduced form; Henry II's "Assize of Arms" of 1166 was designed to provide a well-equipped infantry force to replace it. In France, the *arrière ban* was used to raise men from town and country alike, the same policy being followed across Europe. It became apparent, however, that better-equipped, better-disciplined and better-motivated footmen, even in smaller numbers, were preferable to a mass levy. So rulers struck deals with communities, giving towns charters that laid down the mutual obligations of the two contracting parties, including that of miltary service. They also employed mercenaries widely.

Some areas of Europe did produce dependable footsoldiers. Scandinavian axemen of the Viking type were important until around 1200, when Norse society began to be more feudalized, and so placed an increased emphasis on the mounted man. The poor, mountainous countries of Switzerland and Scotland, for instance, provided pikemen and halberdiers, capable of showing great self-discipline and determination. English archers were nurtured both by individual lords and the state. They operated as mounted infantry. This enabled them to keep pace with the men-at-arms in the strategy of *chevauchée* (literally a ride), the raiding expeditions that were the mainstays of English strategy in the Hundred Years War.

Footsoldiers in the Middle East

In the Middle East, the Seljuk Turks relied upon the nations they had conquered to provide them with footsoldiers; the mountains of Cilician Armenia, for instance, were the home of fine archers and javelinmen. The armies of Fatimid Egypt also had large infantry contingents in their ranks. They included black troops from Ethiopia and the Sudan, equipped with large shields and javelins, and the Iranian Daylamites, who carried battle-axes and fire grenades. In battle, those with shields formed dense ranks, from behind which the missilemen operated. Saladin found this infantry formation useful as well; he also employed professional archers and javelin-throwers to increase its flexibility. Their harassing fire opened the battle of *Arsuf*.

Under the Mamluks infantry were less important, though this was largely because each *Mamluk* was trained to fight on foot as well as on horseback. Dismounted, *Mamluk*

archers could deliver a steady, withering fire, as well as forming a solid defensive block. At *Ayn Jalut*, they were not reluctant to dismount to tackle their Mongol foes, who had taken refuge on a broken hillside.

The Ottoman Turks, while chiefly cavalry orientated, also developed infantry units. These included large numbers of *Azab* irregulars, but centered on the legendary janissaries. These were slave soldiers, raised from a levy of Christian boys, the *devshirme*, who were then indoctrinated into a fanantical loyalty to the Ottoman sultan. Their dependance on him was symbolized by the spoon they carried in the front of their distinctive white hats. They fought in groups of *ortas*, of about 100 men in total, each with a large cauldron from which they ate their rice – the sultan's bounty. Christian military writers deplored the lack of such a reliable force in the west.

Fighting for pay

Men fought for money throughout the period. Even western knights, supposedly fulfilling a feudal duty, were often paid to fight by their ruler, especially since the customary obligation to serve for 40 days was obviously inadequate when men were needed for long campaigns or sieges. Soldiers of lower social rank usually fought at someone else's expense. Specialist troops could always command a price as well. Italian crossbowmen, for example, were in command across western Europe from the 1080s on, and were still employed, though without much success, by the French in the Hund-

red Years War. And the long-handled Viking axe was hefted for pay from Cork to Constantinople.

Eastern rulers employed mercenaries as well. Often these were nomadic peoples fleeing before more powerful forces, such as the Seljuk Turks or Mongols. Though Muslim states tended to prefer the use of slave soldiers, the Ottoman Turks, for instance, bought the services of skilled engineers and artillerymen from the west. One such expert, Urban, a Hungarian, was reponsible for the cannon that battered through the walls of Constantinople in 1453 and brought Byzantium down.

IN THE LISTS *A joust in progress. When the impetus of man and horse was thrown behind the lance's point in the charge, the effect was irresistible.*

Indeed, skilled craftsmen were widely needed in the west as well, often in non-combatant roles. The building of castles required architects, masons, carpenters and a multitude of workmen; destroying them demanded sappers, miners, artillerymen and vast numbers of men for labor and assault. Techni-

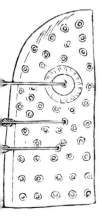

AXES AND BOWS
Battleaxes (top left) were an important infantry weapon up to around 1200; the axemen of the Varangian Guard, for instance, were the Byzantine emperors' elite force. Archers (left) fought in the armies of both east and west, though the way in which they were employed differed.

cal specialists were found rarely on the battle-field (at least before the introduction of gunpowder), but often at sieges. Such men could always command large fees.

On the whole, there was not the same prejudice against mercenary troops as there is today. The rise and fall of the mercenary was bound up with the formation of nation states. Even before the age of the standing armies associated with such states, it made sense to employ veteran, reliable troops, especially for such tasks as garrison duty. As early as 1203, as part of his war effort against John of England, the French king, Phillip Augustus raised a permanent force of 3,033 men. This consisted of a mounted section of 600 knights, crossbowmen and sergeants, 133 foot crossbowmen and the remaining 2,300 being infantry spearmen.

Fighting for money provoked little retaliation unless specific weapons were involved – captured crossbowmen, for example, were liable to death or mutilation at the discretion of knights. The reason for this was simple. The nobility feared and

loathed a weapon that enabled a peasant to bring them low.

On Crusade especially, Saracen crossbowmen were shown no mercy. If they were spared a hanging, such luckless captives had their hands amputated in order to prevent them using their bows again. Similarly, English archers in France could have their middle and index fingers removed to prevent them shooting their bows. This is the origin of the curiously English two-fingered insult; it was an indication that the man who delivered it was able to slaughter the flower of French chivalry.

Training, morale and discipline
It is often assumed that medieval warriors lacked military discipline and it is true that the training of the western knight placed an emphasis on individual skills at the expense of collective ones. As a squire, he learnt to handle horse and arms, finding out how to act in concert with others through hunting; however, there seems to have been no formal drilling. Even the Military Orders, the full-time soldiers of the period, do not seem to have practiced battlefield manoeuvres in groups.

The tournament served to provide such experience. In addition to the individual jousts, there was the opportunity to take part in a large melée, in which men served in the *mesnie* of their lord. This was, in effect, a battle without casualties in which no-one was killed (intentionally), although ransoms were taken. William the Marshal, a friend of Richard the Lionheart, took part in a whole series of such encounters in northern France during the 1170s, where he won a great reputation. Here a man like Henry the Young King, eldest son of Henry II, might learn to wheel and deploy his squadrons, and, under the Marshal's wise guidance, come to realize that the commander who committed his cavalry last into the melée was generally the victor.

Such wargames were all part and parcel of the code of chivalry, which imbued knights with a high sense of personal worth, and hence good morale. This latter could be a disadvantage in battle, however. The French were notorious for their pride and suffered defeat after defeat by allowing their hearts to rule their heads. Under competent leaders, though, western armies could be disciplined and effective. In an age when warfare was, for the most part, an amateur profession, armies that fought together for prolonged periods – Crusaders, members of the Military Orders, the veterans of successive campaigns and many mercenaries – learnt their battle drills through practical experience.

Eastern armies were generally better disciplined. The Mamluks of Egypt issued *furusiyah* (training manuals) to teach their soldiers necessary individual skills and tactical sense. Islam played a large part in maintaining control of the Berber armies who errupted into Spain in two waves in the late 11th and late 12th centuries. The Mongols were renowned for their ability to obey orders and carry out a tactical plan, on pain of dire penalties.

How many fought?

Medieval armies were generally very small in number; the chroniclers, it is clear, exaggerated their size to tens and hundreds of thousands. Soldiers were expensive to equip and maintain, given the revenues of the still developing economies of the west. Knights, therefore, were always few in number, while the slow, cumbersome nature of land transport – ox-carts and pack animals – meant that large armies could not be supplied in the field. There were exceptions, of course. Crusader armies (including many non-combatants) were supplied by Italian fleets on many occasions, while the relative speed and carrying-capacity of water-borne transport meant that campaigns were often closely-connected to inland river lines.

Few armies could afford to live off the land for long, not least because it was approved strategy to lay waste the surrounding countryside in order to deprive the enemy of its resources. Though frugal nomads, such as the Mongols, could survive for longer, even then their horses' need for

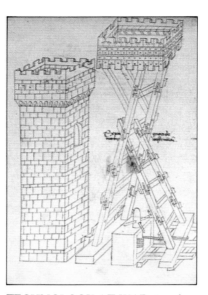

TECHNOLOGY AT WAR *Attackers developed ingenious siege towers (above) and siege engines (below) to deal with the sophisticated defences of the stone-built concentric castle.*

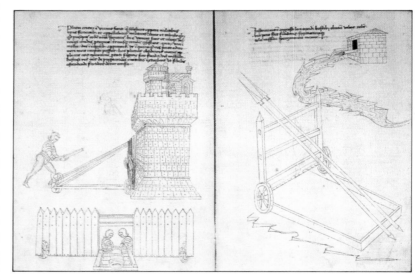

forage presented problems. It is therefore important not to fall into the trap of exaggerating the size of their forces as well.

Accurate numbers can scarcely ever be established before the 14th century. The lists of *indentures*, contracts to provide troops to the English kings fighting in France, and the increasing number of administrative documents associated with centralized government, now begin to provide better information. Even then, given the demands of garrisoning and the ravages of disease, we

have no more than a general indication of the manpower available; what we have to draw on is orders of battle.

Campaigns and sieges

As in all periods of warfare, fortification was an important element in the art of war. The majority of battles were concerned with the siege of a town or castle. Indeed, it has been said that a siege is a kind of long, drawn-out battle, taking place more frequently than encounters in the open field. In the long series of wars between the kingdoms of England and France, the control of a network of castles was crucial to the outcome. Angevin and Capetian fought over Normandy, where Château Gaillard (taken by the French in 1204) was the jewel in the crown. Control of Gascony was disputed between Plantagenet and Valois, each side constructing *bastides* (fortified towns) as part of their frontier policy.

In the Holy Land, castles were huge and sophisticated. Early on, they were put into the hands of the Military Orders, who alone could afford the cost of their upkeep. Crak de Chevaliers, Montfort, Beaufort, Safita and many others all helped to keep the Muslims at bay, until, as a result of the battle of *Hattin*, Saladin killed or captured most of the military manpower of the Crusader states, leaving empty castles to fall, un-

CHRONICLER'S VIEW *The English victory at Poitiers (1356) in an illustration based on Froissart; in fact, the English knights charged dismounted.*

---

defended, into his hands. Properly garrisoned, any fortified place could dominate an area within a day's ride around it. This made medieval campaigns generally slow, step-by-step affairs, as defended positions were reduced one-by-one.

Battles and battle plans

It is in the nature of battles for them to be decisive only in the short term on most occasions. For example, the effects of the great battle at *Antioch*, which put an end to the last Muslim attempt to stop the Crusaders reaching Jerusalem and established

the Duchy of Antioch, were largely undone over the next two generations. The huge losses the Crusaders suffered at Ager Sanguinis – the Field of Blood – owing to the rash behavior of Duke Roger, only 20 years later, went a long way to contributing to the duchy's decline. In the case of *Poitiers*, in which the French were humiliated and their king captured, the victory was not fully exploited by the treaty that followed in 1359. But, as this example demonstrates, the short-term effects of defeat could be disastrous.

What measures did medieval generals take to ensure that their troops had the best possible chance of emerging victorious? Were they capable of devising tactical orders? Unfortunately, battle plans are missing for all but a few encounters.

It can only be assumed that great generals, such as Bohemond, Richard the Lionheart, Saladin and Baibars gave their orders orally; we know that the Mongol system emphasised this means of transmitting commands. The first surviving written examples date from the 15th century.

The main thing to note from this brief introduction to medieval warfare, is that the image of the knight dominating the battlefield with a single charge is a myth. True, this was a powerful weapon, but it had to be used carefully, or it could lead to disaster, as many of the battles described later in this chapter show. Medieval generals were as cautious and capable as those of any age. The art of war, too, did not fall into decline during this period; instead it developed in many ways.

Mediaeval technology

Throughout the medieval period, developments in weaponry led to adaptation of tactics. The first major factor that influenced the conduct of war was the building of castles – first of wood and then of stone.

Castles of stone

The *donjon*, or keep, formed the central part of the typical 12th-century castle, though its origins go back several centuries before this. The earliest example in the west is the two-storey tower-hall at Doué-la-Fontaine in Anjou (c.950). The spread of Norman influence ensured that this style of fortification became the norm from England to Armenia, William the Conqueror's White Tower (London) being a notable example. Surrounded by stone curtain walls, the formidable nature of these new defences meant that the only recourse of a besieging force was to tackle them by mining.

When the British castle of Rochester was besieged by Prince Louis of France in 1216, his miners expertly undercut the foundations of the keep, supporting their

THE AGE OF THE CASTLE *The castle builders of the Middle Ages were supreme architects.*

excavations with timber props. These were then fired to bring about the collapse of one corner, which enabled the French to take the castle. The results may be seen today, with the keep's southern tower rebuilt in the new, round style typical of the concentric castle.

Defensive bastions

The introduction of gunpowder did not mean the abandonment of any other means of attack. The new bombards were slow, inaccurate and dangerous to operate; many notables were blown up by the explosion of their own cannon. Technical progress, however, ensured that, by the mid-15th century, few major rulers lacked guns; France and Burgundy, for example, each possessed extensive artillery trains.

When the Turks shocked Christendom by battering down the previously impregnable walls of *Constantinople* in 1453, fortress designers reacted by improving defences. In Italy, for instance, bastions had become the fashion from the 1420s onward. These were thick banks of earth, designed to absorb the shot that could pierce old-fashioned stone walls. Thus, defensive technology kept pace with that of the attacker in the battle between besieger and besieged.

Weaponry

The basic knightly sword changed little over the period, although there were various additional types from which to choose. The lance grew longer and heavier, so that it had to be cut down for use on foot. True infantrymen used a wide range of polearms.

In the east, the small, but powerful, composite bow remained dominant, while westerners used a simple stave or self bow. This could indeed be a longbow (matching a man's height) but it was not so much the length as the strength and skill of the shooter that mattered. The crossbow, which appeared c.1080, gradually became stronger and heavier, capable of puncturing any armor, but, because it took time to load, it was more suitable for use in defence or during sieges as it was easily outshot by trained longbowmen in open battle. The first guns, developed c.1340, had similar limitations. There was no true field artillerly before the 1470s; despite the successes of the Hussites, the handguns of the time were generally unreliable and made useless by rain.

Tactics and troops

Contrary to the commonly accepted popular view, knightly cavalry did not dominate the battlefield to the exclusion of infantry in the medieval period. Knights, the cream of the medieval fighting forces, often fought dismounted. This mode of fighting was popular in the 12th century – at *Tinchebrai* (1106), The Standard

ARMS AND ARMOR *Knights and charges needed protection from archery in the high mediaeval period (left). The "cavalier" (right) is preparing to fire a petronel from the saddle.*

(1138) and Lincoln (1141), for instance. It was a tactic the English employed in the Hundred Years War to make up for their inferior numbers; it was also adopted by the French at *Poitiers* (1356) and subsequently at *Agincourt* to reduce their casualties from English archery. Fighting on foot was something knights were never too proud to do, whatever their origins. At Damascus, during the Second Crusade, the German dismounted "as is the Teuton custom in a crisis."

Scottish "hedgehogs"

Spears, too, became an important infantry weapon during this period; during the Scottish wars of independence, for instance, infantry spearmen played an important role, beating the English invaders at Stirling Bridge in 1297. Poorly armored though these

FACT AND FICTION *This fanciful 15th-century idea for a war chariot came close to reality with the "battle waggons" of the Hussites.*

spearmen were, they were invulnerable to cavalry attack in a "hedgehog" of pikes, unless the English archers could break up their formation first. Indeed, the Scots paid the penalty for allowing these *schiltrons*, as they were termed, to remain stationary at Falkirk (1298). A barrage of English arrows created gaps in them that the cavalry was quick to exploit.

Handgun and "push of pike"

Infantry, therefore, always had an important tactical role to play throughout the period, and, in the later Middle Ages, they came to dominate the battlefield at the expense of their betters.

Peasant soldiers – whether they were English bowmen, Hussite handgunners or Swiss pikemen – now challenged their social superiors effectively for battlefield supremacy. The Hussites used a barricade of waggons, handguns, artillery and a fearsome collection of polearms to destroy cavalry charges, their tactics being essentially defensive (as at *Kutna Hora*). The Swiss, on the other hand, developed aggressive infantry tactics, using huge masses of men, armed with halberds and close-packed together in a phalanx. Sempach (1386) proved the effectiveness and flexibility of this formation. The halberd remained the dominant weapon, even when pikes were introduced in the mid-15th century – in the typical force of the time halberdiers made up 60 per cent of the total strength and pikemen 20 per cent. However, as it was learnt how important the impact of a massed body of pikemen could be, these proportions were reversed.

Swiss pikemen were well-disciplined and so had the ability to manoeuvre rapidly. They were the most popular mercenaries in the Italian wars of around 1500, and their combination of handguns and pikes were adopted by others and dominated the battlefields of Europe for the next 130 years.

Warfare on the steppes

The harshness of life on the steppes of Eurasia was well-suited to the development of military skills. The steppe warriors were hunter-grazers – their life-style was based on the horse and the herding of animals, and so there was a constant requirement for fresh grazing. From this basic fact, a natural development took place; steppe tribes, with their tents and waggons, migrated in an organized fashion, just like an army on the march. Equipped with hard-hitting composite bows, capable of strategic mobility and tactical flexibility, the nomadic horse archer was a feared opponent throughout the mediaeval period.

During this period, waves of invaders marched westward from the east. They were chiefly Turcic peoples – Pechenegs and Cumans as well as the Turks themselves – who established several states, of which the Ottoman empire proved to be the longest lasting. In the middle of the 13th century, the Mongol hordes proved irrisistable. Although penetrating as far as Germany, crushing all opposition, internal problems led them to withdraw from Europe, though they continued to dominate Russia for another 200 years.

The Seljuk Turks

It was in Asia Minor that the Seljuk Turks made their chief impact. Armenia, the most easterly Christian state, was destroyed by them in the mid-11th century – a victory the Seljuks achieved through their superior archery and their "clouds of arrows", according to the chronicler Matthew of Edessa. Up until then, the Byzantine empire had long been able to repel such nomadic threats, but its army was in decline and received a shattering blow at Manzikert in 1071.

Determined to bring the elusive Turks to battle, the Emperor Romanus Diogenes led a reputedly 60,000-strong army to his eastern border. Sultan Alp Arslan, however, employed the classic steppe tactic of the feigned retreat to deal with the Byzantine attack. When Romanus ordered his men to charge across the open plain, the Turks simply withdrew in front of them until, unable to come to blows with their elusive enemies, the tired Byzantines began to fall back on their camp. The Turks then followed in hot pursuit, their archers harassing the Byzantine cavalry. As Byzantine military manuals recommended, the emperor had arranged his army in two lines to avoid encirclement. But, due either to treachery or confusion, the second line abandoned the first, which, swamped by the Seljuk arrow storm, eventually broke and fled. Romanus was captured and the cream of Byzantium's soldiery killed.

The Mongols

In part, nomadic warfare was an instinctive business – a natural development of the hunting-shooting lifestyle of its practitioners. However, in practice horse-archer armies also planned their tactics, no one being more adept at this than the Mongols. In only two generations, under Genghis Khan and his successors, they rose from obscurity to conquer a world empire. What made them more successful than any nomads before them was their remarkable degree of political cohesion and military discipline, each of which reinforced the other. This centered around a select guard of experienced soliders, which initially was quite small in number, but was increased in strength by Genghis Khan to a total of 10,000 men. The task of this cadre was to provide leadership for the main body of Mongol troops, while, at the same time, forming an élite fighting corps that was totally loyal to the Mongol ruler. The sons of officers were automatically enrolled in the guard, but there was also healthy competition among other warriors to join its ranks.

Foreign observers were most impressed by the iron discipline of the Mongols when it came to care of their equipment, when they were on the march, on guard duty, and, above all, in battle. A system of signalling to indicate tactical moves was developed, making use of the Mongols' celebrated horse-tail standards. The final charge, usually delivered when the enemy was surrounded, followed upon the beating of the giant drums the Mongol army carried into action.

The need to find fodder for their horse herds proved to be the main factor limiting Mongol conquests. When isolated groups reached the Alps and the Adriatic in 1242, far from the grasslands of the Hungarian plain, they could no longer sustain their aggression.

The Ottoman Turks

It was always the ability to keep moving, create widespread havoc and only fight a battle on a site of their own choosing that characterized horse-archer armies, and made them feared for so long. Indeed, horse-archers continued to play an important part in the rise of the Ottoman state; in fact, they formed the bulk of the army, even when the sultans were striving to modernize their forces. Such troops were still invaluable when employed as wide-ranging cavalry raiders against the Byzantine possessions in Asia Minor and Greece. These destructive attacks were led by the so-called *ghazis*, Muslim warrior fanaties who broke the opposition's will to resist by devastating their lands. By means of such *razzias* (raids), the Greeks outside Constantinople were quickly reduced to submission; when the city itself finally fell in 1453, Hungary soon became the main center for their activities.

STEPPE WARRIORS *Brilliant horsemanship, ruthless drive and superb archery made the steppe nomads feared opponents.*

ACRE
THE THIRD CRUSADE
1189–1191

Siege and battles between the Crusaders and Saladin. Several thousand Muslim troops defending the well-fortified city of Acre held off a besieging Christian force, which grew steadily from a few hundred to many thousands as Crusader contingents arrived from Europe. The Christians were themselves hemmed in by Saladin's much larger force, but, despite defeats in the field, Acre eventually fell after the arrival of Richard I of England to take command of the siege.

A surprise attack
King Guy of Jerusalem had led the Christian forces in the Holy Land to their greatest defeat at the Horns of Hattin in 1187. Captured at the battle, and then released after promising not to make war on Saladin, he quickly broke his oath. On returning to the sole remaining Christian stronghold of Tyre, however, Guy found it occupied by his greatest rival, Conrad of Montferrat. With nothing to lose, Guy raised troops and marched to besiege Acre, the chief port and largest city in the Holy Land. In August 1189 he set up camp on the nearby hill of Turon, from which Saladin was unable to eject him.

Disease and defeats
Stirred by this bold action, reinforcements flooded in, and by April 1190 the Christians found it possible to complete a landward blockade of the city. Even though defeated in battle – rashly brought on – in October, their defended camp kept the victorious Muslims at bay. Disease, however, took its toll, including even the highest; Guy's wife, Queen Sibylla, was among those who perished.

Both sides faced stalement. Saladin was unable to raise the siege, while the Christians found themselves unable to seriously trouble Acre's defenders, until the kings of England and France arrived.

Arrival of the Lionheart
Phillip Augustus led the French forces into the Crusader camp on 20 April 1191, but their attacks on the city intensified only when the already legendary Richard the Lionheart landed with his men on 5 June. The city walls were undermined and battered by an array of stonethrowers. Given names like "Bad Neighbor" and "God's Own Catapult" – the money for them being raised by subscription throughout the Crusader ranks – they began to open breaches in the city's walls. Saladin launched a further series of attacks against the Crusaders' stockade with increasing desperation. These culminated in a mass assault on 4 July, which was repulsed. With its walls crumbling, besieged, the city surrendered a week later.

AGINCOURT
THE HUNDRED YEARS WAR
1415

Henry V's army of 900 men-at-arms (each with two retainers) and 5,000 archers faced a French force, whose strength was estimated at 20,000. Suffering from a divided command and over-confidence, the French met complete defeat.

A disastrous campaign
On the evening of 24 October 1415, the eve of the clash between English and French armies at Agincourt, few would have given the English a chance of success in the battle that the heralds of both sides had agreed would take place the following day. Henry's campaign had gone disastrously wrong. After a long and expensive siege of Harfleur, he had embarked on a *chevauchée* (armed raid), intended to take him across Normandy to English-held Calais. But the French advance guard, under the command of the experienced Marshal Boucicault, had foiled him by blocking the passage of the River Somme.

Eventually, Henry got his men over the river some distance upstream of his originally intended crossing point. A French "scorched-earth" policy combined with foul weather to leave his army soaked, starving and riddled with dysentery. Hurrying north once more, he was finally brought to bay at Agincourt.

Pride ruins Boucicault's plan
Fortunately for the English, there were many mutually-jealous French nobles disputing. While they argued, Henry seized the initiative and advanced into a strong defensive position between some woods. His tiny force of armored men held the center, while on each flank the archers stood behind a forest of stakes.

In fact, Boucicault had devised a plan to defeat the English using the advance guard of the French army on its own. The French missilemen were to pin the English

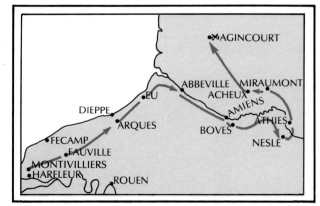

THE AGINCOURT CAMPAIGN *Henry's attack on France was intended as a spoiling raid, rather than a war of conquest.*

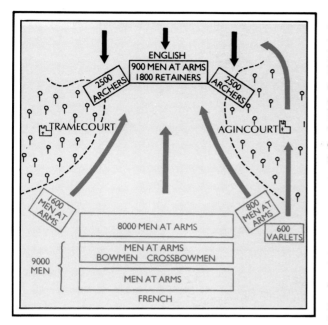

AGINCOURT *French impetuosity and the strong position adopted by Henry V were major factors in the English victory.*

archers down, while a picked body of cavalry charged them in the flanks and a force of "varlets", mounted on their masters' horses, created havoc in the rear. However, the restricted nature of the battlefield, disputes with his fellow nobles and the sheer size of the French host ruined his plan. The flank attackers were forced to charge straight at the archers, and the knights were quickly repulsed, their only minor success being achieved where the stakes had fallen over in the rain-sodden earth. Meanwhile, in the center, the archers and crossbowmen, who should have formed the front line according to Boucicault's plan, were physically pushed back into the second line by the cream of the cavalry of France, thirsting for glory.

France's greatest lords, including Boucicault, d'Albret, Orleans, Bourbon, Eu, Richemont and the Dauphin, led the first "battle" of 8,000 men-at-arms. Having dismounted, they slowly marched through the heavy ground towards Henry's positions. As they approached the waiting English, their ranks were thrown into disorder by the French cavalry and the expected arrow-storm from the English archers. Nevertheless, the English were forced back.

Fighting hand-to-hand
The fighting was hand-to-hand and extremely bitter. Even the archers joined in with their mallets and daggers. Slowly, the tide turned. As the French fell back, they suddenly found their path of retreat blocked by their second line as it pushed forward. They were now packed so tightly that they could scarely use their weapons – yet they fought on. Henry was wounded and his brother, the Duke of York, killed before the French started to flee. Huge numbers of prisoners were taken.

There now followed a discreditable – and uncustomary – massacre of the French prisoners, though why Henry ordered this is unclear. He may have feared an attack on his rear, (which, indeed, had been part of Boucicault's original plan), or may have expected a counter-attack by the remaining French cavalry. In any event, the extent of the massacre have been overstated. The most important result of Henry's victory at Agincourt was that, through the pride that drove all the leading commanders to fight in the front rank, the French had no one left to rally them.

ANTIOCH
THE FIRST CRUSADE
1097–98

The capture of the well-fortified city of Antioch was essential if the First Crusade was to move south into Syria. A nine-month siege and three pitched battles culminated in the defeat of a large army led by Kerbogha, the greatest warrior of the Muslims. This opened the way for an advance on Jerusalem.

Towards the end of May 1098, the Crusaders encamped outside Antioch were desperate. For eight months, they had besieged the city in the face of winter, famine and days of constant fighting, mostly in order to get precious supplies. They knew that soon Kerbogha of Mosul, with a relieving army, would advance on the city, determined to destroy them. Then months of careful planning by Bohemond, a Norman leader, paid off, when the city fell through treachery on 2 June.

Four days later, however, Kerbogha was at the walls. What were the Crusaders to do?

Bohemond to the rescue
The Crusaders had already defeated two relieving forces. Just before Christmas 1097, a large foraging expedition of several thousand knights and footmen had fallen in with the army of Duqaq of Damascus. He had divided his army in two and surrounded Robert of Flanders' detachment. Luckily, Bohemond came to the rescue, routing the Turks with a well-timed charge. Meanwhile, the camp at Antioch had sustained heavy casualties containing a sortie by the city's garrison.

The winter saw starvation and many desertions from among the Crusader ranks. Early in February 1098, Ridwan of Aleppo gathered another relieving force in nearby Harenc. Bohemond suggested an

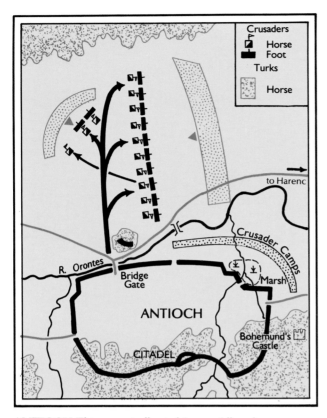

ANTIOCH *This strategically vital fortress fell to the Crusaders after a nine-month siege and three battles.*

immediate attack, to which the other leaders agreed, although it was only possible to scrape together 700 mounted knights for the assault.

In the Battle of Lake Antioch that followed, Bohemond chose a narrow position to fight in, to offset both the superior numbers of the Turks and the tactics they customarily employed of encircling opposing forces. Dividing his army into six "battles", he sent five in line against the enemy, keeping the sixth in reserve under his own command. As Turkish numbers told and the first line began to fall back, Bohemond turned the tables, charging and slaughtering the enemy up to the Iron Bridge.

The final battle

Kerbogha's delay, caused by his decision to besiege Baldwin de Bourg at Edessa for three weeks, saved the Crusaders. Yet they feared to challenge him to open combat. Only the discovery of the Holy Lance, revived their hopes enough to offer battle on 28 June.

The Crusaders advanced cautiously, the foot in front of the knights. The five "battles" of the main line hugged the river at first, before deploying to the left in order to fix that flank on the mountains to the north. Even if they had larger forces than the 260 knights and 900 footmen detailed in one eyewitness account, they must have been stretched to cover the gap that opened in their ranks – and perhaps they could not, for

Kerbogha promptly slipped an outflanking force around the flank and behind their line. Bohemond promptly charged it with the reserve, strengthened by a hastily improvised seventh unit. Meanwhile, Kerbogha was withdrawing in front of the main battle line, behind the usual storm of arrows unleashed by his supporting archers.

To the Crusaders it seemed that "a host of men on white horses" led by St. George, gave them victory. More prosaically, the change in fortune was probably due to the unwillingness of many of Kerbogha's emirs to see him grow still more powerful. As Bohemond forced back his opponents, they fired the grass to cover their retreat. Alarmed by this – and unwilling to fight – the main body fled as the Crusaders charged.

ARSUF
THE THIRD CRUSADE
1191

A classic encounter between Crusaders and Saracens and their two greatest commanders – Richard the Lionheart and Saladin. Attacked on the march by greater numbers of horse archers, Richard managed to restrain his knights' impetuosity and deliver a well-timed charge, which led to a Saracen rout.

On 7 September 1191, Richard led the Crusader army south from Acre towards Jaffa, the jumping-off point for any attack on Jerusalem. The army was rested and well-organized, but had to suffer the constant attacks of Saladin's skirmishers. To counter this harassment, the Crusaders were deployed in three divisions, each consisting of three columns. In the center of each column, rode the knights, plus accompanying baggage; to their left, the foot-soldiers formed a defensive wall protecting the knights against Muslim archery. The infantry's role was to keep the enemy at bay with their own archery fire, while, at the same time soaking up the enemy's arrows and so protecting the valuable cavalry horses. Muslim observers commented admiringly on the way the footmen kept marching on, their padded *gambesons* (protective tunics) bristling with shafts until they resembled porcupines.

Slow but sure

Because this was such an exhausting task, the foot was divided into two halves, one covering the open flank and the other marched along the sea-shore alternately. The sea provided both protection and supplies. The unopposed superiority of the Crusader fleet was vital, for Saladin had ordered a scorched-earth policy to be enforced to hinder Crusader advance.

Despite all Richard's precautions, progress was slow. It took two-and-a-half weeks to reach Jaffa because the speed of the advance was restricted to the pace of the

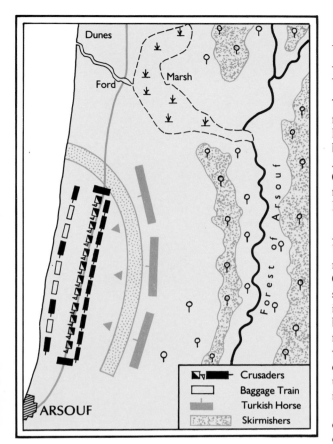

ARSUF *In this classic encounter, Richard I and his heavy cavalry inflicted a decisive defeat on Saladin.*

slowest foot-soldiers. The fact that it was a fighting march delayed things still further, since the rearguard had to turn about constantly in order to repel attack.

A test of nerve
On September 7, Saladin changed his tactics and offered battle. Richard arranged his forces carefully, with his most experienced and disciplined men – the warrior-monks of the Temple and the Hospital – in the van and rear, while the English and Normans formed a central reserve around his dragon standard. The king's main aim was to stop his knights charging too soon, before the enemy wearied, and so becoming scattered and vulnerable to counter-attack.

For most of a long, hot day, assailed by arrows, choking dust and the pounding of the enemy's drums, the Crusaders stood their ground and repelled attack after attack. Eventually, the Master of the Knights Hospitaller, commanding the rearguard, concerned by losses to his knights' horses, led a charge. It was not the moment Richard had chosen, but he reacted quickly, signalling a general advance. The whole Christian line surged forward, taking the Turks by surprise. The reserve with its standard formed a rallying point, as planned. Saladin's army was routed and his prestige destroyed; Richard had achieved a decisive victory.

ASCALON
THE FIRST CRUSADE
1099

The fall of Jerusalem to the Crusaders on 15 July 1099, finally stirred the Fatimid caliph of Egypt into action. A large force of foot archers and lance-armed cavalry, led by his vizier, al-Afdal, moved to challenge the invaders. Although split by internal political tensions, the Crusader leaders rallied together for what was to be the final battle of the First Crusade. The right of Fatimid Egypt was swept away by the Crusaders' charge.

A flexible formation
Under the leadership of Duke Godfrey de Bouillon the newly elected "Defender of the Holy Sepulchre", the Crusaders advanced south to Ascalon. Their formation showed that they had learnt much about campaigning in the Holy Land. The host was divided into nine bodies, arranged so as to present three lines to the front, flanks and rear. In each "battle", footmen armed with spears, longbows and crossbows, marched in front of the knights. This meant that the foot could protect the horses from enemy arrow, while the mounted men, in return, were free to drive off threatening cavalry.

The battle took place outside the harbour-fortress of Ascalon on 12 August 1099. The Egyptians were certainly overconfident, one account stating that they were equipped with water bottles with which to refresh themselves during the pursuit. They were to receive a rude shock, however, for, unlike the Turks, they were composed of lance-armed cavalry, supported by foot bowmen. This provided the Crusaders with a solid

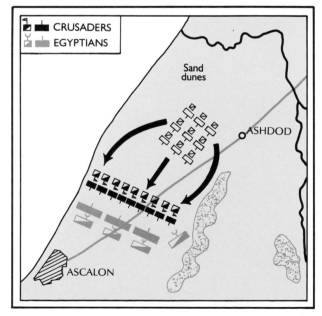

ASCALON *The Crusader knights won the battle with a single charge, cementing their reputation for invincibility.*

target for their knights to charge.

The Arabs probably drew up with their archers on the flanks and cavalry in the centre, while the Crusaders deployed from their march formation into line, infantry to the fore. However, the nature of the two formations had little effect on the outcome of the battle. According to Latin accounts, Robert, Duke of Normandy, took matters into his own hand after an inital exchange of archery. Spying a precious golden ornament on top of the vizier's standard, he charged straight for it, killing the bearer. The rest of the knights followed suit, crashing into the astonished and stationary Egyptians and literally sweeping them from the field. This single impetuous charge seems to have been the deciding factor in the battle.

AYN JALUT
MONGOL ATTACK ON EGYPT
1260

A Mongol force of about 10,000 men under Kitbugha was challenged by the Mamluks as it advanced on Egypt. Sultan Qutuz, with 12,000 men, used the Mongols' favorite tactic of a feigned flight to trap and destroy them.

The sack of Baghdad
In 1258, the great Mongol general Hulagu dealt the Muslim world a great blow with his capture of Baghdad and the execution of its caliph. With Persia and the Seljuk dominions of Asia Minor under Mongol rule, only Mamluk Egypt remained to offer opposition.

Qutuz's task was made easier by Mongol political problems. Hulagu had already demanded that the Mamluks submit to him, but, when the Great Khan Möngke died, he was forced to return to Mongolia for the election of a successor, taking many of his men with him. He therefore entrusted the Syrian campaign to a subordinate general, Kitbugha.

Fewer than expected
Kitbugha had two *tumans* (notionally 20,000 men) under his command, but the forces available to him

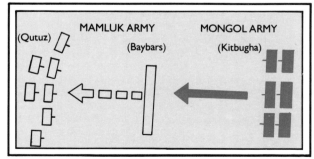

AYN JALUT *The Mamluks employed the Mongols' own favorite feigned flight tactics to defeat their attack on Egypt.*

were substantially reduced in number by a revolt in Damascus and the requirements of garrisoning the Mongol conquests. Also, few of his troops were actually Mongols; for the most part, they were Turks, Armenians and Georgians. Unused to being outnumbered, he also found himself unable to provide the swarms of scouts that contributed so greatly to Mongol victories. Qutuz' force contained Mamluks, *Halga* warriors and many auxiliary, including some unreliable Bedouins.

The trap is baited
The Mamluk vanguard was led by Baybars, who was later to murder Qutuz and prove an even greater ruler than his predecessor. He had his men well in hand when they encountered the Mongol force at dawn on September 3, 1260. The Mamluks fled before the clouds of Mongol arrows and Kitbugha and his men followed, unaware that they were being led into a trap. They rode down the valley to Ayn Jalut, the "Spring of Goliath". Like the Philistine giant the Mongols were about to pay for their over-confidence.

They were still able to break the Mumluk left flank, and charge and counter-charge ensued. Eventually, however, the sultan led an all-out attack that routed the enemy. Many Mongols fled on foot up the nearby hills, the pursuing Mamluks following on foot in order to destroy them. The ruthless Mongols were equally ruthlessly eradicated by the victorious Mumluks; Kitburgha himself was captured and beheaded.

BOSWORTH
THE WARS OF THE ROSES
1485

The battle that ended the long fight for the crown of England between the rival families of York and Lancaster. Although Henry Tudor's army of about 5,000 was outnumbered, his victory over Richard III was ensured by the intervention of Sir William Stanley and the non-participation during the battle of two of the great English nobles – Lord Stanley and the Earl of Northumberland. Despite being one of the best known battles of English history, Bosworth is amongst the most poorly documented.

The prolonged struggle between the rival dynasties of York and Lancaster came to a head in 1485, when Henry Tudor took up the Lancastrian claim to the English crown. On 7 August 1485, he landed at Milford Haven in South Wales with a force of 2,000 to 3,000 men. This force was largely made up of Frenchmen, supplied by Charles VIII of France, and a few hundred English exiles who had joined Henry in Brittany after their unsuccessful rebellion against Richard III's usurpation of the throne in 1483.

THE ROAD TO BOSWORTH FIELD *Henry Tudor's army slowly gathered strength on its march from Wales.*

After marching north-eastwards through central Wales, attracting recruits along the way, Henry's army entered Shrewsbury on 18 August, and after passing through Stafford, turned south towards London. Meanwhile Richard had been mustering his troops at Nottingham, which he left on 19 August to move south to intercept Henry's army. The two armies encountered each other in battle on 22 August near the market town of Bosworth, a few miles to the south west of Leicester.

A fight for a throne

Henry's army was now about 5,000 strong. It consisted of a vanguard, with archers to the fore, under the Earl of Oxford, with wings commanded by Gilbert Talbot and John Savage. Behind came Henry with a troop of horse and a few infantry. They were confronted by the much larger army of Richard, with a vanguard led by the Duke of Norfolk behind which lay the two *battles* of Richard himself and Henry Percy, Earl of Northumberland. Some distances away, observing the activity of the two armies, were the substantial forces of Thomas, Lord Stanley, and his brother, Sir William Stanley.

After initial manoeuvres by Henry to ensure that he kept an area of marsh to his right to stop him being outflanked, the battle began with a clash between the two vanguards. During this struggle, Richard saw an opportunity to win the day with a daring move. Noticing Henry only had a small company with him, he led his own troops around the edge of the fighting and launched a charge against his opponent. The ensuing conflict was very ferocious, with Richard himself killing Henry's standard bearer.

"My kingdom for a horse"

At this point, Sir William Stanley decided to intervene. The way the battle was going gave him a free choice as to which side to support, and he decided to lead his 3,000 troops to the aid of Henry. At the same time Lord Stanley and Northumberland decided to remain neutral, neither coming to the king's support. Richard's soldiers were scattered, and the king himself was killed in the thick of the fighting.

Richard's death brought an end to the battle. The casualties do not appear to have been great, being heaviest in the vanguard, where Norfolk was killed. Large numbers were captured, including Northumberland, who appears to have made no effort to enter the fighting. Through his and Lord Stanley's lack of action and the decisive intervention of Sir William Stanley, Henry Tudor had won the crown of England.

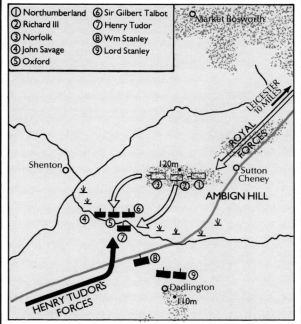

BOSWORTH *After an inconclusive clash between the vanguards, the battle was decided by Stanley's change of sides.*

BOUVINES
FRANCO–ANGEVIN WAR
1214

The battle that led to the collapse of the Angevin empire, built up by Henry II of England. Phillip II, of France led a force of 15,000 against the German Emperor Otto IV, who was an ally of John of England. Otto had perhaps 25,000 men under arms; he forced a battle at Bouvines in Flanders, in which he was totally defeated by the French forces under their able king.

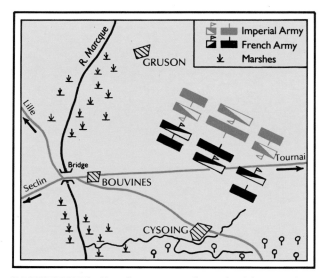

BOUVINES *The French victory was the result of determined cavalry charges against the imperial center and left wing.*

CONSTANTINOPLE
FALL OF BYZANTIUM
1453

The seven-week siege of the previously impregnable fortress-capital of the Byzantine Empire. An army of 100,000 Turks, with a huge fleet and many cannon in support, were opposed by a mere 7,000 defenders and the massive defences of the city walls. After constant bombardment and three mass assaults, the exhausted defenders gave way and the city fell.

In Mehmet II, who became Ottoman sultan in 1451, the fading Byzantine Empire faced a leader who was young, ambitious and determined to conquer. Constantinople stood alone, defended by strong walls, but few men. The emperor, Constantine XI, relied mainly on Italian soldiers and sailors under the command of the Genoan mercenary Guistiniani, but when the Turks arrived before the city on 5 April 1453, only 5,000 Greeks and 2,000 Italians could be found to man the fortifications. Against them Mehmet brought 80,000 men, including 12,000 élite janisseries, and many thousands of irregulars. Sheer weight of numbers, however, was not the main problem facing the defenders – the city's strong defences had defied mere numbers before. But the Turks also brought many cannon with them. Some were so gigantic that they could only be loaded at several hours' intervals, but their destructive power was awesome.

Both sides recognized that the sea was the city's life-line, so the early fighting was mainly naval, as the Turks tried to breach the boom blocking the Golden Horn. Here the Christians had the advantage, since their sailors and vessels were superior to those of their foes. A Turkish naval attack was repulsed on 12 April, while a rash assault on the walls failed a week later. The superiority of their vessels enabled the Italians to defeat

Determined to hold on to his father's territories in France, John had planned a daring pincer attack against Phillip, but was himself defeated by Prince Louis, the French Dauphin, in May 1214 and forced to retreat to La Rochelle. Towards the end of July, however, John's ally, Otto IV, managed to bring Phillip to battle on the plateau of Bouvines. This was the only suitable area for such a conflict, given the marshy, river-intersected nature of the land between the two chief towns of the region, Lille and Tournai.

Both armies deployed in three divisions, infantry drawn up in front of the knights. Otto's foot, which included many Flemish pikemen among its ranks, was superior in quality to that of the French, who soon encountered these formidable troops when they attacked Otto's left wing and center. But, though Phillip's foot-soliders were thrown back in disorder, the French resumed the attack. Guerin de Senlis led the right wing cavalry into the ranks of the pursuing Flemish pikemen and broke them. He then charged on to rout the knights of Hainault stationed behind them.

Both leaders unhorsed

Meanwhile, Phillip himself led similar assaults on Otto's center. Successive charges, by large squadrons consisting of many baronial *mesnies* (retainers) eventually broke through the Germans, but the fighting was very close-matched. The king himself was unhorsed and nearly killed by a Flemish footman, being saved by two knights of his household. Otto also had his horse killed under him and narrowly escaped capture.

The victorious French right and center were now able to turn on the surviving division of Phillip of Dreux. This had held its own against the foe until now, but was soon surrounded and overwhelmed by the new French onslaught. Only the Flemish pikemen fought to the death.

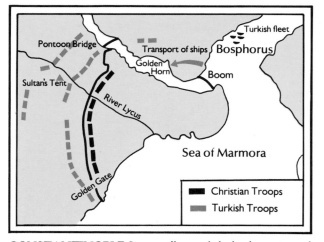

CONSTANTINOPLE *Siege artillery and the land-transport of ships into the Golden Horn were the keys to Turkish victory.*

the Ottoman fleet again on 20 April, but, meanwhile, the Turkish bombardment was opening up breaches in the city walls. These, the defenders quickly repaired.

Incredibly, the Turks now managed to transport part of their fleet on rollers overland into the Golden Horn. This feat neutralized the defenders' sole advantage. Following this, on 7 May Mehmet risked another three-hour assault on a weakened section of wall, which was again defeated. Another attempt on 18 May also failed when the siege tower around which it revolved was set on fire by the Byzantines.

By now, the siege had lasted for seven weeks. Christian morale was higher than that of the Turks; despite their numbers and their cannon the attackers had made little impact on the city's defences. Many advised the sultan to withdraw, but he determined on another assault.

The fall of Constantinople

On the evening of 28 May, Bashi-bazouk irregulars accordingly attacked along the whole length of the walls. After two hours hard fighting they were thrown back with heavy losses, but there was to be no respite for the defenders. Soon, the Anatolian regiments resumed the assault, supported by a ferocious artillery bombardment. When they, too, failed the sultan resorted to his janisseries – fresh élite warriors against men who had already been fighting for four hours. Even then they needed luck in order to succeed.

An unguarded sally port gave the janisseries the opportunity they sought. The wounding of Giustiniani deprived his men of leadership at a crucial moment, and the floodgates opened. The Turks stormed in to capture a city that had stood for a thousand years and Constantine Paleologus, the last Byzantine emperor, was slain in the ruins.

CRECY
THE HUNDRED YEARS WAR
1346

Edward III's *chevauchée* (raiding force) of 8,000 was trapped by Phillip VI of France with an army that may have numbered as many as 20,000. Taking up a defensive position, which the French obligingly, continually and unavailingly charged, the English archers slaughtered the flower of France's chivalry.

Crécy, as far as the English were concerned, was a battle that took place by accident, rather than by design. Indeed Edward III did not intend to fight a major battle at all in 1346. Having captured Caen, he then proceeded to plunder Normandy on his way to the Channel part of Boulogne.

On reaching the Seine, however, Edward discovered that the French had broken the bridges he had counted

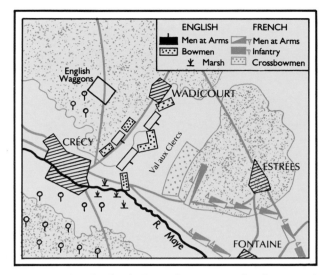

CRECY *Edward's "battles" were drawn up to take advantage of marshy ground and a river. Archers protected the infantry.*

on using to march his force across the river. Consequently he was forced upstream to undertake his own bridge-building work at Poissy. Meanwhile Phillip had used the time gained to gather a substantial force together and, setting out from Paris, he was soon hot on Edward's trail. Forced marches took both armies towards the Somme, where Edward once more faced an obstacle. Denied a passage at three crossing points, he eventually got his men across the river near its mouth at Boismont, the rising tide just cutting off the French pursuit. With the enemy literally on their heels, the English had no choice but to turn and fight.

A good position

Edward chose a good defensive position. His right flank was protected by a small river and some marshy ground, while a damp and reedy hollow, the Val aux Clercs, lay to his front. The English occupied the rising ground, digging pits in front of a hedge to increase its defensive value. They were arranged in three "battles" with the Black Prince, Edward's son, on the right, the Earls of Northampton and Arundel to the left, and Edward in the center. The main body of each "battle" was flanked on either side by archers, thrown forward to enfilade any attack on the men-at-arms.

Longbows versus crossbows

Edward's outnumbered force waited until the late afternoon of August 26 for the expected French attack. Then, probably in defiance of their cautious king's orders, the French nobility charged, the only infantry supporting them being the Genoese and French crossbowmen. Experienced though these were, they managed to loose only three volleys before they were completely outshot by the English longbowmen. Seeing the archers withdraw, the French knights rode through and over the hapless foot in their eagerness to get at the enemy.

Charge to disaster

The English men-at-arms and the archers stood their ground as they watched the cavalry horses slow in the muddy terrain – the rain that had been falling had already played a part in the battle by dampening the cords of the French crossbows, so slowing their rate of fire. Then the English bowmen loosed their shafts, bringing down men and mounts in a welter of confusion. The troops in forward positions were now able to enfilade the now-struggling French.

Wave upon wave of knights rode to defeat in 15 charges as late afternoon turned to dusk. Many, like the blind King John of Bohemia died bravely, but uselessly, in the gathering gloom. The piles of dead men and horses further impeded later assaults. None achieved anything; there was probably no mêlée. By nightfall, the French had been defeated piecemeal and humiliated at the hands of the English archers, losing 4,000 knights, including 1,500 nobles. Edward was free to resume his march to the sea.

DORYLAEUM
THE FIRST CRUSADE
1097

The entire Crusader host of several thousand horse and foot, encumbered by many non-combatants, was ambushed in Central Anatolia by hordes of Seljuk horse archers. This ambush was unsuccessful. While one Crusader column stood on the defensive, the other fell on the Turkish flank and broke the Seljuk army.

The Seljuk ambush

After the defeat of the Seljuk sultan, Kiliji Arslan, on 21 May 1097, at Nicea – a victory that led to the capture of the city – the Crusaders advanced on Dorylaeum, an important crossroads for routes through Anatolia. The sultan, guessing their destination, regrouped his forces for a surprise attack. His task was made easier by the fact that the Crusaders marched in two bodies. The first contained the Normans, from northern France and southern Italy, plus the Flemish contingents; the second, the Provençals, Lorrainers and Hugh of Vermandois' French followers. Accordingly, when swarms of Turkish horse archers fell upon the leading column, the Crusaders marching in it were hard-pressed. Clouds of arrows forced them into a struggling, confused mass.

Only the initiative shown by the Norman leader Bohemond brought order from chaos. While the footmen and the unarmed pilgrims accompanying the Crusaders pitched camp, the knights regrouped behind the defences formed by the waggons, tents and guy ropes. Judicious counter-charges kept their mobile enemy at bay; the Christians, however, lost many men to enemy archery. In the fierce summer heat, thirst was

also a severe problem. Women pilgrims performed sterling service carrying water to the fighting men, but, under the relentless pressure of the Turkish attacks, it was touch and go whether the Crusaders could hold out against their foe.

To the rescue

Then, at the crucial moment, the second Crusader column arrived and fell on the Turkish flank. Whether by luck or good judgement, the Bishop of le Puy, its commander, had achieved tactical surprise. As he led his knights in the charge, Godfrey de Bouillon on his right and Raymond de St Gilles on his left, the Muslims broke and fled. Their sultan narrowly escaped capture, but he was forced to leave his camp unprotected, which the triumphant victors plundered.

Casualties are difficult to assess. The Crusaders, especially the unarmed camp followers, may well have suffered more than the Turks.

KUTNA HORA
THE HUSSITE WARS
1421

Sigismund, the Holy Roman Emperor, led 20,000 men against a Hussite force of 6,000 to 7,000 men (the Hussites were a schismatic religious sect of the time). Through treachery in the city of Kutna Hora in Bohemia (modern Czechoslovakia) the Hussites were trapped outside the walls. Inspired by their leader, Jan Zizka, and their religious fanaticism, the Hussites used their "battle-waggons" offensively to smash through the Catholic encirclement.

Religious rising

The Hussites were followers of Jan Hus, a Bohemian preacher who had been executed for heresy in 1415.

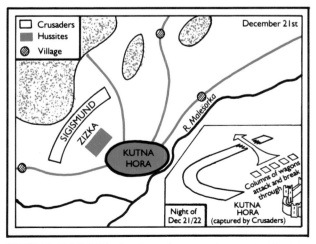

KUTNA HORA *The key factor here was the remarkable night attack made by Zizka's Hussite "battle waggons."*

They were as determined to preserve their religious freedom as the Catholic church was determined to crush the schism, so, when they rose in opposition to their Catholic ruler, Sigismund, he organized a crusade to bring them to heel. This was routed at the Hill of Vitkov, outside Prague, in 1420. Entrenchments and artillery held the best of Sigismund's German troops at bay; seeing them defeated, the rest of his heterogenous force fell apart.

Although a largely peasant army, equipped with flails and clubs, the Hussites became the best fighting force in the Europe of the time. Their leader, Jan Zizka, had been blinded in an accident with gunpowder. This was ironic, since it was his masterly use of handguns and small artillery pieces that made his troops invincible. His army always travelled with what were literally "battle-waggons", which, when drawn up into a waggon-fort, were able to repel enemy attacks and form a base for counter-charges.

In November 1421, however, Sigismund returned to Bohemia with a second crusade. This consisted of a hard-bitten force of Hungarian cavalry with supporting infantry, under the command of the ruthless and experienced Italian warrior, Pipa of Ozara.

Trapped outside the city

The resulting battle was fought outside the strategically important city of Kutna Hora (modern Königratz). Zizka had marched into the city on 19 December; two days later, he moved his small force out to offer battle. The Hussites formed their waggon-fort, which threw back attacks of cavalry and infantry alike, but then treachery came to Sigismund's aid. Many of Kutna Hora's silver miners were loyal to him, and engineered a coup that enabled a force of Crusaders to enter the city. The Hussites therefore found themselves in a desperate position – cut off from food, supplies and even warm clothing on a bitter December night.

Attack by night

Sigismund confidently hoped for a Hussite capitulation; he certainly did not expect a night attack. After dark, however, Zizka marshalled his waggons in columns, and at midnight launched a barrage of shot against his unprepared enemies. Moving swiftly, the Hussites smashed through Sigismund's lines and escaped. The following day, they took up position on a nearby hill, but Sigismund was reluctant to attack. His army's morale had been shattered by this unexpected turn of events; when Pipa finally offered battle at Habry a few days later, his men simply turned tail and fled.

This success was the climax of what had been a magnificent campaign for Zizka. The battle was the turning point of the war, since it gave the Hussites a huge moral supremacy over their opponents. But, though his use of his "battle-waggons" has been seen by some historians as a precursor of the tank, it should be remembered that it was desperation that led to the manoeuvre. Waggon-fort tactics were essentially static.

LIEGNITZ
MONGOLS IN EASTERN EUROPE
1241

In 1241, the northern arm of a Mongol pincer attack on eastern Europe pushed through Poland to Liegnitz on the borders of Germany. Duke Henry II of Silesia led a hastily-collected force against the invaders, but was crushingly defeated by them. The battle was a typical Mongol victory in the face of poorly organized, ill-disciplined opposition.

The Mongol advance

Following the destruction of the Russian principalities in a series of campaigns between 1237 and 1240, the Mongols began to turn further west. The rulers of Central Europe had learnt nothing from the lessons of the Russian defeats; they were divided among themselves and unprepared for the Mongol assault brewing from the east.

After crossing the frozen Vistula in January 1241, the Mongol army divided in two. Kaidu led the northern force, which crossed the Oder in late March. Bypassing the formidable fortress of Breslau, half the Mongols under Kaidu then pressed on into Silesia, while the remainder plundered the countryside. Eager to prevent this destruction, Henry II hurried to meet the nomads in battle. In the van of his force were picked Silesian and Polish knights. Behind them came the Teutonic Knights, under their Grand Master, followed by another Polish division, and finally a solid block of Silesian infantry. We do not know if they deployed from this line of march and it is probable that they went into battle in the same order.

Although Henry's forces were formidable by Western standards, the Mongols showed themselves easily capable of dealing with them. First they burnt reeds to produce a smoke screen, then taunted the knights with showers of arrows before feigning flight. Unable to resist the temptation to pursue, all but Henry's immediate followers were fooled into following in hot pursuit. Suddenly, they came face to face with the heavier Mongol cavalry, who surrounded them. In the rout that followed, some of the finest Western cavalry was swept away, taking with them the helpless infantry, who were hardly able to get in a blow. Henry himself was captured and beheaded.

Western humiliation was bitter, but not total. This came only two days later, when the great Mongol generals Batu and Subadai destroyed the Hungarian army at Mohi on the River Sajó.

MORAT
SWISS–BURGUNDIAN WARS
1476

A large and confident force of 25,000 Swiss surprised and stormed the Burgundian defensive works, despite careful advance preparation. The combined firepower of the Burgundian artillery and archery failed to break up the Swiss infantry blocks, which quickly dispersed Charles the Bold's disorganized army. This victory established the Swiss as the undisputed fighting élite of western Europe.

Burgundian aggression
Charles the Bold, Duke of Burgundy, with one of the most up-to-date and well-equipped armies of the time under his command, was determined to carve out a Burgundian empire in western Europe. The Swiss, however, were determined to foil his plans. Already, in March 1476, their pike columns and handgunners had driven off Charles' finest cavalry and archers, and captured 400 pieces of his carefully-gathered artillery at the battle of Grandson. In June, however, he returned to the attack. With an army of over 20,000 men and 200 cannon, he laid siege to the city of Morat, which was defended by a Swiss force a tenth size of the Burgundian army.

The Swiss Confederation accordingly raised a relieving force of 25,000 of their redoubtable footsoldiers (pikemen, halberdiers, handgunners and crossbowmen), together with 1,800 cavalry led by Rénè, Duke of Lorraine. To counter this threat, Charles constructed an entrenchment, which he planned to pack with infantry flanked by archers, supported on the left flank by enfilading artillery and on the right by 3,000 cavalry.

Charles' plan
Charles' plan was to nullify the impact of the Swiss charge, throwing their advancing phalanx into disarray with arrows and shot, following this by a cavalry charge in the flank to rout them. His first mistake was to underestimate the strength of the Swiss forces; despite a personal reconnaissance, he thought it safe to leave his field fortifications manned by only 2,000 missilemen, backed up by 1,200 cavalry.

The initiative therefore passed to the Swiss, who formed up in an echelon. The advance guard of 5,000 missilemen, stiffened by pikemen, held the right of the line, with the Lorrainer cavalry covering its left flank. Behind them came the main body of 12,000 in a dense phalanx; then came the rearguard, whose task was to swing around the Burgundian right flank to cut off any chance of retreat.

The Swiss attack
The Swiss assault on the afternoon of 22 June 1476 took the Burgundians by surprise, though the archers and artillery in the thinly-defended position nevertheless inflicted many casualties on the Swiss vanguard. The veteran Swiss reacted quickly, manoeuvering to outflank the defence while attacking stoutly with their pikemen. All resistance collapsed as the adeptly-handled main and rear bodies swarmed forward on the other flank. To add to the confusion, the defenders of Morat made a timely sally in the Burgundian rear.

Charles could do nothing to rally his men, who were defeated piecemeal as they arrived in the line to counter the pincer movement the Swiss had launched to win the day. The Burgundians lost 12,000 men in a battle that showed the Swiss virtues of discipline and flexibility in action to the full.

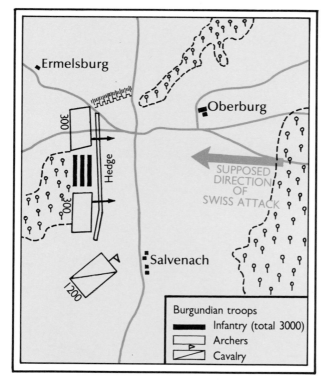

MORAT *Underestimating the strength of his Swiss foes, Charles the Bold left his fieldworks inadequately manned.*

NICOPOLIS
CRUSADERS VERSUS TURKS
1396

The Ottomans demonstrated their strength in this closely-fought battle at Nicopolis (modern Romania). The Hungarian king, Sigismund, commanded c.20,000 troops, together with 6,000 Crusaders. The Turkish sultan, Bayezit, led similar or smaller numbers. Chivalric ill-discipline and the use of oriental massed archery gave victory to the Turks.

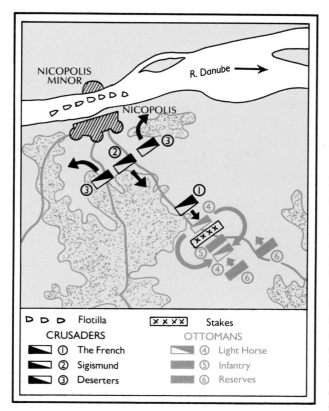

NICOPOLIS *An impetuous charge by the French horse foundered in a field of Turkish stakes and defeat followed.*

Volunteers from the west

As the Ottoman state grew in strength and extent, its new western neighbors became seriously alarmed by the speed of its expansion. The powerful kingdom of Hungary, being the most vulnerable region to Ottoman attack, called for a Crusade to deal with the menace, and a gap in the Hundred Years War ensured a warm reception for the plea. The fortress-city of Nicopolis, which had recently fallen to the Turks, provided a suitable target. France and Burgundy took the lead, although recruits came from all over Europe; some 6,000 knights, squires and mercenaries eventually agreed to serve. They were led by the flower of French chivalry. Jean de Boucicault, Phillipe d'Artois and Jean de Vienne – Marshal, Constable and Admiral of France respectively – Jean de Nevers, heir to the Duke of Burgundy, and Enguerrand de Coucy, an experienced warrior, were among the French nobles who rode east, while the Grand Master of the Knights Hospitaller sailed from the order's base at Rhodes.

The Crusaders took six months to march from their mustering point in Burgundy to Nicopolis, upsetting their Hungarian allies *en route* by carrying out unnecessary massacres in the towns they captured. By the time the combined armies arrived at Nicopolis on 12 September 1396, the two contingents were no longer co-operating. They were also ill-equipped to embark on a formal siege and so resorted to a blockade.

Bayezit's preparations

Meanwhile, Bayezit had led his army in a forced march to the relief of the city, taking up a defensive position on a hillside four miles to the south of Nicopolis on his arrival on the scene. In the first line swarmed his *akinji* (light cavalry), screening a field of stakes "a bowshot wide". Behind this barrier stood the infantry, including the elite janisseries, all of whom were bow-armed. In reserve, the sultan held his mailed *spahi* guard, plus his Serbian allies under Stephen Lazarovic.

A quarrel over tactics

The sudden appearance of the Turks took the Christians by surprise and they immediately quarrelled about what was the best thing to do. Sigismund favored keeping the French knights in reserve, while probing the enemy positions with his own light horse. He felt the hammer blow of the French charge should be held back until it could prove decisive.

However, this eminently sensible proposal outraged the French who, considering themselves slighted, rapidly formed up and advanced against the Turkish cavalry. Their charge scattered the Turks, only to encounter the field of stakes. There, under a galling fire, the knights lost many horses, even though their supporting infantry tried to help by uprooting the obstacles. Some may have dismounted in order to get to grips with the foe. Once the armored knights came to close quarters with Turkish foot they smashed through them, but then were again confronted by the Sultan's light horse, which by this time had regrouped.

Bayezit's coup de grâce

Another French charge split this force asunder and routed it. Exhausted now by the weight of their armor, the heat of the sun and their exertions, the Crusaders now came face-to-face with Bayezit's *spahis*. Largely without horses by this time, the knights' resistance collapsed. Most were taken prisoner.

Meanwhile, Sigismund, who was advancing in support of the French, was deserted by his Wallachian and Transylvanian allies, who could see which way the tide of battle was flowing. The Serbs struck his flank, so shattering the remaining Christian opposition.

Losses were heavy on both sides. The surviving French lords, the guilty parties in the débacle, were held to ransom at a huge cost to their vassals.

POITIERS
THE HUNDRED YEARS WAR
1356

An encounter between a 7000-strong Anglo-Gascon force, under the Black Prince, with a French army of more than double the strength, led by King John. The latter failed to exploit his numerical superiority; instead

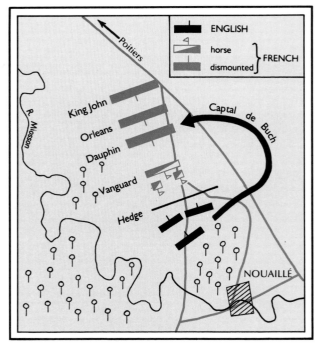

POITIERS *Victory was snatched from the jaws of defeat by a concealed outflanking march and attack on the French.*

he launched frontal charges on the Black Prince's carefully chosen defensive position. Mounted flank and counter-attacks led to a complete French rout, resulting in the capture of their king and many members of the nobility.

The English strike
In August 1356, the Black Prince set out on a *chevauchée* (raid), in a broad sweep from Bordeaux to Bourges and Tours. His army consisted of 3,500 men-at-arms and 1,000 light troops (mainly Gascons), plus 2,500 English archers.

King John could not allow such an attack to succeed, as it would seriously damage both his revenue and prestige. Gathering a force of 8,000 men-at-arms and an equal number of footmen (including 2,000 crossbowmen), he set out in energetic pursuit of the Black Prince's troops. By 18 September, John had caught up with the plunder-laden English just south of Poitiers. Edward at first tried to bargain, offering to surrender his prisoners and booty in return for a free passage, but this was refused.

Fight or flight
The dispositions the English took up the following day suggest that their intention was to flee, rather than to fight. Their waggons were moved under escort to cross the River Miosson, while the rest of the army lined up alongside a hedge and ditch – the latter had been dug during the parley. Arrayed in the usual three "battles", the men-at-arms were flanked by archers.

There was to be no escape, however. The French

advance was soon upon the English ranks – 300 picked knights charging furiously forward. Just as quickly, however, they streamed back in retreat, their charge having been shattered by the English archery.

Attacking on foot
The French king had prepared for this, however. On the advice of a Scot, Douglas, he dismounted most of his men-at-arms. The first division, under the Dauphin, then advanced – slowly, but taking fewer casualties. Once the battle-lines joined, the fight was hotly contested. Gradually, Edward's men gained the upper hand, forcing the French to withdraw.

Now was the moment of the second, mounted, division to fall on the exhausted Anglo-Gascon knights. It did not, since, for some unexplained reason, the Duke of Orleans led his men away from the fight. All was not yet lost for the French, however, as their third and largest division, commanded by the king himself, was ready to deliver a decisive blow.

From crisis to victory
In this extremity, Edward decided to remount his depleted force and counter-attack the advancing French. Every horse that could carry a man – even the pack-horses – was pressed into service, while the archers were ordered to support the advancing knights. Also, unlike the French, Edward now resorted to cunning tactics. While he engaged their attention to the front, he sent the Captal de Buch, a Gascon notable, on a concealed march to take the enemy in the flank and rear. For a time the battle raged fiercely once more, but, when the outflanking force fell on the enemy, a French rout ensued.

Though the English losses were heavy, the French casualty rate was catastrophic. Among the knights, 2,500 were killed and 2,000 captured, including 26 leading nobles, plus their king and the Dauphin. French rigidity of thought and tactics had been soundly defeated by English flexibility and archery superiority.

SLUYS
THE HUNDRED YEARS WAR
1340

A naval battle in which the English king Edward III, with a force of about 200 ships, defeated a much larger French fleet, which had been threatening England with invasion. Sluys is a fine example of medieval naval strategy, in which the ships provided a floating battle ground on which soldiers could employ tactics normally associated with a land battle.

Following the outbreak of the Hundred Years War in 1337, the French had been active in attacking English shipping and raiding towns along the south coast. By the early summer of 1340, it appeared that they were planning an invasion of England; accordingly, a large fleet had been assembled in the estuary of the river Zwin, opposite the town of Sluys. Edward III, who was already preparing to lead an expeditionary force to Flanders, gathered more ships and men on hearing of the French preparations. The core of his fleet was composed of a handful of royal ships, the remainder consisting of merchant ships drawn from the Cinque Ports and other ports along the south and east coasts. These ships – or cogs, as they were known – were specially adapted for warfare with the construction of fighting tops on the their fore and stern castles.

The English set sail
On 22 June 1340, Edward set sail from Orwell near Ipswich. The fleet anchored the next day off Blankenberghe, north-west of Bruges. Scouts were sent out to reconnoitre the enemy strength and reported a force in excess of 400 vessels. These included not only French ships but also Castilian and Genoese contingents, all tightly concentrated into a narrow harbor and commanded by Hugh Quiéret and Nicholas Béhuchet. One chronicler reported they were so densely packed that their masts looked like a forest.

Early the following morning, Edward deployed his fleet into three squadrons, stationing a shipload of men-at-arms between every two of archers. He then sailed toward the enemy, taking advantage of the wind and tide being in his favour. The French had also divided their fleet into three squadrons, one behind the other with the ships lashed together with chains. Barbanera, captain of the Genoese mercenaries, counselled the French commanders to put to sea where they could take advantage of their greater manoeuvrability, but his advice was ignored – both the French admirals, though "right good and expert men of war," were not seamen, while few of the 20,000 men in the fleet had ever seen a battle.

The battle began with a barrage from the English archers, Edward's strategy being to attack the French squadrons one by one, manoeuvring his ships close enough to the enemy for the men-at-arms to board. During the course of the day, two of the French squadrons were overcome in bloody fighting. The chronicler Froissart states: "This battle was fierce and terrible, for the battles on sea are more dangerous and fiercer than the battles on land, for on the sea there is no reculing nor fleeing." Edward himself was wounded in the leg, while both Quiéret and Béhuchet – the former having been badly wounded – were captured and executed. The fighting continued into the night during which the Genoese made their escape, but by morning the bulk of the French fleet had been captured.

Sluys was the first great English victory in the Hundred Years War – it was left to the court jester to break the news to Philip of France. It prevented an invasion of England and gave Edward command of the Channel for the immediate future.

TINCHEBRAI
NORMAN VERSUS NORMAN
1106

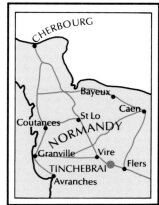

A classic feudal encounter between Henry I of England and his elder brother Robert, Duke of Normandy, in a battle to determine the control of the duchy. They had about 7,000 men apiece under command; the two armies were well-matched in all respects, Henry's victory being due to his superior tactics.

Dismounted knights
The sons of William the Conqueror spent much of their time fighting over his inheritance. Henry, the youngest, seized the throne in 1099, on the death of William Rufus in a hunting accident in the New Forest. When Robert returned from the First Crusade, he attempted to invade England in 1101, but was repulsed. Five years later, Henry crossed the English Channel, determined to deprive his elder brother of his rightful inheritance.

Henry's forces were besieging the castle of Tinchebrai in south-west Normandy when Robert led his army to its relief. On 28 September 1106, the brothers drew up their men for a decisive battle. Both employed large numbers of infantrymen in the fight, Henry and the cream of his knights dismounting to form the second battle line. Cavalry were stationed on either flank, while, further out to the right, an outflanking force under Count Helias of Maine stood in wait.

Robert attacks
Robert also drew his men up in two lines, with footmen (stiffened by dismounted knights) to the rear of his cavalry. Impetuously, and, according to a chronicler, "as he had learned on Crusade", Robert charged with the two wings of the ducal cavalry, each 700 strong, straight into Henry's front line. The left "battle", under the Count of Mortain, almost broke Henry's right wing, driving off the cavalry stationed in its support. However, Henry's infantry stood firm, and the outflanking force – as planned – took the disorganized enemy in the flank and shattered the ducal army.

Robert was captured and imprisoned for the rest of his life (d.1134). Henry's crushing victory had taken barely an hour to accomplish. Only the infantry suffered heavy casualties. What was termed "the brotherhood of arms" meant that the knights spared each other; only three are recorded as being killed.

CHAPTER FOUR
The Gunpowder Revolution

Although artillery had made a major impact at the siege of *Constantinople* in 1453 and a minor one at such battles as *Crécy* and *Agincourt* even earlier, it was under the French King Charles VIII in 1494 that the full potential of gunpowder was demonstrated. With his campaign in Italy, the true transition from feudal to modern warfare began.

The French in Italy

Invading a disunited, yet complacent, Italy in that year, the well-drilled and better-equipped French army outclassed its opponents both in its approach to siegecraft and on the battlefield. Its redoubtable mercenary Swiss and German pikemen were one reason for this success, but of greater significance was the proportion of infantry serving in its ranks, who were carrying the newly-developed arquebus, with its shaped butt and rudimentary firing mechanism. Most important of all these factors, however, was the new artillery in the French ranks. Though the larger pieces were still conveyed in carts, as they had been earlier in the century, the French now introduced the first true muzzle-loading field guns in their support. With their two-wheel gun carriages and primitive trails, the latter were light enough to keep up with marching troops; their cast-iron or bronze barrels could be elevated or depressed; and the iron shot they fired wrought more havoc than the mainly stone projectiles they superceded. This superior and numerically strong artillery arm – the creation of Jacques de Genouillac – ushered in a technological revolution and a new age of warfare that was destined to last for well over three centuries.

If the French inaugurated the age of artillery, the Swiss were the

WEAPONS OF WAR *The Dutch Nassau militia armed with pikes and muskets, the key infantry weapons of the new warfare.*

masters of specialized infantry fighting, with their 16ft pikes and 7ft halberds (combining a spear, axe and a hook). The way in which they used massed columns in attack, or porcupine *schiltrons* in defence earned them a vast military reputation, and many armies hired Swiss mercenaries as a result. Their only rivals – and eventual supercessors – were the German *Landsknechts*. Both types of sturdy foot-soldiers doomed the heavy mediaeval cavalryman to extinction as surely as the stalwart longbowmen of the Welsh marches or the crossbowmen of Genoa.

Cannon – "the last argument of kings"

One contemporary who saw the significance of these developments was Nicolo Machiavelli. In *The Prince* he wrote that a sound military organization was the vital foundation for a successful state. He also appreciated the correlation between military and financial power, and preached the need for balanced, all-arm standing forces to support rulers,

rather than the unreliable *condottiere* (freebooter) companies of his day. War he regarded as a necessary evil to determine which states were to survive and prosper, and which were to suffer eclipse.

With such views being expressed, it is small wonder that the struggles between kings and between the emerging nations took a number of new and dramatic forms from the early 16th century to the mid-18th century. Dynastic rivalries remained as in the past – eventually the main struggle for European predominance developed into a bitter contest between the French Valois dynasty (succeeded by the Bourbons) and the great Habsburg houses of Austria and Spain. But although armed forces remained "the playthings of kings" – it was not without reason that the French King Louis XIV would engrave "the last argument of kings" upon his cannon – there was also a growing fusion of royal and national interests, as the latter became more widely appreciated. This was particularly so in the cases of France, England, the Netherlands, Sweden, and, ultimately, Prussia. For the first half of this period, however, two major causes underlay the great majority of wars – the ideological fervor released by the Protestant Reformation and the Catholic Counter-Reformation, typified by the French Wars of Religion (1559–1610) and the 30 Years War (1618–1648), and the economic tensions fomented by the beginnings of overseas empires in the Far East and the Americas. In later years – after the Peace of Westphalia (1648) – the causes of conflict would largely stem from the rival claims of emerging nation-states, as in the case of the wars of the Spanish, Polish and Austrian Successions.

THE 30 YEARS WAR *Soldiers in camp during the 30 Years War, a conflict between Catholic and Protestant in Germany that gave birth to a military revolution.*

These wars were key contests in the almost constant struggle for European dominance by France and the determined efforts of the other great powers – Austria, Britain and Holland leading the field – to resist her. In the War of the Spanish Succession, for instance, these three powers fought to prevent a Bourbon prince succeeding to the Spanish throne, so uniting the two crowns; in the War of the Polish Succession, the civil war between the two claimants to the throne was exacerbated by the intervention of France on one side and Russia and Prussia on the other. The struggle was renewed in the War of the Austrian

Succession, which was sparked off by Frederick the Great of Prussia's refusal to accept the so-called "Pragmatic Sanction", by which the Habsburg emperor, Charles VI, had attempted to secure the throne for his daughter, Maria Theresa. France allied herself with Prussia, backing the claims of Charles Albert of Bavaria; Britain joined eventually by Holland, supported Maria Theresa.

Spain and the "tercio"
The first clash between Valois and Habsburg was fought out on Italian soil. The French incursion proved hard to check, but an appeal by the kingdom of Naples to Spain did not go unheeded. In 1495, *"el Gran Capitan"* Gonzalo of Cordoba (see p000) was ordered to Naples' aid at the head of 500 light horsemen, 100 mounted men-at-arms and 1,500 infantry. Most of the latter were sword-and-buckler men, but there were some arquebusiers among their number. After initial setbacks, the newcomers – fresh from their final triumph over the Moors in Spain – drove back the French stage by

stage. They began to develop their own pikemen in emulation of the Swiss mercenaries in French service, and to increase the proportion of arquebusiers in their ranks. Gonzalo also employed field fortifications to protect his infantry.

By 1504 the French had been expelled from Italy. They returned – only to meet defeat again. Though the Italian wars continued intermittently until 1559, the period of Habsburg supremacy was inaugurated when the French met defeat at *Pavia* in 1525, a battle that demonstrated the predominance of firearm-bearing infantrymen properly supported by pikemen and field artillery.

Long before 1559 the Spaniards had come into their military prime. One indication of this was their New World, achievement where the mighty Aztec and Inca empires of Mexico and Peru fell to tiny forces of a few hundred men at most, led by commanders such as Hernando Cortez and Francisco Pizarro. Equally impressive was their fighting record along "the Spanish Road" (the lengthy line of communication linking north Italy and the Netherlands by way of the Valtelline passes, the Swiss cantons, Franche Comté and Luxemburg), and through most of the 80 Years War against the Dutch and their allies – at least until *Rocroi*.

The main instrument of Spanish military supremacy was the infantry formation known as the *tercio*. The army of Gonzalo had fought in flexible, balanced 500-strong units, but his successors soon developed 3,000-man (and even larger) *tercios*, which consisted of three columns (*colonellas* – later regiments), each commanded by a "colonel" (hence the rank title). By the mid-1530s the pike-and-arquebus combination resulted in dense bodies of pikemen up to 40 ranks deep. These formed the central nucleus of the Spanish battle formations with "sleeves" of arquebusiers (later matchlock musketeers) deployed in up to 10 ranks along the sides or at the angles. Protected from cavalry attack by the serried ranks of pikemen, the musketeers fired rank-by-rank, before retiring to form a new rear rank, where they reloaded.

The pikes could also be used offensively in massed charges – the so-called "push of pike". During the same period the cavalry became instruments of firepower rather than of shock-action, using their wheel-lock pistols rank after rank before wheeling to the rear in what was termed the *caracole* to reload before coming to close quarters with their foes with the sword.

Masters of the battlefield

Thus, if this period opened with the first serious appearance of artillery in the field, with great implications for the future forms of siegecraft in both the attack and the defence, within half a century the once-scorned firearm-bearing foot soldier had established his place in the battle-line (although for another century the pike still would be regarded as "the queen of weapons"). The Spanish armies were essentially infantry-based; for almost a century, under such commanders as Parma, Alva and Spinola, they knew no military peer. Notorious for looting and rapine, they were also noted for their rigid discipline and ferocious *joie de combattre* in action. Paid (although there were exceptions that from the wealth of the Spanish empire or by loans and taxes raised in the Holy Roman Empire led to mutinies), and increasingly recruited on a long-term voluntary basis by governments in Madrid and Vienna with the necessary administrative organizational base, the proud Habsburg *tercios* became the arbiters of the European battlefield and were widely copied as a result. The first truly regular professional armies of modern history had been born, and refinements in firearms would eventually make the foot-soldier the dominant influence on the field of battle.

Early drawbacks

At first, however, firearms imposed penalties as well as offering opportunities. They were less efficient than the longbow, since their range was far shorter, their rate of fire

CAVALRY AND INFANTRY *Following the reforms of the Swedish king Gustavus Adolphus in the early 1630s, cavalry generally reverted to being a shock force, charging home with the sword, while the infantry became better armed and more manoeuverable.*

slower, and their accuracy inferior. On the other hand, they could be handled by less-skilled (hence cheaper) soldiers.

It was the dense bodies of pikemen, therefore, that first really challenged the supremacy of the cavalry, but, by the 1560s these had also brought the conduct of war to a static and almost moribund condition. Due to their growing bulk, the much-copied *tercios* effectively precluded bold manoeuvre on campaign or on the battlefield; the cavalry, now trained as an instrument of firepower, had also lost much of its shock role in action; the improved heavy artillery had enforced radical changes in field fortification design, which in turn made time-consuming and static siege-warfare increasingly the norm. Battles were bloody, but often

indecisive; even when a true victory was achieved, its effective follow-up was rare, as the long-drawn-out Wars of Religion between Catholics and Protestants in France demonstrated.

The "Military Revolution"

Then came what Professor Michael Roberts has called the "Military Revolution", spanning the century from 1560 to 1660. During this century, the way in which battles were fought changed dramatically, with the introduction of new tactical methods and concepts and the use of the new fighting forces – notably the Swedes and the French – to successfully over-turn the existing status quo in European affairs. The evidence of this period supports the generally held belief that defeat, rather than victory, is often the inspirer of military reform, since it was the hard-pressed Dutch Protestants – almost overwhelmed by their Spanish foes – who began the process. Under Maurice of Nassau's inspiration, they began to replace the cumbersome *tercios* with 500-man battalions (part musket and part pike armed), thereby both economizing in manpower and regaining a measure of flexibility on the battlefield. The Dutch also adopted linear orders of battle (two lines of mutually-supporting formations with a reserve in the rear) – a formation destined to be used, albeit with variations, for over 200 years.

Maurice, however, used these new concepts only defensively, failing to see their full potential, while the Dutch cavalry remained largely as it was. The Dutch Republic – with its growing superiority at sea and aided by English contingents under the Earl of Leicester and other commanders – survived its crisis, but stopped short of implementing a full reform of land warfare.

The rise of Sweden

The completion of the task was left to another Protestant state – the Baltic kingdom of Sweden, led by its great ruler Gustavus Adolphus, who is recognized by all authorities on this period as the effective "Father of Modern War." Gustavus' far-reaching reforms covered practically every aspect of 17th-century land warfare, influencing strategy, tactics and the equally important administrative elements. First, he improved firepower on the battlefield. His infantry were given a lighter wheel-lock musket and a dozen cartridges containing powder and shot, thereby speeding up the reloading process. His pikemen carried a shorter 8ft pike, and retained their aggressive role in battle. Carefully devised tactics were evolved to combine fire-power and shock-action, volley-firing by platoons replacing the rolling fire by counter-marching ranks that had been the hallmark of the *tercios*. His cavalry – following Polish practice – was trained to fight in three ranks, rather than six, to wear the minimum amount of body-armor, and to charge home with the sword, rather than rely on hand firearms.

To support both horse and foot, the role of the artillery was greatly reorganized. Guns were divided into three categories – siege, field and regimental – according to size and role. Improved barrel-casting and carriage design, plus careful training, reduced both the weight of the guns and the size of the artillery trains by half in terms of the horses and waggons they required to get them into action, so vastly increasing their effectiveness in siege or in battle. Salvo-firing by 12pdr field artillery drawn up in "companies" or batteries was supplemented by the light "leather guns" and the later 3pdr regimental pieces. These cannon were revolutionary, since they were actually light enough to keep pace with infantry in action. Their early design (a thin copper barrel wound in rope and plaster within a leather cover) was hazardous, since, despite the rope, the gun was liable to explode in action; by the 1630s the 3pdr *piece suedoise* had an all-metal barrel, but was still light enough to be drawn by a single horse or three men.

Thus was born the idea of the modern "Support Company" (today the mortars and anti-tank weapons attached to an infantry battalion). The use of pre-packaged rounds (cannon-balls attached to hessian bags filled with gunpowder) for all guns also increased the rate of fire; it meant that battle tactics could be evolved around a complex and flexible fire plan.

The success of the new-style Swedish armies during the 30 Years' War rested upon two basic factors – high morale and good administration. To achieve the former, much stress was laid upon discipline and good leadership by junior officers, while the establishment of a standardized drill system and a universally-worn blue uniform led to a sense of professionalism. Where military administration was concerned, much attention was paid to setting up a workable logistical system based upon depots and convoys, while the economy of Sweden was placed upon a war-footing, and the troops received regular rations and pay.

The full impact of this new-style *national* army was experienced at such battles as *Breitenfeld*, Lutzen and Wittstock, and it is hardly surprising that it became the model for many other countries – just as the Spanish *tercio* had been a century before. France, indeed, hired a complete Swedish army in the 1640s, with the major victory of *Rocroi* as the part result. This inaugurated the period of French predominance in warfare under Marshal Condé and, above all, Turenne, the master of manoeuvre warfare, and ended the period of Spain's ascendancy. Similarly, Fairfax's and Cromwell's New Model Army – the force that won the battle of *Naseby* (1645) and with it the First English Civil War – was organized and trained on largely Swedish lines.

Professionals at war

The effects of the "Military Revolution" were thus to bring a new professionalism into war. Although military schools were slow to appear – and tended to train only gunners and engineers when they did – the profession of officer became more sophisticated and demanding. Discipline and drill were more significant than ever, so the ability to train soldiers was vital. The smaller fire-unit required more competent junior officers and NCOs than had previously been the case, while, as firearms improved, more was also expected of the common soldier.

It was soon discovered that it was cheaper to maintain at least a nucleus of trained officers and men in time of peace, than to raise new armies from scratch each time a new crisis occurred. Standing armies therefore make their appearance in the richer countries. The requirements of holding the *Militargrenze* (military frontiers) of the Holy Roman Empire against the Turks, for instance, induced the Austrian Habsburgs to raise a permanent field force. As national and military administrations developed under such ministers as Oxenstierna in Sweden or Michel le Tellier and Louvois in France, so permanent military establishments began to grow until, in the 1690s, Louis XIV could boast a military establishment of over 400,000 in time of war. English armies swung between a mere 7,000 "Guards and Garrisons" and a further 17,000 men overseas in 1660 to almost 98,000 in 1710 (including over 25,000 hired troops). Tiny Sweden briefly supported an army of 110,000, the Dutch 75,000, and Austria about 140,000 troops, while Peter the Great created a Russian army totalling 200,000 by 1712. All armies, of course, were radically reduced in number in times of peace, since it was economically unfeasible for the economies of the day to support huge armies.

Warfare from 1700

By 1700, European attitudes towards warfare were again changing. Religious partisanship had largely subsided, except in wars involving the Muslim Turks, while the days of true national fervour still lay ahead. In line with the dictates of the Age of Reason, rulers and generals alike appreciate the virtues of relative military moderation, and the conduct of war was generally limited in its aims to territorial, commercial or (increasingly) colonial objectives as a result. Indeed fighting and negotiation often went in hand, with peaces such as Utrecht (1713) or Paris (1763) representing compromises, rather than all-out victories or defeats. Of course, there were still severe physical obstacles to reinforce this psychological attitude: factors such as the bad roads of winter and spring, the shortage of fodder and rations, and the problems of recruiting troops all contributed to restricting the "campaigning season" to the months between April and October (although winter campaigns were fought in Spain and eastern Europe). Logistical, topographical, climatic and social factors also had the effect of keeping individual field armies relatively small, averaging between 40,000 and 70,000 between 1680 and 1720, and also channelled most campaigns into areas of high fertility, including the Netherlands, the Middle Rhine and North Italy. Armies, after all, had to be fed.

Limited warfare

These prosperous areas contained wealthy, well-fortified towns in large numbers – desirable acquisitions and also serious obstacles (if untaken) to schemes of manoeuvre. Large guns remained cumbersome and short-ranged, but the developments in defensive fortification were considerable, as 16th- and 17th-century Italian concepts were further developed and refined. In consequence, campaigning became increasingly dominated by the complexities of time-consuming siege warfare – in both attack and defence – and Marshal Vauban's treatises on the

arts of defence and attack became essential reading for senior officers. All-out stormings were discouraged; capitulations on agreed terms after reasonable resistance became the norm. The siege of *Lille* illustrates the problems this type of warfare posed.

Taken together, these factors resulted in a marked limitation of war. Commanders became obsessed with disrupting lines of communication and taking cities. Full-scale battles were avoided almost deliberately, as being too expensive in irreplaceable manpower and material; indeed they could be costly, as *Ramillies* in 1706 and *Leuthen* in 1757 well demonstrated, with the victor suffering almost as severely as the vanquished. Thus it cost Marlborough and Eugene 20% of their troops to win Blenheim in 1704, and 25% to win Malplaquet in 1709 – and the primitive state of military medicine did not help commanders

conserve their effectives, though fewer died of their wounds than might be supposed. Military historians reckon that about one in three battle casualties died of severe wounds. Under these conditions it is not surprising that only a handful of commanders – including Marlborough and Frederick the Great – were willing or able to break away from the military trammels of their day and restore some measure of decision war.

The keys to success

On the battlefield, success or defeat depended mainly on two factors – discipline and firepower. Discipline implies control, so Marlborough's trusted aides were trained to serve as his eyes amidst the smoke and dust of battle. In the matter of firepower, the supercession of the matchlock musket by the superior flintlock and the cumbersome pike by the socket bayonet – a process that was largely completed by 1703 – greatly increased the rate and volume of fire. The English and Dutch were the first to adapt their tactics to make the most of these developments nautical, with the introduction of the platoon-firing system (six at a time) in three ranks. This resulted in a higher rate of more accurate fire – based upon effective fire control exercised by platoon officers and sergeants – than was possible for the French five-ranks-deep formations, employing line, company or full-battalion volleys, to achieve.

The tactical flexibility this method conferred was of considerable importance between 1704 and 1709, for the French and Spaniards were slow to conform to the new system. The infantry principle of "fire and movement" had at last been re-affirmed, however, and by 1710 all European armies were employing the new system with various adaptations. The higher casualty figures involved often made commanders even charier about seeking open battle; as late as the 1740s Marshal de Saxe in his *Reflections on the Art of War* was preaching the virtue of avoiding major engagements. A Marlborough, a Eugene or a Villars – and (later) a Frederick the Great – could prove adept at forcing action upon unwilling opponents by employing night marches, dead (concealed) ground or other ruses to force the issue, but lesser generals found this hard to achieve.

The day-to-day administration of most 18th-century armies left a great deal to be desired. Marlborough's rule-defying march to the Danube in 1704 was far from typical of the age. By dint of careful advance planning, ranging from the opening of new lines of communication up the River Main to the provision of spare boots and saddlery at Heidelberg, Marlborough covered some 250 miles in under five weeks, passing across the front of enemy forces with the aid of feints, and brought his men to the Danubian theater of war in a fit and battle-worthy condition. His concern for his men's welfare was one reason for the high morale in his armies, and made it possible for him to make calls upon their endurance that few others dared to contemplate.

Although infantry was becoming increasingly significant, cavalry (now deprived in most cases of body-armor) retained much of its old prestige, even if its numbers began to dwindle. There was some variance, too, over methods of tactical employment. The French were slow to abandon the fire-power role discussed earlier, but Marlborough and Eugene favoured the Swedish and Cromwellian concept of shock action and cold steel. Cavalry charging at the fast trot, supported by infantry and guns, were the factor that clinched each of Marlborough's major victories, and he habitually retained numbers of horsemen as a reserve for this purpose.

Artillery remained something of a liability on campaign, with its deadening weight, profusion of types, and limited effective range. Few armies could march more than ten miles a day with frequent rest-days during which a fresh four-day batch of bread was baked, while the use of contracted civilian drivers and horse-teams often posed further problems. The creation of regular regiments of artillery during the second decade of the century was an improvement on the older system of depending on quasi-independent Boards of Ordnance, since this reform improved the gunners' integration within the armies, but some organizational problems lingered into the 1770s. A significant tactical advance, however, was the attachment of light guns to infantry battalions for close support – a follow-through of the standard Swedish practice.

Reform proved slow, but, by the time of Frederick the Great, several improvements had been adopted by most armies. An iron ram-rod for the musket replaced the fragile wooden version. Artillery teams were better harnessed in pairs, and improved gun-limbers introduced. Following the Seven Years War, the reforming work of de Gribeauval would reduce the weight and number of types in the French artillery, while greater use of horse artillery and howitzers also became standard. De Saxe experimented with *Legions* comprising detachments of all arms.

From 1740, too, the horizons of warfare were also developing. Central Europe became regarded as a single theater of war. As battles became the decisive factor again in Frederick's time, so the arts of offensive strategy – the seeking of favorable opportunities for action – became more developed. So, too, did the requirements for defensive strategy – to safeguard the territorial gains war achieved – by setting up properly fortified bases. If Europe remained the fulcrum, the establishment of overseas empires also created the need for amphibious operations, marrying the arts of land and sea warfare in both attack and defence,

making logistical support even more complex and costly. Warfare was becoming a science as well as an art – and an ever more costly one.

Early colonial warfare

As European expansion gained momentum – the Portuguese in Brazil and the Far East, and the Spaniards in the West Indies, Mexico, Peru, Florida and the Philippines were the first to create empires – overseas conflicts inevitably proliferated. These were of two main kinds: wars of conquest followed by wars of demarcation and retention. In the first, European technological superiority – above all in cannon and firearms – proved decisive. Small bands of disciplined adventurers could overwhelm vast native armies, as in India. Mounted troops were of equal importance to the *conquistadores* in Central and South America. Disease was a far greater hazard than the local warrior – although in North America the early English, French and Dutch colonists had also to adapt to the conditions of wilderness warfare against the Indians in order to survive. As early colonies began to expand, wars of demarcation became frequent. Thus the Dutch seized most of the Portuguese empire in the east in the early 17th century, and the English attacked parts of the Spanish, whilst the 13 "Old Colonies" in North America were soon engaged in practically endemic warfare against their French neighbors in New France (Canada), as well as against the Indians.

Regular forces were few in North America until the mid-18th century. Mother countries found it hard to transport and support troops across the Atlantic, and from the first the colonists had to rely on self-help. The result was the creation of local militias based upon citizen-soldiery organized first by trading companies and proprietors and later by state executives and legislatures (in the "Old Colonies", only Quaker-founded Pennsylvania refused to raise such a force until 1763). Many militias were inefficient and poorly-led, and many refused to serve outside their counties, let alone their colo-

HEARTS OF OAK
The new age of sail and cannon demanded new tactics. The trim Elizabethan fleet (above) drove off the cumbersome galleons of the Spanish Armada (right) in 1588.

nies. For campaigns of expansion, armies of short-term volunteers had to be called for – with or without a modicum of assistance from England – and, to fill the gap, first the French, then the English colonists used Indian allies.

European warfare had no place in the roadless North American forests, as General Edward Braddock learnt to his cost at Monongahela on 9 July 1755, when his 1,850 regular and colonial troops were routed with 50% casualties – including their commander – by 900 French and Indians attacking from ambush. The better frontier militias adapted themselves to local conditions of warfare by stealth and cunning – and eventually special guerrilla-like formations were raised, such as Roger's Rangers and the Royal American Regiment, which found places in the regular ranks. The favored weapons were the musket, the knife and the tomahawk, although from the 1760s the Kentucky rifle, an extremely accurate long-range weapon, made its appearance. There was no place for cavalry, and artillery was mainly reserved for the strings of forts that sprang up at strategic points, such as Ticonderoga, Crown Point, Duquesne and Louisbourg.

6), King William's War (1689–97), Queen Anne's War (1701–13), King George's War (1743–8) and the French and Indian War (1754–63) often overlapped with major Old World struggles, but the fight in the wilderness went on incessantly, whether war was formally declared or not. From the mid-18th century, larger European armies operated in the New World accompanied by local forces (although most unwillingly), and, ironically, the fate of French Canada was decided by a European-style linear battle at *Quebec*. But then so would the American Revolution a generation later at Yorktown.

The emergence of Prussia

Frederick the Great of Prussia enjoyed one great advantage over his military predecessors: as ruler of an autocratic state he could enforce his concepts, and his reign saw the emergence of both the Prussian state, and of Prussian militarism. Four principles dominated his military philosophy. First, came the imposition of the most rigid type of discipline, designed to make his men fear their officers more than the enemy. Second, he placed great stress on subsistence, devoting much time to the provisioning of depots, the safeguarding of convoys, and the disruption of enemy communica-

tions. Third, he taught the importance of offensive action (at least until his later years), preferring battles to sieges, in marked contrast to many of his contemporaries. His last principle was that of practicability, the application of rationality to matters of strategy and tactics. This was based upon his study of military history. The oblique order of attack – as employed at *Leuthen* in 1757 – was designed to offset his usual numerical inferiority in battle. Sending a small force to distract his opponent's attention and reserves, he massed his main attack against a different sector to gain local superiority in numbers and artillery at the selected critical point.

The Prussian army – its drill, uniforms, tactics and mentality – became widely copied throughout Europe, except by France. That country, after a brief period of martial success under de Saxe's inspiration in the 1740s (exemplified by his victory over the Duke of Cumberland at *Fontenoy* in 1745), relapsed into military decline and consequent humiliation during the Seven Years War. By the 1770s, however, major French reforms were in hand, most notably as regards tactical doctrine and the artillery arm; the first fruits of these improvements would be demonstrated not in Europe but in North America during the American Revolution.

Maritime developments

Sea-power, too, developed greatly over these three centuries. Galley warfare in the Mediterranean reached its ultimate stage at the battle of *Lepanto* in 1571, where Don John of Austria finally destroyed the Turkish bid for naval supremacy. But, though Venetian galleasses, which mounted broadsides of heavy, ship-pounding guns, were a significant development, the future lay with sail-propelled, rather than with oar-driven, naval craft, and with the shot-loaded cannon rather than the ramming spur or beak. The new type of ship's potential was demonstrated in 1588 by the English fleet's defeat of the Spanish *Armada*.

Tactical doctrine emerged from

the hard-learnt lessons of the three Dutch Wars of the 17th century between England and the Netherlands. Dutch naval development had largely paralleled that of England, but admirals such as van Tromp and de Ruyter proved tactically superior in developing the line-ahead battle formation, in which ships entered a battle literally in line. English admirals, such as Blake, preferred the free melée of the Elizabethan tradition, but the Permanent Fighting Instructions (as published in 1691) followed Dutch practice by insisting that the Royal Navy fought in a formalized line of battle. The concept was to persist for almost a century, despite its disadvantages (as Admiral Sir John Byng found to his cost off Minorca in 1757, when his failure to engage the French fleet led to his courtmartial and execution on his own quarterdeck).

As professional armies were established, so, too, were professional navies. Oliver Cromwell was the English progenitor, his work being vastly developed after the Restoration of Charles II in 1660 by Samuel Pepys, Secretary to the Board of Admiralty. In France the great administrator Colbert created a powerful navy for Louis XIV, though, defeated by England in open naval conflict, the French speciality would become the war of commerce waged against merchantmen by privateers. Elsewhere, Swedish fleets contended for Baltic supremacy with the navy of Peter the Great and his successors.

An off-shoot of these naval developments was the growth of amphibious operations, involving both ships and troops. Regiments of marines began to appear in the 17th century, but, for large expeditions, land regiments had to be employed as well. The capture of Gibraltar in 1704 and its retention by the naval battle of Malaga, the celebrated siege and capture of *Quebec* in 1759, and the successive naval reliefs of long-besieged *Gibraltar* (1977–1783) indicate Britain's mastery of combined operatios during the 18th century – but the coordination of military and naval interests was never an easy task, as later wars were to prove.

Siege Warfare in the Age of Vauban

The art and science of fortification has continually evolved to meet developments in artillery, and closely associated with both have been the skills of siegecraft. The subject attracted much attention during the Renaissance from such talented men as Leonardo de Vinci and Albrecht Dürer. The rise of the military engineer to a position of great importance is illustrated by the influence of such men as Niccolo Tartaglia, the celebrated artillery theorist of the first half of the 16th century who also wrote on fortification, Pedro Navarro (the practical soldier-inventor), Vannoccio Biringuccio of Siena, Blaise Francois, Comte de Pagan, and the Jesuit Georges Fournier.

If the states of Italy gave the first great impetus to revised fortress design and siegecraft in the gunpowder age, interest in the subjects soon spread to France and Germany. The great flowering came in the late 17th and early 18th centuries, when the names of Sebastien le Prestre, Seigneur de Vauban, Marshal of France, Menno van Coehoorn, defender of the United Provinces, and the Saxon George Rimpler became synonymous with the skills of siege warfare.

Types and functions of fortifications

There are two main types of fortification and one hybrid variety. Firstly, there are "permanent works", normally constructed as a precaution in time of peace on a large scale and at great expense by governments anxious to protect vital strategic areas from the threat of surprise attack; coastal and frontier fortresses often belong to this category. "Field fortifications", on the other hand, are usually hastily constructed to meet a particular tactical situation in time of war, often taking the form of earthworks, entrenchments and other extemporised obstacles. The third category is best described as "semi-permanent" – defences containing elements of both the main types of fortification.

All fortifications are designed to perform certain basic functions, although priorities alter with changing circumstances. First, there is the element of fire-power: it is axiomatic that all sectors of the defensive perimeter should be covered by fire, and every position should be designed to afford the defenders the free use of their weapons. Second, there is the element of protection; this can be achieved either directly by provision of shot- and shell-proof cover, or indirectly by use of distance. Third comes the element of obstruction, achieved by means of walls, ditches, palisades and other obstacles designed to hinder the enemy's free movement, his use of weapons, and his ability to come to close grips with the defender. Of course, these functions may conflict with one another –

MILITARY MASTER *A crayon portrait of Vauban, hailed throughout Europe for his mastery of the art of fortification.*

so a careful compromise has to be devised to suit particular circumstances.

Design principles

Although weapons change as time passes, certain principles underlie the construction of all effective fortifications. The most significant of these are simplicity of design, strength of construction, the provision of clear fields of fire, the careful adaptation of defence schemes to suit the configuration of the ground, and the utmost economy in the use of manpower.

Two instructive examples of English fortification under the Tudors are the *enceinte* of the town of Berwick-on-Tweed on the Scottish border, and the novel design of Henry VIII's artillery castles, such as Deal and Walmer along the south coast. Designed to hold 50 cannon on a total of three circular tiers of bastions, the whole surrounded by a deep protective ditch, Deal Castle was the most novel design of its day. Yet the attack, defence and construction of fortifications were only to reach their fullest development in the 17th century under the great French soldier-engineer, Vauban (1633–1707), who wrote two treatises – "On the Defence of Places" and "On the Attack of Places".

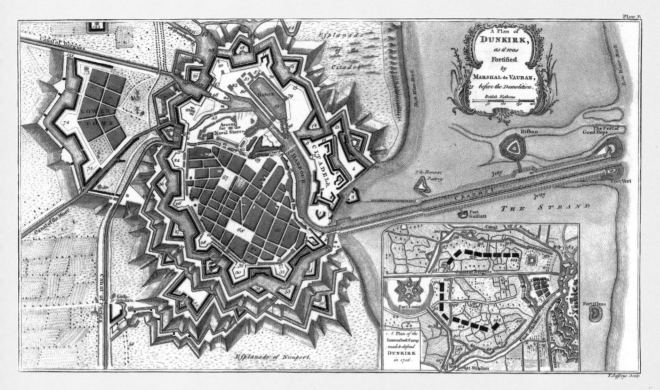

Plate IV

A Plan of
DUNKIRK,
as it was
Fortified
by
MARSHAL de VAUBAN,
before the Demolition.

DUNKIRK *Vauban's fortifications at Dunkirk, with the field defences added in 1706. Note the double counterscarp between the Esplanade de Nieuport and the town's main fortifications.*

"On the Defence of Places"
Vauban built 33 new fortresses – Ypres and Verdun among them – renovated 300 older ones, conducted 53 sieges and took part in 140 engagements. He was awarded his marshal's baton in 1703. It is ironic, however, that his posthumous reputation rests on his reputation as an engineer, for, in fact, he was an advocate of mobile warfare.

Engineers had given up vertical walls for banked fortifications let into the ground, and their defences became increasingly complex as time passed. Vauban described precisely how to build, maintain and hold such places. His designs were based upon simple principles of geometry. The shape of the fortifications around a town or fort was polygonal, each angle of what was termed the trace supporting a bastion, each with an all-round field of fire and covering out-works. Here, to counter the effects of smooth-bore cannon firing from up to 600 yards away, Vauban developed the work of Pagan, making much use of cross-fire to sweep all possible approaches, and employing elaborate supporting defences to protect the parapet. The angle bastions were of stone and earth constructions up to 40ft thick, standing some 17ft over the lip of the ditch and "glacis" – a killing ground devoid of all cover. Ditches were 18ft deep; within them were built "tenailles", "ravelins", "hornworks" and "demi-lunes" – the terms used to describe various types of supporting out-works – to protect the bastions and curtain-walls. "Counterscarp galleries" were let into the outer faces of the ditches, from which musketeers could sweep the foot of the ramparts.

"On the Attack of Places"
Vauban also laid down the proper procedures for attacking a fortress. He stipulated a 48-day average siege timetable – from the start of the blockade, the construction of fortified camps, and the "opening" of the three series of parallel trenches linked by approaches, to the blasting of a practicable breach in the main defences by the siege guns or by mining, and the summons to surrender or face the perils of a storming of the town. His regulations became standard European practice for over 200 years.

Rivals and successors
Many later engineers copied Vauban's concepts and methods wholesale, but certain improvements did appear over the following 150 years as artillery continued to improve in range and fire-power. Indeed, even in Vauban's own day, the Dutchman van Coehoorn stressed the need for an even greater volume of outward fire, while the German Rimpler experimented with a central bastion placed within the *enceinte*. Some experts advocated a mathematically perfect "star trace", which produced strong cross-fire but almost precluded outward bombardment and exposed the parapets to enemy enfilade fire. Such geometrical systems often ignored the natural configuration of the ground. The French engineer Chasseloup-Laubat placed "ravelins" beyond the glacis, while the Prussian Landsberg the Elder and the Frenchman Marc Renée Montalembert dispensed with angle-bastions, replacing them with bomb-proof "caponiers" within the ditch. Like Vauban, Montelambert was also the proponent of a defender waging an active, rather than a passive, defence, and stressed the need for cannon placed in tiers to increase the volume of outward fire.

The Age of Great Captains

In an age dominated by successive conflicts, a large number of notable generals of many nations emerged. Five were exceptional in terms of their achievements in the field and in their contribution to the art and science of war in their various generations.

Gustavus Adolphus, King of Sweden (1594–1632)
Succeeding to the Swedish throne in 1611, "the Lion of the North" served his military apprenticeship fighting against the Danes, Russians and Poles. Realizing that proper organization, equipment and training could transform his peasant-soldiers into a truly professional, national army, Gustavus set in train massive and far-reaching administrative reforms, aided by such men as Axel Oxenstierna and (for the artillery) Lennart Torstensson. To fill the ranks and reduce reliance on hired mercenaries, a system of conscription was imposed on the better-off citizens (so as to obtain well-nourished soldiery with something to fight for). Regular pay was provided during wartime, and veterans were given land-grants or shares in farmsteads to bind them closer to the population they represented.

Gustavus' main tactical and organizational reforms are described elsewhere. The result was the first disciplined, truly modern army, which showed its mettle at *Breitenfeld* (1631) and Lutzen (1632) where Gustavus was killed. Gustavus deserves the title of "Father of Modern War"; his army was widely copied, and for 80 years after his death – until *Poltava* – Sweden was one of the key European powers.

Henri de la Tour d'Auvergne, Vicomte de Turenne (1612–1675)
Together with Louis de Bourbon, Duke of Enghien – "the Great Condé", the victor of *Rocroi* – Turenne was the foremost French soldier of Louis XIV's reign. A nephew of Maurice of Nassau through his mother, he rose to fame in 1638 at the siege of Breisach and through the capture of Turin two years later. Created a marshal of France in 1643, he served with d'Enghien at Freiburg that year, when he revealed his abilities as a master of unorthodox manoeuvre, conducting bold marches to outflank the enemy. Further successes ensued. After deep involvement in the French internal intrigues of the first *Fronde* (a conspiracy of leading nobles against the throne), he remained loyal to the youthful Louis XIV during the second; in 1652, he fought Condé, who had changed sides to join the *Frondeurs*, outside Paris and played a major part in ending the revolt thereafter. In 1657 he again defeated

THE GREAT TURENNE
Marshal Turenne was one of the most respected soldiers of the period. Under him, the armies of France came close to making Louis XIV the military master of Europe.

Condé at the battle of the Dunes, near Dunkirk on the Channel coast, and in 1660 was made Marshal-General.

The Dutch War (1672–8) brought out Turenne's full powers of command. With a small force, he outmanoeuvred larger enemies time after time, winning battles at Sinzheim and Entzheim in 1674, and – following a masterly winter march through deep snow to Belfort – at Turckheim (1675). Later that year he was killed near Strasbourg. Turenne was the greatest field-commander and tactician of his day, beloved by his men, and admired by all, including the young Marlborough, who served under him in 1674.

John Churchill, Duke of Marlborough (1650–1722)
Turenne's apt pupil was destined to become the scourge of France. After a varied early career, including service in Tangier, with the Royal Navy, and under Dutch generals, Churchill served his patron, James II, well at Sedgemoor (1685), crushing the revolt of the Duke of Monmouth, but deserted him in 1688 during the Glorious Revolution. Never fully trusted by William III and Mary II, the newly-created Earl of Marlborough saw more service in Flanders and Ireland before being disgraced following a Jacobite scandal in 1692. He was reconciled with William after Mary's death.

With the accession of Anne to the throne, Marlborough (whose wife was Anne's closest favorite) was appointed Captain-General at the outbreak of the War of the Spanish Succession (1701–13). For ten successive campaigns Marlborough – made duke in 1703 – commanded the main Allied army in the field, masterminded the Grand Alliance, and managed English domestic politics simultaneously. He won the famous battles of Blenheim (1704), *Ramillies* (1706),

THE MIGHTY MARLBOROUGH *A master of both diplomacy and war, the greatest soldier ever produced by Britain.*

Oudenarde (1708) and in 1709, Malplaquet (all shared with Prince Eugene of Savoy except Ramillies), and undertook 30 major sieges (including that of *Lille* in 1708). He always paid close attention to logistics, and was loved by his men.

The duke was indeed a strategist and tactician of consummate skill. Home politics brought about his fall in late 1711. Of his foes, only Marshal Villars, the best of the French generals in the War of the Spanish Succession, came near him in accomplishment.

Hermann Maurice, Comte de Saxe (1696–1750)

An illegitimate son of the Elector Frederick Augustus of Saxony, Saxe saw his first service under Marlborough in 1709. In 1719 he transferred his services to France, where he was destined to become Louis XV's most successful commander. He studied warfare seriously, and in 1732 wrote "My Reflections" (published posthumously), which demonstrate his grasp of war policy. Although some of his tactical ideas were out-dated (he favored the reintroduction of pikes, for example), his concept of the balanced, all-arm "legion" foreshadowed the Napoleonic army corps. He was critical of French discipline and staying-power under pressure, and stressed the use of field fortifications in defence, and (with Chevalier Folard) the advantages of attack in column. He emerged as a lieutenant-general from the War of the Polish Succession (1734–38), but came fully into his own in the War of the Austrian Succession (1740–8). Allied to Bavaria, he captured Prague (1741), and was made a marshal in 1744. Commanding in Flanders, he won the battles of *Fontenoy* (1745), Rocoux (1746) and Laffeldt (1747), and climaxed his career by taking Maastricht (1748). Made Marshal-General, he retired to Chambord. His ideas had great posthumous influence.

Frederick II, King of Prussia, "the Great" (1713–86)

Frederick became a soldier through necessity, rather than by inclination. Succeeding Frederick William I in 1740, he inherited a centralized, but small, state, an army of 80,000 men, a full war-chest – and a ring of potential enemies. Assessing his geographical problems and the capabilities of his army, he coolly seized Silesia from Austria and managed to retain it through the two Silesian wars, though not without difficulty. During the short period between them, he increased the strength of his army to 140,000 men and improved his cavalry and artillery. His invasion of Bohemia in 1744 was too bold, but he recovered from near-disaster at Hohenfriedburg (1745) and established his reputation with that battle. The peace of Dresden that followed finally ceded him Silesia.

Frederick, however, still had many foes, and after increasing his army to 154,000 (utilizing the resources of Silesia), he again struck first in the Seven Years War (1756–63), occupying Saxony. The next year, he won the battle of Prague, but then was defeated at Kolin. With enemies advancing on four sides, he produced a virtuoso performance to save Prussia – winning victories at Rossbach and *Leuthen*. The period from 1758 to 1760 saw three more victories, but Prussia could not afford the casualties these cost, while there were rebuffs as well. Mutual exhaustion – and the death of Frederick's arch-enemy Tsarina Elizabeth of Russia – saved Prussia. Frederick's audacity, his flexibility, eye for terrain and speed had won Silesia for Prussia. However, his later writings on war were notably defensive in tone when compared to the ruthless policies of aggression he advocated in his *Secret Instruction* of 1748. Above all, it was his boldness that earned him the title of "Frederick the Great". His example and army were much copied.

These five men, then, were the "Great Captains" of the 300 years covered by this section. Many more – including the Spanish Duke of Parma (1545–92), Prince Eugene of Savoy (1663–1736) and Charles XII of Sweden (1682–1718), are only excluded with regret, as are several admirals of note – Blake, de Ruyter and the two van Tromps. It was indeed an age of military and naval giants.

THE WILY FREDERICK *Frederick's brilliant use of the military machine he inherited established Prussia's great power.*

BELGRADE
THE AUSTRO–TURKISH WARS
16 August 1717

The siege and battle of Belgrade was Prince Eugene of Savoy's greatest victory. With an army of 100,000 men and 200 guns he besieged the Turkish garrison of Mustafa Pasha (30,000 men, 600 cannon and 70 river-boats) and brilliantly defeated Khalil Pasha's huge relieving army (150,000 men and 120 artillery pieces), thereafter capturing the city.

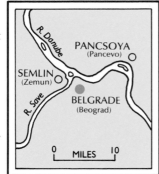

Strategically placed at the confluence of the Danube and Save, Belgrade was the key to Hungary and Turkish expansion westwards into the Habsburg empire. It was the scene of four battles between 1688 and 1717, and since 1690 had been in Turkish hands. The events of 1717 were at last to restore it to the Habsburgs.

The siege opens

Advancing from Futak in the Banat (province) of Temesvar in the spring of 1717 at the head of an imposing army, Prince Eugene advanced well to the east of Belgrade, crossing the Danube at Pancsoya. On 29 June the imperial forces approached the city, and began siege operations. The effects of bad weather soon meant that the imperial camp was decimated by disease, while the city's garrison prosecuted a very active defence; in spite of these problems, Eugene maintained his grip on the situation, surrounding his camp with fortifications, and deploying squadrons of frigates on the Danube to contain the Turkish river craft. Outposts and small islands were gradually captured, and the siege lines crept closer to the city walls, but a successful sortie by the garrison on 17 July towards Semlin caused much damage and many losses.

The besiegers besieged

This gave Khalil Pasha ample time to bring up a huge relief army from Adrianople; by 1 August, this great host had effectively sealed Eugene's army into their positions – thus causing a double-siege. Khalil intended to starve Eugene into surrender, and thus save Belgrade. The summer heat made conditions intolerable, and on 15 August the prince decided to gamble everything on an attack the next morning. By this time, his army was reduced to only 50,000.

Leaving only eight battalions in the trenches facing Belgrade, Eugene's main army began to file silently forward at 1 am, forming into two lines of battle with 30 cannon on each flank. At 4 am the alarm was raised by the Turks, and a desperate battle began. Dense mist confused the imperial cavalry on the right wing, and, in consequence, a gap developed in Eugene's first line. The Turks were quick to exploit this opportunity, and only at 8 am as the fog lifted did the prince realize the extent of the danger. Ordering up his second line, he quickly checked the Turkish break-in.

Meanwhile, on the imperial left, the battle was going better. Despite heavy casualties, the Bavarian contingent stormed and took the Turkish Grand Battery on the Badjina Heights and then turned the captured guns on their foe. This led to the flight of the Turkish formations on their right, and by 10 am Khalil Pasha's entire army was streaming away in full retreat. For a loss of 5,400, the imperial army inflicted an estimated 20,000 casualties, while Khalil Pasha's encampment provided the victors with much booty. Two days later Mustafa Pasha surrendered Belgrade on terms. The siege had cost the garrison 5,000 killed; Eugene's army had lost all of 30,000, mostly from disease.

BREITENFELD
THE 30 YEARS WAR
17 September 1631

Fought north of Leipzig between Gustavus Adolphus commanding the Swedish and Saxon army (40,000 men and 74 guns) and Count Tilly, at the head of the

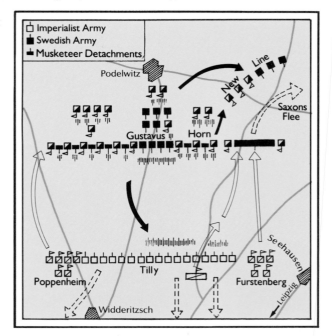

BREITENFELD *The Swedes' newly-developed, flexible tactics brought them victory over the Catholic army under Tilly.*

Catholic League's army (32,000 men and 30 guns), the Swedish victory saved the Protestant cause.

The Swedes intervene

The hard-fought 30 Years War (1618–48) was, by 1629, turning in favour of the Emperor Ferdinand II and the Catholic cause. To rescue the German Protestant princes, and to gain control of the south Baltic coast for Sweden, Gustavus Adolphus joined the struggle in July 1630. At first, the Swedish intervention was ineffectual, as Gustavus lacked German assistance, but when the Emperor sent Count Tilly's army into Saxony in 1631 to punish Elector John George for ignoring an order to disband his army, Gustavus found an ally. Uniting their forces at Duben, the two set out to recover Leipzig.

The armies prepare

Both sides were eager to fight. Encouraged by Count Pappenheim, Tilly selected a battle position five miles north of Leipzig on a treeless plain which would facilitate the manoeuvring of his 14 massive *tercios* and his 11,000 cavalry. Placing his cannon in front of his center, he deployed the imperial cavalry on the right flank under General Furstenberg, and the horsemen of the Catholic League on his left under Pappenheim. A cavalry reserve was placed behind the *tercios* in the center. Despite his inferior numbers, Tilly was confident that his more experienced troops would win the day. Consequently, he made little attempt to prevent the Swedes and Saxons from crossing over the River Lober to deploy in battle order south of the village of Podelwitz.

Gustavus drew up his army in a very different type of formation, reflecting his originality as a tactician. The Swedish troops were placed in two lines, each with its own reserve. Conventionally enough, the cavalry were concentrated on the wings, but unusually for the period the horsemen had detachments of musketeers placed amongst their squadrons, trained to fight in their support. Generals Baner and Horn commanded the Swedish right and left wings respectively, while Gustavus took control of the centre. Here, the seven brigades of Swedish infantry were drawn up in a far more flexible formation than Tilly's unwieldy *tercios*. Besides being supported by a reserve of cavalry, each brigade had six light guns attached to it, which could be manhandled by two men apiece, and so were capable of keeping up with the infantry as it advanced or retired. Much care was taken to place the battalions of the brigades in positions that allowed them to give each other mutual supporting fire. Lastly, Gustavus placed the inexperienced 16,000 men of the Saxon army on his left under command of Elector John George.

Horn survives a crisis

The rival batteries opened fire at about midday, and two hours later Tilly seized the initiative. Intending to outflank his enemies on both wings, he ordered both Pappenheim and Furstenberg to attack. On the left,

Pappenheim swept around Baner's right wing to engage the Swedish reserve cavalry, but the Swedes brought up formations to extend their line to the right to meet this threat. Furthermore, their skilled use of musketry volleys combined with cavalry charges in rapid alternation – the new Swedish tactical concept – baffled their opponents. For three hours a dogged engagement continued, but the Swedes more than held their own.

On the eastern side of the field, however, the story was very different. Soon after Pappenheim had swept forward, Tilly advanced at the head of his *tercios*, a body of cavalry guarding his infantry's left and, with Furstenberg's cavalry on his right, apparently intending to attack the Swedish left wing. However, the *tercios* suddenly veered to the right, and, as they lowered their pike-points to crash into the surprised Saxon infantry, Furstenberg swept round the flank of the Saxon horsemen near Gobschelwitz.

Outnumbered and outclassed, the Saxons soon turned and fled north. The *tercios* then turned against the Swedish left wing, where General Horn (with barely 4,000 men under immediate command) found himself faced on his exposed flank by almost 20,000 victorious foes. Tilly believed he had won the day – but this proved to be a premature assumption. Noting that the imperial forces were taking some time to reorganize their formations after their attack on the Saxons, and that Tilly's supporting cavalry on the left of the *tercios* had interposed themselves between the Swedes and their own infantry, Horn gambled everything by ordering every available man forward to attack the enemy horsemen. This bold movement succeeded. Tilly's cavalry reeled back against their own infantry, throwing them into further disorder and thus again delaying the renewal of their attack.

Profiting from this, Horn now had the time to deploy his local reserve, then formations from the second line, and lastly troops drawn from the far flank to form a reinforced line of battle. A timely change in the direction of the wind blew clouds of dust and smoke into the eyes of the imperials, and the Swedes surged forward to press them back into a disordered mass, their superior numbers proving useless against the flexible Swedish tactics, which used cannons, musketeers, pikemen and charging cavalry in deadly combination.

The Swedish coup de grâce

By 6 pm Tilly's center and right wing were virtually defeated, while Tilly himself had been wounded and forced to leave the field. At much the same time Pappenheim gave ground on the left ' " his horsemen totally exhausted. It was time for Gustavus to launch his attack. Into the large gap that had developed in the imperial centre marched the Swedish centre, overwhelming Tilly's isolated artillery, butchering four regiments that vainly tried to make a last stand, and severing the road towards Leipzig. The Imperialist army broke and fled, only four *tercios* and as many regiments of horse escaping. The imperial army lost 7,600 killed and wounded and 6,000 prisoners on the field, while another 8,000 were rounded up subsequently. The Swedes and Saxons lost an estimated 4,000.

The tactical flexibility of Gustavus's new style of army had been convincingly demonstrated, as well as its staying-power under adverse circumstances. The use of the twin line of battle and the skilled combination of infantry, cavalry and guns in coordinated attacks was to be widely copied throughout Europe.

FONTENOY
WAR OF THE AUSTRIAN SUCCESSION
11 May 1745

Hermann-Maurice, Count de Saxe, commanding the French army (53,000 men and 70 cannon, with 17,000 more besieging Tournai nearby) defeated the Duke of Cumberland and his Allied army (53,000 men and 80 cannon). Each side lost around 7,000 men; the French subsequently conquered most of the Austrian Netherlands.

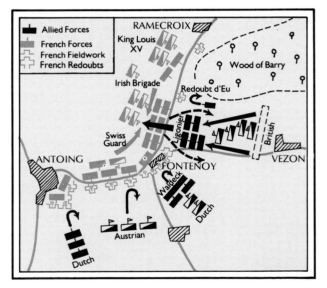

FONTENOY *The British attempt to break through the French center failed due to lack of support on the left.*

Saxe chooses his ground
Tournai was the gateway to western Flanders, and when the French suddenly advanced on the fortress-town on 25 April 1745 and began a blockade, the Allies hastened to try to relieve it. However, their march from Brussels was confused and slow, which meant that Saxe had ample time to select and prepare a defensive position for his covering forces. He chose a battle-site five miles south-east of Tournai around the village of Fontenoy, placing his right wing within rapidly constructed earthworks near the banks of the River

Scheldt, and using the Wood of Barry to protect his left, plus two redoubts. More entrenchments protected Fontenoy itself, with three forts covering the French right-centers – the spaces between them giving Saxe room for manoeuvre. Many of his guns were placed within these positions, carefully sited so as to be able to sweep the approaches from south or east with heavy converging fire.

Calculating that Cumberland would launch his main attack against his left, Saxe – confined to a horse-drawn litter by dropsy – set sharpshooters into the Wood of Barry, with the Irish Brigade in support, and placed his strongest formations in the area. Cumberland obliged, massing his British troops against the northern sector, and leaving General Waldeck's Dutch to attack Fontenoy and Konigsegg's Austrians to assail Antoing. Advancing at 6 am over the open plain, the Allied advance guard suddenly came upon the concealed Redoubt d'Eu, which halted its march. Behind it, the massed British cavalry was forced to halt and came under heavy artillery fire while Brigadier-General Ingoldsby vainly attempted to storm the position. Meanwhile the Dutch and Austrians were proving equally unsuccessful on their sectors.

From advance to withdrawal
Hoping to break the impasse, Lord Ligonier marched his British infantry through the cavalry, and at 10.30 am, with Cumberland at their head, the battalions advanced in superb order. Delaying their fire until the last moment, after allegedly inviting the French Guards to fire first, the British volleys decimated the French first line. Compressed into a single huge column, the British now moved deep into the enemy position, but renewed failure by the Dutch to their left forced them to halt. The French artillery pounded the tempting target the British mass presented remorselessly from all sides, while Saxe – leaving his litter to mount his house – flung in his reserves without hesitation.

Soon after midday Cumberland was forced to order a fighting withdrawal, which was carried out in good order, every yard of ground being contested. But he had effectively conceded the day, and the siege of Tournai continued unabated. The town fell on 19 June, and Bruges, Ghent, Ostend, Nieuport, Oudenarde and Brussels followed.

LEPANTO
THE WARS OF ISLAM
7 October 1571

Don John of Austria's Christian fleet of the Holy League (217 galleys and six galleasses) decisively defeated Kapitan-Pasha Ali Mouenzinade's Ottoman fleet (208 galleys and 66 other vessels) and thus regained Christian naval ascendancy in the

Mediterranean. The Ottomans lost 230 vessels (at least 25,000 killed) to the Christian 12 (7,566 killed) in the last great galley battle in history.

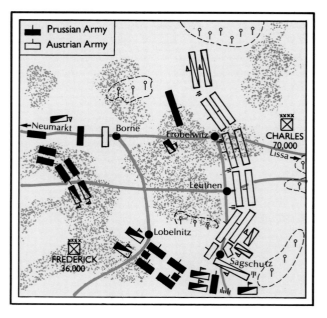

GREECE

LEPANTO
(Navpaktos)

Patras ATHENS

The rival fleets clash

Success at Lepanto stemmed from an original Christian failure. Though intended to raise the Ottoman siege of Famagusta in Cyprus, the Christian fleet was too slow mustering at Messina, and the city in consequence fell to the Turks on 4 August. With Ottoman squadrons ravaging the Aegean and Ionian seas, Don John of Austria sailed from Sicily on 23 September for the Gulf of Corinth. The Kapitan-Pasha assembled his fleet off Lepanto, and the two navies came in sight of one another early on 7 October.

Despite his distance from his base, Don John sought immediate battle. He drew up his five-mile battle line as follows; in his central division he massed 74 galleys, with 53 more on each wing. Each division was led by a pair of large Venetian galleasses, while a reserve of 37 galleys was stationed half a mile behind the main line. Venetian, Papal, Genoese, Tuscan, Maltese and Savoyard detachments were deliberately intermixed. Of the 84,000 aboard, a quarter were soldiers, including many arquebusiers.

For its part, the Ottoman fleet was also drawn up in three divisions and a reserve: the left wing had 95 galleys to the right's 56 (indicating that Ali's probable plan was to envelop the Christian right wing); 40 more were in reserve; the balance in the center. Of 88,000 on board, 16,000 were Turkish soldiers, including 6,000 élite janissaries. Both fleets of galleys had a few cannon in the bows, but the Christians were markedly superior in firearms and defensive armor.

The Christian triumph

The battle opened shortly after 10 am, when the six great galleasses broke through the Ottoman line. By midday the action had become a mass of individual and grouped melées, as the various galleys closed to grapple and board. Under these conditions the superior fire-power of the Christian vessels soon began to make itself felt against the more lightly armed Moslems. The Ottoman right wing under the Bey of Negropont found itself driven ashore, while in the center Don John's flagship engaged that of the Kapitan-Pasha, who was eventually killed.

On the Ottoman left, the fighting was more equal, as the Pasha of Algiers used his superior numbers to partially outflank the wing commanded by Andrea Doria, an Italian admiral. Gradually, however, the superior Christian gun-power again began to assert

itself, and after a desperate three hour engagement Don John triumphed. Only 47 Ottoman galleys were able to disengage and make for home. 117 galleys had been captured, and 10,000 Christian galley-slaves freed. The last galley battle was over.

This decisive victory checked the advance of militant Islam in the Mediterranean, but the Christian fleet returned to its home port on account of the late season of the year. The exploitation of the success was thus postponed until the following year.

LEUTHEN
THE SEVEN YEARS WAR
5 December 1757

Frederick the Great and the Prussian army (35,000 men and 167 guns) decisively defeated Prince Charles of Lorraine and the Austrian army (65,000 men and 210 guns) near Breslau. The Prussians lost 6,400 men, inflicted 22,000 casualties (including 12,000 prisoners).

The year 1757 tested Prussia and its king to the limit, but ended in a blaze of triumph. Taking the initiative at its outset, Frederick invaded Bohemia and achieved a success against an Austrian army outside Prague (6 May). However, he then sustained a sharp defeat at Kolin (18 June), and soon found himself surrounded by converging enemy armies – French and German from the west, Swedish from the north, Austrian from the south and Russian from the east. Fighting for Prussia's very survival, by the year's end Frederick had used his central position to ward off three of these threats,

LEUTHEN *Frederick the Great's oblique attack on the Austrians led to Prussian triumph in his greatest battle.*

winning two major victories in the process – Rossbach west of Leipzig against the French and Germans on 5 November, and Leuthen against the main Austrian army commanded by Prince Charles of Lorraine exactly one month later and 200 miles to the east near Breslau.

Victory at Kolin had inaugurated a period of Austrian successes against outlying Prussian detachments, and they captured both Schweidnitz and Breslau in November. Having dealt with the Franco-German army at Rossbach, it was high time for Frederick to transfer his main army east to counter the Austrian threat. Leaving Leipzig on 13 November, he reached Neumarkt with 35,000 men on 3 December. Despite the superior strength and high morale of his enemies, Frederick felt that boldness and surprise might make up for his numerical inferiority, and he ordered an immediate attack.

Taken by surprise

Early on 5 December the Prussians advanced through dense mist in four columns toward Breslau. Frederick's advance guard cavalry routed an Austrian force at Borne, but the warning this gave enabled the Austrians to take up a strong four mile long position between Nippern and Sagschutz, the village of Leuthen being at their left center. After reconnoitring their battle-line, Frederick ordered part of his force to mount a feint attack against the Austrian right near Frobelwitz, while the main body wheeled south behind a convenient ridge to head unseen towards the enemy's left. The Austrians obligingly fell for the bait. Considerable numbers of horse and foot were transferred to reinforce the northern flank, and when it was realized that the Prussians were still marching in the distance, it was concluded by the Austrian high command that there would be no major action that day.

As they moved southward, the Prussians skilfully reordered their four marching columns into twin lines of battle. Emerging from concealment in a dip in the ground at about midday, they swung half-left and advanced in oblique order, right wing forward, the remaining battalions echeloned back to the left rear. It was this daunting spectacle that presented itself to the surprised Austrians. In the first wave of attack came Prince Karl of Bevern with six battalions, his open right flank guarded by General Ziethen's 53 squadrons of cavalry. Next came General von Wedell with three battalions, while behind him came the bulk of the army in echeloned formation. Supported by several 12 pdr. cannon brought well forward, Wedell swung half-left and stormed the Kiefenberg feature. Bevern moved half-right in support of Ziethen, heavily attacked by General Nadasti's Austrian cavalry, who were repulsed with loss. Eleven battalions of Wurttembergers, after a fair show of resistance, suddenly broke and ran, and the entire Austrian left wing fell back towards Leuthen village. By this time the Austrian high command had realized its earlier miscalculations, and steadily began to transfer more and more troops from their right. This movement led to much confusion and over-crowding, and the Prussian massed guns on the Judenbeg caused heavy Austrian casualties before moving forward to deploy on the Kirchberg's slopes.

The second stage

Having given up Sagschuz to the Prussians, the Austrians eventually managed to form a new battle-line extending for a mile both east and west of Leuthen, facing south. After a pause to reorder their ranks, at 3.30 pm the Prussian battalions again swept steadily and remorselessly forwards, and a desperate struggle began for possession of Leuthen, which was now in the centre of the new Austrian line. The battle swayed to and fro, centering around the church, but ultimately the Prussians were not to be denied, and again the Austrians found themselves driven back – this time on to the plain north of the village. Emerging from the village itself, the highly disciplined Prussian battalions again halted to reform their ranks before resuming their seemingly inexorable advance.

The Austrians had one last card to play. General Lucchese and the 70 squadrons of the Austrian right wing suddenly swept down at 4.45 pm to assail the left flank of the Prussian infantry. Fortunately for Frederick, Lieutenant-General von Driesen, commanding the Prussian cavalry on the left wing, realized what was afoot, and counter-charged with the five squadrons of the Bayreuth Dragoons, with 35 squadrons of heavy cavalry close behind, to take the advancing horsemen on their right flank. A desperate cavalry melée resulted. At first the outnumbered dragoons found themselves in a difficult situation, but they were rescued by the arrival of the Prussian cuirassiers in strength. Once again the cavalry battle escalated to new heights, but the arrival of 30 more Prussian squadrons from reserve clinched the engagement. The Austrian horsemen were routed in short order. Driesen promptly reordered his cavalry and then charged the right flant of the exhausted Austrian infantry, who, after a show of resistance, broke and fled from the field.

Frederick strikes

However, the seemingly tireless Frederick was still not satisfied. As dusk fell, he personally organized a force consisting of three battalions of grenadiers and the Seydlitz Cuirassiers and set off at their head to capture the bridge at Lissa a mile and a half to the east, seeking to stop the Austrians from making any attempt to reform their shattered ranks behind the protection of the River Weistritz. Prince Charles of Lorraine and the remnants of his army thus had no other option but to retreat to the mountains on the frontier, leaving a force of 17,000 isolated in Breslau, which surrendered 15 days later. Prussia's hold on the province of Silesia had been confirmed, and Frederick was now free to turn north to check the advance of the Swedish army threatening Berlin and Potsdam.

SIEGE OF LILLE

THE WAR OF THE SPANISH SUCCESSION
12 August – 10 December 1708

The 120-day siege of Lille in north-eastern France demonstrated Marlborough's and Prince Eugene's mastery of siegecraft and conventional warfare. The Allied forces (100,000 men and 80 siege guns) ultimately compelled Marshal Boufflers and his 16,000-strong garrison to capitulate. The siege cost the Allies 10,000 casualties and the French 7,000.

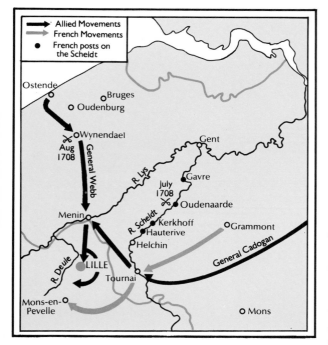

LILLE *Marlborough's field army maneuvered to stop the French relieving Lille while the siege was under way.*

The descent on Lille
After defeating the French field army at Oudenarde (11 July 1708), Marlborough and Eugene decided to besiege Lille, the most important city in north-eastern France which was considered to be Vauban's masterpiece of defensive engineering. Covered by the Allied field armies, two great convoys of guns and siege stores escorted by General Cadogan moved from Brussels to Menin, arriving there safely on 25 July.

The siege opened on 12 August, when Prince Eugene with 50 battalions opened the blockade of Lille, while Marlborough covered the operation with the main army from Helchin on the Scheldt, ready to intercept any French attempt to raise the siege. By 22 August Eugene had completed a ring of fortified posts around Lille, and now started work on trenches facing the north-eastern side of the city – the River Deule and the swampy ground between it and the Marque ruling out any other line of attack. On 27 August the siege guns opened fire.

Countering the relief
Louis XIV was determined that Lille should be saved, and an army of 110,000 men duly assembled at Grammont and Tournai to raise the siege. As this force marched towards Lille, Marlborough moved his army to come between the French and the siege lines, summoning Eugene and 30,000 men from the trenches. A sortie by Boufflers on 5 September was repelled by the remaining besiegers' and after a two-week confrontation near Mons-en-Pevelle, the French fell back on 17 September, not daring to engage.

Meanwhile, between 7 and 9 September, several Allied assaults on Lille's outer defences had only led to small gains, and Eugene himself was wounded. Marlborough now took overall command; when he did so, he was alarmed by the low reserves of supplies, powder and shot. The garrison was also running short of ammunition, though it had received some supplies on 28 August, when 1,000 dragoons broke through the lines, each soldier carrying a musket and 60lbs of powder.

The French now decided to try to sever the besiegers' communications to both Brussels and Ostend in order to deny them munitions and other supplies. They seized the line of the Scheldt to achieve the former, and, by flooding the coastal sector, isolated Ostend. A crucial Allied convoy escorted by General Webb (11,000 men) set out from Ostend and forced its way through the floods on 28 August only to find General La Motte and 22,000 French blocking the road to Lille at Wynendael. In a sharp action, Webb defeated the superior French force and triumphantly brought his waggons safely to the siege lines two days later. Furious at this, Marshal Vendome challenged Marlborough's covering force to battle at Oudenburg, but thought better of it on 7 October, retiring to Bruges. Somehow, the supply line to Ostend continued to operate.

Marlborough and Eugene triumph
At Lille, several breaches had been made in the defences by 20 October; on 23 October Boufflers agreed to surrender the town but withdrew into the strongly fortified citadel. So a second siege had to be opened. Yet again Louis XIV ordered a relief attempt – this time sending the Elector of Bavaria to create a diversion by besieging Brussels from 22 November. Marlborough's response was immediate: in a concerted operation he attacked the French posts on the Scheldt early on 26 November and took them all. This was sufficient to make the French before Brussels flee for Mons, abandoning their wounded, guns and convoys. Aware that there was no further chance of relief, Boufflers and his starving garrison finally surrendered the citadel on 10 December 1708.

MALTA
THE WARS OF ISLAM
19 May – 8 September 1565

Jean de la Valette, Grand Master of the Order of St. John, at the head of the Christian garrison of Malta (700 knights, 8,500 men-at-arms, and 80 cannon) defied Mustapha Pasha and Admiral Piali commanding the Turkish army (6,300 Janissaries, 26,000 troops and 100 cannon), who were striving to capture the island. Casualties on both sides were extraordinarily high.

The bulwark of Christendom
In 1565 the island of Malta found itself the foremost bulwark of Christendom against the westward advance of the Ottoman Turks in the Mediterrean. Suliman the Magnificent had driven the Order of St John from Rhodes in 1522, and now was determined to add Malta to his conquests as a useful base from which to launch a future invasion against Sicily.

For several years Jean de la Valette had been preparing for just such an eventuality; the defences of Forts St Elmo and St Angel on each side of the Grand Harbour had been put in good order, as had those of the promontories of Birgu and Senglea and the inland town of Mdina. The storehouses were full, and the seven *langues* (national companies) of Knights of the Order were at full strength. In the event of an attack, the declared strategy was to move the population within the strongpoints, burn the crops and poison the wells, and hold out until a Christian relief army could be assembled.

The Turkish onslaught
On 18 May the first Turkish ships were sighted, and soon their army was landing in Marasirocco Bay in the south-east of the island. Mustapha Pasha at once attacked the defences of Birgu, only to be repulsed. He then established his camp near Marsa Creek, and turned his efforts against Fort St Elmo, which was held by 53 knights and 800 soldiers. The struggle lasted for 31 days, but although their defences were ruined, the garrison – reinforced each night across the Grand Harbour – repelled almost daily assaults. Only after the corsair Dragut had taken control of the siege did matters become critical, and on 23 June the Turks at last triumphed. However, the fort's capture had cost the Turks 8,000 casualties, including Dragut himself.

The Turkish slaves next dragged 70 cannon to face Birgu and Senglea, while as many galleys were dragged overland and relaunched on the Marsa, as Mustapha now intended to assault simultaneously by land and water. The great attack against Senglea came on 15 July; on the landward side the Knights, reinforced over a bridge of boats from Birgu, held their own, while the amphibious attack also came to grief under fire from a hidden battery on Fort St Angelo. Day after day the attacks were renewed heedless of loss, but even the explosion of a large mine did not help the Turks in their attempts to break through; the breach in the Castille defences was remanned, and two Turkish assault towers and an "infernal machine" were destroyed – even though by 18 July the garrison was down to 600 men fit to carry arms. Mdina also held out.

As dissension raged in the Turkish camp as to whether the siege should continue, the Christian relief fleet at last arrived from Sicily – and the 10,000 reinforcements it brought soon decided the issue. By 8 September the last Turks had put to sea. Malta had been saved and the Ottoman threat to the Mediterranean had been checked, if not halted.

NASEBY
FIRST ENGLISH CIVIL WAR
14 June 1645

This battle was the first clash in the English Civil War between the Royalists and Cromwell's New Model Army. Both sides were seeking a victory that would decide the outcome of the war. In addition the Puritans hoped to avenge the recent storming of Leicester, and to recapture that town. The contending forces were the 13,000-strong New Model Army, under Sir Thomas Fairfax, and the 8,300-strong Royalist army, under Charles I and Prince Rupert of the Rhine. The two armies consisted of 6,000 horse, 7,000 foot and 13 cannon and 5,000 house, 3,350 foot, 12 cannon and two mortars respectively.

The New Model Army had been formed at Windsor in April 1645. It was made up of troops from the old Parliamentarian armies of the Earls of Essex and Manchester and Sir William Waller and the intention behind its formation was clear – to create an efficient war-winning force. The king for his part moved out from Oxford on 7 May, and the scene was set for a major campaign. Both sides needed a decisive battle, and neither lacked confidence, for their leaders all had several years campaigning behind them.

Manoeuvres before battle
The opening moves of the campaign were somewhat tentative. Fairfax, after relieving Taunton, alarmed the Royalists by appearing before Oxford. Rupert struck

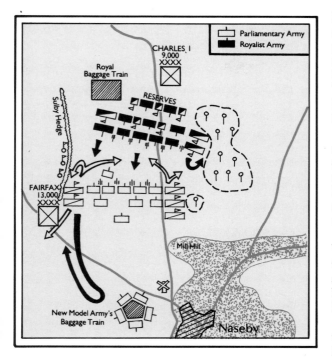

CHARLES I
9,000
XXXX

Royal
Baggage Train

RESERVES

Sulby Hedge

FAIRFAX
13,000
XXXX

Mill Hill

New Model Army's
Baggage Train

Naseby

Parliamentary Army
Royalist Army

NASEBY *The Royalist infantry's destruction by Cromwell's disciplined cavalry was the battle's turning point.*

back by storming Leicester. Determined to avenge this defeat, Fairfax now advanced to meet the king, making contact with the Royalists on the evening of 13 June. The Royalist commanders, who had been making for their strong-hold at Newark-on-Trent, now held a midnight council of war and decided to risk a battle. By 8 am the following morning, the Royalists had taken up position two miles south of Market Harborough, but dissatisfied with the report of his scouts, Rupert, himself rode out to see what was happening.

Fairfax, for his part, had marched at an early hour. When eventually the two armies caught sight of each other, they were about four miles apart – the Roundheads marshalling on the Naseby ridge, while Rupert deployed the Royalists upon Dust Hill.

The two armies drew up for battle in the straightforward fashion favoured by most generals of the period. Fairfax showed a touch of tactical skill by placing Okey's Dragoons in Sulby Hedge, where they outflanked Prince Maurice's wing of cavalry. But on the whole there was little subtlety about the deployment of either army.

A kingdom at stake

The Parliamentarians seem to have outnumbered the Royalists by about 4,000. Even so, according to Lord Digby, the Cavaliers were confident of success. When the Royalists came in sight, Fairfax "drew his line back 100 yards . . . so that the Cavaliers might not perceive in what form our battle was drawn, nor see any confusion therein". This move made the Royalists think that the New Model was falling back on Northampton. Rupert

hurried forward to engage, and at about 10 am, began a general advance. Seeing this, Fairfax resumed his position on the ridge and sent his cavalry and Skippon's foot forward. Rupert, instead of staying with Charles, led on the cavalry (1,760 to 2,000) of the Royalist right. Then, doubtless not wishing to get too far ahead of Lord Astley's foot, he made a brief halt. Ireton also halted to let his squadrons "recover their stations".

Charge and countercharge followed with mixed success. Some on either side charged home and others did not. Some fled carrying their neighbours away with them. Ireton, seeing Skippon's foot hard pressed by Sir Bernard Astley's brigade, led his right squadron against some Royalist foot, who slew his horse, wounded him twice, and took him prisoner.

Rupert, though outnumbered, eventually drove Vermuyden and the remains of Ireton's wing from the field. The Lifeguards of the two Palatine princes, supported by Sir William Vaughan and the Earl of Northampton then broke right through the Roundhead left. Some 1,750 horse had routed 2,700.

"The enemy," wrote Joshua Sprigge, "having thus worsted our left wing, pursued their advantage, and Prince Rupert himself prosecuted his success upon our left wing, almost to Naseby town, in his return summoned the Train, offering them quarter.' The prince, his summons rejected, galloped back to rejoin the king. In his absence, Lord Astley's foot, some 3,500 strong, had driven back Skippon, who may have had as many as 6,400 men under his command.

The New Model Army's artillery fired five rounds, all of which overshot their targets. The Royalists pressed forward until they were in carbine range, but the cost was heavy; Skippon himself fell severely wounded, and the lieutenant-colonel of his regiment, Francis, was killed. Fairfax's own regiment, with no Royalist regiment opposite it, held firm. Sir Edward Walker, who was with the king's entourage, saw the Cavaliers fall on their foe with swords and butt of musket, the Parliamentarian banners falling, and their foot in great disorder. Some of their officers withdrew with their colours and rallied on the second line, "choosing rather there to fight and die, than to quit the ground they stood on." The three regiments of the second line – Rainsborough's, Hammond's and Harley's – now advanced and came to "push of pike" with the main body of Cavalier foot.

Astley had done well, but disaster was at hand; with his left flank in the air, he was about to receive the onslaught of some 3,000 horse – Cromwell's famed Ironsides. This formidable body had already had a rough bout with Langdale's Northern Horse, some 1500 strong. The latter were to a large extent officers and gentlemen, survivors of Newcastle's army, which had been destroyed at the battle of Marston Moor (2 July 1644).

Langdale, advancing at the same time as Rupert and Astley, was met by some of Cromwell's best regiments. Sprigge records that the northerners "made a very gallant resistance; and firing at a very close charge, they came to the sword." Overwhelmed by the weight of numbers opposing them, Langdale's men took shelter to the rear of Prince Rupert's Regiment, where they tried to rally. Sending four regiments in pursuit of the Northern Horse, Cromwell now fell upon Lord Astley with the rest, some 2000 strong.

A fatal intervention

The time had come for the king to counterattack. He still had his Lifeguard as well as the Newark Horse, and it may be that these would have sufficed to turn the fate of the day. At this instant the Earl of Carnwarth seized Charles' bridle, and shouting "Will you go upon your death?" led the king rearwards. At this critical moment, someone gave the order "March to the right hand". Thereupon, says Walker, . . . 'we turned about and ran on the spur almost a quarter of a mile, and then the word being given to make a stand, we did so: though the body could never be rallied. Those that came back made a charge, wherein some of them fell.' The miserable failure of the king's reserve left Cromwell to destroy Astley's infantry at his leisure.

Charles and Rupert were still on Dust Hill with several thousand horse. But even the best of them thought they had done enough. Fairfax was quick to reform his army, and launch his cavalry in a relentless pursuit, which did not finish until the Ironsides came within sight of Leicester.

The Civil War decided

The battle cost the Royalists their main army. They lost nearly 5,000 prisoners, 200 carriages, all their artillery, 40 barrels of powder, 8,000 arms amd 100 colors. About 100 camp followers were massacred. Though the war dragged on for another year, the ultimate issue was settled by this decisive action.

PAVIA
THE FRENCH WARS IN ITALY
25 February 1525

The Habsburg emperor Charles V, fighting France for control of Italy, sent a 20,000-strong army, consisting mainly of Spanish pikemen, but with 17 guns, nominally under Charles de Lannoy but in fact commanded by the Marquis of Pescara against the army of Francis I of France (20,000 men and 53 guns) that was beseiging Pavia. In the resulting battle, the imperial forces inflicted at least 8,000 casualties for the loss of 800, and took Francis himself prisoner. The tactics employed in the battle ushered in a new period in warfare, as well as marking the end of the long struggle between the two rival Habsburg and Valoi dynasties for dominance in Italy.

A diversion fails

On 28 October 1524 the French army attacked Pavia; failing to take it by storm, the French undertook a winter siege. The imperial generals did not feel strong enough to attempt the city's relief until they heard that Francis I had detached one-third of his army to launch an attack on Naples. Lannoy and Pescara then approached the French lines from Lodi, hoping to lure the French away from Pavia. The king did not oblige; instead, he positioned his army within entrenchments along the Vernavola stream, facing east, with the high-walled Mirabello Park protecting (as he thought) his left flank, and continued with the siege. In late January 1525 the imperial forces dug positions facing the French, and deadlock ensued.

A bold overnight march

Aware that the French were suffering from desertions, and that their own men were mutinous for lack of pay, Lannoy and Pescara determined on a daring plan. Leaving a small force to hold their positions, the imperial generals led their army north through a wet and windy night to the north-east corner of the park, knocked three breaches in the wall undetected, and passed their five formations through them before daybreak. They then began to form a line of battle threatening the left wing of Francis's army, and captured much valuable booty in an unguarded camp.

Taken by surprise

Taken completely by surprise, the French monarch summoned his forces, but made the mistake of feeding them piecemeal into the developing battle. He personally led the *Gendarmerie* (French élite cavalry) in a successful series of charges against the outnumbered imperial horsemen, and Pescara's men hesitated. However, the French infantry were slow in appearing on the scene, so the imperials were afforded time to deploy their cannon and recover. A sally by the besieged garrison led to some delay, and several French formations never entered the fray.

Disaster for Francis

Soon 1,500 Spanish arquebusiers, supported by some pikemen, manoeuvred so as to fire into the *Gendarmerie*'s rear from cover; this fire led to heavy losses and their defeat. The 5,000 German *Landsknechts* in French pay now plunged into the battle, only to find themselves receiving heavy arquebusier fire in their turn, and then were beset on two sides by halberdiers, who duly annihilated them. The French army's Swiss detachments fought poorly, and soon left the field. Disaster now ensued for the French: their last infantry was rounded up, their king was taken captive, and many distinguished officers were slain.

This conflict effectively inaugurated a long period of Habsburg rule in Italy. It had been a confused battle, but the superior surprise, fire-power and coordination of the imperial forces had won the day decisively.

POLTAVA
THE GREAT NORTHERN WAR
13 July 1709

Peter the Great's victory on the River Vorskla over Charles XII of Sweden marked the emergence of Russia as a major power. The Russian army (77,000 men and 100 guns) defeated the Swedish army (16,000 men and 8 guns plus 5,000 besieging Poltava), inflicting 7,000 casualties and losing only 1,300 men.

The Tsar's response

Charles XII's rash invasion of Russia was already in dire straits when he decided to besiege Poltava. Not only had the Swedes failed to secure the support they had hoped for from Mazeppa, leader of the Cossacks in the Ukraine failed, but September 1708 had seen the loss of a vital supply convoy, while the bitter winter that followed had decimated the Swedish army.

The Swedish king opened the siege of Poltava in May 1709, but once the tsar had completed the subjugation of the Ukranian and Don Cossacks, he began to collect a large army to relieve the town and on 4 June arrived near Poltava. Peter placed his army in a large entrenched camp on a low ridge with forests on two sides and the River Vorskla behind, 3½ miles from the Swedish camp, and built a series of 10 redoubts to guard the only open approach from the south. After some skirmishing, these were completed on 25 June – a day on which Charles XII was badly wounded in the foot.

Boldness brings disaster

Charles rejected his generals' advice to retreat before such a strong enemy, and ordered General Rehnsköld to launch all-out attack. Charles accompanied his army in a litter. Advancing shortly after midnight, the 18 battalions and 12 squadrons of Rehnsköld's force hoped to rush the Russian outlying forts and then to rout their cavalry and storm the Russian camp. Unfortunately the key Swedish generals were at loggerheads, and the dawn attack only took five forts; even worse, General Roos's infantry became tied-down and isolated amongst the remainder. The weakened main body continued to advance, but by now Peter the Great had his army in full readiness. Nevertheless, General Creuz's cavalry managed to rout the Russian horsemen, and the remaining Swedish infantry moved along the edge of the forest to assault the main camp from the north-west. Meanwhile, Roos was surrounded by 10,000 Russians under General Rensel, and after trying to escape towards the Vorskla his men were forced to surrender.

The Swedish main body – which by now had also lost its supporting artillery – was waiting to charge the Russian entrenchments. Even Charles realized that this was hopeless, and accordingly he ordered a southwards retreat. However to do so involved passing across the front of 40,000 deployed Russians, so the king changed his mind and ordered a frontal attack. Pounded by 40 Russian guns, the Swedes gallantly tried to press their charge home, but were repulsed with heavy loss. The survivors began to flee towards their distant camp, but their disabled monarch managed to rally them.

The Swedes, joined by the 5,000 men who had been left besieging Poltava, now began a headlong retreat. Charles and his 1,500-strong escort fled south across the Dnieper and eventually reached Bender in Turkey. The main army, perhaps 14,000 strong, under the command of General Lewenhaupt was trapped on the river and forced to surrender to the pursuing Russians. Owing to the rashness of its commander, the Swedish army had thus been virtually eliminated. Peter was well on the way to making Russia a great European power.

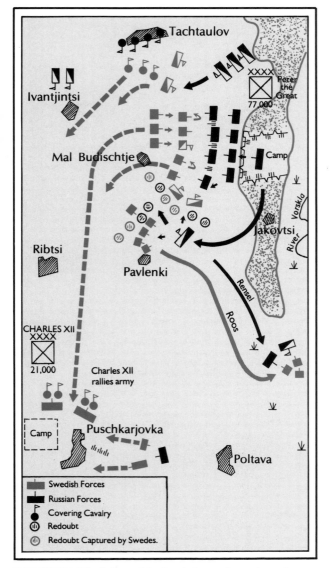

POLTAVA *The failure of the Swedes' second attack on the Russian entrenchments led to retreat and surrender.*

QUEBEC
THE SEVEN YEARS WAR
27 June – 18 September 1759

Siege and battle that virtually completed the British conquest of French Canada. Major-General James Wolfe's army (14,000 men) and Admiral Charles Saunders' fleet (22 ships of the line and 12 frigates) besieged and ultimately defeated Louis, Marquis de Montcalm, and Governor Pierre de Vaudreuil (14,000 men and 4,000 Indians, and 100 guns). Both Wolfe and Montcalm were killed in the deciding battle.

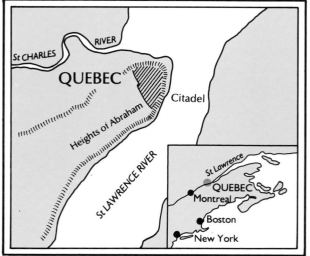

QUEBEC *A 15-minute battle on the Heights of Abraham opened the way for French defeat and the fall of the city.*

Key to the St Lawrence

After the capture of the fortress of Louisbourg in Nova Scotia on 27 July 1758, the British forces made rapid progress in their conquest of Canada. Next year Prime Minister William Pitt the Elder ordered expeditions against Fort Niagara, Fort Ticanderoga, and the city of Quebec, which dominated the St Lawrence River. Command of the third operation was entrusted to the 32-year-old James Wolfe, and on 26 June he was landed from Admiral Saunders' fleet on the Ile d'Orléans downstream from Quebec and on the opposite bank of the St Lawrence, the west bank being strongly held. The upper town of Quebec stood on a high rock and was deemed impregnable.

Although Montcalm and Vaudreuil were on bad terms, they conducted an active defence from the outset. French fireships were launched twice against the anchored fleet, but achieved nothing. By early July the British had captured Point Lévis nearer to Quebec, and also established their main camp near the River Montmorency on the St Lawrence's west bank facing the strong Beauport Lines held by Vaudreuil. But Wolfe was a sick man and often at odds with his three Brigadier-Generals, Monckton, Townsend and Murray,

and was much criticised when an attack on the Beauport Lines was repulsed on 30 July.

A new plan

Changing his strategy, Wolfe sent Murray past Quebec by water on 5 August to threaten the French lines of supply – a move that induced Montcalm to detach 3,000 men from his main force. Having achieved Wolfe's aim, Murray's troops then returned to Wolfe's camp. Admiral Saunders' anxiety lest the river should freeze up and trap his fleet made Wolfe decide to adopt a bold plan of attack to finally take the city. After evacuating his west bank camp, he massed his army on the east bank facing Quebec.

On the night of 12 September Wolfe quietly embarked 4,000 men and two light cannon in ships' boats, and rowed over the river to the Anse de Foulon, where a steep and ill-guarded path had been discovered leading up to the Heights of Abraham close to Quebec, a diversionary attack against Beauport being launched to distract the French. At dawn the next day, Montcalm heard of Wolf's deployment south of the town. Returning from the Beauport Lines, Montcalm collected 4,500 men (but no cannon) and at 10 am sallied out to attack the British. The clash lasted barely 15 minutes. The British held their fire until they were barely 10 yards from the French, when then their volleys caused heavy losses, though both Wolfe and Monckton fell under the French fire at the onset of the action. As Wolfe died the French began to retire, pursued by Monckton's brigade, while Murray led his men to cut the French off from the bridge over the St Charles River. Townsend – now in command – regrouped his men and advanced. As the battle ended, Montcalm fell mortally wounded. Each side had suffered some 800 casualties. Vaudreuil decided to evacuate the Lines, and on 18 September Quebec surrendered.

This success clinched the British conquest of most of Canada (the entire country finally came under British control on 8 September 1760). The British had displayed their skill at combined operations involving both troops and ships, even though Quebec had defied them for almost three months.

RAMILLIES
THE WAR OF THE SPANISH SUCCESSION
23 May 1706

Fought on Whit Sunday, between the Duke of Marlborough's Allied army (62,000) and Marshal Villeroi's French army (60,000), the battle resulted in the total defeat of the French (13,000 casualties.) Ramillies was Marlborough's greatest success. At Blenheim (1704), Oudenarde (1708) and Malplaquet

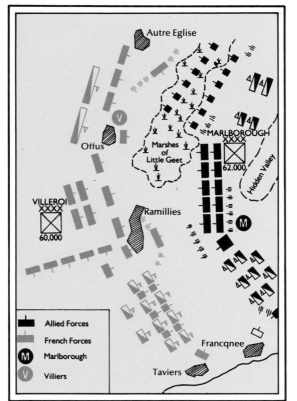

RAMILLIES *Marlborough's masterly ability in switching his troops' positions enabled him to break the French line.*

(1709), he shared the victories with Prince Eugene of Savoy, but in May 1706 he was in sole command and produced a virtuoso performance of generalship.

Taking the opportunity

At the outset of the campaign Marlborough's expectations were limited: French offensives on the Rhine ruled out his first plan to transfer his army to North Italy, and he had scant hope of achieving much in Flanders. However, it was at this moment that the pride of Louis XIV played into his hands. Louis ordered Villeroi to avenge the disgrace of Blenheim, and the French accordingly advanced from Louvain and crossed the River Dyle to seek battle. A gratified Marlborough at once summoned his outlying formations, and advanced early on 23 May, intending to pitch camp near Ramillies. As the fog cleared, his advance guard discovered the position already occupied by the enemy in full strength. Learning of this, the duke ordered his men to speed up their rate of march, while he himself rode forward to reconnoitre. He found the French occupying a concave four-mile ridge, their extreme right wing protected by the River Mehaigne and two occupied villages, their left and part of their center positioned behind the marshes of the Little Geet, with the villages of Ramillies, Offus and Autre Eglise strongly held behind the stream. To hold the only area of open ground south of Ramillies, Villeroi had massed 82 squadrons supported by infantry brigades.

A cunning plan

However, Marlborough realized that the French were over-extended – this meant that it would take them time to transfer troops from one wing to the other. It was on this realization that he based his plan. Although his Prussian units had still not arrived on the scene, he determined to attack without delay. He drew up his army along a shorter, three-mile line on a plateau facing the French.

At 1 pm the 120 Allied guns engaged the French 70; an hour later, Marlborough launched his first attacks against each extremity of the French position. In the south, the Dutch Guards and Danish cavalry rapidly captured Franquinacy and Taviers, aided by two cannon brought well forward. In the north, Lord Orkney led the English infantry through the Geet's marshes towards Autre Eglise. Villeroi, unknown to Marlborough, had specific orders from Louis XIV to pay special attention to where the red-coats attacked, and began moving infantry from his right center to reinforce his left. More units were sucked into the fighting around Taviers. As a result, the French right-centre was being weakened. Marlborough clearly had the initiative, and was beginning to impose his will.

The day was still far from won, however, and at about 3 pm a major crisis occured on the open plain south of Ramillies. As General Schulenburg advanced his infantry in the center, the Dutch commander Overkirk moved his 69 squadrons in support – and was promptly charged by 68 French squadrons – who eventually drove the Allied horsemen back in disarray. Realising that this would threaten his center, the watchful Marlborough took three quick decisions. First, despite its progress, Orkney's attack must be recalled. Second, 18 squadrons, followed by 21 more, should move from the right wing through the dead ground of the hidden valley without delay to reinforce his battered horsemen on the left. Third, as this move would take some time, the duke would intervene in person at the head of his staff to rally Orkney's command and lead them forward.

Crisis averted

Marlborough led two charges in person, was unhorsed, and might have been captured or worse, but for his trumpeter's bravery before cavalrymen and two battalions from the center arrived to rescue him. As he mounted, his equerry was killed holding his stirrup by a French shot which missed the duke by inches. But his intervention had won the time that was needed for the squadrons from the right to enter the fray and the French were flung back in their turn. Struck on the flank by the Danish cavalry, the entire French right swung back, pivotting on Ramillies (where a French battery of triple-barrelled cannon was causing much execution), until they formed some sort of a line at right angles to their original front, but seriously hindered in this new deployment by the tents of their camp. Marlborough prepared to smash the hinge.

The decisive blow

Meanwhile, it had taken ten messages to induce Orkney to abandon his attack on Autre Eglise – which he had all but taken – despite the unfavorable terrain – and to fall back grudgingly to his original position on the Allied right. He was promptly ordered to send his rearward line of six battalions down the concealed re-entrant to reinforce the impending grand attack in the centre. Villeroi, suspecting a trick, kept all his massed infantry and 50 squadrons of cavalry on his left, cautiously reoccupying part of the ground Orkney had so unwillingly vacated. By 6 pm, Marlborough had everything prepared, and a general attack was ordered. Ramillies and Offus were captured, and the French army dissolved. At a cost of 3,600 casualties, the Allies had inflicted at least 13,000 on the enemy and scattered many more in a pursuit that lasted throughout the night. Marlborough only dismounted 12 miles beyond the field, after 20 hours in the saddle.

Extensive exploitation

Ramillies displayed Marlborough at his battle-winning best. His grasping of the initiative, eye for critical terrain, personal battle-control, and exploitation of success marked him out as the great general of his age. The fruits of victory were impressive. With several months of good weather available, the Allies – reinforced to 100,000 men – cleared the French from the Spanish Netherlands. Brussels was taken, and, so demoralized were the French, a dozen fortresses surrendered after offering only token resistance. Seldom has a victory been more dramatically exploited. To cap it all, in late September news arrived of Eugene's corresponding triumph at Turin in North Italy.

ROCROI
THE THIRTY YEARS WAR
18 & 19 May 1643

Fought near the French north-east frontier between the Duke of Enghien's French army (23,000 men and 12 guns) and Don Francisco de Melo's Spanish army (27,000 and 28 guns) to the south-west of the fortress of Rocroi, this celebrated battle signalled the passing of the Spanish period of European military predominance and its replacement by that of France.

A challenge accepted

To prevent the Spaniards from capturing Rocroi (an important fortress on France's north-east frontier), the 21-year-old Louis de Bourbon, Duke of Enghien (later the great Prince de Condé) advanced from Aubenton on 18 May 1643 to challenge the besieging Spaniards. De Melo accepted the challenge, and the two armies drew up for battle to the south-west of the town. Although stronger, de Melo's line was 500 yards shorter

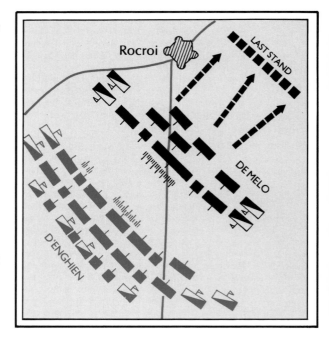

ROCROI *French victory at Rocroi marked the end of the battlefield dominance of the Spanish infantry tercio.*

than that of his opponent, because he had placed his *tercios* in a deep central formation.

The day of decision

The battle started slowly. All that occurred on the first day was an artillery bombardment and one indecisive cavalry clash on the Spanish right wing. The two armies lay on their arms that night divided by only 1,000 yards. The next morning, however, Eughien ordered both formations of cavalry on his flanks into the attack. On the right, General Gassion manoeuvred as if intending to outflank the Spanish horsemen of General Albuquerque in the hope of inducing him to form front of his flank. When he duly obliged, Enghien led the rest of the French right wing cavalry to attack Albuquerque's exposed flank, and after an hour's hard fighting finally routed him.

On the French left, however, different fortunes prevailed. General La Ferte-Senneterre duly charged General Isembourg's Spanish horsemen, but was defeated. The Spaniards rode forward to assail the open flank of d'Eprenan's French infantry, and captured their guns. Fortunately the aged Marshal d'Hopital counterattacked with a scratch force of horse and foot, and recaptured the cannon – albeit only briefly, as a new Spanish infantry attack retook them, and turned their fire against the French.

The fire of some 30 cannon at close range was hard to bear, and General La Vallière ordered a retreat. Fortunately the French reserve under the veteran General Sirot (like Gassion a veteran who had served under Gustavus Adolphus) was still intact; Sirot managed to halt his retiring compatriots and then led them forwards to attack the *tercios* of de Melo's first line. This coincided with a determined attack by Enghien on the third line of *tercios* in de Melo's centre, which found themselves pressed back into the rear of the formations of the second line, causing much confusion with many turning to flee. Noting this, the French reserve repulsed Isembourg's renewed cavalry attack, and then plunged forward to assail the troubled Spanish infantry in the center. These began to withdraw to the north-east.

After reordering his line of battle, Enghien advanced to close range. The French were repulsed three times by the Spanish salvos, but when Enghien massed his guns against an angle of the Spanish square formation, some officers signalled a surrender. Enghien, however, was fired upon as he rode forward, and it took a further furious French onslaught to clinch the day at 10 o'clock, just as some Spanish reserves arrived too late to intervene. For the loss of 2,200 casualties the French inflicted 14,500 on the Spaniards.

THE SPANISH ARMADA
THE ANGLO-SPANISH WARS
29 July – 9 August 1588

A running naval engagement in the English Channel between the 130 Spanish vessels of the Duke of Medina Sidonia (23,000 men and 1,500 cannon) and the English fleet (120 ships) commanded by Lord Howard of Effingham, resulting in the thwarting of the Spanish plan to invade England and the subsequent scattering of the Armada as it returned to Spain.

Spanish preparations had been delayed by Sir Francis Drake's pre-emptive raid against Cadiz in April 1587, and this – the celebrated "singeing of the King of Spain's beard" – postponed its sailing until the following year. Philip II's plan was for the Armada, which eventually included 24 galleons, four galleasses and 102 smaller craft, to sail up the Channel defeating the English fleet en route, to link with the Duke of Parma's veteran army in Flanders, and then to convoy it to make a landing in the Thames estuary.

Fighting up the Channel
Sailing from Lisbon on 28 May 1588, bad weather and water shortages forced the Armada to put into Corunna for a month, and it was not until 29 July that it was sighted off Cornwall and the news of its approach reported to Lord Howard at Plymouth. The English fleet put to sea, and by adroit manoeuvring placed itself up-wind of the Armada's crescent-shaped formation. The first clash between the two fleets took place off Plymouth on 31 May, when two Spanish ships were crippled and subsequently captured.

Employing "tip-and-run" tactics, and relying on cannon fire (limited although its effects were on the stout Spanish vessels) to harrass their opponents, the English captains denied the Spaniards any chance to close and board – their favorite tactic.

Frustrated by the English ability to avoid close action, the Armada eventually anchored off the Calais roadstead. The English – plagued by munition shortages – anchored nearby, and, after being joined by Lord Seymour's 35 ships from off Dover, sent in eight fire-ships on the night of 7 August against the massed Spanish shipping. In panic the Spaniards cut their cables, and headed for the open sea. Howard attacked the scattered Armada off Gravelines on the 8th, and sent boats to loot the stranded galleass *San Lorenzo*. A second Spanish ship also became a victim amidst the shallows. All this while Parma had been waiting at Bruges, but, blockaded as it was by Dutch ships, his army could not put to sea from its camp at Dunkirk. Despairing of linking with the army, on 9 August Medina Sidonia abandoned what Philip had grandly termed "the Enterprise of England", and hotly pursued set off up the North Sea to round Scotland and thence head for Spain down the west coast of Ireland.

THE ARMADA *Though the unwieldly Armada kept its formation well, it was unable to bring the English fleet to battle.*

CHAPTER FIVE
The Age of Revolution

On 19 October 1781, the British and Hessian troops of Lord Cornwallis marched out from the defences of *Yorktown* and laid down their arms in the presence of the Continental Army and its Bourbon allies to the ironical strains of the popular tune of the time – "The World Turned Upside Down". On the evening of 18 June 34 years later, a dejected Emperor Napoleon transferred from his large coach, trapped in the midst of the remnants of his fleeing army near Genappes in Belgium, to mount a horse and escape in the gathering gloom with Field-Marshal Blücher's Prussian cavalry hot on his heels.

These two events were climacteric moments in world history. Although few recognized it at the time, the first marked the final collapse of British political and military power in the North American colonies. The second marked the final eclipse of Napoleon's empire, although the events of the war-scarred period between 1789 (the outbreak of the French Revolution) and 1815 (the year of *Waterloo*) would leave equally indelible marks on the world's future as the earlier triumph of the American Revolution (1775–1783) had in creating the United States.

The 40 years between 1775 and 1815 were some of the most remarkable – in both revolutionary and evolutionary terms – in all of military history. The period saw the demise of the 18th-century's concept of limited war (battered although that had become by the period of Frederick the Great), and the onset of two generations of almost total war – fought between whole peoples, rather than just governments, by larger armies and navies (from 1792) than had been seen for many centuries in pursuit of, or to counter, ideological objectives that threatened to overturn the old order of monarchical government.

INDEPENDENCE *The Declaration of Independence in July 1776 set the scene for total war with Britain.*

A new type of war

In many respects, the War of American Independence was transitional in its nature, reflecting both old and new political concepts, and foreshadowing important new military developments that would come to full fruition at the close of the century. The American Revolution was essentially a political, not a social, upheaval.

The issues hinged upon the right or otherwise of the government of George III to tax the colonists without either consultation or granting them representation in Parliament. The unwillingness of the colonial legislatures to pay for their own defence, and the incapability of most of the local militias to carry this out in any case, together with colonial dislike of the British liberal Indian policy and restrictions on westward expansion by the settlers, made it necessary for the British government to provide both troops and enforcement policies. In London, it seemed eminently reasonable that the colonists should pay part of the costs of their own defence. To American patriots, on the other hand, this demand appearanced to signal a further tyrannical invasion of the rights of the individual.

After a long period of growing dissent, stemming from the Stamp Act of 1764, and later attempts to levy duties or taxes on various imports, including tea, the moment of explosion came in Boston in December 1773 with the famous "tea-party", in which a band of patriots, thinly disguised as Indians, boarded an East India Company ship and threw its cargo into the harbor. The Continental Congress met the next September in Philadelphia, and the first shots were fired in April 1775, as British troops attempted to sieze munitions at the two New England villages of Lexington and Concord. As the fighting spread, the situation worsened, and in July 1776 the ultimate political act of rebellion was committed with the passing of the Declaration of Independence. A full-scale popular war based upon ideological concepts rapidly developed in the Americas.

The search for an army

Thus, in 1775 the focus of attention switched from an old-world Europe, exhausted by a whole series of wars, to an unanticipatedly serious struggle for independence by Britain's 13 New World colonies. At the onset, few – if any – outside observers believed it would prove possible for the founding fathers of the United States to achieve the objectives set by the Continental Congress, and in the process humiliate the power of Britain. However, by the time the Peace of Paris was signed in 1783 after seven years of variable fortunes in America, on the intervening ocean, and (latterly, and on a far smaller scale) in Europe, this, indeed, proved to be the case. Only the West Indian naval victory of *The Saints* (1782) and the successfully sustained siege of *Gibraltar* (1779–83) would go some way towards redeeming the reputation of British.

The higher leadership of the American rebel forces at first posed great problems. George Washington was appointed commander-in-chief of the embryonic Continental Army in June 1775 on the strength of his colonelcy in the Virginia Militia, but in reality he was a land surveyor and country gentleman, rather than a professional soldier. Among the others, Horatio Gates and Charles Lee had minimal military experience, but Nathaniel Greene was an iron-forger, Henry Knox a bookstore keeper and Benedict Arnold (not until 1780 an object of American hatred for desertion to the English) is variously described as an apothecary's apprentice, a merchant in drugs and a Caribbean smuggler.

Such homespun generals were unlikely to impress the victorious comanders of the Seven Years War – but ultimately they earned more than English respect, particularly Washington. Fortunately, he could call on the services of two European advisers – the youthful French volunteer, the Marquis de Lafayette (from August 1777), and (from February 1778) the Prussian drill-master Frederick von Steuben. Between them, the two men began the process of turning militiamen and farmers into something approaching trained regular soldiers.

Nor was leadership the only problem the colonists faced. Congress and the State Assemblies proved most reluctant to form a long-service army. To the politicians, brought up on dire English Whig legends of Cromwell and the rule of the Major-Generals in the 1650s, permanent forces spelt both expense and the possibility of tyranny. Only in 1776, when the first regiments melted away as the original volunteers returned to their homes, did Congress offer inducements for three-year enlistments, or for service for the duration of the war. Despite the large reservoir of available manpower, however, men still did not enlist in adequate numbers. Realizing the problem, Congress called for nine-months compulsory service – a form of conscription – in early 1777 but this also failed, as the states

SPIRIT OF INDEPENDENCE
Colonial backwoodsmen proved their worth in guerilla-style conflicts against the British in the War of Independence.

applied the draft to only their n'er-do-wells. So the cash and land-grant bounty system had to continue, but, despite ever-rising inducements, men still refused to come forward. The simple reason for this reluctance was that the cash bounties of $750 per man were paid in increasingly worthless paper money, while civilian labourers could earn almost 30 times as much as a soldier's daily pay. Year after year, therefore, many of Washington's regiments were at least one-third below establishment.

Therefore, the popular image of patriots eager to serve against British tyranny should be qualified. As late as 1780, only a quarter of the Continentals were serving on over nine-month enlistments, which meant that replacements had to be trained continually, while desertion was rampant. However, large numbers of negroes were willing to enlist to fight. Though the ban on negro recruitment in the southern states

encouraged many to join British Loyalist formations, this response helped fuel the early call for emancipation of the slaves in the northern states. Thus the war had some important long-term social, as well as political, effects, preparing the way for the mid-19th century confrontations that led to the US Civil War.

Officering also posed problems. There were plenty of men of varying ability willing to serve at the outset, but disillusion soon spread because of an inequitable promotion system. The system was that Congress appointed all general officers, while the state legislatures commissioned more junior ranks, but favoritism was rife, and Washington's recommendations of the deserving were often ignored. So officers began to press for pensions of half-pay for life; after much opposition and delay, Congress had to concede this in 1780 to stem the flood of resignations.

Equipment, weaponry and finance were also hard to procure in a mainly agricultural society. Manufacturer goods were brought in from Europe, while Philadelphia became the center of the native war industry, such as it was. Ambassadors abroad – Benjamin Franklin in Paris, for instance – purchased and shipped French and Dutch munitions; the successful American privateers brought in the weapons and supplies they had taken from their prizes, but at a price, and there was inevitably corruption and profiteering to be countered as well. Food was available in quantity, but distribution was the difficulty in a country of few roads, and salting meat for winter use in sufficient amounts proved difficult.

Congress's increasing reliance on a debased and devaluing paper currency lay at the root of many problems. The selfish jealousy with which individual states guarded their "inalienable" rights, heedless of the common purpose, underlaid many more. An orthodox system of regular taxation was unthinkable, as that was the burden the patriots were fighting to have removed. Interest rates on loans soared, and reliance on French assistance (such as the million *livres* secretly loaned in May 1776), became greater and greater as time went by. Thus the creation and maintenance of perhaps the first truly "national" war effort in history was far from effective, and yet – somehow – the Continental Army survived, and the war would be won.

The British riposte

In early 1775, General Thomas Gage – with 3,500 regular troops (nine battalions) under command in Massachusetts out of 8,000 in the whole of North America – advised London that it would require 20,000 men to pacify New England. It took the costly storming of Bunker Hill on 17 June, and the subsequent British evacuation of Boston (March 1776), to convince Lord North's government that such a force was indeed needed, but to provide it was not easy. In Britain, professional soldiering was still unpopular; so, because of cost, was the maintenance of a standing army of any size in time of peace. Thus much reliance was placed on the hiring of German mercenaries (available from Hesse and Hanover and neighboring princely states) to make up the

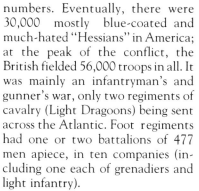

AID FROM FRANCE *Man for man, the US infantry (above left, right) and the British (above center) were an even match, but French aid to the Americans made a major difference, particularly at Yorktown, where Washington inspects a French battery (right).*

numbers. Eventually, there were 30,000 mostly blue-coated and much-hated "Hessians" in America; at the peak of the conflict, the British fielded 56,000 troops in all. It was mainly an infantryman's and gunner's war, only two regiments of cavalry (Light Dragoons) being sent across the Atlantic. Foot regiments had one or two battalions of 477 men apiece, in ten companies (including one each of grenadiers and light infantry).

The British red-coat was equipped and armed much as his forebears had been. His uniform had evolved a little to a trimmer cut, but he still carried the "Brown Bess" musket, a bayonet and 60 rounds of ammunition. Grenadiers now wore fur caps, rather than miter-hats (though Hessians still wore brass-faced miters), while the reintroduced light infantry companies had caps and a shorter red jacket. Brigades were still the largest fighting formation.

Tactics – which had developed to permit some open-order fighting in the Seven Years War – had by now retrogressed to follow standard European linear concepts; Bunker Hill, for instance, was fought following normal 18th-century precepts. However its cost in casualties hastened the relearning of old lessons, and, indeed, the British Army proved itself more adept in fighting under wilderness conditions than is often realized. Discipline, however, was draconian, pay and rations poor,

and leadership highly variable.

Gage's successors were men of fair ability – Generals Howe and Clinton almost won the war by taking New York after a successful combined operation in September 1776 – and Howe's victory at *Brandywine* in 1777 led to the capture of Philadelphia itself. The defeats and capitulations of Generals Burgoyne and Cornwallis at Saratoga (October 1777) and *Yorktown* (1781) – though strategically and psychologically of the greatest importance – should not lead us to overlook the skill of the former's troops in bushwarfare, or the abilities of such commanders as Tarleton, Ferguson and Simcoe as leaders of light troops.

In the hated Banastre Tarleton, who was much feared by the Americans, the British Army had a highly-effective intelligence chief and commander of light cavalry and Loyalists. Similarly the victories at Savannah, Charleston and Camden were far from negligible — at one stage much of the south was pacified. Large numbers of Loyalists (or "Tories") also rallied to the Union flag (at least a fifth of the population supported the crown). But the British effort, impressive though it was, proved insufficient to force the

patriots to abandon the war. They, too, had their victories – at Trenton (1776), Princeton (1777), King's Mountain (1780) and Cowpens (1781) – and they won through to eventual success, though, at times, it was a "near-run thing".

The French to the rescue
American diplomacy played a critical role in the drive to eventual victory. French shipments of arms and stores were as important in the early years as American "Lend-Lease" would be to Britain in 1940. Over 80 shiploads of supplies were shipped to America from Bordeaux alone in 1777. Several hundred unemployed French officers followed Lafayette over the Atlantic to help train and lead the Continental Army, which, after numerous early setbacks and narrowly surviving a desperate winter in Valley Forge in the winter of 1777–1778, emerged from its encampments drilled by von Steuben into an effective, 10,000-strong-force.

An event of crucial importance was the formal Treaty of Amity and Commerce, which the Americans signed with France on 6 February 1778. This was made possible by skilled exploitation of the news of the victories of Saratoga and Germantown the previous September by envoys Silas Deane and Benjamin Franklin in Paris. By the terms of the treaty, not only would an expeditionary force of 5,000 French regulars be sent to America under General Rochambeau, but it was also agreed that the French fleet would attack Britain's over-stretched lines of communication across the Atlantic. In addition, the so-called "First Armed Neutrality", proclaimed by Catherine the Great of Russia and joined by most of the other powers of Europe, greatly increased the stress and expense of the struggle to Britain, especially when the Spanish and Dutch joined the French in open war.

Just as the presence of North Vietnamese regular forces in South Vietnam helped the *Vietcong* to victory from 1967–1975, so the presence of French regulars helped convert the Continental Army and the State Militias into a war-winning force. Some 7,500-strong, they proved their worth in the decisive *Yorktown* campaign, a triumph which was made possible, in turn, by Admiral de Grasse's naval victory at the Capes. This ended all hope of British aid arriving from New York to relieve Cornwallis.

Congress and its soldiers
The fact that French intervention proved of key importance should not be taken as denying the abilities of Washington and Greene, or the capabilities of the best of their native-born soldiers. But, from first to last, the attitude of Congress remained ambivalent – and often obstructive. Civil-military relations were not the strongest suit in the colonists' hand, with Samuel Adams declaring in 1776 that "a standing army . . . is always dangerous to the liberties of the people . . . Such a power should be watched with a jealous eye."

Without such a staunch leader as Washington, the American war-effort would have collapsed on several occasions for want of political support by both Congress and the state legislatures. As it was, he faced several serious mutinies by disillusioned troops in 1781 over pay and poor enlistment terms, and, even when the war was won, the "Newburgh Affair" of 1783 almost led to aggrieved and disaffected officers mounting a *coup d'état* against Congress to install Washington as a military dictator. Only Washington's firmness and some overdue Congressional concessions averted the danger; and the army, still disgruntled, agreed to disband and go home. Even later, however, the garrison of Philadelphia mutinied and surrounded Congress. It is small wonder that distrust of standing armies became more and more engrained in the minds of American politicians.

Why the Americans won
One of the main reasons for the eventual American triumph was the lack of strategic grasp displayed by the British government at home and its senior commanders in the field. For too long, they regarded the struggle as purely a military one, ignoring its political and cultural aspects. Slowly, the British came to realize to the full the difficulty of fighting a war 3,000 miles and an ocean away from home – a task that rapidly became impossible when a powerful French fleet intervened. The failure to prevent the war from

spreading to involve France, Spain, Russia and other European countries was a further major British setback, so, in the end, sea power and diplomacy largely decided the issue.

Secondly, tribute must be paid to the fighting ability of the Continental Army. However shaky its earlier performances, its resilience after defeat enabled it to present a steady focus of continuing opposition of British pacification that kept alive the revolutionary cause.

Thirdly, the role of the French alliance cannot be over-estimated. Money, weapons, volunteers, and then the expeditionary corps tipped the balance in the patriots' favor at several critical moments. The key contribution of the French fleet has already been mentioned, while the revolutionary cause was substantially boosted by France's psychological support and diplomatic recognition.

Fourthly, incompetence at winning over American hearts and minds – and the mishandling of the loyalist element in the population – underwrote the British political failure. All sides were guilty of occasional atrocities, not least the loyalists and the militias, but it was these aspects of the struggle that destroyed all hope of genuine pacification for the British.

Fifthly, at the military level, there were great contrasts in leadership. The British tended to be weak. The well-meaning Howe gave away the possibility of an early overall victory through his indecisiveness, while Burgoyne, Clinton and Cornwallis proved incapable of effective co-ordination – indeed it was the lack of effective centralized direction that led to the final British failure. And, of course, the strength of will and strategic and tactical capabilities displayed by George Washington deserve full recognition. Despite weak political and logistical backing for much of the time from both the Continental Congress and the State Legislatures, his determination, courage, integrity and self-effacing modesty inspired both his army and the newly-emerging nation, as well as earning him the respect of his opponents.

VALLEY FORGE *An American Continental at the Valley Forge encampment. Though battered and tattered, Washington's army survived winter.*

The revolution's significance

Seen from one angle, the War of Independence can be regarded as the prototype for all struggles for colonial independence in modern history. It started as a popular insurrection, which was sparked off by a few determined and able men, who appreciated the political nature of the challenge they were posing, even if their grasp of military realities was slight. From this, it developed into a nationalist crusade.

It was a struggle that came to involve every type of conventional and unconventional warfare. The Continental Army and the French represented standard European-type warfare, which the British and Hessians were well-suited to fight. But the scorned they might have been militias, however incompetent in the regular line of battle, became the soul of the partisan and guerrilla campaigns – particularly on the southern front, where, for a time, they operated alone. They also provided effective support in the northern and eastern theaters. The British Army proved as incapable of dealing with all these problems simultaneously as Napoleon's marshals in Spain or Russia, Hitler's armies in Yugoslavia or the USSR,

or, in the 1960s and 1970s, the Americans in Vietnam.

Lastly, the struggle created, for better or for worse, the American military and naval tradition; it reinforced the distrust of standing armies for almost 150 years – but ensured the maintenance of civil supremacy. In the methods by which it came to be fought, it also inspired considerable changes in tactics and strategy (see p114). From 1776 onwards, all armies would employ light infantry units and methods, while many (although not, interestingly enough, Britain) would abandon their reliance on linear tactics.

The use of mercenary troops would lessen (except, again, in the British Army, which, to the present day, employs Gurkhas from Nepal). And gradually all warring nations and armies would become imbued with a sense of strong national spirit and urgency that saw one of its first manifestations in the American Revolution. The reliance on the militias to support and feed recruits to the Continental Army would lead to the concept of conscript armies and the idea of the "nation-in-arms". It became the duty of every adult citizen to answer his country's call, not only with courage but with intelligence and understanding. It is true that the flame flickered from time to time between 1776 and 1783, but the American patriots' concept of fighting a just war in a just cause ultimately triumphed, and implied that an important ideological element would be present in almost all future conflicts.

Most miraculous of all, perhaps, was the way this hard-fought and bitter struggle did not lastingly poison relationships between the former colonies and the mother country. It is true that 1812–15 would see a renewal of the conflict between the two, but the special relationship of today would eventually emerge.

"The first modern war"

The French Revolutionary and Napoleonic Wars (1792–1815) lasted for the greater part of $23\frac{1}{2}$ years – virtually a complete generation –

with only two short interludes of general peace – October 1801 to May 1803 (the Peace of Amiens), and April 1814 to March 1815 (though, in fact, the War of 1812 between Britain and the USA continued throughout this second period). The struggle spread to most parts of the globe, involved seven successive coalitions against France, caused several million casualties and disrupted the lives of many millions more people. Professor A.J.P. Taylor's claim that it constituted "the first modern war" is sustainable as far as the actual conduct of the struggle and the growing scale of national involvement are concerned.

The causes of this vast struggle were complex, but were inevitably bound up with the development of the French Revolution from 1789. This subject is too vast to be treated in detail here; it is sufficient to point out that political, social and economic problems were inextricably involved, and that in three ways the preceding American Revolution played a part. First, some influential soldiers (including both Rochambeau and Lafayette) returned to France imbued with democratic ideas learnt in the former Thirteen Colonies, and swelled the growing ideological and political debate. Second, the cost of the support Louis XVI had provided for the American patriot cause (largely in order to spite Britain, France's oldest and inexorable foe, was a major factor in causing the financial crisis of 1788, which compelled the king to summon the States General the next year. It was this meeting that, in turn, triggered the Revolution. Third, not a few of the military lessons of 1776–1783 would be incorporated in several of the many armies of the period.

Each of the many wars that make up the period had its own particular causes, but all can be said to have sprung directly or indirectly from those of the First Coalition (June 1792–October 1797). There were three deep-seated causes: the links between the French and Austrian thrones, dating from the formal alliance of 1756 and cemented by the marriage to Louis XVI; the Habs-burg princess, Marie Antoinette, the continual Franco-British feud (although this would only lead to war on this occasion in 1793, following the execution of Louis XVI); and the problems associated with an emerging Russia over Poland and declining Ottoman Empire over the Balkans.

Then there were the immediate causes. An early degree of acquiescence over the events in Paris on the grounds that they would plunge France into chaos (and thus remove her influence as a serious European power for years to come) gave way to repugnance over the fate of the Bourbons; then fear of the full implications of the French Revolution quickly became a factor, for the other monarchies of Europe once French republican armies began to advance on the Rhine and into the Low Countries (the safety of the River Scheldt particularly exercising Britain). Although each side misunderstood the other's intentions and capabilities, there were faults on both sides. The French resented the presence of *emigré* armies of French exiles on Austrian territory, while the hysterical atmosphere of the French Assembly and its violent rhetoric was hardly likely to convince Vienna or Berlin that France's intentions were peaceful. The issues that finally led to war being declared on 20 April 1792 by the French Girondin government were Austrian fears for the sanctity of treaties over the future of the small states of Trèves and Trier, and the opportunism of French politicians hoping to use the hostilities for their own ends.

Once the die was cast, there was no turning back, and France was drawn from one war into another in pursuit of what she, and, from late 1799 onwards, Napoleon, considered to be her rightful interests. National feelings reached new peaks. Victories and dictated peace treaties never won more than a brief respite. British hostility, once aroused, was implacable – pursuit of its campaign against France even led to a further war in 1812 with the USA, brought on by problems over the British determination to search neutral shipping for contraband war mater-ials, as well as other issues (including the fate of exiled American loyalists in Canada.

Changes in scale

As a direct result of the French Revolution, the art of war underwent a considerable transformation. The event was the prelude to a period of total war. In marked contrast to the 18th century, whole populations became engaged in struggles for national survival, and entire economies and societies became geared to the maintenance of large armed forces. Thus was born (on a larger scale than had previously been the case in America) the concept of the "nation-in-arms" – first in a France desperately trying to preserve the principles of the Revolution and the sanctity of her boundaries, and then progressively throughout continental Europe, as Napoleon's adversaries adopted his own methods to defeat him. In Portugal and Spain (from 1808), and in Russia (1812), guerrilla and partisan wars strengthened the commitment of the common people to these nationalistic struggles.

As countries mobilized their resources for war, larger armies came into existence. In 1792, faced by a hostile Europe, Revolutionary France mobilized armies totalling over 600,000 men; this astonishing achievement marked the appearance of the first truly citizen-armies of modern times in Europe. However, reliance on volunteers alone could not provide the manpower needed, so the *levée-en-masse* followed as a natural consequence; from 1798, a form of conscription was adopted, whereby all French males between 18 and 45 became liable for service in annual classes. Within a generation Prussia, Austria and, to a lesser extent, Russia, would be driven to adopt similar measures.

The conscript armies

The new type of conscript soldier was noted for his patriotic zeal and higher level of intelligence than his predecessor. A revised tactical system was introduced to make the most of these characteristics – and, at the same time, to allow for the general lack of experience in the conscript ranks. Troops were trained to fight either in skirmishing order, or in columns of attack, as at *Valmy* (1792); the psychological shock effect of the threatened bayonet charge was accorded higher priority than volume of musketry fire. Larger casualties could be accepted because of conscription.

In the French army, new-style divisions became standardized from February 1793 onwards. These consisted of several *demi-brigades* (formerly regiments) of line infantry; another of light infantry; a *demi-brigade* of cavalry; two *compagnies* (or batteries) of cannons; a divisional artillery park and a self-contained divisional staff – this last was a complete novelty. The total strength of such a division was around 8,000 men.

The flexibility of these new major formations was enhanced by a new doctrine of subsistence – living off the land. The idea of leaving the troops to fend for themselves (after central provision of basic rations) became a central feature of the French system of warfare. The reduction in the size of waggon trains this brought about, plus a lessening of the reliance on pre-stocked depôts, gave the French a crucial advantage in mobility over their convoy-bound foes.

The new leadership

Coordination and leadership posed great problems at first, with the flight of many experienced officers abroad. Experiments with election proved unsatisfactory, so gradually the principle that promotion would be based solely on professional competence and political acceptability took root. At a higher level, Lazare Carnot, the so-called "organizer of victory", instituted a rudimentary form of general staff in his *Bureau Topographique* (Map Office), and set up a system of political commissars, who were empowered to enforce the orders of Paris on the armies at the front. The development of an effective signalling system based upon the Chappe visual telegraph further

assisted in the transmission of orders and reports, so helping the efforts on the various war fronts to be coordinated. The degree of centralization still left something to be desired, however, for Carnot at one time had no less than 13 separate armies in existence.

ORGANIZER OF VICTORY *Lazare Carnot tried to bring order and discipline to the armies of the French Revolution, setting up a primitive general staff.*

Nevertheless, the new arrangements encouraged talent to show itself and natural leaders began to emerge, including such commanders as Jean Moreau, Charles Pichegru, Jean-Félix Kléber and Jean-Baptiste Jourdan, all of whom acquired their reputations fighting on the Rhine fronts. Most outstanding of all, however, was destined to be a Corsican captain of artillery, Napoleon Bonaparte, who would acquire his reputation in northern Italy. There also emerged a group of other notable, mostly young, soldiers – André Massena, Louis Davout, Michel Ney, Jean Lannes, and the rest of the quarrelsome, dynamic warriors who would make up the famous 26 marshals of the First Empire. Some were notable men in their own rights, but none equalled "the Little Corporal," as his soldiers dubbed Napoleon.

Napoleon's emergence

Napoleon was an adventurer from first to last, but his martial talents amounted to genius. After unsuccessful adventures in his native

Corsica, he moved to the French mainland, and in 1793 began his dramatic rise to power. In a matter of eight weeks, he rose from the rank of Captain to that of *Général de Brigade* as a result of his achievements at the siege of Toulon. Just three years later, he had won his appointment as army commander in Italy through a combination of military skill and political opportunism. A mere four years on, he was First Consul and *de facto* ruler of France, despite a failed campaign in Syria (where he was badly defeated at the siege of *Acre* (1799), from which he escaped by deserting his men in Egypt.

Memory of this *debacle* was soon overshadowed by his second campaign in northern Italy and the battle of Marengo in 1800, which, together with Moreau's success at Hohenlinden, led to the Peaces of Leoben and Amiens. Years of great constructive work in France followed, and in December 1804 Napoleon, aged 35, crowned himself Emperor of the French. Not since Alexander the Great had a man enjoyed a more meteoric career, destined to last a further 11 years, during which he destroyed one after another three hostile coalitions created by British diplomacy and backed by British gold in such great campaigns and battles as those of *Austerlitz* (1805), *Jena-Auerstadt* (1806), Friedland (1807), and Wagram (1809). By 1810 Napoleon was master of almost all western and central Europe. But flaws were already showing in his imperial edifice.

Decline and fall

Only Britain, secure from invasion behind the English Channel even before Nelson's great confirmatory victory at *Trafalgar* (1805), defied Napoleon's will with isolated impunity. Indeed, the period 1793–1815 was to prove the great age of sail and wooden ships of war.

During this period, the Royal Navy, under such fine commanders as Lords Howe and St. Vincent, and, of course, Horatio Nelson and his "band of brothers," confirmed its overall superiority in battle, blockade and convoy duties. There was one exception to this, however. In the War of 1812, the superior American frigates proved doughty adversaries in the Atlantic, while Lieutenant Thomas Macdonough's fine conduct of the decisive naval battle of *Lake Champlain* (1814) further demonstrated American naval capabilities.

When Napoleon turned to an economic blockade to break British trading prosperity, he was lured into the Iberian peninsula – a step that eventually allowed the British Army under Sir John Moore and then Sir Arthur Wellesley (later the Duke of Wellington) to intervene first in Portugal and then in Spain. This ability was in large measure due to the backing and support of the Royal Navy, exercising its hard-won "command of the seas." As at Toulon and Acre, Napoleon had good reason to rue Britain's mastery of the waves.

From 1809, or possibly even earlier, French fortunes began to change. The task of holding down the vast territories France had conquered proved to be such that greater reliance had to be placed on troops from Italy, Holland and Westphalia, while Napoleon's invasion of Russia in 1812 placed still more strain on the imperial military machine. An inconclusive battle at *Borodino* and the resultant capture of Moscow led only to a disastrous winter retreat – the entire campaign cost Napoleon 500,000 men. Spurred on by this disaster – and British success in Spain – Napoleon's reluctant allies, Prussia and Austria, deserted him; the 1813 campaign he fought to defend his position in Germany cost him half a million more.

In 1814, after a virtuoso performance at the head of a small army against vastly-superior foes, the mutiny of his Marshals at Fontainebleau forced Napoleon to abdicate. After a spell in exile on Elba, he escaped back to France in March 1815, only to meet decisive defeat at *Waterloo*, followed by a second abdication and exile – this time on the lonely South Atlantic island of St.Helena, where he died in 1821.

Napoleon as general

Napoleon was no great innovator as a soldier; his genius was practical rather than theoretical. As has been well said, "he added nothing to the armies of France – save victory." He found a weapon largely ready to his hand in the French army he inherited from the Revolution as described above, although it should be noted that he also owed a debt to reformers who had been active in the years immediately before 1789, making good the damage sustained by French arms and martial reputation during the Seven Years War.

During this period, De Gribeauval had transformed the artillery arm, for example, by lightening the cannon, organizing regular batteries, and standardising the field pieces into four calibres. Guibert had produced a philosophy of total war, and at the tactical level had helped the evolution of the *ordre mixte* formation of infantry drawn up in column and line in mutual support. Marshal de Broglie had conducted experiments, based on de Saxe's earlier concepts, with mixed divisions. On to this generally battleworthy army, Napoleon imposed further improvements, but he owed much to his predecessors.

Napoleon's specific achievements were several. First, he greatly developed the staff organization at army, corps and divisional levels, achieving a proper chain of command and facilitating a high degree of coordination on campaign and battlefield alike. Next, at the level of army organization, he perfected the adoption of the *corps d'armée* as the standard major formation. The subdivision of his army into these large self-contained formations meant that it could move in a number of

IMPERIAL EAGLES *Napoleon distributes eagle standards to his army on the Champs de Mars in December 1804. These veteran soldiers were to march in triumph into every major European capital, bar London.*

widely-spread columns, rather than in a single dense mass, yet concentrate quickly for battle. This facilitated living off the country and spread the load over the available roads. Each corps was a miniature army in itself, with its own infantry and cavalry divisions, guns, supply trains and headquarters, and could fight several times its own number for a limited period, if necessary, pending rapid reinforcement. What this system could achieve was convincingly demonstrated in the manoeuvres leading up to Ulm in 1805, and in the movement of the *bataillon carrée* before *Jena-Auerstädt* the next year. In the former case, 210,000 men in eight columns swept from the Rhine to the Danube in a matter of 11 days.

The flexible French army corps can thus be considered the secret weapon of these wars. Not since the Roman legion or the Mongol *touman* had there been as effective a major formation, and not until the German Panzer divisions of the Second World War would Europe see another to compare with it. Small wonder that by 1812 all major powers, save Britain alone, had adopted similar organizations.

Napoleon also expanded the practice of massing much of his heavy cavalry and many of his guns into army reserves, to be retained for use at the critical moment in a campaign or battle. As might be expected as a trained gunner himself, he continued the work of reforming the artillery arm as a whole. As First Consul, he effectively militarized artillery drivers, deploying them in battalions. As the wars progressed, Napoleon steadily increased the proportion of guns to men, until they had reached four to five for every thousand troops. He also created a *corps d'elite* in the form of the Imperial Guard, which grew from the size of a small division in 1806 to a veritable army of 112,000 by 1812.

Napoleon's art and science of war

As a grand strategist, Napoleon's preference for short, sharp wars led to a long series of crushing victories, between 1805 and 1809, but no lasting peaces. As already mentioned, the development of long wars of attrition in Spain – the notorious "Spanish ulcer" – and Russia in pursuit of his Continental System led to catastrophe, and doomed both Napoleon and his empire to defeat. As a strategist, however, Napoleon had no peer. Setting himself to make the most of the superior mobility and enthusiasm of his armies, he devised, and time and again employed in varying form, two main strategic systems, which were designed to exploit numerical superiority or allow for numerical inferiority on campaign. His whole aim was to achieve superiority on a decisive battlefield, where the grand (or operational) tactics Napoleon often employed closely reflected his favorite strategic system of envelopment. Indeed, his greatest contribution to the art of war lay in his fusion of fast marching, hard fighting and then relentless pursuit into one continuous and remorseless process.

Success in action, as on campaign, depended in large measure on securing and retaining the initiative, and on launching properly coordinated all-arms attacks. The French tactical sequence frequently followed this set order to achieve this result. After a heavy bombardment, the light infantry would advance to skirmish and reconnoiter. Cavalry attacks would then often be launched both to defeat the enemy's horsemen and pin down his infantry in formed squares – ideal targets for the horse artillery batteries that accompanied the cuirassiers. Infantry columns would hasten forward to deploy into line for fire action, or, if circumstances were favorable, to charge home with the bayonet to achieve a breakthrough, which would at once be exploited by the waiting regiments of dragoons and light cavalry – hussars, horse-chasseurs and (from 1810) lancers. Only when all these methods became stereotyped and predictable did French failures begin to mount.

Perhaps the most important secret of all was Napoleon's mastery of man-management. Time and again, he showed himself capable of inspiring officers and men alike to heroic and sustained efforts. He believed in seeing and being seen, holding ceaseless reviews of the army, visiting units day after day, and sleeping in their midst on the eve of battle. He was quick to reward, creating in the *légion d'honneur* the first mass honors system, awarding princedoms, dukedoms and even crowns to his senior subordinates. He was equally quick to criticise shortcomings, and his furious reprimands were greatly feared. Not without cause did Wellington once remark, "I used to say of him that his presence on the field of battle was worth 40,000 men." Quite simply, he was a military genius, and even his eventual failure was that of a titan surrounded by pygmies.

Napoleon's opponents

Over the years, several worthy opponents appeared, including the Archduke Charles of Austria, Baron Barclay de Tolly and Prince Kutusov of Tsarist Russia, and the great Prussian organizer, von Scharnhorst. These commanders copied French organization and method in the years after the Peace of Tilsit in 1807, and eventually made their armies more battleworthy as a result. One of France's enemies, however, proved resistant to change, though, paradoxically, she eventually emerged as the most successful of all. This was Britain.

The British Army seemed to have learnt little from its North American experiences, except the need for light infantry, and doggedly clung on to Frederickian concepts of linear tactics, though reducing the battalion battle-line to a depth of only two ranks. The musket was still the "Brown Bess," supplemented by the Baker rifle carried by some of the light infantry – a force which was greatly developed from the late 1790s by Sir John Moore and other enlightened commanders at Shorncliffe Camp in Kent. The 9-pounder was the standard field gun, the 6-pounder for horse artillery; here the employment of Lieutenant Shrapnel's invention of the exploding shell packed with musket walls was a significant development.

Wellington as commander

What the British did produce was a commander of considerable brilliance – the Duke of Wellington. He had four great strengths as a commander-in-chief. Firstly, he refused to be psychologically dominated by the French systems or reputation, and soon saw ways of countering them. Secondly, he realized that his main role in Spain was to assist the Portuguese partisans and the Spanish guerrillas by mounting diversionary attacks to draw off the vastly superior French forces (there being over 320,000 imperial troops in the peninsula until 1812). This left the

guerrillas free to operate, while carefully preserving Wellington's own Anglo-Portuguese Army, which rarely numbered more than 46,000 men before 1812. He enhanced the security of his base at Lisbon by building in 1809–10 the famous 29-mile broad triple Lines of Torres Vedras with the help of Royal Engineer officers aided by 10,000 Portuguese peasants – one of the best kept secrets in military history. Thirdly, he appreciated that the great French weakness amidst the largely barren plains and mountains of Spain and Portugal was in finding sufficient food to feed its men.

In 1810, having taken great pains to build up a sound logistical system of his own workable – based upon

his hard-learnt experiences in India (where he had won the celebrated battle of *Assaye* in 1803), Wellington deliberately lured Massena's army by way of *Bussaco* towards the hidden and impregnable lines north of Lisbon, before which lay a belt of "scorched earth" – countryside completely cleared of crops, cattle and peasantry. The same scorched-earth policy was operated against the French with even greater effect during the invasion of Russia (1812). Massena was so daunted by the appearance of the outer line of detached forts commanding the hills that he never dared to launch a serious attack and his army was eventually starved into retreat. Fourthly, Wellington developed

RUSSIAN RESISTANCE *The Russian generals Bagration (above) and Kutusov (below) led the Russians against the French invaders in 1812. Bagration fell in action at Borodino.*

NAPOLEON'S NEMESIS *As Napoleon's enemies finally became accustomed to his methods, his campaign became more costly and failures more frequent. The 1812 disaster in Russia was the turning point in his fortunes, but the rot had already set in with the Peninsula War in Spain, in which Wellington (above) was to defeat the best of Napoleon's marshals. The two men confronted each other for the first time at Waterloo in 1815; it was Napoleon's defeat here that was to lead to his final exile to St Helena (left).*

great skill in minor tactics. On many occasions, he chose to fight tactically on the defensive. He would habitually choose positions with secure flanks and affording as much cover as possible; the troops, drawn up out of sight on the reverse (or rearward) slopes, missed much of the effect of the French cannonades, only the British guns being in action along the crests with the light infantry pushed forward to contest every yard of no-man's-land against the advancing French. This often confused the foe as to Wellington's exact positions: when the French columns stumbled to the crest, they found themselves facing a blast of well-directed volleys, followed by the feared British cheer and a bayonet charge. Many Peninsula battles were decided at the tactical level – and so, too, was the great battle of Waterloo in 1815.

Waterloo - the end of an era

The events of 18 June 1815 – the great, first and final confrontation between Napoleon and Wellington, respectively the great masters of strategy and tactics in their day, was a fitting climax to this long period of multifaceted conflict. Perhaps of the greatest significance for the future was the growth of widespread guerrilla warfare in Spain and partisan warfare in Russia. In Spain, the French lost an average of 100 men a day over seven years, half their casualties being lost to the guerrillas, and a quarter each to Wellington's battles and disease. Here was a foretaste of things to come, of irregular methods which would still be posing a challenge to accepted rules of conventional warfare 150 years later. The lessons of the Napoleonic Wars were carefully analyzed by the Swiss soldier and historian, Baron Jomini, sometime Chief of Staff to Marshal Ney, and above all by the Prussian Colonel Carl von Clausewitz in his famous work *Am kreig* ("On War"), a book destined to lay down the parameters of serious warfare for the next century and is still of relevance today. The age had proved itself to be a time of military giants.

"UP GUARDS AND AT 'EM!" *The flank company of the Coldstream Guards holds out against French attack at the strong-point of Hougoumont on the west of the Allied line at Waterloo in 1815. Napoleon had intended this attack only as a diversion to conceal his real intentions–a mass onslaught on the Allied center–from Wellington, but the British commander was not to be fooled. Relying on the Guards to hold their ground, he sent only minimal reinforcements to their aid, while, during the course of the day, almost an entire French army corps was dragged into this secondary action by Napoleon's subordinates.*

Napoleonic Warfare

Napoleon's influence on the conduct of land warfare in this period was dramatic. Distrusting positional warfare based upon sieges after his experiences in besieging Mantua (1796) and *Acre* (1799), he consistently sought a decisive battle in order to break his opponent's political will, and so induce him to agree to a profitable peace that suited France. Above all, Napoleon's methods fused marching, fighting and pursuit into a single remorseless process. The all-arm *corps d'armée* — in effect, miniature armies capable of marching and indeed fighting alone against superior numbers for up to 24 hours if need be — was the ideal instrument for this direct and brutal strategy. Though the *corps* was not Napoleon's invention, as in so many other ways he exploited other men's ideas to the limit and even beyond it; through his sheer audacity and opportunism, he achieved brilliant successes. As the Abbe Siéyès acutely remarked: "He knows everything; he understands everything; he can do anything." Many of his ideas were borrowed from his wide-reading of military history and earlier experts, while both the old Bourbon army and that of the Revolution had included many of the novel features that he later incorporated into his *Grande Armée*.

Grand strategy apart (both the Spanish and Russian invasions were grave mistakes, as was the economic blockade of Britain from 1806 with the establishment of the so-called "Continental System"), matters generally went Napoleon's way until at least 1812, although there was something of a falling-off in the effectiveness of his methods from late 1806 onwards. In the end, however, he became unoriginal and hence predictable, while his foes learnt how to devise counter-measures to deal with his newly-understood approach

to war. "I have fought 60 battles and I have learnt nothing I did not know at the beginning," was Napoleon's own boast, but, on analysis, this can be shown to be a damningly revealing statement. When it came, his fall was colossal and deserved – but so, too, was his genius. There is no doubt that Napoleon left an indelible imprint on the conduct of war that had lasted to the present day – and will almost certainly continue to do so.

The central position
Napoleon used adaptations of two main general strategic systems, and, though every time their detailed execution differed, the underlying principles were one of the two. If the French were faced by superior foes, Napoleon sought to divide them, and then defeat each section in detail in turn, relying on local, rather than total, superiority.

Using his questing light cavalry and other sources of intelligence to learn the approximate locations of his enemy's main formations, Napoleon would strain every nerve to interpose his army between them. Then, leaving one or two corps to keep half the enemy at bay for up to a day – fighting a spoiling battle against seemingly overwhelming odds, which only the all-round flexibility of the *corps d'armée* system made possible – Napoleon would mass the remainder of his army in superior strength against the second opponent, and hopefully defeat him heavily on the main battlefield. Having forced the enemy body into retreat, the emperor would detach his light cavalry and one or two corps and send them in pursuit of the beaten adversary, while force-marching the remainder towards the flank and rear of the secondary opponent, who would then be defeated in his turn – this time decisively.

The strategy of envelopment
From Napoleon's point of view, the central position manoeuvre had one serious drawback in that it left one part of the enemy force still capable of offering further resistance, so robbing him of the complete victory he always set out to obtain. When conditions made it operable his favored strategy was, therefore, envelopment. This manoeuvre pre-supposed an overall French superiority of strength.

Using a part of his army to distract the enemy's attention in an irrelevant direction – by launching a secondary offensive, or possibly feigning a retreat – Napoleon would launch the remainder in a forced flank march, his aim being to swing round to threaten the enemy's flank and rear, while, at the same time, cutting all his foe's lines of communication. Then, selecting his battleground with care, Napoleon would fight a "reversed front battle" – in other words, each

CONSERVATIVE *Surprisingly, Napoleon did not make the most of technological innovation, disbanding the balloon corps.*

opponent would be facing towards his own base – on greatly superior numerical terms. If defeated, the enemy had nowhere to go: the victorious main French army was between him and his bases, whilst the original French pinning attack would now be advancing to close the trap. The result would be, at least in theory, the annihilation of the enemy army; its stark choice would be to surrender or die.

But there were counter-measures available, as the allies eventually learned. To frustrate the central position strategy the answer was for the armies under attack to keep in contact – even in defeat – as at *Waterloo* on 16 and 17 June 1815. To defeat the "manoeuvre of envelopment", the secret was to ignore Napoleon's arrival behind the army, but to press ahead deep into French territory, ignoring Napoleon's posturing in the rear. This required sufficient reserves, supplies and munitions to be in hand, but the idea worked to perfection in April 1814 when the allies pressed on Paris while a mutiny by his marshals forced Napoleon to abdicate at Fontainebleau.

The Napoleonic battle system

Everything in Napoleonic warfare was designed with one goal in mind – a decisive battle fought at the right moment at the correct place under the most favorable conditions. His favorite battle (or grand tactical) system grew out of his strategic systems. Using part of his army to pin the enemy army to a known location, Napoleon would order up some nearby corps to escalate

AUSTERLITZ *In this battle, Napoleon demonstrated his tactical mastery to the full. Having lured his enemies into stripping their centre to launch a massive out-flanking attack to the south, he ordered a sudden surprise attack to storm the key central heights. Its success meant that the French were now able to envelop either enemy wing–Napoleon chose to smash the Austro-Russian left, trapping Buxhowden's troops and attacking them on three sides.*

Napoleon would order up some nearby corps to escalate the battle, while sending another part of his force on a distant, concealed enveloping march to threaten the foe's line of communications, or line of retreat. Meanwhile the French reserve would mass unseen behind the sector of battlefront nearest the enemy flank about to be threatened.

When he was convinced that all enemy reserves had been drawn into the frontal battle, Napoleon would signal his outflanking force (by pre-arranged distinctive cannon-volleys) to reveal its presence and attack. As the foe desperately switched troops from his front to his flank to meet this new threat, Napoleon would unleash his pre-positioned reserve in the decisive break-through attack – and the battle would be won. Only rarely did conditions permit this system to be employed – at both Castiglione (1796) and Bautzen (1813) it was imperfectly implemented and only at *Austerlitz* was it fully effected (and then in an adjusted format). But Napoleon clearly preferred this method to frontal battles, such as *Borodino* in 1812 or Leipzig (1813).

ACRE
THE FRENCH REVOLUTIONARY WARS
18 March – 20 May 1799

Defended by Djezzar Pasha (5,000 men, 250 guns – aided by Royal Naval landing parties and shipping) against Bonaparte's Army of the Orient (13,000 men, 60 guns), Acre was the turning-point of the French campaign in the Middle East. The failure of the siege marked Bonaparte's first significant set-back in a major operation of war, and the successful resistance of the city, the key to Palestine, thwarted Napoleon's plans.

Following his successful invasion of Egypt in 1798, Napoleon and his army were trapped there after Nelson's destruction of his fleet at the battle of the Nile. This British success hastened the formation of the Second Coalition against France; of more immediate importance for Napoleon, it also induced the Sultan of Turkey to take action to recover his lost province. To forestall the arrival of the Turkish Army of Damascus (35,000 men), Bonaparte decided to strike into Palestine and Syria, and, accordingly, leaving 10,000 men to garrison Egypt, he advanced into the Sinai desert on 6 February 1799. After delays before the fort at El Arish and at Jaffa (where his army massacred captured Mamelukes and Bonaparte made his famous visit to the Pestiferies or plague-hospital), his army arrived before Acre on 18 March.

The Royal Navy to the rescue
Acre stands on a peninsula jutting into the Mediterranean. In 1799 its defences were ancient, but

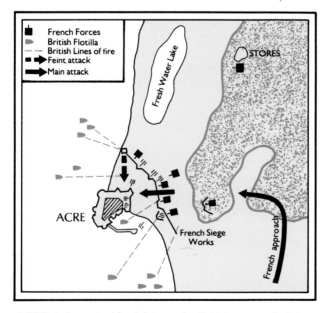

ACRE *A determined land defence plus British command of the sea led to the failure of the French siege of this key port.*

massive, while in its defender, Djezzar Pasha – popularly known for good reason as "the Butcher" – the French faced a determined opponent. Bonaparte was aware that a Turkish army was forming in Galilee, and so he immediately detached troops under Generals Junot and Kléber to cover the impending siege operations.

From the start, the French were laboring under serious disadvantages. First, plague was rife among their ranks. Second, their lack of sea-power as a result of the Nile was now wreaking havoc on their coastal communications, especially when faced with the prompt response of the Royal Navy. Commodore Sir William Sidney Smith, with two warships – the *Theseus* and the *Tigre* – appeared off Acre on 15 March, having captured intact a flotilla of small French craft carrying munitions and half Napoleon's siege guns. The guns and munitions were put ashore, and a strong party of sailors and marines was also landed to strengthen the town's defences. Amongst these was a French *émigré* engineer officer, Colonel Phélippeaux, a one-time classmate (and personal foe) of Bonaparte at the School of Brienne.

A hard-fought siege
Without heavy guns, the siege was slow to make any progress. The need to send a force to defeat the Army of Damascus at the battle of Mount Tabor (16 April) was a major distraction, while all the time the sick list was growing. A battery of Sydney Smith's guns sited on the lighthouse mole enfiladed the French trenches, while the *Theseus* and the *Tigre* stood close inshore to add the weight of their broadsides to the bombardment. Supplies, of course, continued to reach Acre by sea.

In growing desperation, Bonaparte resorted to eight costly – and unsuccessful – storming attempts from 28 March onwards. On 1 April the explosion of a large mine beneath the "Tower of the Damned" failed to create the hoped-for breach, merely cracking the masonry. Djezzar Pasha sat in state, paying gold for every infidel head brought to him, while Bonaparte had to pay for recovered cannon-balls.

When the remainder of his siege train arrived overland, it was too late, and, on 10 May, after another failed attack, Bonaparte decided to retreat. Ten days later the French burned their camp, and set off on the long march back to Egypt. With them went 2,300 sick and wounded; a further 2,000 lay dead behind them.

ASSAYE
THE SECOND MAHARTTA WAR (BRITISH CONQUEST OF INDIA)
23 September 1803

Major-General Arthur Wellesley (13,500 troops and 22 guns) decisively defeated the Princes of Scind and Berar (95,000 troops and 98 guns) on the banks of the River Kaitna (or Kelna) in central India. This success,

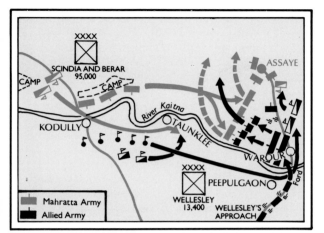

ASSAYE *Wellington's oblique attack on the Indian position was modeled on the tactics of Frederick the Great.*

together with that of Argaum later in the year, extended British control over large areas of the Nizam of Hyderabad's possessions, although the war continued until 1805.

Robert Clive's victory at Plassey in 1757 over Siraj-ud-Daula gave the British East India Company control of Bengal, and, despite considerable local opposition (often backed by French money and men), the company's rule rapidly spread over further large areas of the sub-continent. In 1803, the Governor-General, Lord Mornington, ordered General Lake to march into northern India with one Company army, while he entrusted his younger brother, the 34-year-old Arthur Wellesley (the future Duke of Wellington) with a second force to operate against the powerful Mahratta Confederacy and its allies.

A battle against long odds

Wellesley found his opponents elusive; it was only after six weeks of marching that his force of European soldiers and Indian sepoys caught up with the Princes of Scindia and Berar near Assaye, when he found them occupying a seven-mile long position behind the River Kaitna. Their army was dauntingly strong in terms of size. Besides 20,000 Mahratta cavalry – renowned for their hard-fighting qualities – there were as many infantry and perhaps 55,000 irregular soldiers, plus numberless servants.

Realizing that a frontal attack against an army of this size holding so large a position was out of the question, Wellesley decided to mount an oblique attack in the style of Frederick the Great. To draw the enemy's attention, he sent the British and sepoy cavalry under Colonel Maxwell on to the plain south-west of Assaye, while he himself advanced with his British infantry from the village of Paugy on the River Pirna to seize a ford opposite Waroor, one and a half miles to the south-east. Maxwell was under orders to return to the main body with his cavalry once this manoeuvre was completed. Then the British line would

swing westwards to attack the extreme left of the enemy position, securing its own flanks on the banks of the Kaitna and the Juah beyond.

A ferocious assault

Maxwell successfully drove off a Mahratta attack on the far left, but the enemy realized what Wellesley's plan was faster than he had intended. Aided by a German mercenary, Pohlmann, the princes redeployed many of their guns to face the developing threat to their left flank, while regiments of regular Scind infantry moved up in their support. British and sepoy casualties rapidly mounted, but Wellesley pressed on to storm the low heights and silence the guns placed there. However, Assaye itself proved too strong to take, while suddenly a swarm of Mahratta horsemen swept past the town to attack the British right wing. The situation might have been a serious one, but, fortunately, Maxwell was at hand to repulse the fierce horsemen. The respite allowed Wellesley to attack the Scind infantry, who soon fled in their turn.

His right flank secured, Wellesley, relying on Maxwell to guard his open flank, now wheeled his troops northward in a tight arc to fall upon the masses of the princes' army, who now were formed with their backs to the Juah. The flank fighting intensified as a hot afternoon drew to its close, but the enemy eventually broke and fled for the river hotly pursued by Maxwell, who was killed. At 6 pm the princes abandoned the field to the exhausted Wellesley and his men. This had proved one of his toughest battles, and ably demonstrated his offensive skills.

AUSTERLITZ
THE NAPOLEONIC WARS
2 December 1805

The so-called "battle of the three emperors" took place east of Brunn in Bohemia (today Czechoslovakia). The Emperor Napoleon's *Grande Armée* (73,200 men and 139 guns) decisively defeated General Kutusov's Russo-Austrian Army (85,400 men and 278 guns), which was accompanied by Tsar Alexander I and the Emperor Francis I of Austria. The battle destroyed the Third Coalition. It is widely regarded as Napoleon's tactical masterpiece, and he himself is known to have thought highly of his own performance – so much so that he refused to award the title of Duke of Austerlitz to Marshal Soult. Its fame was to be his alone.

By late November 1805 the *Grande Armée* was in a dangerous situation. After Napoleon's dramatic sweep from the Rhine to the Danube in August and September, the almost bloodless success over General Mack's Austrian Army at Ulm on 20 October, and the subsequent occupation of Vienna, his position had

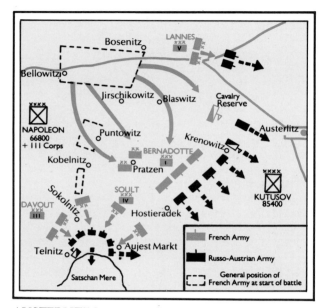

AUSTERLITZ *By stripping their center to attack the French right, the Allies were open to counter-stroke.*

seemed assured. However, the wily General Kutusov, avoided being trapped south of the Danube and skilfully retired north towards Olmutz with the remnants of the Austrian Army. There, he linked up with a second Russian force commanded by General Buxhowden, bringing the combined Russo-Austrian strength to over 85,000 men. The French main body was in hot pursuit, but, owing to necessary detachments, Napoleon had only about 53,000 men under his immediate command by late November.

Napoleon was aware that he could advance no further than Brunn, and that he could hardly force a major battle against such unfavorable odds, as even a minor reverse could rapidly become a disaster so far from his center of operations at Vienna, 70 miles away – especially as there were strong signs that Prussia was about to enter the war against him. However, it was essential for him to fight a decisive battle before his position in Moravia became untenable, for any retreat would be considered a strategic defeat. His reputation – and that of the French army – was at stake.

Coping with the crisis

Napoleon was never better than when facing a crisis, and set about turning his numerical and strategic weakness to his advantage. First, he lured his foes forward from Olmutz by feigning a panicked withdrawal by his outposts from the vicinity of Austerlitz, and also by indicating that he was ready to negotiate. Scenting victory, the Russo-Austrian army advanced south-west towards Brunn – and were allowed to occupy the key terrain of the Pratzen Heights unopposed on 1 December. Parleys continued as Napoleon continued to feign weakness. Both armies camped for the night, facing each other over the Bosenitz and Goldbach streams. Around the campfires, only the bravest slept.

Some days earlier Napoleon had sent urgent orders of recall to Bernadotte's I Corps at Iglau to the west, and to Davout's III Corps at Vienna to the south. The former rejoined the *Grande Armée* on 1 December, raising its strength to 66,800. Davout's leading division – by dint of herculean marching – covered 60 miles in under 72 hours, and its 6,600 men and corps cavalry were near the main army by the following night.

Trusting that the arrival of these reinforcements had been hidden from the allies by the French cavalry screen – as indeed was the case – Napoleon, having gained the opportunity he sought – now proceeded to induce his still superior and over-confident foes to attack him where he wanted them to. To achieve this, he deliberately massed most of his army on his left, where Lannes' V Corps occupied a small, but steep, feature called the Santon, with Bernadotte concealed behind it, and on his center. This was placed on and around the Zurlan feature overlooking the Bosenitz stream; the troops involved included Oudinot's division of grenadiers, Murat's cavalry, and Generals Vandamme and St.Hilaire at the head of their divisions of Soult's IV Corps. His right wing – holding a very extended position along the Goldbach from Puntowitz to Telnitz – was entrusted to Soult's third division under General Legrand. This was the tempting bait Napoleon dangled before his adversaries, who had no knowledge of Davout's concealed approach to reinforce this wing from the south.

The chilly night passed slowly for Napoleon, but his men formed a torch-light procession in his honor to mark the first anniversary of his coronation. Over on the Pratzen, the allies held a long conference to decide their plan of attack. While Kutusov unashamedly slept through the proceedings, it was decided to make a major attack with 45,000 men under Buxhowden's command against the weak French right wing to cut off their line of retreat to Vienna, using all the allied troops of the right wing and most of those of the center for the purpose; on the northern side of the battlefield, Bagration was to attack the Santon with 13,000 men. The enemy had thus obligingly taken Napoleon's bait: not only would they find the French right stronger than they expected, but they had also stripped their center – and it was towards the Pratzen Heights that Napoleon intended to launch his major counter-stroke.

Battle in the mist

Dawn on 2 December was cold, with dense fog cloaking the valleys. At 4 am the Russians were on the march, but the mist threw their columns into some confusion as they headed towards Sokolnitz village to carry out their great enveloping move. Soon a fierce, if muddled, fight was raging around the houses, and eventually both Sokolnitz and Telnitz fell into allied hands. Then, at 8 am, Davout's footsore, but determined, brigades counter-attacked, and a surprised Buxhowden reacted by summoning yet more troops from the Pratzen.

Warning Oudinot's grenadiers to prepare to support the right wing, Napoleon carefully scrutinised what he could see from his post on the Zurlan above the mist. On the left, fierce fighting was taking place around the Santon, where Lannes was holding his own aided by Bernadotte; on his right Murat's squadrons were about to clash with – and ultimately defeat – Lichtenstein's horsemen in a massive engagement involving 10,000 cavalry. Below the Zurlan, completely concealed in the fog, Soult's two divisions strained at the leash. Turning to their commander at his side, Napoleon asked: "How long will it take you to storm the Heights?" "Twenty minutes, Sire," replied Soult. "Very well then, we will wait another quarter of an hour." Timing was of the essence – Napoleon wanted to give the allies all the time they needed to remove their troops from the Pratzen, but he could not delay too long in case his valiant, but still massively-outnumbered, right wing should succumb to the allied pressure. As a precaution, Oudinot was now sent to Davout's and St. Hilaire's aid.

The sun of Austerlitz

AT 9 am Napoleon gave the signal. Muffled drums beat, and rising out of the thinning fog – the newly-revealed sun glinting on their myriad bayonets – Vandamme's and St. Hilaire's divisions emerged. Now Kutusov finally realized what was happening, and tried to recall troops from his left, but it was all too late. Napoleon countered by calling in Bernadotte to Soult's support, and, after some heavy fighting, the French were firmly ensconced on the Pratzen by midday, repulsing Kutusov's counter-attacks from 10.30 am onwards. The last such counter-attack came at 1 pm when the 10,000 men of the élite Russian Guard Corps attacked from the east, but, coming up hill, were taken at a disadvantage after initial success by a counter-attack by Bessières and Rapp at the head of the cavalry of the French Imperial Guard, and by one of Bernadotte's divisions. Defeated, the mitre-hatted guardsmen retired, and Napoleon was indeed master of the Pratzen, and of the battlefield.

It only remained to turn victory into triumph. Moving the Imperial Guard and the rest of Bernadotte's corps on to the Pratzen, Napoleon swung Soult's men south to the edge of the heights, brought up cannon, and from 3.30 pm, began to pulverize the ice of the frozen meres to its south, around and over which Buxhowen's troops were trying to escape. Some were drowned, while many more panicked. The Allied monarchs quit the field, and Bagration retreated from the Santon.

A great victory had been won. For the loss of over 8,000 killed, wounded or missing, the French had inflicted 27,000 casualties on the allied armies (including 11,000 prisoners) and captured 180 cannon and 45 regimental colors. Next day, as the Russians marched hard for Poland, Francis I met Napoleon and sued for an armistice. A dictated peace on French terms followed in late December.

BORODINO
THE NAPOLEONIC WARS
7 September 1812

Napoleon, commanding the multi-national *Grande Armée de Russie* (130,000 men and 587 guns), indecisively defeated the Russian army commanded by Field-Marshal Golenichev-Kutusov (120,000 men and 640 guns), 70 miles west of Moscow. The battle cost the French 30,000 casualties, and the Russians 44,000. Napoleon duly occupied Moscow on 14 September, but a month later he began a forced retreat to Poland.

The French invasion of Russia began on 24 June 1812, when the Central Army Group (three armies under Napoleon, Prince Eugène, and King Jérôme respectively) crossed the River Niemen. Some 449,000 men and 1,000 guns made up the first wave, including a detached corps on each flank; these were supported by a further 165,000 reserves. Successive attempts to trap the two outnumbered Russian armies of Barclay de Tolly and Prince Bagration into separate decisive battles failed one after another, and the French were drawn ever deeper into Russia. The two Russian forces joined at Smolensk on 4 August, but, after a two-day major battle (17/18 August) they were able to resume their retreat. Only when Tsar Alexander I sent Kutusov to take command (29 August) did the Russians decide to make a real stand at a position selected around Borodino on 5 September.

The build-up to battle

Kutusov used the 5 and 6 September to prepare his battle position. His right wing (under Barclay) was

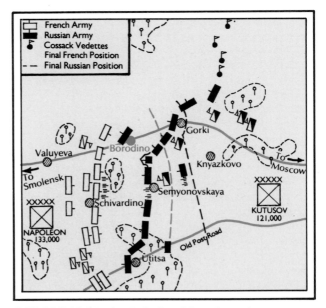

BORODINO *Napoleon's flank and frontal assaults met fierce Russian resistance and the battle became a slogging match.*

behind the River Kalatsha, its left hinging on Borodino village through which ran the old Smolensk road. The center was anchored by the *Raevski* (Great) Redoubt (holding 18 guns), and then stretched south past the three redoubts (or *flèches*) of Semonovskoi with ravines and a stream to the fore. This, with the left wing (partly shielded by woods and the town of Utitsa and its knoll, past which ran the new Smolensk road) was commanded by Bagration. The Russian headquarters was at Gorki.

Napoleon placed himself 1½ miles west in the Schivardino Redoubt, which he captured on 5 August. He rejected Marshal Davout's suggested southerly outflanking manoeuvre, preferring instead to launch a frontal assault on the Russian right and center, while Prince Poniatowski attempted an outflanking move around Utitsa, Eugène was to storm Borodino and the Raevski Redoubt, while Davout and Ney assaulted Semonovskoi. Junot, Murat's cavalry, and the Imperial Guard were held in reserve. 120 guns gave these forces massed support.

"Bravo Messieurs! C'est superbe!"

At 6 am on 7 August the battle proper opened, the delay being caused by the need to resite the guns. Ney and Davout began their attacks over broken ground in fine form, gaining even Bagration's admiration. Progress was slow and costly, so at 8 am Napoleon sent Junot's corps to extend the battle to the right. Poniatowski moved on Utitsa, but Bagration prevented any break-through, aided by strong troop transfers from the Russian right as ordered by Kutusov.

Eugene's attacks eventually took Borodino, but, despite reinforcement, he failed against the Raevski Redoubt. A lull in the center permitted more Russians to move from right to center; Bagration, however, now fell mortally wounded, and Utitsa fell to the south – but still the Russian line held firm. Some cavalry and cossacks outflanked Borodino, and had to be driven off, delaying the main attack on the Raevski Redoubt.

A large cavalry attack by Murat in the center was bravely met and repulsed, as was Eugène's first major onslaught against the smoke-ringed Redoubt – the key to the battlefield. Only at 3 pm did Eugène's second onslaught make ground, when a cuirassier division at last broke into the position's rear. A huge cavalry battle ensued, the French holding their gains. Grudgingly the Russian line gave ground, but only to the next ridge.

Napoleon refused repeated entreaties to send in the Imperial Guard, and the battle petered out indecisively. The worst single-day's fighting in all history was over. Both armies were exhausted. Overnight Kutusov retired from the field.

A week later Napoleon occupied a deserted Moscow, but on 15 September a great fire destroyed most of the city. Hoping that the Tsar would sue for peace, Napoleon lingered in Moscow for a month, but on 19 October he left the Kremlin. The onset of the Russian winter – not for nothing did the Russians

count "General Winter" as one of their key generals – the threat posed by the converging Russian armies and ruthless partisan activity virtually destroyed the *Grande Armée*; at the end of December, only 94,000 French survivors managed to limp back into Poland. Napoleon's reputation was shattered – but two more year's hard fighting lay ahead before France was finally defeated at *Waterloo* and its emperor at last securely exiled on the South Atlantic island of St. Helena.

BRANDYWINE
THE AMERICAN WAR OF INDEPENDENCE
11 September 1777

General William Howe (15,000 men) outmanoeuvred and defeated General George Washington (11,000 men) at the Brandywine River, near West Chester in Pennsylvania. This setback threatened the security of Philadelphia, the American capital, and almost led to Washington's downfall as commander-in-chief of the Continental army.

On 14 June 1775, the Second Continental Congress had appointed George Washington commander-in-chief of the forces available to defend the interests of the thirteen colonies. His scratch army suffered many reverses at the hands of British and Hessian regulars in 1775 and 1776, but Washington's successes at Trenton

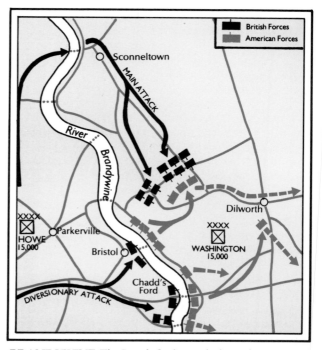

BRANDYWINE *The British flank attack threw the Continentals into confusion, paving the way for the main thrust.*

(26 December 1776) and Princeton (2 January 1777) served to rally American morale.

The British high command thereupon implemented an ambitious strategy, based upon three major complementary offensives. General John Burgoyne was to strike southwards from Canada with 10,500 troops against Ticonderoga and then march towards Albany; General St. Leger, with a small force of 2,000 men, was to advance west from Oswego on Lake Ontario to threaten Albany up the Mohawk River; General Howe, with 18,000 men, was to strike north from New York. The aim was to unite all forces at Albany, and thus win control of the River Hudson, so isolating New England, the heart of the American resistance. This, the British hoped, would lead to the collapse of the Americans.

Howe alters the plan

The British plan called for miracles of coordination, as all three forces would be out of contact with, or supporting distance of, one another as they advanced through the dense forest until they approached the rendezvous. Even worse, there was no overall commander in charge of the approach – indeed, all three generals had explicit clauses in their orders to allow them to vary the plan, if, in any of their opinions, the need arose to do so.

Howe soon decided to exploit this factor. Leaving General Clinton to execute the northern advance from New York with 3,000 men, he loaded his supporting fleet with 15,000 troops and sailed south for Chesapeake Bay, determined to capture Philadelphia, the American capital.

Battle at Brandywine Creek

Howe's movement by sea was slow, and, by the time he landed, Washington was aware of his intentions and waiting for him. The British found the Delaware river leading to Philadelphia strongly fortified, so had to advance overland, while the Continental army took up a defensive position on ridges overlooking the Brandywine facing west towards the British line of advance on the city.

Howe was not to be tempted into launching a major frontal assault, however. While General Knyphausen, with 5,000 men, advanced towards Pyle's Ford to distract the American, the British commander sent General Cornwallis and 10,000 men on a circuitous route towards Jeffry's Ford, with orders to cross the river there near West Chester and envelop Washington's right flank. It was the same manoeuvre that had worked well at New York in 1776, and which was to be much used by Napoleon a generation later in his greatest campaigns.

The enveloping move, which began at 5 am on 11 September, was beautifully executed. Washington was almost fatally fooled by Knyphausen's approach at 10 am and, when Cornwallis revealed his presence on Osborne Hill on the American flank at 2 pm, panic began to spread through the Continental army's ranks.

Fortunately, Washington proved capable of forming a scratch force under Generals Sullivan and Alexander, and formed a new flank near Birmingham with them to meet the new threat. Sullivan and his men fought heroically while slowly giving ground, while Washington personally rallied the troops. Thus the Continental army was able to extricate itself and retreat on Wilmington, but only at a cost of 1,000 casualties and the loss of 11 guns. Philadelphia duly fell to Howe with many supplies; only Washington's extemporised attack at Germantown – failure though it proved – in early October helped restore both his reputation and the morale of his men.

Elsewhere, however, 1777 had gone well for the rebels. St. Leger had been repulsed by Benedict Arnold at Fort Schuyler, and had retired. Putnam worsted Clinton near West Point on the Hudson, but then retired on New York. Most significant of all, however, "Gentleman Johnny" Burgoyne, after a brilliant start to his campaign was ultimately forced to surrender to General Horatio Gates at Saratoga on 7 October. The British overall strategy thus foundered, while news of Saratoga was enough to persuade the French government of Louis XVI to sign a formal treaty of alliance with Congress the following year. Thus, despite the setbacks at Brandywine and Germantown in the south, the year 1777 saw the war reach a decisive turning-point in favour of the Americans.

BUSACO
THE PENINSULAR WAR
27 September 1810

Lord Wellington's Anglo-Portuguese Army (51,340 men and 60 guns) severely checked Marshal André Massena's of Portugal (65,974 men and 114 guns) on a steep ridge north of Coimbra, thus winning time for their further withdrawal to the secret Lines of Torres Vedras protecting Lisbon. The French lost 4,486 men to the Allies' 1,252.

After the loss of the fortresses of Cuidad Rodrigo and Almeida on the Spanish-Portuguese frontier to Massena, Wellington began a retreat towards Lisbon. The French pursuit was dilatory, so giving Wellington the time to select an eight-mile battle position in very broken country seven miles north of the River Mondego, where he turned on his enemies. He had seven divisions under his overall command.

Placing only two divisions under Generals Leith and Hill to hold his right, Wellington massed the remaining five on his center and left, so as to command the two roads crossing the ridge from Moura and San Antonio de Cantara respectively at the foot of the facing valley. As usual, most of his men were concealed from view, ready to take the enemy by surprise.

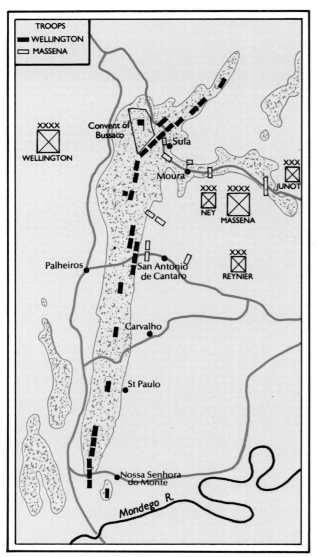

BUSACO *Defeating Massena at Busaco gave Wellington time to retreat to his prepared defensive lines at Torres Vedras.*

Massena attacks

Approaching Busaco on the 26 August with three corps, the French marshal erroneously believed he was facing only a rearguard. He ordered a double attack for early the next morning – by Marshal Ney's 6 Corps from Moura towards the Convent near the Coimbra highroad, and by General Reynier's 2 Corps from San Antonio de Cantara further east. General Junot's 8 Corps was held in reserve behind Ney.

Owing to the steepness of the ridge, few of the French cannon could be brought to bear, but a thick mist shielded their infantry's approach. At 5.45 am Heudelet's and Merle's columns emerged from the shadows to attack Picton's 3rd Division on the right center. Hill and Leith moved part of their men to reinforce Picton, and after three failed attacks the French were hurled back downhill by 6.30 am.

At 8.15am, unaware of Reynier's defeat, Ney's

divisions under Loison and Marchand breasted the slope towards the convent, pushing back Crawfurd's riflemen before them, and captured the outlying hamlet of Sula. However their further advance was halted by accurate British fire from the main position, and, above all, by the use of shrapnel (explosive shells filled with musket-balls) by the Royal Artillery for the first time. Eventually Marchand almost reached the Convent, but was repulsed by Pack's Portuguese. At 4 pm Massena called off the battle without sending forward his reserve under Junot, preferring to see if his cavalry could find a way round the Busaco position from the west.

A retreat in good order

The threat this posed induced Wellington to resume his retreat through Coimbra towards his defences at Torres Vedras. Arriving there without further incident in early October, he again turned at bay. For a year, British engineers and Portuguese labor had been toiling to prepare three lines of detached forts and battery positions, two of them along the steep heights north of Lisbon (Wellington's base) and the third to protect his potential embarkation points at St. Julian to its south, should he be forced to evacuate his army. The forward line, running from the Atlantic coast near Torres Vedras to the Tagus near Alahandra, consisted of 32 redoubts, holding 158 guns and 10,000 men. The main line to its rear, contained 65 redoubts, mounting 206 guns and holding 14,500 men. These two sets of lines extended for 29 and 22 miles respectively. The third required 4,000 men to hold 4,000 men and 83 guns in 11 redoubts. A further 42 positions were placed to strengthen key sectors.

Massena was astounded when he first approached the Lines on 11 October, since no hint of their existence had reached French intelligence. After probes near Sobral in the center between 12 and 14 October, the French commander decided to play a waiting game, hoping to lure Wellington out of his redoubtable defences. Wellington, however had no intention of obliging the French, and eventually starvation forced Massena to fall back – first to Santarem, then, in March 1811, towards the frontier fortresses. Wellington then emerged from his positions to beat the French at Fuentes de Oñoro in early May. The invasion of Portugal was over.

GIBRALTAR
WAR OF AMERICAN INDEPENDENCE
24 June 1779 to 7 February 1783

General Eliott's heroic defence of the Rock of Gibraltar for 3½ years from 1779 (with a garrison of initially 5,500 men and 412 fortress guns) frustrated the Spanish General Don Alvarez's besieging force (originally 14,000 men and 150 guns but rising ultimately to 40,000 men after the arrival of the Duke of Crillon and Admiral Morena), and redeemed the reputation of British arms after the defeats in North America.

Ever since its capture by Admiral Sir George Rooke during the War of the Spanish Succession in 1704, the Spanish had sought to regain Gibraltar, the key to the Mediterranean. The great siege that began in 1779 was the severest test of British determination to retain the rock, but the valor of George Augustus Eliott and his garrison, combined with the skill of the Royal Navy, succeeded in thwarting all Spanish and French efforts to reduce the British positions. Appointed Governor of Gibraltar in 1777, Eliott had greatly improved the fortifications before the supreme test came, but, at the onset of the siege, the defenders of the rock had food for only five months.

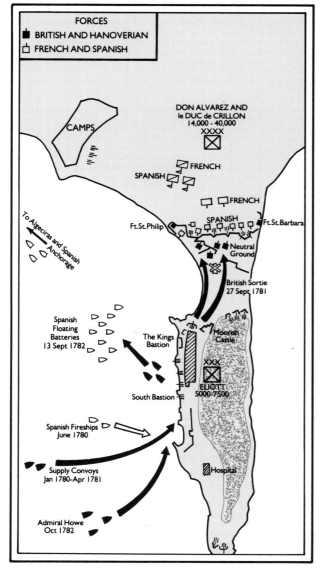

GIBRALTAR *Determined resistance plus naval support led to the raising of the siege after 1,320 days.*

The siege begins

At its outset, the siege was little more than a close blockade of the three-mile peninsula by land and sea, and some supplies continued to reach the garrison from Morocco. In mid-January 1781, the Royal Navy breached the blockade with a convoy carrying supplies and 1,000 reinforcements; on 12 April Admiral Darby repeated the feat, so raising the garrison's strength to 6,500 men. The Spanish then began a sustained bombardment of the town and its defences with 150 guns – this continued for 13 months, causing much damage. Morale occasionally fell under the strain, but Eliott firmly restored discipline and enforced rigid rationing. He organized a most successful sortie by 2,000 men on the night of 27 November 1781, causing much damage to the siege works on the isthmus of Las Lineas (the Lines), and spiking several guns at the cost of only 22 casualties.

The grand assault

In February 1782, however, the Spaniards received French reinforcements, bringing the attackers to an eventual strength of 40,000 men and 40 ships. Following six months of careful preparation, a full-scale assault was launched early on 13 September by both land and sea. Ten floating batteries were positioned 1,000 yards off the King's Bastion on the rock's western side, and a devastating bombardment began. Eliott's guns replied to good purpose, however, and by 1 am the following day six floating batteries were ablaze, as well as two supporting warships. A sortie in boats under Captain Curtis RN increased the havoc, and by dawn the assault was over.

Much of the heart had now gone out of the besiegers; in October, Admiral Howe successfully brought a new relief convoy with a further 1,000 reinforcements safely into harbor after weathering a gale. The siege continued in a half-hearted fashion until 5 February 1783, when the investing forces withdrew. Eliott – nicknamed "Old Cock o'the Rock" – had withstood 1,320 days of siege, sustained 1,780 casualties (including 536 deaths from sickness) and inflicted an estimated 5,000 losses on his foes. For his services, he was knighted and created Baron Heathfield. His epic defence – together with Rodney's naval victory at *The Saints* did much to re-establish the prestige of British arms after the blunders in North America.

JENA-AUERSTÄDT
THE NAPOLEONIC WARS
14 October 1806

A notable double-battle on the banks of the River Saale in Saxony, which saw the massive defeat of the Prussian army. At Jena, Napoleon (96,000 men and some 120 guns) heavily defeated Prince Hohenlohe and General

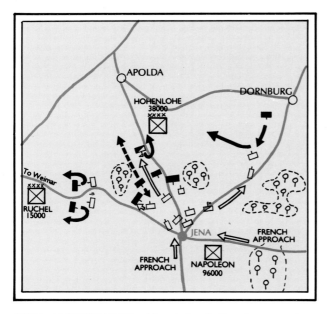

JENA-AUERSTADT *In this twin battle, French opportunism and speed of reinforcement led to Prussia's total defeat.*

Rüchel 53,000 men and 120 guns), inflicting 25,000 casualties at a cost of 5,000 French losses. The same day, at Auerstädt, ten miles to the north, Marshal Davout (27,000 men and 40 guns) routed the main Prussian army under King Frederick William IV and the Duke of Brunswick (63,500 men and 230 guns), inflicting 21,000 casualties for a loss of 7,700 men. The double-victory led to the rapid conquest of most of Prussia by the French.

Aware that Prussia was about to declare war on France, Napoleon struck first by a bold advance from Würzburg into Saxony on 8 October, and crossed the difficult Thuringian forest in three columns. Brushing aside small Prussian forces near two exits from the passes, he advanced north expecting to fight on the Elbe near Leipzig. However, late on 11 October, intelligence reports revealed the Prussian army to be, in fact, near Erfurt to the west; accordingly Napoleon wheeled his 180,000-strong army towards the River Saale the next day, now anticipating battle on 16 October.

Anticipating the enemy
Once again, events dictated otherwise. On 13 August, Marshal Lannes, commanding Napoleon's advance guards, reported many Prussian troops near Jena on the Saale. Overnight, Napoleon ordered 120,000 of his men to converge on the town with all speed, while III and I Corps (under Marshals Davout and Bernadotte respectively) were to sweep further north towards Auerstädt to cut the Prussian line of retreat towards the Elbe. That night, Bernadotte chose not to obey his latest orders, and, instead, left Davout and marched on Dornburg. Meanwhile, unknown to the French, the main Prussian army was already retreating north,

leaving Hohenlohe near Jena (supported by Rüchel's 15,000 men near Weimar) to cover the move.

Napoleon and the Imperial Guard had joined Lannes late on the 13 August, and the emperor supervized the cutting of a track up the Landgrafenburg. By 10 am on the foggy morning of 14 August, he had 50,500 men on the field, with 70,000 more approaching. As soon as Ney's VI Corps had arrived, with Augereau and Soult nearby, Napoleon launched Lannes forwards with Ney in support. Hohenlohe – already outnumbered – fought back desperately; an error by Ney caused a crisis at 10 am, which took a massed battery of guns and some time to remedy. However, Augerau and Soult were in action on the flanks by midday, while Murat's arrival with much of the cavalry brought the French strength up to 96,000 as opposed to only 38,000 Prussians (Rüchel not having arrived on the scene). By 3 pm the Prussians were in flight towards Weimar, carrying Rüchel's tardily arriving forces with them, with Murat in hot pursuit.

Against long odds
Napoleon believed he had won a major battle. However, he was in for a surprise late that afternoon. Away to the north, Davout had advanced alone through thick fog to pass the Saale and the Kosen defile beyond it. Abruptly, Gudin's division ran into Brunswick's flank-guard, and a fierce battle grew around Hassenhausen. Gudin performed wonders, but all depended on reinforcement. Heavy Prussian infantry and cavalry attacks were somehow repulsed – then, at about 11 am Vandamme's division arrived on the scene. More Prussians also entered the fray, but the mortal wounding of Brunswick threw the Prussian command into confusion, which permitted Friant's division to appear. Even now, Davout faced unfavorable odds of two against one, and losses were mounting. However, he exploited the Prussian hesitation with consummate skill, and about 4 pm, Frederick William IV (who had belatedly assumed command), believing that he was facing Napoleon in person, ordered an immediate retreat, which fast became a rout as the Prussian forces crumbled under Davout's pressure.

At first Napoleon would not believe the news from Auerstädt, but in due course gave Davout his deserved credit. Bernadotte was almost court-martialled, but redeemed himself by an energetic pursuit of the Prussians, reaching the Baltic coast three weeks later. Meanwhile fortress after fortress surrendered, as Prussian morale sagged and then collapsed. Soon almost 150,000 prisoners-of-war were in French hands, and three-quarters of Prussia, including Berlin, its capital was occupied as the most effective exploitation of a victory in modern history was ruthlessly carried out. However, Frederick William unexpectedly refused to sue for peace, and the war did not end until July 1807 with the Treaty of Tilsit, after two more hard campaigns against the Russians, as well as the remnants of Frederick William's once-proud army.

LAKE CHAMPLAIN
WAR OF 1812
11 September 1814

The critical naval battle of the War of 1812 fought on 11 September 1814 on Lake Champlain, near Plattsburg, New York, between a British squadron of four major warships and twelve small gunboats, commanded by George Downie, and an American flotilla, comprising four sizeable men-of-war and ten tiny gunboats under the command of Thomas Macdonough. The latter's victory forced George Prevost's British army of over 11,000 men to retreat from Plattsburg.

Having won a majority of the land battles on three northern fronts in the first two years of the War of 1812, some 11,300 British troops – seasoned veterans of Wellington's Peninsular War army, backed by a reserve of 3,700 more – were led southward from Montreal by Sir George Prevost to Lake Champlain in the late summer of 1814. Confronted at Plattsburg near the Saranac River by over 4,000 American troops of all descriptions under the able Alexander Macomb, Prevost hesitated and decided to await the outcome of an impending naval clash in the vicinity.

Evenly-matched fleets
The two naval forces were evenly matched. The brilliant 30-year-old Macdonough had under his command the frigate *Saratoga* (flagship, 26 guns), brig *Eagle* (20), the schooner *Ticonderoga* (17), the sloop *Preble* (7), and ten gunboats mounting a total of 16 guns between them. The experienced Downie had the frigate *Confiance* (flagship, 37 guns), the brig *Linnet* (16), the sloop *Chubb* (11), the sloop *Finch* (11), and twelve gunboats, carrying a total of 17 guns. Macdonough wisely determined to fight in position, with spring lines and kedge anchors, behind Cumberland Head, near Plattsburg.

Battle of the flagships
Before 9.00 am on 11 September, Downie's fleet rounded Cumberland Head and the battle commenced. Contrary winds handicapped the British, and the engagement was close and unrelenting. Macdonough aimed a number of the guns himself, and, though knocked down and rendered momentarily unconscious on several occasions, each time he managed to recover quickly. Early in the action, Downie was killed instantly when an American shot hurled a British cannon upon his groin. *Confiance* engaged *Saratoga*, and seemed to be having the better of it until Macdonough wound his ship 180 degrees on its spring lines and anchors, thereby bringing his undamaged broadside to bear. When *Confiance* attempted to do likewise, she fouled her lines halfway through the turn, was raked severely, and had

to strike her colors. She had been hulled 105 times to *Saratoga*'s 55.

The Americans victorious
As the desperate battle continued, *Preble*, *Chubb*, and *Finch* were shattered and put out of action. Then *Linnet* received a broadside from *Saratoga*, and had to surrender. While a few of the small British gunboats fought well for a time, the others fled. The *Saratoga* herself was so badly damaged that she later had to be scuttled; the same was true of all of Downie's warships.

In this pivotal battle, the Americans lost four officers and 48 men killed and 58 wounded (a casualty rate of 13 per cent) while the British lost five officers and 49 men dead and 116 wounded (an 18 per cent casualty rate.

The consequences were dramatic and immediate. After only light skirmishing at Macomb's lines, Prevost, although outnumbering the American troops almost three to one, seeing the crushing defeat of Downie's fleet, supinely gave up the contest and retreated with his troops to Canada.

THE SAINTS
THE WAR OF AMERICAN INDEPENDENCE
9 and 12 April, 1782

The Royal Navy (36 ships-of-the-line), under Admiral Lord Rodney, defeated the French fleet (33 ships-of-the-line and two 50-gun ships escorting 150 sail of merchant shipping), commanded by Admiral Comte de Grasse, off Les Saintes Islands between Guadeloupe and Dominica in the West Indies. The British success, however, was poorly exploited.

In 1781, at the Battle of the Capes, Comte de Grasse's French fleet had played a vital part in ensuring ultimate American success at *Yorktown* by preventing its relief by sea, and so enabling Washington's army to force British capitulation. The following year, the French and Spanish admiralties ordered de Grasse to escort an invasion force of 20,000 troops from Haiti to attack the British colony of Jamaica. The British admiralty, learning of this scheme, ordered Lord Rodney to prevent the junction of the escorting fleet and the invasion shipping.

A preliminary engagement
Rodney – altered by his "eyes", the frigates – was soon on de Grasse's trail after the French admiral sailed from Martinique on 5 April; on 9 April, de Grasse signalled the convoy to head for Guadeloupe as a precaution. The two fleets came into contact that same day, their first clash being a complex affair, made the more difficult by a flat calm, succeeded by only light breezes.

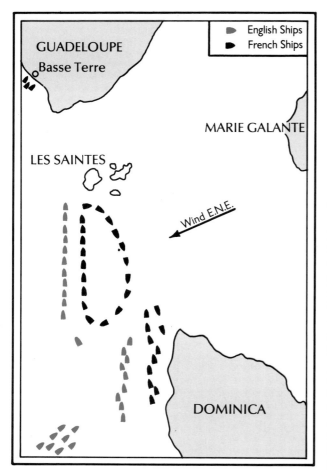

English Ships
French Ships

GUADELOUPE
Basse Terre

MARIE GALANTE

LES SAINTES

Wind E.N.E.

DOMINICA

THE SAINTS *By abandoning the traditional battle line to attack in columns, Rodney defeated the confused de Grasse.*

At 9.30 am de Grasse, who had the windward advantage, ordered his vanguard of some 15 ships to engage several British vessels bearing down on two isolated French warships in the Saints' Channel.

Using his advantage skilfully, de Grasse sailed his fleet in line-ahead parallel to Rodney's ships, his ships carrying out a wide continuous circling movement to come back into action at the back of the fighting line in turn. Using the fluky breezes with great skill, Rodney and eight ships of the main fleet worked their way between the French van and their main fleet off Dominica; seeing this the French broke off the attack at 11 am to rejoin de Grasse.

Half an hour later, the action resumed. Because there was still a substantial distance between Admiral Hood's vanguard and Rodney's main fleet, the French hoped to gain a local advantage, but failed in this intent, since the fickle wind improved to allow Rodney's division to catch up with Hood. At 1.15 pm the French fell away.

The fleets come to blows
The action to date, therefore, had been indecisive, neither side sustaining many losses. Both fleets repaired

the minor damage they had suffered at sea, and next day Rodney resumed his pursuit. The French drew ahead, but that night two French ships collided, forcing de Grasse to return to their aid on 11 April. This he effected, but, on the following night, the *Zélé* hit a fellow French ship for a second time – this time none other than de Grasse's flagship – and had to be towed to Guadeloupe.

These French problems permitted Rodney to make up the lost ground, and, at 5.30 am, he bore down on the confused and scattered French. Sending four ships to threaten the disabled *Zélé* as a bait to draw the main French fleet further to leeward, Rodney was in action against the French line of battle at 7.40 am. At first, the action followed the conventional line-against-line pattern, the two fleets sailing parallel to one another and passing on opposite tacks, but a sudden major shift of the wind from east to south-south-east at about 9 am caused the French to veer closer to the British. The British center and rear responded – whether deliberately on orders, or instinctively, remains in doubt – by turning towards the French fleet in two columns, and crashed through their opponents' line in two places, splitting it into three.

Totally confused by this highly irregular attack, the French lost all cohesion. A hard pounding ensued, until at about 4 pm de Grasse signalled his ships to disengage, abandoning his more battered ships to their fate. His own flagship, *Ville de Paris*, was captured after a hard fight, together with four other French ships, Grasse himself being taken prisoner. Rodney had won an important, but not wholly decisive battle, for his pursuit was later much criticised. However, the French never invaded Jamaica, and Rodney had regained overall command of the West Indian oceans. And, by luck or judgement, the sacred "Fighting Instructions", enjoining action to be always in line-of-battle, had been breached; Rodney's example was to be followed 23 years later by Nelson against the Franco-Spanish fleet at *Trafalgar* with far more impressive results.

SALAMANCA
THE PENINSULAR WAR
22 July 1812

Fought to the south of the major Spanish city of Salamanca, between Lord Wellington's Allied Army (48,569 men and 60 guns) and Marshal Marmont's Army of Portugal (50,000 men and 78 guns), this battle resulted in a great Allied victory. At a cost of 5,214 casualties, the allies inflicted 14,000 on the French, and captured 20 cannon and two *tricolors*. The battle led to the temporary liberation of Madrid.

In the fourth year of the Peninsular War, Wellington launched a telling offensive deep into French-occupied

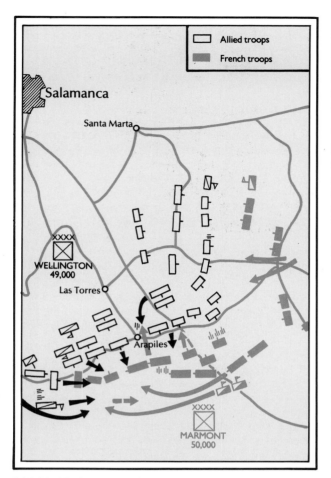

SALAMANCA *By mistakenly over-extending his line of advance, Marmont invited Wellington to defeat him in detail.*

Spain. Capitalizing on Napoleon's reduction of his forces to 220,000 in preparation for the invasion of Russia, and utilizing his base at Lisbon supported by the Royal Navy, Wellington first captured the two key crossing points from Portugal into Spain – the fortress-towns of Cuidad Rodrigo and Badajoz – albeit at heavy cost. He then mounted several feints to confuse the French as to his intentions, before suddenly moving through Ciudad Rodrigo on 13 June with his main army into northern Spain.

A period of shadow boxing

The French were taken completely by surprise, with the result that Salamanca – less its three forts, which held out until 27 June – was speedily occupied. There followed a period of fast marching and manoeuvring, as Wellington and the newly-appointed Marmont played cat-and-mouse along the River Douro to the north of the city, seeking a favorable opportunity for battle.

Learning that Marmont was expecting reinforcements from Madrid, Wellington decided to retreat towards the Portuguese frontier. On 15 July, a confident Marmont launched his offensive, and pursued Wellington back towards Salamanca, the two armies

being in close proximity. The Allies reached the city on 21 July, crossed the River Tormes, and took up a position in hilly ground to the south, while their hospital and supply trains began to move off towards Portugal. That afternoon and evening, there was skirmishing to the east between the French advance guard and the Light Division near Calvarasa de Abajo.

Wellington grasps his opportunity

Early on 22 July Wellington made a deliberate decision not to occupy the high hill of the Greater Arapiles. By noon, his left wing, comprising the Light and 1st Division, was facing east, while the main body (facing south) held the Lesser Arapiles feature. Here, Wellington established his forward headquarters with the 6th Division and Pack's Portuguese. Three more infantry divisions, the bulk of the cavalry (including Spanish troops), were to its west, with General Pakenham's 3rd Division and D'Urban's Portuguese cavalry fast approaching from Salamanca to form the extreme right flank. In typical Wellington fashion, most of these troops were kept out-of-sight of the enemy behind protective ground.

Marmont was fooled by this – and by the dust clouds created by the departing convoys – into believing that Wellington was already in full retreat. He determined to out-march the Allies by a southwards sweep to sever their line of retreat. Placing many guns on the Greater Arapiles, the marshal ordered Curto's cavalry and General Thomières' leading division to march hell-for-leather westward, followed, after a short interval, by the divisions of Maucune and Brennier with Boyer's cavalry, and then (more than a mile further back) by those of Generals Clausel, Bonnet and Ferey, with Foy's command bringing up the rear. Misunderstanding the situation, and under-estimating Wellington's generalship, Marmont thus allowed his army to become very over-extended in three disconnected sections – inviting defeat in detail – and was also marching straight across the front of a strong, concealed enemy.

Wellington was at lunch when he heard of this development. "By God! That will do!", he exclaimed. Riding fast, he joined Pakenham, and ordered him and D'Urban to attack the leading French troops head-on near Aldea Tejada after making a rapid two-mile hidden approach march. "I'll do it, my lord," agreed his brother-in-law.

The battle opens

Pakenham's sudden attack at 4.45 pm took Thomières completely by surprise. Outflanked by D'Urban's horsemen and charged frontally by the 3rd Division's infantry, his men – and Curto's – turned and fled. Next Wellington's 5th Division revealed itself, attacking Maucune, who also received a brilliant cavalry charge from Le Marchant's British cavalry, which then shattered a square formed by part of Brennier's infantry, next in line (at the cost of Le Marchant's life).

If not exactly defeating "50,000 men in 50 minutes", almost half Marmont's army had been scattered. Even worse for the French, their commander was seriously wounded at this juncture by a shell-burst, and his second-in-command, General Bonet, fell a minute later. General Clausel assumed command.

By this time, Wellington was launching his main attack from the center. The 5th and 4th Divisions, flanked by the two Portuguese brigades, and supported by the 6th and 7th Divisions in their rear, swept forward. But Clausel was made of stern stuff. Pack's Portuguese failed to storm the smoke-shrouded Greater Arapiles and, in falling back, unwittingly uncovered the flank of General Lowry Coles' advancing 4th Division. Against it Clausel launched Bonet's men – burning to avenge their fallen chief – and Cole's men, outflanked, reeled back.

For a time, it appeared as if Clausel was turning the tide of the battle, driving a deep salient into the Allied line, but, fortunately, Wellington deployed Clinton's 6th Division to meet the threat, which he did manfully at a loss of one third of his men over a desperate five minutes. This gallant action won time for Beresford to coolly take stock of the situation and counter-attack with Spry's Portuguese brigade of 5th Division. These measures succeeded in stopping the rot, and the French were driven back. It was now about 7pm.

Attack and disappointment

Wellington now launched his second major attack. Clinton advanced to be held by Ferrey's division until guns were rushed forward to support the 6th Division. Ferrey's troops were scattered, and Clinton stormed the Greater Arapiles. Only Foy's division remained intact, which proceeded to carry out a masterly rearguard action as dusk fell. Leading the pursuit, Wellington was slightly wounded by a spent musket ball, as the French streamed away towards the bridge at Alba de Tormes.

Wellington's staff were jubilant, for, in anticipation of just such an outcome, a Spanish force had been sent to occupy that bridge earlier in the day. Unfortunately, Carlos d'Espana had abandoned the position without orders, so the French were able to pour away over the Tormes unhindered. Undaunted, the Allied pursuit headed for the bridges at Huerta, where they hoped to trap the French in an angle in the river. Foiled again, it was only the next day that Foy was brought to bay at Garcia Hernandez, where the heavy cavalry of the King's German Legion broke a formed square and scattered a column, inflicting 1,400 casualties. The French flight resumed.

Although two-thirds of the Army of Portugal survived to fight another day, Wellington's victory brought him, in Foy's opinion, "... almost to the height of fame of the Duke of Marlborough." Using concealment to brilliant effect and sound tactical insight, Wellington had skilfully exploited Marmont's errors, demonstrating his ability to win a major offensive battle.

TRAFALGAR
THE NAPOLEONIC WARS
21 October 1805

Fought off Cape Trafalgar in south-eastern Spain, between Rear-Admiral Lord Nelson and his fleet (27 ships-of-the-line) and Vice-Admiral Pierre de Villeneuve, commanding the Franco-Spanish fleet (18 French and 15 Spanish ships-of-the-line, and seven frigates). The five-hour battle resulted in a resounding British victory. The French and Spaniards lost 18 vessels and 14,000 men; the British lost no ships and 1,500 men, including Horatio Nelson.

Although usually popularly associated with the frustration of Napoleon's plans to invade Britain, Trafalgar, in fact, was fought one month after Napoleon had abandoned the project: he and the Grande Armée were campaigning on the River Danube in late October 1805, when Nelson and de Villeneuve met in one of the decisive battles of naval history.

A frustrating pursuit

Earlier in the year, however, de Villeneuve's activities had been closely linked to the threatened invasion of British shores. On Napoleon's orders, he had successfully linked up with Admiral Gravina's Spanish squadrons from Cadiz, lured Nelson's fleet to the West Indies in May, and then doubled back to European waters once he learnt that his red herring was working. There, he was supposed to link with Admiral Bruix's

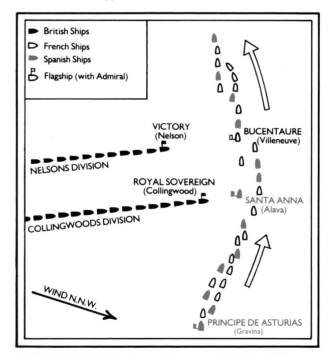

TRAFALGAR Nelson's two columns smashed through the Franco-Spanish battle line, so splitting it into component parts.

blockaded squadron in Brest, before sweeping down the Channel to convoy Napoleon's invasion barges during the trans-Channel crossing; instead, he exploited a loophole in his orders when he found that British ships were on his trail, and, after an inconclusive brush with a squadron under Admiral Calder, he had sailed into the Spanish port of Ferrol.

There, however, de Villeneuve was hounded out to sea again by new orders from Napoleon, which called for him to sail into the Mediterranean to support a French offensive in Italy. The Franco-Spanish fleet duly reached Cadiz.

Meanwhile Nelson, having failed to catch Villeneuve and Gravina in the West Indies, had disconsolately sailed back to Gibraltar, and from there to England, where he spent three weeks with his mistress, Lady Hamilton. On 14 September, however, he rehoisted his admiral's pennant in HMS *Victory* at Portsmouth and sailed to rejoin the fleet off Cadiz on 28 September, where Admiral Collingwood had been deputising in command.

Villeneuve puts to sea

Nelson lost no time consulting with his captains – his "band of brothers" – to devise his tactics in case a battle was to materialize. He decided that the fleet would close on the enemy in two lines ahead, aiming to pierce the Franco-Spanish line of battle about one third from the van and so forcing a close engagement, ship against ship, which he was confident that superior British naval gunnery and ship handling would win. But would the French put out from Cadiz?

Napoleon again played unwittingly into Nelson's hands by insisting that de Villeneuve should leave harbor and head for the Straits of Gibraltar. The brow-beaten admiral – despite personal reservations as to the wisdom of this order – obeyed his emperor, and, on 19 October, the combined French and Spanish squadrons put out to sea. Unknown to him, Nelson was waiting for him over the horizon, kept in touch with every move of Villeneuve's squadrons by his watchful screen of shadowing frigates.

The fleets engage

The two fleets came into visual contact early on 21 October. Obeying their admiral's plan, the windward British column closed up around HMS *Victory* while the leeward section gathered behind HMS *Royal Sovereign*, carrying Collingwood's flag. One look was enough for Villeneuve, who at once turned and ran for Cadiz, but he had little chance of eluding Nelson. The British admiral retired to his cabin to frame his famous Trafalgar prayer, and then ordered the celebrated signal to be hoisted – "England expects that every man will do his duty."

Shortly after midday, Collingwood's squadron engaged the rear of the combined fleet, piercing its line as intended, and then breaking off to fight a series of ship-to-ship duels. By 1 pm, *Victory* was also in action at

the van of the windward column; soon Villeneuve's van was sundered from the rest of his fleet, while vessel after vessel of his center and rear found itself being pounded by the superior gunnery of one or two British ships of the line.

"They have done for me at last"

Nelson was on the brink of total victory, but he was not to live to enjoy its glory. At about 1.15pm, the *Victory*'s quarterdeck came into the sights of a French marksman in one of the *Redoubtable*'s fighting-tops, and a single shot felled Nelson – an obvious target owing to his medals and orders, which he insisted on wearing in action. Shot through the shoulder and spine, he was carried below. There he survived for three hours – long enough to learn that 18 French and Spanish ships had struck their colors, and that Villeneuve himself had been taken prisoner. "Kiss me Hardy" said the dying hero to his Flag-Captain, and then died.

The Nelson touch

Nelson's body was placed in a wine-cask to preserve it for a formal state burial in England, and Collingwood assumed command of the fleet and its battered prizes. As he was convoying these towards Gibraltar, a great gale blew up, in which all but four of the captured ships foundered. Nevertheless, Trafalgar set the seal on British command of the seas. Although Napoleon would be able to mount some form of naval threat for eight more years – causing the Royal Navy to maintain a costly blockade of the key naval ports of the continent – French and Spanish pretensions to true naval power lay shattered beyond recovery.

VALMY
THE WARS OF THE FRENCH REVOLUTION
20 September 1792

North-west Verdun in France, Valmy and its windmill was the scene of a decisive battle in the early wars of the French Revolution, when Generals Kellermann the Elder and Dumouriez (52,000 men and 40 guns) managed to halt the advance towards Paris by the Duke of Brunswick's Prussian Army (34,000 men and 36 guns). The French lost 300 casualties to the 180 they inflicted, but they had saved Paris, and, with it, the Revolution.

The "cannonade of Valmy" (it hardly deserves the name of a battle) is an example of a minor military engagement that was almost indecisive in its tactical terms, but politically was of the greatest significance. When France brought on itself the War of the First Coalition in April 1792, the result was almost disastrous. Her armies were filled with untrained volunteers and lacked sufficient officers, many having fled overseas. Facing the experienced regular armies of Austria and Prussia, it is little wonder that all the opening moves of the war went against the French, as the allies invaded her territory and marched on Paris. Prussian successes at Longwy and Verdun – where the *sans-culottes* fled – caused panic in Paris, leading to the notorious "September Massacres."

Dumouriez to the rescue

With only a demoralized force of unblooded troops at Châlons ahead of him, total victory appeared to be within Brunswick's grasp. Fortunately General Dumouriez rose to the occasion, and boldly marched his ragged and weak army to cut the Prussian lines of communication at Sainte-Menehoud to create a distraction. There he was joined by General Kellermann with part of the Army of the Center on 19 September. He had brigaded one battalion of regular troops with two of volunteers throughout his force, so bringing a little discipline to his motley forces.

Brunswick, accompanied by King Frederick William III marched south-east to destroy what he regarded as an impudent rabble. The French – after some confusion – eventually took up a semi-circular position, with General Stengel on the right, Kellermann around the windmill in the center, General Chabot on the left, and with Dumouriez in reserve.

A cannonade saves France

Dawn on 20 September was misty. The French soon lost the village of La Lune, and the Prussians slowly drew up their battle-line between La Lune and Somme Bionne – under one mile from Kellerman's main position. About midday the rival batteries opened fire. Kellermann's hillside was the main Prussian target, but his mixed-brigades stood their ground manfully. An hour later, the Prussians began a ponderous advance, but only covered 200 yards before French cannon fire brought them to a halt. Then, a lucky shot exploded three French ammunition waggons near the windmill. The troops almost ran, but Kellermann rallied them, while Dumouriez sent forward more guns and ammunition to reinforce the shaken sector.

The Prussians made no attempt to exploit this fleeting advantage, and the day passed in desultory exchanges of fire until 4 pm, when a torrential downpour sent both armies looking for shelter. The aged Brunswick had already left the field, and the cannonade of Valmy was over. Nothing much appeared to have been decided, but at least the French had stood their ground, and the Parisian propagandists immediately inflated this into a major victory.

The psychological impact of Valmy was indubitably immense – and the Revolution had surmounted its first great external challenge. Years later on St. Helena, Napoleon remarked of Kellermann's position: "I am probably the boldest general who ever lived, but I wouldn't have dared to take post there."

WATERLOO
THE NAPOLEONIC WARS
18 June 1815

Fought between the Duke of Wellington's Allied army (68,000 men and 156 guns), reinforced by Field-Marshal Blücher's Prussian army (72,000 men and 126 guns) during the afternoon, and the French *Armée du Nord* (72,000 men and 246 cannon) commanded by the Emperor Napoleon I. The total defeat of the French led to Napoleon's second abdication, the second restoration of King Louis XVIII, the Allied occupation of France, and the end of the French Revolutionary, Consular and Napoleonic Wars.

After Napoleon's return to France on 1 March 1815 from exile on Elba, and his resumption of power in Paris on 30 March, it was only a question of time before a major trial of strength would result. Hoping to forestall the advance of large Russian and Austrian armies across France's eastern frontiers, the emperor suddenly launched an offensive over the Belgian border at Charleroi early on 15 June, intending to drive a wedge between the Allied and Prussian armies (based on Brussels and Namur respectively) before defeating them separately and occupying the Belgian capital. However, although Blücher was heavily defeated at Ligny on 16 June (losing 25,000 casualties to the French 11,000) – the same day that Wellington was held to a draw after a long encounter battle against Marshal Ney at Quatre Bras some six miles to the west (resulting in some 5,000 losses on each side – both armies retreated northwards towards Wavre and Mont St. Jean.

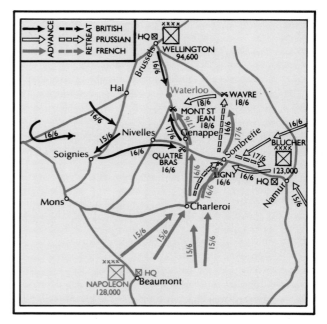

WATERLOO *Wellington's determined defence gave Blucher's Prussians time to come to his aid on the French right.*

Very untypically, the French pursuit was dilatory, but, by the next evening, Napoleon had 72,000 men facing Wellington's 68,000 across a shallow valley facing the ridge of Mont St. Jean. The evening of 17 June proved as wet as had the afternoon, and both armies endured a wretched night huddled around their smoking campfires, divided by barely a mile.

Napoleon attacks

Overnight, Wellington received assurances that Blücher would march from Wavre to his assistance in the morning with at least two corps. Accordingly, he deployed his army along the 2½-mile ridge, placing 17,000 men to the west near Hal to intercept any French outflanking attempt. He stationed the greater part of his strength on the right wing and right center (relying upon the Prussians to reinforce his left), with a screen of light infantry pushed forward into no-man's land. Forward strong-points were established (from west to east) at Hougoumont Château, the massive farm of La Haie Sainte, and the hamlets of La Haie and Papelotte respectively.

Wellington concealed most of his troops behind the ridge; behind his line was the village of Mont St. Jean and the forest of Soignies. His strategy was to hold this position until Blücher could arrive from Wavre, seven miles to the east. In the two integrated corps under Wellington's command, less than a third of the troops were British, owing to the despatch of a large force to North America to fight in the War of 1812 and, only one division (Picton's 5th) could be described as veteran.

Napoleon – scorning his opponents – devised what was for him a simplistic battle plan. His intention was to crush the Allied center to the east of the central axis formed by the main Brussels highway passing La Haie Sainte, after a softening-up bombardment by 70 massed guns, and the mounting of a diversionary attack against Hougoumont to the west. However, he postponed the opening of the battle to allow the sodden ground to dry, and, as an afterthought, summoned Grouchy's wing from Wavre. There, however the single Prussian corps of General Thielmann (17,000 men and 48 guns) would pin down Grouchy's two corps (33,000 men and 82 cannon) all day, while his chief, "Papa" Blücher, pipe in hand, was urging the remaining three Prussian corps towards Mont St. Jean.

Fighting around Hougoumont

At 11.30 am, the French guns spoke, and Prince Jerôme Bonaparte led his division of General Reille's 2nd Corps against Hougoumont. Both events achieved less than expected. Many cannon-balls lodged in the mud short of Wellington's concealed formations – save for Bylandt's unfortunate brigade left to the fore of the ridge, which received heavy casualties – while the attack on Hougoumont was held off by its garrison of British Guards. This aroused the fury of Jerôme, who called almost the whole of another French division to

support his attack. Thus, whereas Wellington sent only minimal reserves forward to Hougoumont's support, the larger part of a French corps was soon pinned down in a secondary engagement. The fight for the Château would continue until 9 pm. Even though the Château was ablaze by 3.30 pm, it never fell; though the French once forced an entry into the courtyard, they were promptly expelled.

An equally disappointing fate awaited Napoleon's main attack. At 1.30 pm, General d'Erlon's 1st Corps attacked Wellington's left-center. Owing to a confused order, two of his four divisions advanced in massive, outdated formations, presenting targets the British gunners could not overlook. Further, although his better-deployed flanking divisions made rather more progress, and Bylandt's decimated brigade gave ground, the main attack struck the sector held by Picton's veterans. Though Picton was killed, his men held firm and repulsed the French, whose retreat became a rout as Lord Anglesey's Household Cavalry Brigade crashed into their left flank, while the Union Brigade – including, contrary to their orders, the 2nd North British Dragoons (Scots Greys) – charged through their center.

The fortunes of war

Unfortunately, the Scots Greys and other horsemen pressed their attack as far as the French gun line, where they were to be taken in flank and severely mauled by Jacquinot's lancers. Nevertheless, the French 1st Corps had been repulsed, so winning Wellington invaluable time. Now, the first Prussian troops finally began to appear near Planchenoit on the French right flank.

Napoleon reacted to this unwelcome news by sending his 5th Corps (General Lobau) to meet the newcomers, thus forming a new flank, but from 4.30 pm onwards the Prussian threat became ever more serious. Eventually the Young Guard, followed by part of the Old Guard, had to be sent into the fluctuating contest for Plancenoit. By late afternoon almost all Napoleon's reserves had been committed.

Meanwhile, from 3 pm, Marshal Ney had been hurling massive cavalry attacks against the Allied right-center. Believing that Wellington was retreating, Ney failed to give his cavalry horse artillery and infantry support. The ground was restricted by Hougoumont and La Haie Sainte, and very muddy, while the allies formed up in 20 fire-fringed squares, which the horsemen could not pierce. They also failed to spike the temporarily abandoned British guns. The survivors were extricated only with great difficulty by General Kellermann.

At about 6 pm, however, yet another attack on La Haie Sainte brought Ney his one success of the day. Major Baring and his King's German Legion battalion ran out of ammunition, and lost the post. Ney rushed up some guns to almost point-blank range of Wellington's center, which began to waver under the fire. Ney appealed to Napoleon to send up the Imperial

Guard to clinch the victory, but owing to the Plancenoit fight there were no troops available until 7.30 pm. By then, Wellington – always quick to respond to a crisis – had brought up his cavalry from the left and a few infantry reserves, to strengthen his center. But the situation looked grim. "God bring me night or bring me Blücher", the Duke remarked. It was the Prussians of Ziethen's Corps that timely arrived.

Napoleon's last throw
At 7.30 pm, a lull settled over the field, as 11 battalions of the Middle Guard were led forward by Napoleon in person before he handed command of them over to Ney. The most feared veteran troops in Europe crested the slope, but veered to their left, and thus came up (in part) against the British Guards, lying waiting for them amidst the man-high corn. "Now Maitland, now's your time!" ordered Wellington, and the Guards rose to pour deadly volleys into the heads of the French columns.

The Imperial Guard stopped, and hesitated. Then, taken in flank by more British infantry, the French veterans began to retire. The rest of the tired French army received this news with incredulity, and then despair. At the same time, Zeithen's Prussians, whose approach Napoleon had announced to his men to be that of Marshal Grouchy, opened fire. A shout of "Treason!" went up. Judging his moment with skill, Wellington thrice waved his hat in a pre-arranged signal, and the whole Allied line swept forward with a cheer. The French army's cohesion snapped, and it was soon a horde of fugitives. Napoleon sought shelter in a square formed by the Old Guard, but was persuaded to leave the field. The square held firm, and covered the flight of their comrades until the Old Guard was mown down by Allied guns brought forward after General Cambronne had refused an offer to surrender with the famous one-word "Merde!". Waterloo was over.

As the Prussian cavalry took over the pursuit, Wellington met Blücher near the farm of La Belle Alliance. "Quelle affaire!," the aged Prussian remarked, ". . . which was about all the French he had" Wellington later commented.

YORKTOWN
THE AMERICAN WAR OF INDEPENDENCE
28 September – 19 October 1781

The siege, battle and capitulation of Yorktown was the decisive event in the struggle for American independence, though French sea power, rather than American military superiority, was probably the determining factor. General George Washington (16,000 men and an estimated 100 guns) forced Lieutenant General Lord Cornwallis to surrender at the head of almost 8,000 men. Although peace was over

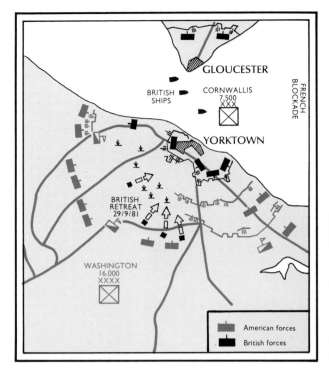

YORKTOWN *Penned into a corner by Washington and cut off at sea by the French fleet, British defeat was inevitable.*

two years away, the issue of the war was decided. Though it can be argued that General John Burgoyne's surrender with 3,000 men at Saratoga on 17 October 1777 was the turning-point in the American War of Independence, there is no doubt that the disaster that overwhelmed Lord Cornwallis at Yorktown in Virginia four years later was the decisive event in the revolt of the American colonies. Although substantial British and Hessian forces remained in America, this event broke the resolve of the British to continue.

An uncertain strategy
Although Washington was aware that the overall situation was moving in his favor by mid-1781 as further French military and naval aid arrived, he was by no means certain how to achieve final victory. His main aim was to recover New York from the British, and to this end considerable time and effort was expended probing the British defences in the so-called "Old Colonies". It needed the threat from Admiral de Grasse that he would withdrew the French fleet from American waters in mid-October to induce the commander of the Continental army to make up his mind. Leaving half the Continentals to contain General Clinton within the defences of New York, Washington assigned the remaining American troops under General Lincoln, and the complete French expeditionary corps under the Marquis de Rochambeau, to attack Cornwallis in his strong position on the bluffs overlooking the York river.

Throughout this campaign, sea-power played a

determining role. De Grasse's naval victory of the Virginia Capes on 5 September over Admiral Graves' fleet meant the completion of Cornwallis's isolation and the ending of any hopes of his being reinforced from New York – or, alternatively, being evacuated – by sea. By the same token, French command of the seas ensured the safe arrival of a convoy of artillery and munitions for Washington at Jamestown.

As the American and French troops steadily converged on their objective (some French conducting a long march, the rest being landed by de Grasse at Jamestown), Cornwallis found his outlying posts being driven back step by step, until, on 28 September, his 8,000 men and their 65 guns were wholly contained within the defences of Yorktown on the south bank of the James River, save for a 1,000-strong detachment under Banastre Tarleton that was holding Gloucester on the north bank. The small British naval flotilla in the York was wholly dominated by de Grasse's blockading squadron; thus the British were effectively besieged by both land and sea.

The siege opens
Anxious in case the reported arrival of British naval reinforcements at New York would induce de Grasse to bring forward his announced departure date, Washington prosecuted the siege with determination and vigor. His camps established from the York River in the north-west to the Wormley Creek in the south-east, he began to push forward to within cannon range of the British defences. These made use of creeks, marshes and cliffs to create a fortified line, strengthened by ten redoubts, one "horn-work" athwart the Hampton Road, and 14 battery positions. To the south-east were two detached positions – Redoubts No. 9 and 10; to the north-west was the detached "Fusiliers Redoubt", manned by the 23rd Foot. The position was strong, but supplies for the British troops were already short. The latter fact was to prove Yorktown's Achilles' heel.

The Americans and French began to sap their way forward towards Yorktown, employing the standard methods of siege warfare. By 6 October, Washington was ready to open his first parallel; this was done two days later, 1,500 men digging the 2,000-yard trenches, while a further 2,800 guarded the sappers against a possible British sortie. The next day, the heavy batteries opened fire – Washington in person firing the first cannon. Progress was slowed by determined British counter-battery fire, and there were several hard fights between small parties of troops for domination of no man's land between the two forces, Major-General von Steuben directed the siege operations aided by the gunner, Brigadier-General Knox.

From 10 October a constant two-day American bombardment of Yorktown caused heavy damage, Cornwallis's headquarters being rendered uninhabitable. As house after house was damaged, many British troops moved into caves in the cliffs,

whilst the hapless inhabitants who had remained in the town survived as best they could. On 10 October, HMS *Charon* and two transport vessels were set on fire by red-hot shot, the first mentioned being totally destroyed. Early on 12 October the besiegers were able to start their second parallel still closer to the main Yorktown defences, but this trench could not be completed at its eastern end because of the enfilade fire the works attracted from the two British detached redoubts – Nos. 9 and 10 – on the right flank. Clearly, these posts would have to be neutralized or taken.

The assault on the redoubts
To distract the British from his main intention, Washington ordered diversionary attacks against Gloucester Point over the York River and also against "Fusiliers' Redoubt" on the north-western side of Yorktown. Then, at 8 pm on 14 October, two strong assaults were suddenly launched from the second parallel under cover of darkness. Redoubt No. 10 was attacked by 400 Americans from Lafayette's command under Lieutenant-Colonel Alexander Hamilton, carrying unloaded muskets in case an accidental shot might reveal their intentions. Charging over the ditch and through the barriers of stakes protecting the redoubt's earthern scarp face, the post was carried at bayonet point in just ten minutes.

Simultaneously, 400 French soldiers under Colonel Deux Ponts rushed forward to attack Redoubt No. 9. This assault was pressed home rather less boldly than the American attack had been, and a bitter and costly hand-to-hand fight developed. After half an hour the French planted their colors on the captured parapet.

"The World Turned Upside Down"
The writing was now on the wall for Cornwallis. The Americans speedily completed the second parallel and dragged up their heaviest guns to close by Redoubt No. 9 – within easy range of the main fortifications. The British replied by sending out a sortie of 350 men under Lieutenant Colonel Robert Abercrombie on the night of 15 October. Some damage was caused to the siege battery before the British had to withdraw, but within a day the cannon they had spiked were back in action. Next, Cornwallis planned to move all his men over the river to Gloucester to attempt a break-out, but a storm wrecked this plan. He now accepted the inevitable.

At 10 am on 17 October, a British drummer beat a "parley". Talks were opened, and at 11 am two days later agreement was reached. An hour after this, two redoubts were occupied by the Americans. At 2 pm Cornwallis's 8,000 survivors marched out under command of Major-General O'Hara, their commander-in-chief being indisposed. The troops had been issued with new red-coats for the occasion; the bands played "The World Turned Upside Down" as the men piled their arms. The siege of Yorktown was over. So, effectively, was the war. America had won its independence from Britain.

CHAPTER SIX
Towards Total War

The era between the end of the Napoleonic wars and the start of World War II falls into two quite disparate periods. Up until the Crimean War (1854–56) the great powers of the world – the European empires of Great Britain, France, Austria Russia and the emerging new world nation of the USA – had lived in peace among themselves, thanks to the balance of power devised by the Austrian foreign minister Prince Klemens von Metternich at the Congress of Vienna in 1815. The Crimean War shattered the balance, however, and the next 60 years saw several major wars, the emergence of three new great powers – Germany, Italy and Japan – and the bloody US Civil War, which settled the future direction of development of that increasingly powerful country. The European nations gradually coalesced into two great blocs, the *Entente Cordiale*, between France and Russia joined later by Britain and the Triple Alliance of Germany, Austria-Hungary and Italy. Their mutual antipathy would lead directly to that world shattering event, the First World War.

Naturally enough, both these periods were speckled with minor conflicts – some of which were not quite as minor as others. Yet the two periods were quite different. The emerging nationalism, the accelerating Industrial Revolution, the quantum jump in military technology, the political schisms between conservatism and liberalism all conspired to make warfare in the second part of the period more likely and more intense after the consensus established in 1815 evaporated.

The Industrial Revolution
The use of steam power to replace muscle power had started in the 18th century, but it was not until late in that century and early in the

INFANTRY IN ACTION A French infantryman of 1869 in action with his *Chassepôt rifle. France's military dominance was to end with the Franco-Prussian War.*

1800s that steam power came into extended use. It revolutionized armies and navies in several ways. It enabled men and supplies to be moved rapidly and economically by steamship and by railway. It made it possible to make arms and armaments quickly and in great quantity. As a result of the development of rifled small arms and cannon and the appropriate projectiles, the invention of the percussion cap and breech-loading mechanisms, the armies of the world became much more lethal and the battlefield greatly expanded in depth. Tactics accordingly had to change to meet the new conditions.

Navies, too, were not exempt. Cannon of much greater power firing explosive shells hastened the adoption of first armored-plated wooden vessels and then the all-steel warship. The first use of exploding shells by the Russians and the resulting devastation of the Turkish fleet at Sinope early in the Crimean War gave notice to the world's admirals that times were changing.

The Industrial Revolution also changed warfare in that the development of manufacturing capacity and agricultural machinery enabled warring states to mobilize and put a much greater proportion of their manpower into the field without running the risk of starving the civilian population. Mass armies, the first of which were raised in the Napoleonic era, became the rule, not the exception. Another result was the need to obtain raw materials to feed the voracious appetites of the factories. Colonialism flourished, which in turn required large colonial armies to keep the natives in check and prevent other powers from encroaching on imperial preserves. The British altitude in India demonstrated the point.

The growth of nationalism
It was Napoleon who unleashed the powerful force of nationalism, which continued to spread unabated in the 19th century from Europe across the world. People with a common language and culture tended to have similar beliefs, attitudes and feelings, which encouraged them to value their heritage and make them willing to make sacrifices to preserve it. Nationalism was expansionist where a people wished to consolidate within one nation the similar peoples in neighbouring states. Examples are the creation of Germany, centered around Prussia, while Italy became unified around the kingdom of Piedmont in Savoy. Nationalism also led to the fragmentation, or attempted fragmentation, of established empires. Italy, for instance, gained much of its territory at the expense of Austria-Hungary and that large and diverse empire was continually battling to keep the Hungarians, the Serbians or other nationalities of the realm from establishing their own nations. The Ottoman Empire faced the same problem as its Balkan territories, rose in revolt.

The Greek revolt

One of the earliest nationalist revolts was the Greek War of Independence, which was sparked off in 1821 by the massacre of 10,000 Turks garrisoning Tripolitsa in the Morea area. Turkey responded by capturing the rebel island of Chios and killing or selling into slavery almost all of its inhabitants. The Greeks were quite successful in maintaining their independent state, repulsing both a 30,000-man Turkish army at the fortress of Missolongi – where the poet Byron died in the siege – at the mouth of

the Gulf of Corinth and destroying a Turkish fleet.

The Turkish sultan, however, called on his vassal state of Egypt for support, and, by 1826, had reconquered practically all of Greece. This alarmed the French, the Russians and the English, who asked that the Egyptians be withdrawn. When the Sultan refused, the fleets of the three powers entered the harbour of Navarino, which was sheltering the combined Turkish and Egyptian fleets, and destroyed it on 20 October, 1827. Finally in 1833

RAILWAYS AT WAR *A Russian troop train under Japanese artillery fire during the retreat from Mukden. Railways were now an integral factor in war planning.*

Otto, a prince of Bavaria, became the first king of the constitutional monarchy of Greece. The Turks, after three centuries, had lost their stranglehold on the Balkans.

US expansion

When the guns fell silent in January 1815, signalling the end of the fight-

ing in the War of 1812, the USA's search for a viable peacetime military policy – interrupted by a number of armed conflicts – followed a tortuous course. Several nasty little Indian Wars reared their heads, followed by an expansionist policy at the expense of Mexico. The fall of the Alamo in 1836 in San Antonio, Sam Houston's victory over the Mexicans at San Jacinto, and the resulting creation of the "Lone Star" Republic of Texas were merely harbingers of a full-blown war between the USA and Mexico, commencing in 1846, as a result of which the USA gained California and another large block of territory in the south-west.

South American independence
Dating back to the early 16th century, when the Spanish colonies in the New World first attempted to assert their independence from the motherland, the movement for South American independence had to wait until the 1800s to gain any real impetus. With the home government distracted by the Peninsula War with Napoleon, the patriots saw their chance – especially when an enfeebled Bourbon government tried to reassert itself after the restoration.

The leading figure in the struggle for independance was José de San Martín. Having raised and trained an army at Mendoza in Argentina, which had declared its independence in 1816, San Martín crossed the Andes with 5,200 men in February 1817, defeated the Spanish forces and occupied Santiago. After beating back a royal army from Peru a year later, the independence of Chile was proclaimed. Moving north by sea, he gained control of the capital, Lima, and proclaimed the independence of Peru on 22 July, 1821.

Meanwhile, Simón Bolívar had been leading the revolutionary armies in the north. Despite earlier defeats in Venezuela, he led an army, including British volunteers, into Columbia and, in a battle that was to prove decisive for the future of northern South America, he defeated the Spaniards at Boyaca on 7 August 1819. Together with his lieutenant, Antonio de Sucre, he went on to liberate Ecuador in 1822, and on 26 July met San Martín at Guayaquil. Bolívar assumed command of the combined forces and in a climactic battle at Ayacucho, where 14 Spanish generals were captured, Spanish control of their South American colonies was finally lost once and for all.

The Crimean War
In Europe, however, the status quo in military matters established by the Congress of Vienna lasted until the 1850s. Then, the system started to crumble insofar as relationships between the powers were concerned. The first sign of this was the outbreak of the Crimean War between Russia and Turkey, allied to Britain and France. The bulk of the action took place in the Crimean Peninsula, where the Allies sought to destroy the Russian fortress and naval base of Sevastopol. It lasted from September 1854 until the capture of Sevastopol a year later. The war was notorious for the military incompetence of the commanders on both sides, notably in the battle of *Balaclava*.

The unification of Italy
The next major incident on the European scene was the unification of Italy, which had been an objective

of many statesmen and many uprisings among its peoples prior to 1859. In 1848, for instance, the kingdom of Sardinia had spearheaded a revolt in northern Italy and declared war on Austria, only to be soundly trounced by the Austrian forces under Marshal Josef Radetzky. So matters rested for a decade, until King Victor Emmanuel II of Piedmont and his premier Count Camillo de Cavour secretly met with the Emperor Napoleon III, when Napoleon agreed that France would support the unification of Italy – even at the expense of war with Austria.

Piedmont mobilized in March 1859,
Austria invaded Piedmont in April,
French reinforcements arrived, and,
in the battles of Palestro (30 May)
Magenta (4 June) and Solferino (24
June), the Austrians were bested.

On 11 July, Napoleon III and the
Austrian Emperor Franz Joseph met
and agreed that most of Lombardy
would be ceded to Piedmont, while
Austria retained Venetia. This outraged most Italians, who saw Venetia
as part of their rightful claims. The
result was further outbreaks of revolution in Sicily and the Papal states,
which were ultimately successful.
On 17 March 1861, the kingdom of
Italy under King Victor Emmanuel
was proclaimed. In the meantime,
Piedmont had ceded the provinces
of Nice and Savoy to France for her
help in the 1859 war. Final unification, however, had to wait. In
1866, Venetia was ceded to Italy as
part of the settlement after the
Austro-Prussian War, and in 1870
Rome finally became united Italy's
capital.

The American Civil War 1861–1865

The USA, though well removed in
temperament and by distance from
these European conflicts, now faced
a great war of its own – an internal
struggle between the North and
South. When the diverging political,
economic, and social views of the
two sides finally led to formal civil
war in April 1861, with the Confederate attack on the Federal garrison
of Fort Sumter in the harbour of
Charleston, South Carolina, a dis-
passionate comparison between the
two sides would have shown the
north well ahead of the south in
almost every way, as far as industrial
and human resources were concerned. Much was expected of the
Confederate President Jefferson
Davies; but, while he did well in
many respects, he was eventually
surpassed in overall performance by
Union President Abraham Lincoln,
who slowly and often painfully grew
in ability and stature as Federal
commander-in-chief. Both sides
raised very large and courageous
volunteer armies, while the Union
navy gradually tightened a decisive
blockade of the Confederate Atlantic
and Gulf coasts.

The first major land battle occur-
red on 21 July 1861 near Manassas,
Virginia, along the Bull Run, where
Irvin McDowell's Union army of
some 32,000 was defeated by a
Confederate force of about 28,000
under Generals Beauregard and
Joseph E. Johnston. Then the young
Union commander George B. Mc-
Clellan masterfully moulded the
Army of the Potomac into an
effective Federal striking force –
only to be checked just short of the
Confederate capital of Richmond,
Virginia in the spring of 1862 in his
ambitious "Peninsular Campaign"
by Robert E. Lee.

With the Army of the Potomac
withdrawn – despite McClellan's
protests – from near Richmond to
the Washington front, its new
commander, the bombastic and inept
John Pope, sallied forth recklessly,
only to be trounced at Second
Manassas in late August, 1862.
When Lee countered by invading

Maryland in September, however,
he was thrown back by the reinstated
McClellan at South Mountain and
Antietam – victories that enabled
Lincoln to issue his Emancipation
Proclamation. The president, however, thought "Little Mac" too slow
and cautious, and replaced him with
the incompetent Ambrose E. Burnside. The latter surged forward in
mid-December 1862, only to shatter
his army against Lee's nearly-im-
pregnable defences at Fredericksburg,
Virginia. The two rival armies then
went into winter quarters.

Meantime, both sides – especially
the Federals – were building armored warships. The first naval battle
between ironclads occurred in
Hampton Roads, Virginia, on 9
March 1862, when the John Erics-
son-built *USS Monitor* checked the
CSS Virginia (ex-*Merrimack*) in the
latter's sinking of wooden Northern
warships. Throughout the remainder
of the war, ironclads clashed on the
inland rivers and in coastal waters,
while Confederate sea raiders –
notably Raphael Semmes's *CSS
Alabama*, which took 69 Union
prizes – nearly ruined the US merchant marine.

In the western theater, Federal
armies scored an almost-unbroken
series of successes. Ulysses S. Grant,
aided by the Union navy, captured
Forts Henry and Donelson in Tennessee in February, 1862; but, caught
napping, he barely managed to
repulse Albert Sidney Johnston's
attacks at Shiloh (6–7 April 1862).
A menacing Confederate invasion
of Kentucky by Braxton Bragg was
turned back by the cautious Don
Carlos Buell at Perryville in October;
and Buell's successor, the erratic,
but frequently brilliant, William Rosecrans, captured Nashville, Tennessee, plus beating off Bragg's counter-
stroke at nearby Stones River
(Murfreesboro) at the end of December 1862. Then, in the spring of
1863, Grant – initially frustrated by
his repeated failures in the so-called
"bayou expeditions" – finally managed to capture the important Confederate citadel of *Vicksburg* on the
Mississippi on 4 July through skill
and grim tenacity. The Southerners

won a rare victory in the west in mid-September, when Bragg whipped Rosecrans at Chickamauga in northwestern Georgia, and besieged Chattanooga, Tennessee. However Rosecrans' successor, Grant – reinforced by railroad – redeemed the situation by defeating Bragg and driving him away from that important city in late November.

In the east, after an auspicious beginning, "Fighting Joe" Hooker was beaten by Lee at *Chancellorsville*, Virginia, in early May 1863. Then, when Lee invaded Pennsylvania with some 75,000 men in June, the 93,000-man Army of the Potomac – now under the steady George G. Meade – after an initial setback on 1 July 1863 – bloodily repulsed Confederate assaults over the next two days at *Gettysburg*, a battle that compelled Lee to retreat back into Virginia again.

In the spring of 1864, Grant – now Federal General-in-Chief – advanced against the outnumbered Lee in Virginia in May; and, although he was heavily repelled in his assaults at the Wilderness, Spotsylvania Court House, and Cold Harbor, he finally besieged Lee at Petersburg. Meanwhile, the equally able Sherman captured the vital rail-hub of Atlanta, Georgia, in September, and then embarked on his celebrated "March to the Sea," which resulted in the fall of Savannah in December. Sherman then campaigned successfully through the Carolinas in early 1865, finally forcing the surrender of Joseph E. Johnston at Durham Station in April. In the same month, Grant occupied Petersburg and Richmond, thereby impelling Lee to surrender at Appomattox Court House, thus effectively ending the War. The Civil War had cost the Federals some 360,000 dead out of 1,556,000 troops raised, as compared to Confederate dead of 260,000 out of perhaps 800,000. The outcome of the war settled the divisive issue of slavery once and for all and impelled the USA on a course of industrialization rather than agricultural development.

The tactics and strategy employed in this war were studied in war

GETTYSBURG *A Union cannon at Little Round Top. Northern industrial muscle proved a major deciding factor.*

colleges throughout the world. In particular, the use of the railways and the engineering techniques developed for the rapid repair of damaged tracks and bridges were of great interest to military men. The employment of field fortification on both sides were noted as well, while the campaigns of Lee, Grant and Sherman became standard entries in military manuals and textbooks.

The Franco-Prussian War
While North and South were locked in battle in America, the scene was

being set in Europe for an equally decisive military clash between the supposedly leading power of the day – Napoleon III's Second Empire – and Otto von Bismark's Prussia, now attempting to unify Germany as Italy had been unified a few years before. By 1870, both the French and the Prussians seemed to be eager to provoke war. The French had been alarmed by the Prussian defeat of Austria during the "Seven Weeks War" of 1866, which culminated at the battle of Königgrätz, where the Prussians lost 10,000 against 45,000 Austrian casualties. They were equally alarmed at the success of Bismark in forming the North German Confederation under Prussian leadership after the Austrian defeat. Prussia, in turn, was concerned by France's alliances with Austria and Italy, and, as a counterbalance, attempted to put a member of the Prussian royal family on the Spanish throne. This was the last straw as far as the French government was concerned, and popular pressure and belief in the invincibility of the French army drove the reluctant Napoleon III to declare war on 15 July, 1870.

The French forces, optimistically named "The Army of the Rhine", set out well provided with maps of Germany and none of France, but they were soon to be undeceived. With the armed support of the south German states, three Prussian armies crossed the French frontiers: General Karl von Steinmetz with the 85,000-man First Army advanced from the Moselle, Prince Friedrich Karl led the Second Army of 210,000 towards Metz and Crown Prince Friedrich Wilhelm and the 180,000-strong Third Army marched on Strasbourg. While nominally under the command of Wilhelm I of Prussia, the army commanders were under the effective control of Marshal Helmuth von Moltke, one of the greatest generals and strategists of the day, and the superb Prussian General Staff.

Success soon crowned the Prussian efforts. After an initial minor setback at Saarbruken, the Crown Prince won victories over Marshal

MacMahon at Weissenburg and Wörth, put Strasbourg under siege and advanced toward Nancy and Toul. The First and Second Armies soon had Marshal Bazaine and the cream of the French Army forced back into the fortress at Metz. In heavy fighting at Mars-la-Tour and Gravelotte, Bazaine's attempts to break out were repulsed and by 19 August Metz was besieged.

In a desperate attempt to meet the situation MacMahon reconstituted an army at Châlons and started out with 120,000 men on 21 August to the relief of Bazaine. However he was blocked by the Prussians, and, in the battle of Sedan on September 1, the defeat of the French field armies was completed. The Prussians marched on and invested Paris, which capitulated after an epic siege on 28 January 1871. By the terms of the Treaty of Frankfurt, signed on 10 May 1871, Alsace and a part of Lorraine were

ceded to Germany and an enormous war indemnity of five billion francs imposed on the French.

As a result of the war, the empire of Napoleon III (who personally surrendered to the Prussian king at Sedan) was overthrown and the third French Republic came into being, as did the German empire, with the union of the states of north and south Germany. When Wilhelm I of Prussia was proclaimed Emperor of Germany in the great hall of mirrors in the Château of Versailles on 18 January 1871, the event marked the beginning of German predominance in continental Europe.

GERMAN TRIUMPH
An engraving of a triumphant Prussian Uhlan (above left) reflects the patriotic fervor that greeted the overthrow of France by newly-united Germany in 1871, despite dogged French resistance after their initial set-backs (left). Superb staff work forced the main French armies into encirclement and surrender at Metz and Sedan.

Developments in America
If 1870 saw the emergence of another great power in Europe, the last decade of the century saw the first stirrings of another sleeping giant insofar as the international scene was concerned in the USA. The beginning of this awakening were seen in the War of 1898 with Spain, which marked the start of a policy of expansion that was ultimately to make the USA a Pacific power. When war came, George Dewey won the pivotal naval victory of *Manila Bay* in the Philippines, and an American fleet under William T. Sampson and Winfield S. Schley crushed another decrepit Spanish squadron off Santiago, Cuba. Over 200,000 volunteers were enrolled into the army, and a mood of patriotism swept the nation as an American force of some 16,000 under William R. Shafter defeated an enemy army at San Juan Hill, near Santiago, and forced it to

surrender. Nelson A. Miles then captured Puerto Rico, and another US ground force under Wesley Merritt succeeded in forcing an enemy surrender of Manila, thereby ending the war. American army contingents also performed creditably in China during the Boxer Rebellion of 1900, and participated in suppressing the brutal Philippine insurrection (1899–1902).

The rise of Japan

The same decade that saw the start of the USA's Pacific expansion also saw the rise of another new Pacific power – imperial Japan. On 23 July 1894, coveting Korea, a vassal state of China, the Japanese seized the royal palace at Seoul, captured the reigning queen and appointed a puppet regent, who promptly declared war on the Chinese. As a result China and Japan declared war on each other. After easy victories on land and sea, the Japanese forced China to accept the Treaty of Shimonoseki on 17 April 1895. By its terms, Japan gained the Pescadores Islands, the Liaotung Peninsula with its coveted warm-water harbor at Port Arthur, and Formosa. Korea became nominally independent. However, shortly after, France, Germany and Russia, at the instigation of the Russias, forced Japan to relinquish the Liaotung Peninsula in return for an increased indemnity. This caused bad blood between Russia and Japan, who henceforth were rivals for the control of Korea and for the Port Arthur naval base, which China soon leased to Russia.

In 1904 the Japanese decided to resort to war to implement their expansionary plans at the expense of Russia; on 8 February 1904, they attacked the Russian fleet at anchor in *Port Arthur*, without formally declaring war as with Pearl Harbor 37 years later. On 10 February, war was declared and by the end of May Port Arthur was under siege. After heroic resistance, it surrendered on 2 January 1905. Russian forces were defeated at the Yalu River and at Liao-Yang, forcing a withdrawal to Mukden, where they were again defeated in March.

JAPAN EMERGES *Japanese warships go into action at Tsushima (above), while a Russian prisoner of war is brought into the Japanese lines during the siege of Port Arthur (left). Japan's victory brought her world-power status.*

The Russians' last throw came in late May 1905, when the Baltic Fleet, which had been dispatched from Kronstadt seven months earlier, finally reached Japanese waters. This was destroyed at the battle of *Tsushima Straits* and, as a result Tsar Nicholas II was forced to accept the mediation of President Theodore Roosevelt. At the Treaty of Portsmouth, signed on 5 September 1905, Russia agreed that Korea, in effect, became a Japanese vassal, plus ceding the southern half of Sakhalin Island, the lease of Port Arthur and the Liaotung Peninsula to Japan. By late 1910 Korea had been formally annexed by Japan, and, by 1912, Japan had secured Russian recognition that Manchuria was a legitimate sphere of Japanese influence on the Chinese mainland.

These developments were dramatic and totally unexpected – even by the British, who had made an alliance with Japan in 1903. By 1914, however, it was clear that Japan had become the pre-eminent force in the Far East and was well on the way to emerging as a world power.

Queen Victoria's wars

After the Crimean War, Britain was not directly involved in any European conflict until the First World War. It was a different story in Africa and Asia, however, as Britain's imperial role involved her in many minor wars in both continents. The largest of these clashes came in South Africa. In 1880, the so-called First Boer war between the Boers and the British erupted over control of the recently discovered diamond and gold fields. The Boers won, and by the treaty of Pretoria (April 5 1881), the independence (under British suzerainty) of the two Boer republics – the South African Republic and the Transvaal – was recognized. By October 1899, however, the British felt the Boers were determined to drive them out of southern Africa, while the Boers, in their turn, were convinced that the British planned to acquire the rich Transvaal region. The Second Boer War broke out on 12 October 1899.

At the outset, the British had only some 25,000 troops to oppose a much larger Boer force, which was well equipped with small arms and had in addition some modern breech-loading cannon made by Krupp in Germany and by Creusot in France. The Boers were accomplished marksmen and horsemen, superb irregular soldiers and used to the climate, geography and terrain of the area. The British forces were well-disciplined, but were trained for combat in the style of the Crimean War; nor had their equipment altered much from that issued to them in that era.

The Boers were very successful in the beginning, winning such battles as Laing's Nek, Nicholson's Nek and besieging Ladysmith, Mafeking and Kimberly. The British attempts to relieve Kimberly and Ladysmith were frustrated at Magersfontein and *Colenso*. Heavily reinforced and with a new supreme commander in Field Marshal Roberts, with General Kitchener as chief of staff,

ON COMMANDO *Well-equipped Boer commandos successfully resisted the might of the British Empire.*

the tide started to turn in Britain's favor. The turning point came with the relief of Ladysmith on 28 February 1900. The Orange Free State was overrun and annexed as a British colony in May, the Transvaal was similarly annexed that September, and, by the treaty of Vereeniging (31 May 1902) the Boers accepted British sovereignty. All of southern Africa with its wealth was effectively under British control.

This was the last major conflict involving Britain prior to the First World War; it also marked the end of the self-proclaimed period of "splendid isolation" that had lasted since the Crimean War. It also sparked off a period of army reform, though, unlike their European rivals, the British still relied totally on a small professional army, rather than on large conscript forces.

By the end of the period, therefore, things had changed out of all recognition since 1815. France and Russia were now allied, joined by a reluctant Britain in the Triple Entente. Italy and Germany had emerged as new factors on the European scene – and had joined the fading light of Austria-Hungary in the Triple Alliance. Europe was a powder keg waiting for the spark. In world terms, the USA had embarked on the path that was to make her a force on the world scene, while Japan was rapidly emerging as a militaristic world power.

What few of the leaders involved – generals and politicians alike – saw was that the notion of the "nation at arms", allied to the revolution that had occurred in weaponry as the result of the Industrial Revolution, meant that a truly major war might well be more protracted and costly than ever before. The lessons of the US Civil War, which had shown the power of the defensive, were quickly overlooked in favor of the *élan* and dash of the all-out offensive. The cost of this was to be borne by a generation from August 1914 to the 1918 armistice.

INTO THE CHARGE *This was how Victorian imperialists liked to see their wars – bold, brave actions in which civilization swiftly triumphed over the ignorant natives. British victory at Omdurman was not clinched by this romantic cavalry charge, however. It was the result of the superb fire of the squares of infantry.*

Railways, Communications and Warfare

After Waterloo, as armies became larger and more mobile, commanders were faced with more demanding logistical problems, so it is astonishing that there was considerable delay in employing the railroad to convey soldiers and supplies. As early as 1830 – only a few days after the official opening of the Liverpool and Manchester Railway – Britain moved troops by rail between the two cities, but, for many years, this remained an isolated example, rather than rule.

In the Crimea in 1854–55, the British used a small amount of standard-gauge track and railway equipment locally, but this action had scarcely any lasting impact on the quartermaster branch of the British Army. Despite a few stirrings in Prussia, the realization that railroads could be useful in wartime had to await the US Civil War.

The North, the South and the railroad

When the war between the states broke out in 1861, both the Federals and Confederates showed little interest in railroads at first, save for their use in army mobilization. The situation changed, however, when it was seen that the war would be a long and costly one. Before too long, existing railroads, augmented by river steamboats, were increasingly pressed into service to move tens of thousands of troops and animals and

mountains of supplies and equipment; as the war progressed, major military campaigns were planned around the need to capture, or defend, important rail lines and junctions. Sweeping cavalry raids were launched to tear up track, burn railroad bridges, and seize vital rail hubs. Indeed, as the conflict dragged on, many Federal and Confederate leaders came to realize that control of the railways could well determine the difference between victory or defeat.

This became clear as early as the First Bull Run campaign in July, 1861, where P.G.T. Beauregard's Confederate army near Manassas – threatened by Irvin McDowell's superior Union force – was reinforced decisively at the last moment by rail. The timely arrival of Joseph E. Johnston's Confederate troops from the Shenandoah Valley, enabled the graycoats to defeat the Northerners and force them into rapid retreat. But the most impressive use of railways came after *Gettysburg*,

RAILWAYS AT WAR *The Union locomotive (below) still bears Confederate bullet scars; (right) successful Union sabotage.*

when, in the Chickamauga campaign in Georgia in September 1863, Braxton Bragg's Confederate army was massively reinforced by rail by James Longstreet's 12,500 troops from Virginia – a reinforcement that enabled Bragg to gain one of the South's few victories in the western theater of operations. This Confederate success was short-lived, however, when Ulysses S. Grant was reinforced by some 20,000 soldiers under Joseph Hooker – again sent by rail from George G. Meade's Army of the Potomac in northern Virginia. These enabled Grant to turn the tide and smash Bragg's army at Chattanooga, Tennessee.

As far as other forms of communication were concerned, flares and wig-wag flags were still employed in wartime and peacetime, as was the heliograph in the south-west. Balloons, too, were widely used for military purposes, the most prominent Federal aeronaut being Professor Thaddeus S.C. Lowe. However it was the widespread use of the telegraph for rapid military communications that had a more lasting effect. The clicking instrument was employed constantly by both Union and Confederate sides during the civil war, for both strategic and even tactical purposes. Experiments, too, started with homing pigeons.

In the late 1870s in America, shortly after its invention by Alexander Graham Bell, the US Army was experimenting with the telephone; by 1892, of the 99 garrisoned military posts in the USA, 59 had telephone equipment to supplement their existing telegraph services. When war broke out with Spain in 1898, President William McKinley set up a "war room" in the White House in which 25 telegraphs and 15 telephones were placed, so speeding up communication with distant departments, posts, and headquarters. European powers followed suit.

The military railway

Railways soon became an integral factor in the waging of war in Europe as well. In the Franco-Prussian War,

for instance, while the French employed their railways largely to evacuate refugees, the Prussians planned the use of their rail network extremely effectively, both to move their troops and their equipment and to keep them well stocked with supplies.

All of these uses thus far of railways for military purposes, however, were of existing systems. The first attempt to construct a solely military railroad occurred in 1882 when General Kitchener, the British commander in the Egyptian-Sudanese campaign, built a standard-gauge line from his Nile river base into the interior. While this track was soon torn up by his Dervish opponents, it set an example for more distinctly military employment of railroads. This was seen in the Boer War at the end of the century, when the British used no less than 20 armored trains – not only to fight the Boers, but also to protect the many miles of track being used increasingly by the advancing British forces for logistical purposes.

Other nations noted this British practice. The German regular and reserve companies of railroad engineers were increased in number, while the French 10th Section of military engineers was reorganized as a railway force. By the early years of the 20th century, the British railroad branch of the Royal Engineers maintained two permanent railroad companies, who even had their own lines to train on at Chattenden in Kent and at Longmoor in Hampshire. And much military railway development by several European powers took place in their colonies, including the use of semi-portable track. The Americans made considerable military use of their existing civilian rail lines in the 1898 war with Spain.

On the eve of the First World War, the great powers had developed light narrow-gauge rail lines that could be laid quickly – even over rough terrain – to serve the front lines. By 1914 the Germans were undoubtedly the leaders in railroad development for military purposes, but all the warring nations utilized their railways to the full during the ensuing four years. Of course, once the armies had left their railheads they were largely dependent upon horses and their own muscles.

WAR NEWS *Union engineers construct telegraph lines (below left), which reporters (below right) used to flash news home.*

ANTIETAM (SHARPSBURG)
US CIVIL WAR
1862

This battle, fought on 17 September 1862, was the bloodiest single-day conflict of the US Civil War. Federal victory here marked the repulse of General Robert E. Lee's first invasion of the north. The Confederate Army of Northern Virginia numbered perhaps some 52,000 men, as contrasted with about 75,000 effectives serving in Union Major-General George B. McClellan's Army of the Potomac.

Following the disastrous defeat of John Pope's Federal army at Second Manassas at the end of August 1862, the Confederate commander Robert E. Lee promptly invaded Maryland, his combined army soon reaching Frederick. On the Union side, George B. McClellan, reinstated in command of the Army of the Potomac, pushed his forces westward from Washington, D.C., to

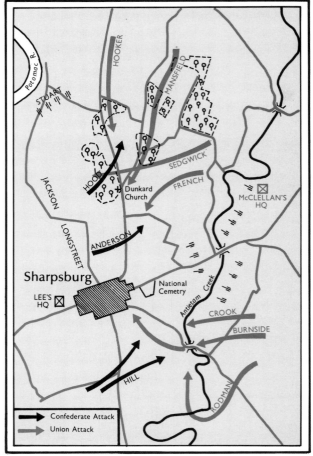

ANTIETAM *Delays by Burnside on the Federal left enabled Lee to contain McClellan's attacks and counter-attack.*

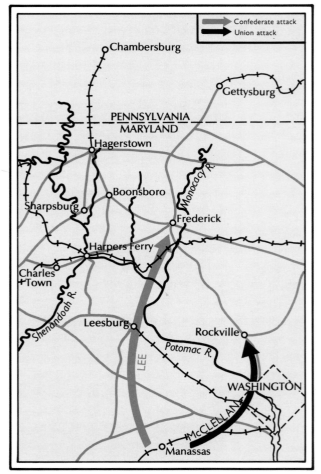

LEE IN MARYLAND *Though a tactical success, the campaign was a setback for Lee as his invasion was blocked.*

confront Lee, but he could not convince the inept Federal General-in-Chief, Henry W. Halleck, to withdraw 12,500 Federal soldiers from a virtual death-trap at Harper's Ferry; they were captured there by the Confederate cavalry leader Stonewall Jackson.

Union initiatives

From his cavalry reconnaissance – confirmed by a captured enemy order – McClellan correctly guessed that Lee had daringly split his army. Half under Jackson were moving to invest Harper's Ferry, and half under James Longstreet were marching from Frederick towards Hagerstown. Pressing forward, McClellan won the Battle of South Mountain on 14 September, thereby wresting the all-important initiative from Lee. The latter was now obliged to concentrate his army in a cramped defensive position behind the Antietam creek near Sharpsburg, Maryland.

Advancing to the attack, McClellan delayed opening the battle in earnest until 17 September. His plan was to assail the Confederates first with his right, followed by his left, and finally his center. In heavy morning fighting, Union troops made gains against Jackson in the East Woods, the Cornfield, and the

West Woods, and against Longstreet at the Sunken Road ("Bloody Lane"); however, inexcusable delays throughout the morning by Ambrose E. Burnside on the Federal left enabled Lee to successfully shift troops from opposite him to eventually contain McClellan's other attacks. When Burnside finally captured the bridge that bears his name, and advanced toward Sharpsburg, the move was too late, since he was promptly counter-attacked on the left flank and checked by A.P. Hill, who had arrived from Harper's Ferry just in time to make the move.

So, after 14 hours of desperate fighting, the bloodiest day in all of American military history to that date ended. Confederate casualties were around 13,724 as opposed to Union losses of 12,410. The clash forced Lee to retreat into Virginia, and McClellan's success gave Abraham Lincoln the opportunity to issue the Preliminary Emancipation Proclamation. It also ended a real threat of British diplomatic recognition of Confederate independence.

BALACLAVA
CRIMEAN WAR
1854

Fought on 25 October 1854, when British, French and Turkish forces totalling some 10,000 men, plus 20 cannon, under Lord Raglan prevented the capture of the key supply port of Balaclava by Count Liprandi's Russians (25,000 men and 78 guns). The victory meant that the siege of the great Russian naval base of Sevastopol could continue; it is also notable for the ill-fated charge of the British Light Brigade.

In late October 1854, Prince Alexander Menshikov, commanding the Russian field armies in the Crimea, sent a force of 25,000 men and 78 guns under Count Liprandi to capture the British supply port of Balaclava and thus force the lifting of the siege of Sevastopol. The attack took the small British and Turkish forces in

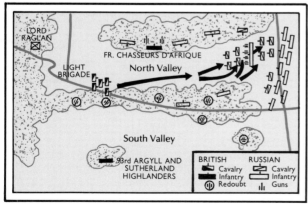

BALACLAVA *A misunderstood order sent the British Light Brigade charging into the "valley of death".*

the area by surprise; the Turks, who were manning six redoubts along the Causeway Heights, were soon driven out of their positions in complete rout. Following this, the Russian cavalry advanced to the south, their advance remaining unchecked until they came upon a battalion of the 93rd Highland Regiment, commanded by Sir Colin Campbell, which was guarding the approaches to the port. This was the first memorable moment of this famous battle. As the *Times* war correspondent, William Howard Russell, described it, the Highlanders formed "a thin red streak with a line of steel." A volley from their Minié rifles stopped the Russians in their tracks; a second volley drove them back in full retreat.

The Heavy Brigade charges
Meanwhile, the Russian cavalry to the north of the Causeway Heights had also turned south toward Balaclava. As the 3,000 Russians were halfway down the Heights, however, Sir John Scarlett ordered his 800-man Heavy Brigade of the British Cavalry Division to charge them at full gallop. This completely unorthodox manoeuvre – the text books laid down that cavalry could not charge up hill and the standard response would have been to prepare to receive the Russian charge – took the Russians completely aback. Thrown into confusion, they suffered substantial losses and were forced to retreat back to the North Valley. The victorious squadrons of the Heavy Brigade were too disorganized to pursue.

The misundertood order
Count Liprandi reorganized his cavalry, positioning most of it behind 12 artillery pieces at the east end of the North Valley. The North slope of the valley held eight of his battalions and 14 guns, while the remainder of his forces were strung along the eastern half of the Causeway Heights.

Lord Raglan, who was watching the progress of the battle from the heights north-west of the valley saw the Russians start to remove the guns from the redoubts they had taken from the Turks. Forgetting that this would be invisible to the men on the field, he sent an order to Lord Lucan, commanding the Cavalry Division, ordering him to move forward to prevent the removal. The imprecision of the order was to lead to disaster. Lucan, assuming the cannon in question were those in front of the Russian cavalry, promptly ordered Lord Cardigan to attack them with the Light Brigade, and, after registering a protest, Cardigan courageously led his men in the charge up the valley.

As the ranks thinned in the face of a hail of Russian fire from the front and both flanks, the British troopers manoeuvred as precisely as they would have done on the parade ground, drawing in to fill up the ranks and continue the charge to sweep through the Russian artillery. The attack finally spent itself on the cavalry massed at the head of the valley. Returning through the shot and shell from the cannon to the south, little fire was received from the north, as the French 4th Chasseurs d'Afrique had silenced the northern guns with a similarly heroic charge.

"Someone had blundered"

Of the 673 officers and men of the Light Brigade who went into action at the start of the 20-minute engagement, 247 men and 497 horses were lost. Celebrated in Alfred, Lord Tennyson's stirring poem "The Charge of the Light Brigade", the action was pithily summed up by the French general Pierre Bosquet, who aptly commented to Lord Ragland: "It is magnificent, but it is not war."

The port of Balaclava, however, was saved – though the severing of the crucial supply road almost led to the starvation of the British army the following winter. What the action demonstrated was the incompetence of the senior commanders on both sides and the courage and gallantry of the combatants. This was to be a characteristic of the conduct of the whole of the war, though, as far as military medicine was concerned, Florence Nightingale's crusade to improve medical conditions was directly aided by the wretched conditions this incompetence provoked. The costs, however, were high, slightly more than 250,000 men perishing on each side.

BUENA VISTA
MEXICAN WAR
1847

Buena Vista – fought on 22-23 February 1847 – was a decisive battle of the Mexican War and one which the USA could have ill afforded to lose. Some 4,800 US troops, under the command of Zachary Taylor ("Old Rough and Ready"), repulsed the assaults of about 15,000 Mexican regulars under Santa Anna.

Having won three victories earlier in the war at Palo Alto, Resaca de la Palma, and Monterrey, Zachary Taylor, protecting his main advanced supply base at Saltillo, now stood on the defensive on the fingerlike, ravined plateaus to the east of the main road at a defile known as the Angostura, near the hacienda of Buena Vista. He had approximately 4,800 mostly inexperienced soldiers under his command. Having intercepted a message from American General-in-Chief Winfield Scott to Taylor which not only revealed to the Mexican leader the dwarfed size of Taylor's force near Buena Vista, but also the plans for Scott to land a sizeable army at Vera Cruz and push toward Mexico City, Santa Anna correctly determined to crush Taylor first and then turn to deal with Scott.

A hard-fought battle

Consequently, on 2 February 1847, Santa Anna pressed

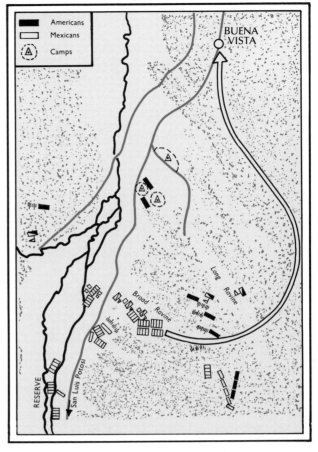

BUENA VISTA In this hard-fought battle, the day was won by masterful handling of the US "flying artillery" batteries.

northward from San Luis Potosi in a forced march through desolate country with some 15,000 wiry Mexican soldiers; and, on 22 February, he launched several impetuous, but indecisive, assaults on part of Taylor's force, under John E. Wool, to the east of the road near the Angostura. The main battle was joined the following day, desperate Mexican attacks initially driving some Americans back on their left and critically endangering Wool's entire position. Only the masterful handling of the so-called "flying artillery" batteries by Braxton Bragg, John Paul Jones O'Brien, John M. Washington, and Thomas W. Sherman saved the day for the USA.

At the crisis of the battle, Taylor hurled his last reserves from the ranch-house at Buena Vista into the fray, and finally rode on to the battlefield himself. Invaluable counterattcks by these troops – including Jefferson Davis' First Mississippi Rifles – and other Americans succeeded in checking the Mexican onslaught. Savage hand-to-hand fighting occurred at places. Although hindered by an abortive American charge and a terrible rainstorm, Taylor managed to repel a final Mexican attack against his center, a repulse that induced Santa Anna to fall back, and then to retreat from the field to the south to defend his capital.

US casualties at Buena Vista totalled some 746, as contrasted to Mexican losses of at least 3,700. The battle resulted in the all-important strategic initiative in the war shifting decisively to the US side, thus foreshadowing Mexico's ultimate defeat.

CHANCELLORSVILLE
US CIVIL WAR
1863

One of the major battles of the US Civil War – often called General Robert E. Lee's most brilliant victory – fought on 1–5 May 1863 in Virginia. Lee's success there paved the way for the Confederacy's second invasion of the North. His Army of Northern Virginia numbered approximately 62,000; it was pitted against Major-General Joseph Hooker's Union Army of the Potomac, which consisted of some 132,000 men.

Following the disastrous defeat of the Federal army under the inept Ambrose E. Burnside at Fredericksburg, Virginia, in mid-December, 1862, President Abraham Lincoln replaced Burnside with "Fighting Joe" Hooker. Successively an able brigade, division, corps, and grand division commander, the new Union leader initiated a number of helpful administrative reforms of the Army of the Potomac in the early months of 1863. When the campaign season opened that April, Hooker wrung from Lincoln approval of his plan of operations. This was to leave some 40,000 soldiers under John Sedgwick to hold the Confederate army at Fredericksburg, while

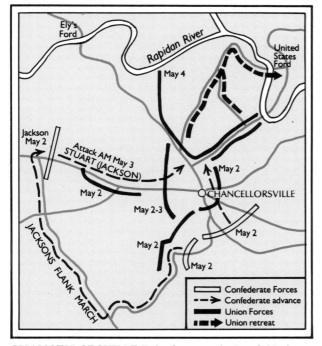

CHANCELLORSVILLE *Federal commander Joseph Hooker squandered an advantage and was then outgeneralled by Lee.*

marching the rest of his army westward up the Rappahannock river, and then crossing the river to move against Lee's rear.

Stroke and counterstroke
Hooker's was a sound plan, and, in its initial stages, he outgeneralled Lee. In an adept manoeuvre beginning on 27 April, the Union commander succeeded in moving several of his corps in three days to Chancellorsville, a strategic crossroads in a tangled area known as the Wilderness, some ten miles west of Fredericksburg. Lee, however, reacted enterprisingly. Leaving some 10,000 troops under Jubal Early to hold Marye's Heights at Fredericksburg, he himself marched with the rest of his badly outnumbered army to confront Hooker at Zoan Church at the eastern edge of the Wilderness, some three miles east of Chancellorsville.

A loss of nerve
Expecting that Lee would withdraw his entire army southward toward Richmond, Hooker was astounded by the bold Confederate countermove. He lost his nerve, and on 1 May pulled back to defend the Chancellorsville crossroads. Lee moved forward, and ordered Stonewall Jackson to attack the exposed right flank of Oliver O. Howard's 11th Corps, which was posted on the Orange Plank Road just west of Wilderness Church. In one of his greatest feats, Jackson, late on the afternoon of 2 May, smashed Howard's force and sent it reeling eastward toward Chancellorsville. Just as the Confederate attack was losing momentum and grinding to a halt, Jackson was mortally wounded, by his own men, who mistook their general and his staff for Federals in the gathering dusk. The following day, Lee resumed the offensive and gradually pushed the Federal forces back to Chancellorsville and then north of the town. Hooker was wounded in the fighting, but unwisely retained command.

Meanwhile, Sedgwick's 6th Corps had attacked Early's Confederates at Fredericksburg, driven them off Marye's Heights, and advanced westward toward Lee's rear. The Southern commander, however, marched swiftly eastward with a part of his army, and, reinforced by Early, defeated Sedgwick at Salem Church on 3–4 May, and forced him to withdraw. The demoralized Hooker then retreated to his starting point.

COLENSO
THE ANGLO–BOER WAR
December 1899

A serious defeat inflicted on General Sir Redvers Buller (13,500 men and 44 guns) by the Boer leader, General Louis Botha (5,000 Boers and 15 guns) near Colenso, while the former was attempting to relieve the besieged

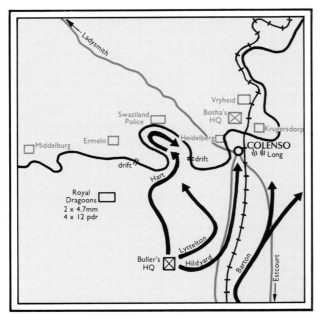

COLENSO *Buller's cumbersome frontal attack on 6,000 entrenched Boers across the Tugela was a costly failure.*

garrison of Ladysmith. As the third setback of what the British termed "Black Week", it led to the replacement of Buller by Lord Roberts as commander-in-chief.

The Anglo Boer War (1899–1902) saw the full military might of the British empire being deployed to crush the two tiny Boer republics of the Transvaal and the Orange Free State in southern Africa, but, as Colenso was to show, this was to prove no easy task. Determined to raise the Boer sieges of Kimberley, Mafeking and Ladysmith in the last months of 1899, Buller's forces advanced in three columns. Two of these, under Generals Gatacre and Methuen, were defeated at Stormberg (10 December) and Magersfontein (11 December) respectively. The third, under Buller's personal command, was to fare no better at Colenso two days later; this setback, together with the earlier pair, earned the period the nickname of "Black Week" in the British army.

An incompetent plan
Approaching the River Tugela, only 14 miles south of Ladysmith (where General White's garrison had been besieged since 2 November), Buller, without conducting a thorough reconnaissance, ordered an immediate attack on the Boers holding the river's further bank. This was in fact what Botha – planning to trap the British once they were over the river – hoped he would attempt. However, the British advance was not going to follow Buller's plan, despite his original intentions before action was joined.

Buller ordered the Irish Brigade (four battalions strong) to cross the Tugela on the left near Bridle Drift. The 2nd Brigade (also four battalions) was to attack in the center, cross the river over bridges at Colenso, and

to take the Boer held *kopjes* (low hills) beyond, while, on the right, Lord Dundonald's mounted brigade was to occupy Hlangwane Mountain and support the main attack with flanking fire. To support this three-pronged advance, (but especially the attack on Colenso), Colonel Long was ordered to move forward two Royal Field Artillery batteries and six naval 12pdrs. In the event, this last element in Buller's plan – as erroneously executed – was to determine the outcome of the battle.

The bungled attack
From the outset, everything went wrong. On the left, Major General Hart and his Irishmen were diverted into a loop of the Tugela, and would have crossed straight into a Boer trap had not their opponents opened fire too soon and pinned them down on the south bank. Only when Buller had sent in Major-General Lyttelton's 4th Brigade was Hart extricated. On the right, Dundonald's assault on the Hlangwane feature was stopped in its tracks by its 800 Boer defenders and a fast-firing pompom gun. This pinned them down until the end of the battle, when the Mounted Brigade was successfully withdrawn.

It was in the center, however, that the critical events took place. Long moved his guns far further forward than ordered, advancing ahead of the main infantry of Major-General Hildyard's 2nd Brigade. The guns were soon under accurate enemy fire, and running out of ammunition, the British gunners were ordered to leave their pieces and seek cover while awaiting resupply. Noting that the guns were unmanned, and believing all their crews to be dead, Buller rode forward to organize the rescue of his supposedly-abandoned guns by volunteers. Two guns were brought back, but casualties mounted, Lord Roberts' son being killed (earning a posthumous Victoria Cross).

Buller now ordered a general withdrawal, and abandoned the remaining ten guns to the Boers. These might have been recovered by Dundonald's retiring cavalry, but the presence of field-ambulances nearby dissuaded him from the attempt. The total cost of the battle to the British was 71 officers and 1,055 rank and file, the Irish Brigade taking about half these casualties.

Buller replaced
Botha was disappointed by Colenso's outcome, as he was convinced that he could have inflicted a major defeat on Buller had the British crossed the river. Nevertheless, Buller had given him a success. This defeat, added to the earlier setbacks the British had suffered that same week, completed the discrediting of Buller. He was relegated to command of only the Natal front, while Lord Roberts, with Lord Kitchener as his chief of staff, took over as commander-in-chief. Colenso – and other events of the three-year Anglo-Boer War – awoke Britain to the need for military reforms. These were carried through just in time for the outbreak of world war in 1914.

DELHI
INDIAN MUTINY
1857

Brigadier-General John Nicholson at the head of 4,000 British soldiers captured the city of Delhi defended by Badahur Shah and 30,000 mutineers on 20 September 1857. The British success signalled the beginning of the end of the great Indian Mutiny.

The sepoys rise
The great Indian Mutiny of 1857–58, although based on numerous grievances, was sparked off by an entirely unforseen event. The improved Minié cartridge, introduced in 1857 for the weapons of the native armies of the East India Company, required its user to bite off the end of the paper cartridge before loading it into the gun. The problem was that the cartridge was greased with a combination of pork fat (abhorrent to Moslems) and cow tallow (sacred to Hindus). Soldiers of both faiths objected to the new cartridge, and, on 10 May 1857, sepoys at Meerut, near Delhi, mutinied and killed all the European men, women and children they could lay hands on.

The Delhi garrison joined the mutineers, and a general massacre of Europeans took place. At Cawnpore, an especially barbarous event occurred when, after promises of good treatment, the British troops surrendered and were promptly slaughtered to a man. Their women and children were imprisoned and later hacked to death on the eve of the recapture of the city by a relief force.

The siege of Delhi
So matters rested until June, when a relief force of 3,000 British soldiers under the command of Sir Henry Barnard reached Delhi. The force was not sufficiently strong to capture the city, or even to invest it completely. However, on 8 June, the British did manage to capture the Baddi-Ki-Serai ridge, which overlooked the city, and, despite attacks by the mutineers, they successfully maintained their positions there for the next month and into July.

In early August additional reinforcements, led by General John Nicholson, arrived. After completing the encirclement of the city, they called on the defenders to surrender, but Badahur Shah, commanding some 30,000 mutineers, refused.

The fall of Delhi
After a heavy bombardment starting on 10 September, four columns of 1,000 men each assaulted the city four days later. Despite heavy losses – the gallant General Nicholson was among those who fell – the British finally succeeded in penetrating the city. Six days of heavy and vicious street fighting followed before Delhi was finally subdued. Among those captured was Badahur Shah, whose sons were summarily executed in reprisal for the Cawnpore massacre.

The capture of Delhi marked the beginning of the end for the mutineers. From then on, the British moved swiftly to reassert their control of India, even though the Indian sub-continent was not completely subdued until the next summer.

GETTYSBURG
AMERICAN CIVIL WAR
1863

A three-day battle from 1 July to 3 July 1863, that marked the climax and failure of Confederate General Robert E. Lee's second and final invasion of the North during the US Civil War. Lee's force – the Army of Northern Virginia – numbered approximately 75,000; the Union Army of the Potomac, under Major-General George G. Meade, comprised some 93,000 men.

Gettysburg was one of the crucial battles of the US Civil War – yet it was an engagement into which both sides stumbled unexpectedly. For almost a month after Lee had moved from Fredericksburg, Virginia, where his army had been barring the advance of Union forces under Major-General Joseph Hooker, both Confederate and Federal intelligence had been faulty, and neither commander knew precisely where the other was

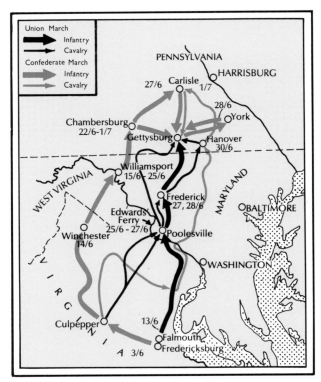

GETTYSBURG *The Federal lines were anchored on Culp's Hill in the north and Little Round Top in the south.*

located. After his plan to advance upon Richmond, the Confederate capital, had been vetoed by President Abraham Lincoln, Hooker's aim was to manoeuvre his army between the rebels and Washington, D.C. Lee, for his part, marched his forces northward up the Shenandoah and Cumberland valleys into southern Pennsylvania. However, the Confederate cavalry, under the dashing "Jeb" Stuart, was absent on an ill-advised raid around the Federal army; the exhausted Southern troopers would not rejoin Lee until the afternoon of the second day's battle.

This was the situation on 28 June when Lee received the unexpected news that the Army of the Potomac was not in Virigina as he had confidently supposed, but just 25 miles away at Frederick, Maryland. He also received the unwelcome word that the more competent Meade had replaced Hooker as the Union commander.

The first clashes

Lee immediately ordered the three corps of his army to concentrate near Cashtown, while Meade moved northward toward the road-hub of Gettysburg. On 30 June, elements of two opposing brigades spotted each other just to the west of the town; the battle proper

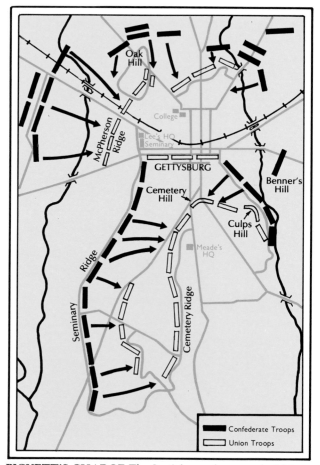

PICKETT'S CHARGE *The Confederate charge on the Union right-center was the last-ditch throw of Lee's army.*

opened the following morning. Neither army commander had sought the clash, so there was little initial overall plan on either side. Instead, reinforcements were thrown piecemeal into the fray as they arrived on the field.

Fortune favored the Confederates at first. By the end of the first day's fighting, A.P. Hill's 3rd Corps and Richard S. Ewell's 2nd Corps had got the better of the outnumbered Federals; in eight hours of heavy fighting, they pushed them back from the north-west to the south of Gettysburg. Meade had been absent from the field. Lee, who by late afternoon had arrived on the scene, ordered Ewell to attack the commanding eminence of Cemetery Hill, but added the fatal words "if practical" to his order. The cautious Ewell confined his efforts merely to reconnoitering and light probing.

This gave the battered Federal forces time to regroup. They assumed positions on Cemetery Hill, Culp's Hill, and along Cemetery Ridge, anchoring their left flank at two hills – Little Round Top and Big Round Top – thereby establishing a strong defensive position against the Confederates.

The decisive day

During the night, both sides brought up reinforcements, while the commanders drew up their plans for the next stage of the contest. Lee ordered James Longstreet's 1st Corps to attack the Union left wing, thereby rolling up the defences along the Emmitsburg Road and Cemetery Ridge, in conjunction with an assault by Ewell against Cemetery and Culp's Hills. The plan, however, called for both attacks to be coordinated – but they were not. Longstreet's delayed attack at 4.00 pm did drive Daniel Sickles' Third Corps back from the Peach Orchard, Wheatfield, and Devil's Den, but Longstreet could not break through the main Union line.

Yet, perhaps Longstreet had the opportunity to do this. The Confederates had failed to try to take advantage of the disorganization of the Federal forces at the end of the first day's battle. Now, they missed another chance of decisive victory. Before Longstreet moved to the attack, Sickles, acting without orders, had moved his troops off Cemetery Ridge and Little Round Top, and had formed a weak salient at the Peach Orchard in front of the main Union line.

If the Confederates could take Little Round Top, they would be able to enfilade most of the Federal line and probably sweep the Army of the Potomac from the field. Fortunately for Meade, Gouverneur K. Warren rushed Northern infantry and artillery to the summit of Little Round Top just as the Southerners started their assault upon the key hill. The Confederates were repulsed and the Union army saved. Ewell's later attack on East Cemetery Hill was repelled, but he did gain a lodgment on the lower slopes of Culp's Hill.

The charge of Pickett and Pettigrew

During the night of 2 July, the arrival of fresh Union reinforcements swung the balance in Meade's favor.

The next morning, a heavy seven-hour Federal counterattack, beginning at 4.00 am, drove Ewell's troops from the ground they had gained at Culp's Hill. In a desperate bid for victory, Lee ordered George E. Pickett and J.J. Pettigrew, with nearly 15,000 men, to launch an all-out assault on the right-center of the Union line in association with a cavalry sweep by Stuart toward the rear of the Union army.

After a preliminary artillery bombardment of an hour and 50 minutes, Pickett and Pettigrew led the cream of the Confederacy forward in a magnificent charge at 3.15 pm toward the Federal line – nearly a mile away – on Cemetery Ridge. Their orders, which Longstreet thought impossible to execute successfully, were simple – to break the Union center – but, even more unfortunately for the Confederates, Meade had anticipated Lee's move. Cut down by cannon and musketry fire, only some 150 Southerners reached the Federal lines, where they were promptly overwhelmed.

The great charge of Pickett and Pettigrew cost the Army of Northern Virginia at least 7,000 casualties. Simultaneously, Lee learned that Stuart's cavalry had been repulsed by David M. Gregg and George A. Custer at the Rummel Farm. Though the two exhausted armies held their positions for a further day, the South had lost the crucial battle and, that night, Lee began a skilful retreat into Virginia.

The casualties at Gettysburg were approximately 23,000 Federal to 28,000 Confederate. This advantage was enhanced by the North's ability to replace its losses to a far greater degree than could the Southerners. From then the South was on the strategic defensive.

HAMPTON ROADS
US CIVIL WAR
1862

This naval action, fought on 9 March 1862 in Hampton Roads, Virginia, is significant as the first engagement in history between ironclad warships. Although the battle was a draw, the fact that the Union's *Monitor* thwarted *Virginia*'s (ex-*Merrimack*) further destruction of wooden Union men-of-war near Norfolk enabled Major-General George B. McClellan's 95,000-man Army of the Potomac to land safely at Fort Monroe and commence

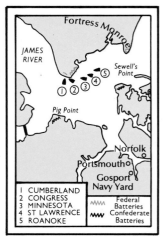

1 CUMBERLAND
2 CONGRESS
3 MINNESOTA
4 ST LAWRENCE
5 ROANOKE

Federal Batteries
Confederate Batteries

When the Federals prematurely evacuated the Norfolk Navy Yard on 20–21 April 1861, the screw warship USS *Merrimack* – needing engine repairs – was scuttled. She was salvaged by the Confederates, given a 170-ft-long superstructure armoured with four inches of wrought iron, provided with a ram and six 9-inch Dahlgren smoothbores and four rifled guns of 6-inch and 7-inch, and rechristened CSS *Virginia*. Her captain was Franklin Buchanan. *Monitor* – a completely revolutionary vessel designed by John Ericsson – had a 172-ft-long deck, almost awash, upon which were mounted a four-ft-high pilothouse and a revolving cylindrical turret armored with eight inches of iron plates and carrying two mammoth 11-inch Dahlgrens.

Clash of the ironclads
On 8 March 1862, *Virginia* entered Hampton Roads and destroyed the wooden Federal warships *Congress* and *Cumberland*. Buchanan was wounded and succeeded in command of *Virginia* by Catesby ap R. Jones. When the Confederate ironclad returned the next morning to attack *Minnesota*, however, she saw *Monitor* – the "cheese-box on a raft" – barring her path. The two ironclads immediately engaged at 9.00am in a desperate, indecisive, but historic, battle at close quarters for nearly three hours. When *Monitor*'s captain, John Lorimer Worden, was temporarily blinded by shell splinters, the command fell to Samuel D. Greene, but only light damage was inflicted upon each vessel. The stalemate was finally broken by *Monitor*'s withdrawal.

The struggle between the two ships was not to be renewed. With the landing of McClellan's army at Old Point Comfort, *Virginia* was blown up by her own crew because her deep draught of 22 feet did not allow her to withdraw up the James River. *Monitor*, which foundered in a gale off Cape Hatteras on 31 December 1862, gave her name to an ensuing class of Union ironclad warships bearing one or two revolving turrets – a class of warship lasting well into the 20th century. The historic duel of the two Civil War ironclads had ushered in a new and revolutionary type of technology and naval warfare.

MANILA BAY
SPANISH-AMERICAN WAR
1898

The naval battle of Manila Bay – fought on 1 May 1898 between the American Far Eastern Squadron of six warships commanded by George Dewey, and Patricio Montojo y Pasaron's flotilla of ten decrepit men-of-war – was decisive not only in crushing the Spanish fleet

MANILA BAY *Dewey's five broadside attacks on the Spanish fleet reduced it to scrap within three hours of battle.*

Attack at dawn

Just before dawn on 1 May, led by *Olympia*, Dewey's fleet entered Manila Bay, and exchanged a few indecisive shots with the enemy shore batteries. At 5.30 am, at an average range of 3,000 yards, Dewey opened fire on the Spanish ships near Cavite. Steaming in eliptical courses to starboard and making a total of five broadside passes at the Spanish flotilla, Dewey continued his cannonade until 7.36 am, when he paused to allow the gunsmoke to lift and to send his crews to breakfast. After firing had been renewed briefly, the American commander saw that Montojo's fleet had been reduced to scrap iron and lumber. Each enemy ship was shattered beyond repair, and 381 Spanish sailors had been killed or wounded. Only a few light hits were sustained by the American vessels; no sailors had been killed and only eight slightly wounded.

Dewey's victory at Manila Bay was critical for US military plans in the Pacific, since it made possible an ensuing landing by US troops under Wesley Merritt. The end result was the surrender of Manila and all Spanish forces in the Philippines and the eventual cession by Spain of the entire Philippine archipelago to the USA. This territorial acquisition meant that the USA was embroiled in Far Eastern affairs into the latter quarter of the 20th century.

and helping gain the Philippine Islands for the USA, but also in thrusting the USA squarely into the power politics of the Far East.

Assistant Secretary of the Navy Theodore Roosevelt was instrumental first in securing for George Dewey the Far Eastern command and then, when war came on 11 April 1898 following the destruction of the US battleship *Maine* in Havana harbour – this mysterious sinking sparked off the declaration of war – in issuing him orders to destroy Montojo's fleet in the Philippines. A hero of the US Civil War, the 60-year-old Dewey was a thoroughly competent and widely-versed perfectionist, who had his squadron in excellent condition when he steamed from Hong Kong via Mirs Bay toward Manila. His force consisted of the protected cruiser *Olympia* (flagship, 5,870 tons, 38 guns of varying sizes), four smaller cruisers, and a gunboat. In position inside Manila Bay, near Cavite, were the ten men-of-war of Montojo, all in pitiful condition. Dewey was also faced with a few ineffective Spanish mines in the water near the mouth of the bay and a number of shore batteries – mostly composed of obsolete guns.

OMDURMAN
BRITISH RECONQUEST OF THE SUDAN
1898

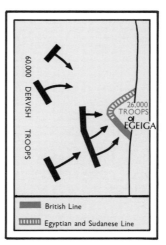

Major General Kitchener, *Sirdar* (commander-in-chief) of the Egyptian army, with 25,000 British and Egyptian soldiers, defeated more than 50,000 Dervish followers of the Khalifa Abdulla on 1 September 1898. The victory restored Anglo-Egyptian control of the Sudan and avenged the death of General Gordon at Khartoum 13 years earlier.

The battle of Omdurman came at the end of Kitchener's 1,000-mile trek south from Cairo into the Dervish heartland. Initially, he had his troops and stores transferred in convoys of steamers up the Nile to the First Cataract, some 500 miles south of Cairo. From there, he built a military railway to terminate at the junction of the Nile and Atbara rivers, where he set up his rail head. Having beaten off a group of some 16,000 fanatical followers of Khalifa Abdulla, to secure this, Kitchener and his men embarked on a 200-mile march on the main Dervish army; by 1 September 1898, he was approaching his main objective – the twin cities of Khartoum and Omdurman, the latter being the Dervish capital.

Bivouacking that night on the banks of the White Nile behind a *zereba* (rampart) of closely-packed thorn bushes, Kitchener's 25,000-man Anglo-Egyptian force slept fitfully. Cavalry patrols had reported some 50,000 Dervishes stationed behind a low ridge, only five miles away from the *Sirdar's* camp.

At daybreak Khalifa Abdulla's warriors moved to the attack. By 7.30 am the 46 pieces of Kitchener's artillery had opened up at a range of 2,000 yards and shortly thereafter the machine gun troop of 20 fully automatic Maxims joined the fray. Finally the infantry, armed with bolt action Lee-Metford rifles opened fire, the net result being that the howling Dervish horde was halted in its track with heavy casualties without ever reaching the *zereba*.

The second phase

To Kitchener, it appeared as if the battle was decided, and, eager to occupy Omdurman before the defeated stragglers could find shelter within its walls, he started his march on the town. The 21st Lancers, one of whose subalterns was the young Winston Churchill, was ordered to cut between the enemy and the fortress and harry their retreat. But there was fight left in the Dervishes.

As the Lancers started out on their mission they were suddenly fired upon from a fold in the ground. Wheeling and charging, the Lancers discovered a line of whiteclad warriors a dozen deep hidden in the wadi and extending to their flanks. Accelerating their charge, their momentum swept them through and dispersed the Dervishes, but a cost of a quarter of their strength.

At almost the same time, a large force of Dervishes attacked the right flank and rear of Kitchener's column. The rearguard was composed of the superbly trained 2nd Sudanese Brigade commanded by Lieutenant-Colonel Hector MacDonald, a skilled and gallant officer who had been commissioned from the ranks. "Fighting Mac", as MacDonald was nicknamed, dispersed the attack with heavy volleys of rifle fire and then skilfully re-aligned his brigade to meet and defeat a second onslaught of 20,000 fresh Dervishes. When relieved by the Lincolnshire Regiment the Brigade was down to its last few cartridges.

The battle of Omdurman was over with 10,000 of the Khalifa's warriors dead, another 10,000 wounded, 5,000 captured and only 500 casualties among Kitchener's soldiers. The victory re-established Anglo-Egyptian control of the Sudan, subdued the fanatical Dervishes and convincingly demonstrated to the world the power that the fully-automatic machine gun and rapid fire rifle gave to modern armies.

SIEGE OF PORT ARTHUR
RUSSO–JAPANESE WAR
1904–05

On 2 January 1905, General Maresuki Nogi with 80,000 men and 475 guns, captured Port Arthur, Russia's chief base in the Far East together with the bulk of the Russian Far Eastern fleet, and the survivors of General Anatoli Stössel's defending force (41,000 men and 500 guns.) This ended an epic 11-month siege and opened the way for Japan's total defeat of Russia.

Determined to enlarge the Japanese empire by expansion into Korea and Manchuria, Japan had first to neutralize the Russian Far Eastern fleet. The war began on 8 February 1904, when Admiral Heihachiro Togo launched a surprise torpedo boat attack on the Russian fleet at anchor in its home port of Port Arthur – as with Pearl Harbor in 1941 the Japanese did not bother with a formal declaration of war – following this up by a sea blockade.

By 25 May, Port Arthur was under land attack, and the 3rd Japanese Army, commanded by Nogi, soon had the port invested. On 7 August came the first major Japanese assault. The eastern hill positions took the brunt of the attack, and, by the evening of the following day, they had fallen to the determined Japanese. They kept up the pressure with attacks, mostly at night, from 19 August to 24 August. The tactics the Japanese employed were primitive, however, relying on massed frontal assaults in close order against the port's north-eastern fortification and 203 Meter Hill. In both cases, the Russians used their searchlights to good effect, and their machine guns caused carnage in the massed Japanese ranks. When the attacks subsided, the Russian defences were substantially intact, while their losses of about 3,000 were only a fifth of the 15,000 Japanese casualties.

Nogi changes tack

Nogi, who had captured Port Arthur from the Chinese during the Sino-Japanese War of 1894–5, was determined to succeed and so modified his tactics, employing the classic siege warfare methods of sapper trenches and subterranean mines. On 15 September, massive mines blew up the forts in the northern and north-western defences and waves of Japanese infantry attacked the survivors. Despite heroic Russian resistance, the forts had fallen by nightfall on 20 September; however, the key strongpoint on 203 Meter Hill remained in Russian hands until its few remaining defenders were overrun on 27 November. This opened the harbor to direct artillery fire and in a few days the Russian fleet was immobilized. On 2 January 1905, Stössel surrendered Port Arthur, with its surviving

10,000 starving defenders.

This siege is noteworthy for its extensive use of the machine gun and indirect artillery fire in defence. These caused most of the 59,000 Japanese casualties (disease claimed 34,000 more). The cost to the Russians was some 41,000 killed, lost to disease, or captured. For the first time, an Asiatic power had decisively defeated a large European force. Coupled with the Russian naval defeat of *Tsushima* in May of 1905, the image of European invincibility was forever shattered.

SEDAN
FRANCO–PRUSSIAN WAR
1870

On 1 September 1870, General de Wimpffen surrendered the encircled remnants of the 124,000 man Army of Châlons to the Prussian 3rd Army under Crown Prince Friedrich Wilhelm and the Army of the Meuse, commanded by the Crown Prince of Saxony, totalling almost 200,000 soldiers. This opened the way to the Prussian advance on Paris and the eventual French surrender on 10 May of 1871.

In mid-July 1870, France, alarmed by the Prussian attempt to install a member of their ruling Hohenzollern family on the Spanish throne and thus menace France from two sides, declared war. Emperor Napoleon III, putting his faith in the traditional *élan* of the French solider, had an exaggerated idea of the capabilities of the French Army, which in reality was ill-prepared for combat. Its training had suffered in the years since the 1859 war with Austria and, though French equipment was good, its use had been little tested in manoeuvres or training exercises. As an example, the *mitrailleuse* (an early form of machine gun), developed and manufactured in conditions of such secrecy that the tactics for its employment had not been defined, and the troopers little trained in its use.

The road to Sedan

After a series of defeats in early and mid-August, Marshal Achille Bazaine and the main French army in the field had been forced back to the fortress of Metz, where he was promptly besieged. Marshal Marie de MacMahon, after his defeat at Wörth on 6 August, had fallen back to Châlons-sur-Marne, where his surviving units, together with hastily formed reinforcements, were assembled into the Army of Châlons. Napoleon III joined the force but did not assume command.

Directed by the Minister of War, General Charles, Cousin-Montauban, Count de Palikao, to break through to Bazaine and so relieve Metz, MacMahon started north-east towards the Belgian frontier on 21 August, planning to later head south towards Metz around the flank of the besieging Prussian army. After several sharp clashes with the Army of the Meuse, under Crown Prince Albert of Saxony, and the Third Army, commanded by Crown Prince Friederich Wilhelm, both under the overall command of Field Marshal Count Helmuth von Moltke, MacMahon decided that his best move was to concentrate his forces around the fortress of Sedan.

Trapped by the Prussians

During 30–31 August the army of Châlons straggled into the triangle roughly bordered by the rivers Flaing to the north-west, the Meuse on the south-west and the Givonne to the east. The small fortress of Sedan was ill prepared to receive this force of more than 120,000 infantry and cavalry with over 400 fieldguns and *mitrailleuses*. The garrison had only about 200,000 rations on hand – enough to feed the arriving army for less than two days. A train with 800,000 rations was shelled before it could be unloaded and returned to Mézières some 15 miles to the west.

In the meantime, von Moltke had issued orders to the two German armies to press the French into the "narrowest possible space between that river (the Meuse) and the Belgian frontier". The Army of the Meuse was to bar escape to the east, while the Third Army was to push against the front and right flank of MacMahon's troops. The French withdrawal to Sedan greatly simplified the carrying out of the German plans.

Early on 31 August, a detachment of the 1 Bavarian Corps found the railway bridge south of Bazeilles intact and crossed, only to be pushed back by a counter-attack by the French XII Corps under Lebrun. However, before the bridge could be blown up, it was recaptured

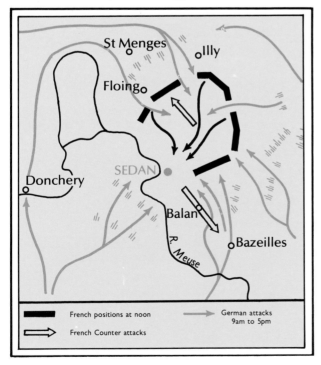

SEDAN *The French withdrawal to Sedan meant that over 120,000 men became trapped in a salient banded by three rivers.*

by the Bavarians and early on the morning of 1 September they advanced as far as Bazeilles under cover of a dense fog. At first light the French XII Corps again counter-attacked and again drove the Bavarians back. But now fate took a hand. As the fighting raged around Bazeilles, Marshal MacMahon himself was severely wounded by a shell fragment at around 7.00 am. He named General Alexandre Ducrot of the I Corps to assume command of the Army of Châlons.

Three commanders in two hours

When at about 8.00 am Ducrot learned of his promotion, he immediately decided to withdraw to the plateau of Illy to the north of Sedan, as this was a much more defensible position than the bowl in which the French had found themselves. However, a strange event now occurred. General Emmanual-Felix de Wimpffen, in Paris on 29 August en route to take command of the V Corps, had been given a letter from the Minister of War, Count Palikao directing him to take command of the Army of Châlons if MacMahon should be wounded. Though de Wimpffren had arrived at Sedan early on 31 August to take command of his corps, he had mentioned the letter to no one. Now, on learning almost simultaneously of MacMahon's wounding and of Ducrot's orders to pull back to the Illy plateau, he reacted violently. Ignorant of the real situation, he thought that the success of XII Corps' counter-attack against the Bavarians would enable the French to drive the Germans into the Meuse and win a great victory. He therefore produced the letter placing him in command and countermanded Ducrot's orders.

"Nous sommes enmerde"

However, the Army of Châlons, already under attack from the east and south was soon to be completely surrounded. The German XI Corps of the Third Army had crossed the river at Donchéry, and, by 10 am, was moving towards Illy. Despite a gallant cavalry charge, the French were pushed back with heavy losses. The German V Corps soon joined the XII, and, with a combined total of 140 guns, silenced the French batteries, already under fire from the east from the Army of the Meuse. Before noon, the two armies made contact near Illy and the encirclement was complete.

Despite heroic cavalry charges attempting to open an escape route to the north-west, and a last desperate attempt to break through to the south, the French were trapped. The Germans occupying the heights to the north and east implacably shelled the evermore constricted French. The fire of the 426 guns they used in their day-long bombardment demoralized the defenders – whole units broke up and sought shelter in the ruins of the town.

Napoleon surrenders

Finally, at about 6 pm, Napoleon who was in considerable pain from a kidney stone and so had taken little part in the battle, decided that further French sacrifice would be useless and ordered the white flag raised. He then went out to surrender personally to the Prussian king. Though de Wimpffen first of all repudiated the order to surrender, the Army of Châlons eventually laid down its arms practically unconditionally.

Napoleon's surrender led to revolution in Paris and the overthrow of the dynasty. The Sedan campaign had cost France 17,000 killed and wounded, plus 3,000 stragglers interned in neighbouring Belgium; 104,000 prisoners, 419 field guns, 139 fortress guns and 6,000 healthy horses were surrendered. The cost to the Germans was some 9,000 officers and men killed or wounded. As the official German war historian wrote, "The victory at Sedan crowns the united efforts of the German leaders and their men with a success almost unprecedented in history."

Though the war dragged on until the treaty of Frankfurt was signed on 10 May 1871, the defeat at Sedan made the outcome inevitable. The German Empire, proclaimed in the Hall of Mirrors at Verserilles in 1871, succeeded France as the dominant military power on the European Continent, a position it was to hold until the end of the First World War.

TSUSHIMA
RUSSO–JAPANESE WAR
1905

Naval battle in the straits of Tsushima between Korea and Japan on 27–28 May 1905 in which Admiral Heihachiro Togo's fleet of four battleships, 8 cruisers, 21 destroyers and 60 torpedo boats sank or captured most of the Russian Baltic fleet of four new battleships, and 35 other ships under command of Vice-Admiral Zinovy Petrovich Rozhdestvenski. It is one of the most decisive sea battles in history.

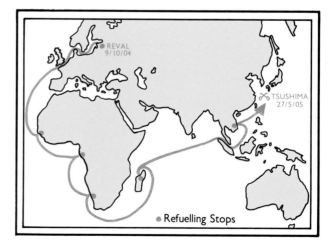

TSUSHIMA *The Russian Baltic fleet steamed around the world, only to meet destruction in a few hours of battle.*

In mid-1904 the Russian Ministry of Marine in St. Petersburg (now Leningrad) decided to send a force to relieve their Far Eastern Fleet, which was bottled up in *Port Arthur* by the Japanese. The only available ships were in the Baltic Fleet and were mostly old and slow, the exceptions being four new fast cruisers and four 15,000-ton 18-knot battleship, which were just being fitted out in the naval dockyards at Kronstadt. These four ships – the *Suvorov* (the flagship), *Alexander III*, *Borodino* and *Orel* – had four 12 inch guns with a range of 10,000 yards arranged two each in fore and after heavily-armored turrets as their main armament. In addition, they carried 12 six inch cannon, plus 56 rapid firing anti-torpedo boat guns. The armour was an impressive ten inches thick at the waterline and four inches over the decks. Unfortunately late changes in the design specifications, which greatly enlarged and heavily armoured the officer's quarters, made the ships top heavy and steam low in the water.

From the Baltic to the Pacific

On 20 June 1904, Tsar Nicholas II appointed Vice-Admiral Rozhdestvenski commander of the new 2nd Pacific Fleet. Although lacking in command experience, Rozhdestvenski was considered one of the ablest of Russian flag officers. This was just as well considering the daunting nature of his mission. In three months he had to whip his heterogeneous fleet into readiness for combat and lead them on an 18,000-mile voyage half way around the world. Then he was to defeat a much more modern, although smaller, Japanese fleet in its home waters.

Despite dire predictions to the contrary, Rozhdestvenski managed to get his unwieldy armada to the Sea of Japan relatively intact, though the voyage was not without incident. Prior to sailing, rumors abounded that the Japanese had dispatched a torpedo boat squadron to attack the Russian fleet in the North Sea. On October, nine days after sailing, in an afternoon fog near the Dogger Bank, the *Kamchatka*, a repair ship that had managed to steam ahead of the fleet, reported that it was being chased by eight torpedo boats. This threw the Russians into a state of panic, even though the *Kamchatka* soon signalled the boats had disappeared.

At around midnight, the fleet came upon a group of British fishing trawlers, and, to alert the fleet to their presence, the fishermen fired a couple of flares. The Russian response was prompt – the trawlers were lit up by searchlights and fired upon. Three were hit, several fishermen killed, many wounded and one trawler, the *Crane*, was sunk. The fleet continued on its way, celebrating the great "victory". Not until reading the newspapers a week later at Vigo in Spain did the Admiral realize that the "attackers" were fishing vessels and not Japanese torpedo boats – the nearest of which was some 17,000 sea miles away. It was only with difficulty that war with Britain was averted.

The Russian fleet at Port Arthur had been lost with the port's surrender on 2 January 1905, but the 2nd Asiatic fleet plodded on, now heading for Vladivostok, the Siberian naval base. After many vicissitudes, including a near mutiny, the great fleet finally reached the straits between the island of Tsushima and the Japanese coast on the morning of 27 May 1905. Had they fooled the Japanese? No Japanese vessels were in sight, yet the narrow waters of the Tsushima straits were the logical place to expect the enemy.

Clash of iron

Admiral Heihachiro Togo and his fleet was fully aware of the location of the Russians, however, for despite orders, one of the Russian hospital ships had kept its navigation lights blazing throughout the night of 26–27 May. While Togo's fleet of four battleships, eight cruisers, 21 destroyers and 60 torpedo boats was numerically inferior in capital ships, it could steam almost twice as fast and overall was much more modern than the Russian fleet.

On the morning of 27 May, Admiral Togo kept close tabs on the progress of the Russians through radio reports from his scouts. This was the first major naval engagement in which radio communication played any role. The Russians in contrast to the Japanese, used it sparingly, relying mainly on signal flags.

The Japanese battle line heading south-east overshot the Russians advancing to the north-east. In order to get to windward, Togo changed course to the west and then south-west. Finally coming in sight of the Russians, he found himself on an opposite, but parallel, course to them. Making a daring decision he made a U-turn within range of the Russian guns. As he turned, his flagship *Mikasa* came under fire and was hit several times. Each succeeding ship was fired on as it made the turn, but none was seriously damaged. At a few minutes after 2.00 pm, as *Mikasa* straightened into a parallel course, the Japanese opened fire.

The Russian fire was concentrated on the *Mikasa*, which was hit 15 times in the first half hour of the battle. The *Suvorov*, Rozhdestvenski's flagship, received the heaviest Japanese fire and soon was badly damaged. Her control tower was destroyed and the admiral severely wounded. The rudder was disabled and *Suvorov* started to circle. In the meantime, the old battleship *Oslyabya* had been hit repeatedly and at 3.15 pm she pulled out of line, turned turtle and sank. The destroyer *Buiny* came alongside *Suvorov* and took off the admiral and most of his staff, leaving in command Midshipman Werner von Kursel who refused to leave the sinking ship. The battle then turned into a Russian rout, with the battleships *Alexander III*, *Borodino* and *Suvorov* all sinking a little after 7.00 pm.

A decisive victory

Rear Admiral Nicholas Nebogatov, aboard *Nikolai I*, had succeeded to the command of the battered fleet at about 6.00 pm. Not much remained of the powerful 2nd Asiatic Fleet – and what was left was fleeing in confusion. During the night, some of the cruisers headed for internment at Manila and three of them arrived. One cruiser and two destroyers reached Vladivostok. The five ships with Nebogatov, having successfully fought off torpedo attacks during the night, were encircled by the Japanese the next morning. Nebogatov then surrendered.

VICKSBERG
US CIVIL WAR
1863

The 1863 Vicksburg campaign of the American Civil War was decisive in the eventual Federal capture of the Confederate "Gibralter of the West," located on high bluffs on the eastern bank of the River Mississippi. It resulted in the opening of the great river to the Union and the consequent denial to the Confederacy of the invaluable supplies of the rich territories to the west of the river. Federal forces of 40,000 and eventually 71,000 troops under Ulysses S. Grant were matched against initially 45,000 and finally 22,000 Southerners under John C. Pemberton.

The vital Confederate river port of Vicksburg, Mississippi at first defied capture. In the summer of 1862, Admiral David G. Farragut moved his Union warships up the Mississippi from New Orleans, bombarded Vicksburg heavily, but failed to capture it. Obeying literally President Jefferson Davis' order to hold Vicksburg at all costs, John C. Pemberton unwisely kept his army anchored inflexibly near the stronghold.

Union forces under U.S. Grant were unsuccessful in their first attempts to capture the stronghold. When Grant moved southward along the railroad from Holly Springs in December, 1862, toward the Mississippi state capital of Jackson, located to the east of Vicksburg, he was forced to give up the campaign and fall back when the Confederate cavalryman Earl Van Dorn captured

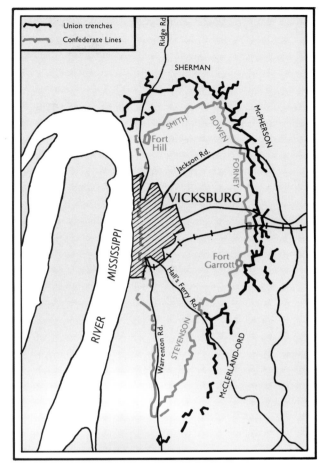

VICKSBURG *Grant's siege and capture of this major fortress was a grueling early lesson in trench warfare.*

his major Holly Springs base in a surprise raid. Then, in the spring of 1863, Grant likewise failed in a series of five so-called "Bayou Expeditions" to the north and west of Vicksburg.

Finally, Grant succeeded when Federal Admiral David Dixon Porter was able to run the batteries of Vicksburg with his warships, supply vessels, and troop transports, and land Grant's army at Bruinsburg, to the south of Vicksburg, on 30 April 1863. From there, in a masterly campaign, Grant fought and won five battles (at Port Gibson, Raymond, Jackson, Champion's Hill, and Big Black River) and began a siege of Vicksburg from the east. Pemberton unwisely allowed his army to be bottled up in Vicksburg instead of manoevering it to link up with Joseph E. Johnston's ill-trained force at Jackson. Although he repulsed Grant's initial attacks on 19 and 22 May against Vicksburg, Pemberton, after a 47-day siege during which his soldiers and the townspeople were reduced to eating dogs, cats, and even rats, was forced to surrender remnants of his forces to Grant on 4 July 1863.

The capitulation at Vicksburg, following by one day the repulse of Pickett's Charge at *Gettysburg*, sounded the eventual death-knell of the Confederacy.

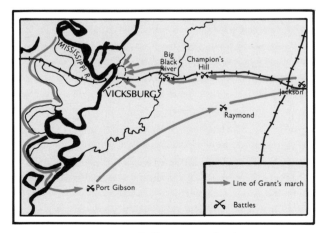

BEFORE THE SIEGE *A brilliant series of preliminary manoeuvres by Grant led to Confederate entrapment.*

CHAPTER SEVEN
The Two World Wars

The first 45 years of the present century witnessed the waging of the first total wars – that is, wars on a world-wide scale in which millions of casualties were inflicted on civilians and fighting men alike. In both world wars, modern technology combined with national ambitions to broaden the scope – and the expense – of conflict to a point where it could be almost as costly to win a war as it was to lose it, as the course of history in France after the First World War and in Britain after 1945 both demonstrate.

Causes of the world wars

The long-term causes of the First World War have their roots in the conflicts of the 19th century. During the latter part of the 1800s, the weakness of Austria-Hungary and of the Ottoman Empire, and the tensions between them, allowed the Balkans to become a major source of instability in eastern Europe. The assassination of the Archduke Franz Ferdinand, the heir to the Austro-Hungarian throne, in June 1914 by Serbian nationalists convinced Austria-Hungary that the domination of Serbia was essential to her security; however, for both strategic and political reasons, it was impossible for Russia to tolerate this. Nor, for technical reasons, was it possible to limit the scope of the conflict by ordering partial mobilization – or to stop general mobilization, once it had begun. Once Austria-Hungary had launched its attack on the Serbs, Russian, German and then French mobilization inevitably followed. Britain, having emerged from "splendid isolation" to informally ally herself with France, was drawn in by the German attack on Belgium, the neutrality of which both powers had guaranteed.

By contrast, the causes of the Second World War were short term,

WAR'S IMAGE *This propaganda painting of purposeful soldier of Hitler's Wehrmacht glamorized the image of war.*

the result of the explosive political changes born of the Treaty of Versailles and the economic conditions of the 1920s. The unspoken aim behind European diplomacy in the decade that followed Versailles was the desire to restore the *status quo* – but a *status quo* without a pre-First World War Germany, and relying on a cluster of small states on the new Germany's eastern borders, instead of the imposing presence of Tsarist Russia, to provide a check on any resurgence of German ambitions. The conditions necessary to achieve a balance of power simply did not exist, especially since the USA had retreated into isolationism. Nor could traditional 19th-century economic policies stand the strain of post-war upheaval. The prolonged economic crisis of 1929–1932 produced stresses that combined with other factors in the two strategically important nations of Germany and Italy to lead to economic autarchy, totalitarianism and militarism.

Japan, too, benefited from the moribund state of the former great powers. Her victory over Russia in 1905 had given her tremendous self-confidence; the naval strengths of the European empires in the Far

East were ones that she could easily surpass. She, too, was surrounded by power vacuums – China, the eastern provinces of the USSR and the Pacific Ocean – and it was in the first that she began her policies of military expansion, starting by supporting the puppet state she had set up in Manchuria and then embarking on open war in an attempt to conquer China from 1937 onwards.

The shape of modern war

The two world wars were both total wars. The participants stood or fell by their capacity to supply their fighting forces with weapons and food. All the resources of the contending nations were engaged. In both wars, political and, above all, economic considerations dictated military decisions. The farmer and the factory hand were as important as the soldier. The technological and industrial advances of the 19th and early 20th centuries erupted on to the battlefield, with the consequences, as foreshadowed in the US Civil War, of enormous costs in men and material.

The first element in this new equation of war made itself felt even before war was declared. The huge conscript armies of the European powers were mobilized by railway, and complicated timetables were required to ensure a smooth and rapid build-up of forces at the required point. Once this process was unleashed, it was almost impossible to stop, without giving an opponent a decisive advantage. This was what the Austrians found in 1914 when their General Staff could not alter a mobilization plan that called for the cream of the Austro-Hungarian army to be deployed against Russia, rather than Serbia. The logistics of railway mobilization were thus a decisive factor in the outbreak of war.

Railways had a further impact on the conduct of war. They could deliver millions of men to the battlefield, even though these men thereafter depended on their feet, or on horse-drawn transport, for mobility. The cavalry, formerly charged with keeping war on the move, was now too vulnerable to the weapons the infantry carried to be of effect, while, although cars and trucks existed, their numbers were inadequate to affect this state of affairs. Railways, too, could also deliver artillery and munitions to the battlefronts on an unprecedented scale.

DEFEAT AT DUNKIRK *Germany's campaign against France and Britain in May 1940 was a triumph for the Blitzkrieg tactics of armored warfare. Within days, the northern Allied armies had been cut off; with their backs to the sea, the British were forced into evacuation from Dunkirk (above).*

AUGUST 1914 *Volunteers flock to the colors on the outbreak of war (right). However, the realities of modern war were soon driven home to the men in the field, as this view of an exhausted British cavalry trooper shows (below). The war was not "over by Christmas".*

From offensive to defensive

Given enough room, these armies were capable of manoeuvre. The German assault on Belgium and France, their battles on the Eastern Front, the battle of the *Marne* and the subsequent "race to the sea" were all engagements of manoeuvre on a huge scale. However, the number of men-per-mile that railways made it possible to deploy was such that the space available was soon filled, particularly on the Western Front. The decisive advantage given to the defence by rifled infantry weapons, entrenched fortifications, massed artillery fire and barbed wire immediately became apparent, inhibiting the offensive and enforcing stalemate, as the battle of Ypres and the *Gallipoli* campaign demonstrated.

It was also not just the destructive power of the weaponry available to the defenders that inhibited the offensive. Command and control of armies occupying large tracts of land was in itself a major problem, as the German chief of the general staff von Moltke found in 1914 when trying to keep track of his advance formations. In the defensive, field telephones could be used, but these

were not sufficiently mobile to be used to control an offensive thrust. Advancing troops still had to communicate by flags, runners, carrier pigeons or by similar more or less primitive means.

Despite this, many attempts were made between 1914 and 1918 to break the deadlock on the Western Front. Most of these held the seeds of future success, even though they failed when first introduced. The British, for instance, deployed the first tanks on the *Somme* in 1916. Though the tanks failed here, they were used with greater success at *Cambrai* the next year. But, even though they proved that they could break through the front line, the battle also showed that the problem of mobility still had not been resolved. The initial British success petered out, as their tanks broke down or ran out of fuel; no suitable mobile reserve existed to back them up, or to exploit their breakthrough. Both sides, therefore, embraced the empty doctrine of attrition at one time or other; many historians think, for instance, that the German High Command failed to seize the opportunity of breaking through the French defences at *Verdun* in 1916

because of their insistence on "bleeding France white" by deliberately prolonging that battle.

Breaking the deadlock

It is not surprising that the Germans, with their experience of open warfare on the Eastern Front, were the first army to break the trench deadlock effectively. Freed by the Russian collapse in 1918 to transfer massive reinforcements from east to west, they were able to fling their extra divisions against a key sector of the Allied lines in France.

These troops were rehearsed in tactics, that had proved themselves in Russia, and, sensationally, at *Caporetto*, in Italy, when a combined Austro-German army smashed through the Italian line. Gone were the long preliminary bombardments of conventional battles. In their place, novel artillery and infantry tactics, based on infiltration and rapid support, enabled the Germans to penetrate the front line, by-pass strongpoints and press on to the rear. The Germans came within an ace of success, but again the problem of mobility eventually halted them before a truly decisive breakthrough could be achieved.

War in the air and at sea

The culminating battles of the First World War witnessed the concerted use of infantry, artillery, armor and aircraft on a massive and co-ordinated scale, as at *Amiens* in August 1918. Despite this, however, the pace of battle was still determined by the speed at which the infantry could march. In addition, the final ingredient of modern warfare – instant voice command over long distances and down to sub-unit levels – still had to be provided.

In the air, the First World War saw the development of air power; from primitive beginnings, this had reached a sophisticated level by 1918. The fully-aerobatic fighter, armed with a forward-firing machine-gun, proved a revolutionary weapon, both in aerial combat and when turned against ground formations, as in the aftermath of *Megiddo* in 1918. The role of aircraft as reconnaissance vehicles on land and at sea was exploited, and bombing aircraft made their appearance.

At sea, Britain and Germany fielded the largest battle fleets the world had ever seen. These, however, clashed on only one abortive occasion at *Jutland*. The naval war centered on Germany's attempt to starve Britain into surrender by sinking her maritime commerce with submarines. As with aircraft, these new weapons increased in complexity and effectivenss during the war, threatening not only merchant shipping, but even the mighty battle squadrons, which never again were able to ride the seas and oceans with full confidence.

The implications of technology

At the end of the First World War, therefore, most of the ingredients required to overcome the defensive power of modern weapons were present. The internal combustion engine had now been developed to a point where it could provide mobility for armored cross-country vehicles, infantry-carrying vehicles and for artillery. One additional element was needed to fuse the new techniques together – a means of exercising command effectively over long dis-

THE AIR WAR *Preparing for photo-reconnaissance (above) and Britain's first strategic bomber (top).*

tances and at speed. This was provided by wireless.

When the Second World War broke out, therefore, the necessary technological basis for rapid mobile warfare, battles of manoeuvre and successful offensives had been established. The armored division, backed up by motorized infantry and artillery and preceded by supporting air strikes, was to be the decisive land weapon until the advent of the atomic bomb in 1945. In 1939, Germany, with its revolutionary *Panzers*, led the world in armored warfare; as a consequence, she was rewarded with a string of victories – over Poland, Denmark, Norway, Holland, Belgium, France and in the Balkans – which gave her effective control of the European continent. Paradoxically enough, the German *Wehrmacht* was not the most mech-

anized army of its time – its second-line supporting troops depended on their feet and on horse-drawn transport, just as their fathers had a generation before in 1914.

Until the German armies were finally halted on the Eastern Front, the series of stunning victories continued. Faced with these successes, the Allied powers were forced to specialize in an equally dramatic and logistically highly complicated technique – the combined operation. Armies disembarking from ships have always been vulnerable, as the Gallipoli campaign demonstrated in 1915, but this was never more the case than in the Second World War, given the advantage that air power and accurate massed artillery fire theoretically gave the defence. Nevertheless, in North Africa, Italy, on countless Pacific islands, and, above all, on the *Normandy* beaches, the Allies perfected this hazardous operation of war. Success, they realized, depended on achieving air superiority and then using naval gun-fire to support the infantry during and after the landing until a firm bridgehead was established.

Atlantic and Pacific

As Germany again attempted to strangle Britain into surrender with its U-boat fleet, and as the Japanese resisted the US drive to dislodge them from their gains in the western Pacific, the oceans of the world witnessed naval fighting on a scale that had not been seen since the Napoleonic Wars between Britain and France. One significant change was the eclipse of the "big-gun"

PEARL HARBOR *The devastating surface attack on the US Pacific Fleet by the Japanese demonstrated the power of the carrier-based strike force.*

battleship by the aircraft carrier, using its aircraft not just as fleet auxiliaries, but as a decisive striking force, as at *Pearl Harbor* in 1941. The overwhelming US victories at *Midway* and later at *Leyte Gulf* confirmed this new ascendacy, though, where no aircraft carrier was present, ship-to-ship actions remained the rule.

Next to the carrier, the dominant naval weapon was the submarine. The Germans came very close to victory over Britain by attacking Allied merchant shipping with their U-boat "wolf packs". Drawing on their First World War experiences, the British were quick to re-adopt the convoy system, but, despite this, losses in the battle of the *Atlantic* continued to mount. The U-boat threat was not brought under control until 1943 and it was not entirely eliminated until land forces isolated the U-boat bases on the French Atlantic coast the following year. In the Pacific, US submarines enjoyed an even greater success, almost completely eliminating the Japanese merchant marine.

Technological advances had the same impact on naval warfare as they did on every other field of war. Long-range, land-based, radar-equipped aircraft were a key factor in the battle to beat the U-boat menace, while wireless made the instant transmission of orders to widely dispersed fleets routine. Radar enabled ships to detect invisible enemies, and improved communications enabled "command ships" to carry both the naval and military staffs in combined operations. Improvements in naval gunnery – in particular, the adoption of radar control – meant that, in amphibious operations, land forces could be provided with massive artillery support from the start, thus bridging the dangerous gap between the moment of the initial infantry landing and the subsequent arrival of supporting artillery.

The advent of air power
In one respect, the Second World War differed from all previous conflicts. This difference was due to the scope and importance of air operations. From the short-range aircraft operating in support of ground forces to the strategic bomber, it is clear that air power was the decisive weapon of the war. No operation could succeed without air superiority being secured – or, at the least, the ability to battle the enemy's air strength effectively. Command of the air could be seized directly by successful air combat, or indirectly by the destruction of enemy air strength on the ground – usually by bombing, but sometimes by the advance of ground forces.

The first true air battle was the Battle of *Britain*; the RAF won this because of its technological, if not numerical, superiority (radar and the superiority of the Spitfire over the *Lufwaffe's* Me 109), its superb tactical dispositions and its system of ground-to-air control. In addition, the *Luftwaffe* made a fatal tactical blunder in dispersing and over-extending its resources.

The war also witnessed the whole-scale bombing of industrial and civilian targets. Initiated by Germany in Poland, Holland and in the "blitz" against Britain, the same strategy was pursued even more wholeheartedly by the Allies against both Germany and Japan in an attempt to wear down their war-waging capabilities. There were two schools of thought – the RAF favoring blanket night bombing of major industrial areas, while US air chiefs argued for pin-point daylight raids on key strategic targets. The *Ploetsi* raid illustrates the latter trend. How effective the strategic bombing campaign bomber actually was is still a matter of considerable controversy, but it cannot be doubted that, at the end of the war when married to the atomic bomb, the long-range strategic bomber became, for a short time, a decisive weapon.

Aircraft were also used as troop transports and, as in the case of *Crete* and *Arnhem*, as paratroop deliverers. In the Burmese and Chinese theaters of war, whole armies were supplied from the air by transport aircraft, dropping supplies by parachute or landing on improvized landing strips. The German failure to keep their army in *Stalingrad* supplied showed what could happen if the system failed; the battle of *Kohima-Imphal* on the border between India and Burma, showed how it could bring victory.

The new warfare
The size and complexity of Second World War military operations – particularly in the USSR in battles such as *Moscow* and *Kursk*, or sieges like those of *Leningrad* and *Sebastopol* – made enormous demands on the support services of the armed forces, many of which expanded far beyond their pre-war roles. Engineers,

cavalry, that moved at the pace of the infantry, and in some cases, still wore uniforms reminiscent of the days of Napoleon. It ended with the advent of mass armored forces, air fleets, submarines, and the atomic bomb. It encompassed the attritional slaughter of Verdun, the use of poison gas, a desert war between Axis and British and Commonwealth armored armies, and the amphibious reconquest of the western Pacific by the USA. It included the greatest land battles ever fought, between Nazi Germany and the USSR, and a combined civil and anti-Japanese war in China whose astronomic cost in terms of human life can never be calculated. It witnessed the destruction of the old European empires, the conquest and occupation of half of Europe by the USSR and the rise and fall of Japan. It signalled the end of European hegemony in the colonial world and ushered in the era of "superpower" dominance by the USA and USSR.

On the ground, the period witnessed the advent of armoured, fast-moving ordinance, a major improvement in the fire-power of the infantry, and great advances in the accuracy, speed and concentration of artillery fire. From the air, the machine gun, the bomb and the torpedo revolutionized tactics on land and at sea, where the carrier-borne aircraft and the submarine ended the days of battleship dominance. Wireless brought these innovations together, enabling commanders, for the first time, to exercise effective control over dispersed and fast-moving forces.

No other period of military history has seen such rapid change. It is therefore ironic that the era closed with an event that threatened at the time to make all these dramatic innovations obsolete – the explosion of the first atomic bombs over Hiroshima and Nagasaki.

medical services, supply organizations – all had to adapt to the demands of the new warfare.

Perhaps the most important of all these services was intelligence. Two strokes of luck enabled the Allies to read the Japanese and German wireless codes for the bulk of the war. These were the discovery of a dead Japanese naval officer, with the Japanese naval codes on him, by the Americans and the breaking of the German naval and diplomatic codes by British cryptographers, using the "Enigma" machine. These two events gave the Allies an insight into enemy intentions of an accuracy that had never been enjoyed by any commander of the past. So vital was the latter source that elaborate deception operations were mounted to conceal it from the enemy.

Warfare revolutionized

The period from 1914 to 1945 was a period of rapid and determined change. It began with the mobilization of armies that still contained

Great Commanders of the The Two World Wars

Great wars breed great commanders, as the two world wars fully demonstrate, even though modern military historians have challenged many of the views and opinions of the commanders of the time that were current when these wars were fought. A classic example is the case of Field-Marshal Haig, the commander-in-chief of the British forces in France during the greater part of the First World War. Vilified by many subsequent historians as an unimaginative, unintelligent leader, whose tactics led to the mass slaughter of Britain's conscript armies, his reputation is still a controversial one. Here, six "great captains" of the period have been singled out for special examination, since their claims to fame are indisputable.

Zhukov, Georgi Konstantinovich (1896–1976)

When war broke out with the Nazis in 1941, Zhukov swiftly emerged as one of the key men in the Soviet military machine. His first major task was to stabilize the *Leningrad* front; in September 1941, he was brought back to the central front, where he took over the defence of *Moscow*, halting the German drive on the Soviet capital. Then, on 6 December 1941, with 100 divisions on a 200–mile front, he launched the first of his great counter-offensives, driving the Germans back from the city and scoring the first major Soviet success of the war.

Zhukov was now regarded by Stalin as the toughest and ablest troubleshooter in the Soviet Army. Accordingly, in the autumn of 1942, he was sent to *Stalingrad* to organize the defence of the city; then, as deputy commander-in-chief, to direct the Ukraine offensive of 1943. Next, as commander of the 1st White Russian Army, he was the mastermind behind the great operation that led to the reconquest of White Russia. It was this army he led to the gates of *Berlin*. As a commander, Zhukov was decisive and inventive; he was also noted for his ruthless disciplinarianism, using the firing squad and the penal battalion as weapons to whip his subordinates into line.

Yamamoto, Isoruku (1884–1943)

Probably the greatest naval leader of either world war, Yamamoto was quick to appreciate the changes that the development of air power had wrought in naval strategy; in 1939, he was appointed commander-in-chief of the Japanese Combined Fleet. He opposed war with the USA and Britain on the grounds that Japan could not win a prolonged conflict against both powers, but, with the growth of the war party in Japan, he set to

WAR PLANNER *Yamamoto masterminded the Japanese triumphs of the war's early stages.*

work to devise a strategy to achieve such rapid victories that Japan's enemies would be forced to the conference table in six months from the outbreak of war.

Though Japan's astonishing successes between December 1941 and May 1942 bear eloquent testimony to his genius, Yamatoto's plans were fatally flawed by the Japanese failure to destroy the entire US Pacific Fleet at Pearl Harbor – in particular, the survival of the US carrier force – was to play havoc with his plans, as Japan's defeat at *Midway* showed.

MacArthur, Douglas (1880–1964)

MacArthur came from a military family, his career in the US Army starting in 1903 when he was commissioned into the engineers. As a young officer, he served in the Philippines; he was then ADC to his father, the US military attaché in Tokyo, where he was stationed during the Russo-Japanese War. After holding various staff appointments and seeing active service in Mexico, he went to France in 1917 as chief-of-chief of the 42nd Division. He had a dramatically successful war, winning the *Croix de Guerre* and reaching the rank of Brigadier-General when only 38 years old.

As Allied supreme commander in the South-West Pacific from 1942, MacArthur showed himself to be perhaps the greatest master of combined operations that the world has yet known. Using island after island as his stepping stones, he defeated or contained the Japanese forces opposing him, cutting Japan's supply routes and gradually coming closer and closer to the home islands. In pursuit of this policy, forces under his command successively recaptured *Guadalcanal*, Luzon, Iwo Jima and *Okinawa*. He showed his continuing mastery of this type of operation at *Inchon* at the outbreak of the Korean War, but when he called for an expansion of the war into China, however, President Truman relieved him of his command.

CONQUERING HERO *MacArthur (seated left) was a strongly individualistic commander with a flair of showmanship.*

Foch, Ferdinand (1851–1929)

During his career in the French Army, Foch had three chief periods of influence – before the First World War at the Ecole de Guerre, during it as an army commander and, in 1918, as generalissimo of all Allied armies on the Western Front. Believing that France had lost the Franco-Prussian War through being forced on to the defensive, he preached the virtues of the all-out offensive, although with qualifications that were often ignored by his disciples on the French general staff –and, unlike them, learnt quickly from his experiences. The failure of the Somme offensive, however, led to the fall of Joffre, the French commander-in-chief, and Foch fell with him, due to his close association with Joffre's strategy. However, he was recalled as chief of the French general staff in May 1917 and, the next year in the face of the final German offensive of the war, he became generalissimo of all Allied armies in France. Here his leadership was of decisive importance, not only in staving off the German offensive, but also in co-ordinating the Allied counter-offensives that brought the German armies to their knees.

Slim, William Joseph (1891–1970)

Though he never saw action in Europe in the Second World War, in the eyes of the British Army "Bill" Slim ranks with its greatest captains – Marlborough and Wellington. A master of the arts of deception and manoeuvre, his fame rests on his leadership of 14th Army against the Japanese on the Indian-Burmese frontier and in the subsequent reconquest of Burma. He led 14th Army from humiliating defeat to the greatest land victory gained over the Japanese in the Second World War in the reconquest of Burma. He firmly grasped the two main problems that confronted him – how best to train a part-European army so that it could live and fight in the jungle and how to keep large forces supplied in terrain that was totally unsuited to the use of motorized transport. His aim was to make his troops as accustomed to jungle life as were his Japanese opponents, and, by perfecting the logistical art of air supply, to enable them to take on their enemy on superior terms.

BURMA TRIUMPH *Slim's leadership of 14th Army in its defence of the Indian border and subsequent reconquest of Burma was a masterpiece of tactical and logistical planning and showed his grasp of the arts of deception and manoeuvre. The 800-mile advance the campaign involved culminated in a brilliant encircling action at Meiktila in early 1945.*

Guderian, Heinz (1888–1954)

Heinz Guderian was without question one of the founding fathers of armored warfare as the originator of the armored warfare tactics and techniques that Hitler's *Panzers* were to put into practice with devastating success in the *Blitzkriegs* of the opening campaigns of the Second World War. He reached pinnacle of his success as a field commander in May 1940, when his *Panzers* emerged from the Ardennes to smash through the French defences at Sedan and drive across France to reach the Channel coast within a week of the initial breakthrough. However, he clashed with Hitler over the conduct of the Russian campaign and, as a result, was largely unemployed from 1942 to 1943.

After 1943, as Inspector-General of Armored Troops, Guderian, often without success, sought to prevent Hitler – and some of his generals – frittering away tanks in piecemeal actions. He became Chief of the Army General Staff in July 1944, but, unable to influence Hitler's increasingly irrational decisions, he was eventually relieved of his command in March 1945.

The Advent of Air Power

Throughout military history, commanders have always longed to see "the other side of the hill". In 1908, when the first aircraft came into military service, this became possible; reconnaissance, indeed, was the aircraft's first battlefield role and one in which it remained pre-eminent throughout this period. The natural progression from this was to devise a means of destroying the intelligence gatherer – hence the evolution of the fighter. Conversely, it was also quickly recognized that an aircraft capable of observing an enemy position was equally capable of dropping explosive on it, so leading to the development of the bomber.

The three roles of aircraft in battle – reconnaissance, air combat and acting as an extension of artillery through bombing – thus evolved side by side. So, too, did aerial tactics. It is a peculiarity of air combat that, even when the strategic purpose of the battle is defensive (as the battle of *Britain* was from the British viewpoint), the tactics of both sides are offensive. Only in the case of large bombing formations attempting to beat off fighter attack is anything like a defensive posture assumed.

Adapting to air warfare

Evolution, however, is the operative word as far as the story of air combat is concerned. As the size and range of aircraft increased, three further roles were added to their repertoire. These were strategic bombing (the massed bombing of civilian and industrial targets in isolation from ground operations); transport; and airborne troop landings. Together, these functions added a new dimension to land warfare, both on the battlefield and beyond it.

From the aircraft-delivered message that alerted Joffre, the French commander-in-chief, to the German First Army's fatal change of direction at the battle of the *Marne* (1914) to the detailed and exhaustive aerial photography that preceded the major operations of the Second World War, the aircraft revolutionized both the volume and quality of intelligence available to commanders, especially as far as enemy deployments and probable intentions were concerned. Concealing ground dispositions from the probing cameras carried by aerial reconnaissance patrols led to the development of camouflage as a major art, while establishing air superiority over the prospective battlefield to deny the enemy this all-important "oversight" became a vital prerequisite for any major operation. It was the *Luftwaffe's* loss of air superiority in the West, for instance, that made the *D-Day* landings practical.

As a weapon of interdiction, the aircraft developed only slightly more slowly. Light bombers were in existence by 1917, while one of the duties of the "scouts" – as fighters were then named – was the "strafing" of enemy ground troops with machine-gun fire. Both bombing and strafing were carried out extensively in the Allied offensives on the Western Front in the summer of 1918. These roles were even further elaborated in the Second World War, when aircraft of many types supported ground troops with machine-guns, cannon, bombs and rockets. The great German *Panzer* advances, for instance, were preceded by conventional and dive bomber attacks on key targets in the enemy's defences and in his rear. The Germans saw their tactical aircraft as a natural extension of their artillery, with greater range and the ability to deliver more high explosive more accurately.

The development of air transport

The aircraft was not far enough advanced to be used as a means of transport during the First World War, although an unsuccessful attempt was made to resupply the beleaguered British-Indian forces at *Kut-el-Amara* in early 1916 by air. Even with the larger aircraft of the Second World War, a prodigious carrying capacity was needed to resupply ground forces successfully; Goering's pledge to keep the German 6th Army supplied from the air at *Stalingrad*, for instance, proved impossible to fulfill, with catastrophic consequences for the *Wehrmacht*. It was in the British 14th Army's reconquest of Burma from the Japanese in 1944 and 1945 that air supply came into its own, when an advance of 800 miles by an army of upward of 100,000 men was largely supplied from the air.

VAIN BOAST *Goering's pledge that Stalingrad would be supplied by air was a promise his Luftwaffe could not fulfil.*

BATTLE IN THE CLOUDS *By 1917 air warfare was assuming a sophisticated pattern.*

As a transporter of airborne infantry, however, the aircraft brought another revolutionary element to the battlefield earlier in the war. Either as glider-borne infantry, or as paratroops, a relatively small formation, landed in the enemy's rear, could dislocate his command system, or circumvent a fortified position – both capabilities that had been eagerly sought by commanders throughout history.

Aircraft at sea

At sea, the aircraft's great range and the fact that it could drop bombs vertically on to inadequately armored decks made it a war-winning weapon in the Second World War. It could also deliver torpedo attacks. Its introduction, especially when carrier-born, meant the end of the battleship; as the crippling losses inflicted by the *Luftwaffe* on British shipping during the invasion of *Crete* by the Germans in 1941 showed, it meant that warships and merchant vessels alike could not survive for long unprotected when faced with unrelenting air attack.

Against submarines, too, the aircraft played a vital role. Active long-range patrolling compelled submarines to travel submerged, so curtailing the amount of time they could spend underwater and shortening their cruising life. Indeed, it is arguable that, if the resources committed to the strategic bombing offensive by Britain in the Second World War had been allocated instead to long-range air patrols of the Atlantic approaches, the immense shipping losses of the battle of the *Atlantic* might have been checked sooner.

Strategic controversy

As a strategic weapon, therefore, the aircraft was of less certain value. It is doubtful whether the strategic bomber could ever have been a war-winning weapon in itself, as was claimed by its proponents. The results of the Allied bombing offensives against Germany in the Second World War suggest strongly that the accurate interdiction of communications, weapon sites, and key industrial installations was the only profitable form of strategic bombing, as opposed to the "blanket" bombing of cities and industrial areas, such as the Ruhr.

Nevertheless, at the end of the war, the bomber did become the decisive strategic weapon for a brief period. This, however, was not brought about by the massed bombing fleets of the Allied air forces; rather, it was brought about by a single bomber, the *Enola Gay*, which dropped the first atomic bomb on Hiroshima.

THE AGE OF THE BOMBER *B-17 strategic bombers cruise the skies on a daylight pin-point raid against Hitler's industries.*

AMIENS
FIRST WORLD WAR, WESTERN FRONT
8 August 1918–4 September 1918

A three-week Anglo-French offensive in the Somme region, which broke the will of the German army on the Western Front; its first day was so successful that Ludendorff called 8 August "the black day of the German army in the war".

By August 1918, the force of the German offensives had spent themselves and the Allies were ready to reply. Around Amiens, the British Fourth Army (Rawlinson) and the French First Army (Debeny) planned their attack on the German 18th Army (von Hutier) meticulously and quickly. In Fourth Army's area alone, 14 infantry and three cavalry divisions, 2,000 guns and 450 tanks were secretly assembled. Security was paramount. Artillery registration was carried out according to an elaborate plan, so that no dramatic increase of fire from the British positions would alert von Hutier to the imminence of the attack.

"The black day"
At 0420 on 8 August, the Canadian and Australian

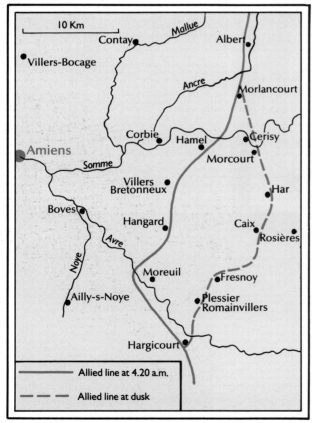

AMIENS *The Allied counter-offensive opened up a salient 10 miles deep in 24 hours, so finally breaking German morale.*

infantry of Fourth Army, preceded by tanks and a rolling barrage, attacked the German forward positions in dense fog. Surprise was complete and success instantaneous, more than 400 guns and 15,000 prisoners being captured. On the right, after a preliminary bombardment, the French attacked with equal success. Despite all attempts to hold their ground, the German forces finally started to crumble. On 10 August the French Third Army (to the right of First Army) captured Montdidier: the following day, Haig, in overall command, called a halt to regroup.

Fourth Army resumed the offensive on 22 August, and was joined by the British Third Army (Byng) and the First Army (Horne), both to its left. Ludendorff ordered a general withdrawal, but his plans were frustrated by the Anzacs' brilliant capture of Peronne , and the fall of Queant to the Canadians. The Germans were forced to fall back to the Hindenburg Line with a loss of more than 100,000 men (including 30,000 prisoners). Allied losses were 22,000 British and 20,000 French. Amiens marked the breaking point of the morale of the German armies. Never before had so many surrendered to the Allies.

CAMBRAI
FIRST WORLD WAR, WESTERN FRONT
20 November–5 December 1917

A 15–day battle fought on the Western Front by General Sir John Byng's British Third Army (19 divisions and 3 tank brigades) against part of General van der Marwitz's German Second Army (six divisions, subsequently reinforced to 20 divisions). Though the battle finally ended in stalemate, it convincingly demonstrated the potential of tanks used *en masse*, together with infantry infiltration tactics. The British lost 44,000 men, while the battle cost the Germans 53,000 casualties.

Late 1917 was the nadir of the First World War for the Allies. Russia was in revolution, the submarine war had bled Britain white, the Italians had suffered heavily at *Caporetto*, as had the British at *Third Ypres*, while the French army, having been bled white in a futile offensive in Champagne, was suffering from demoralization – indeed, some units were in a state of mutiny. To bolster Allied morale before yet another dismal war-time winter set in, Field-Marshal Haig approved Byng's proposal for a surprise attack – or at least a raid in strength – at Cambrai.

The plan of attack
The area the British had chosen for their attack was relatively uncratered by shells, so providing their tanks with good going on which to manoeuvre. These

HINDENBURG DEFENCES
- - - - Outpost Zone
- - - - - Hindenburg Line
-·-·-·- Hindenburg Support Line
············ Siegfried Line II

BRITISH POSITIONS
———— Front Line, dawn 20/11/17
+++++ 1st Objective where different from Hindenburg Line
•••••• 2nd Objective where different from Hindenburg Support Line
— — — Gains by night of 20/11/17
—·—·— Maximum consolidated gains
············ Maximum position held only temporarily

CAMBRAI *This was the first battle to demonstrate how a massed tank attack could break the trench stalemate.*

vehicles had been first used at Flers in September 1916 and on several occasions since then; however, they had never seen action in force. Now, the plan was to launch 476 (including 376 MkIV battle tanks) at the German trenches, with the intention of breaching the German Hindenburg Line on a five-mile front. The next objective was Bourlon Ridge, to serve as an observation post, after which five cavalry divisions would be unleashed in a broad sweep around Cambrai to sever the German road and rail communications.

Tanks, cavalry and infantry were assembled in great secrecy and trained in new battle tactics devised by Colonel Fuller, GSO1 to Brigadier-General Hugh Elles, the commander of the Tank Corps. Although there was to be no prolonged preliminary bombardment, 1,000 guns were positioned ready to fire as the tanks moved forward. By 19 November the assault forces were ready on the start line in and around Havrincourt Wood. Immediately ahead of them were only two German divisions and 150 guns.

A brilliant opening
At 6.20 am the following day, a sudden bombardment heralded the attack. As the tanks moved forward, working in teams of three, followed through the wire by infantry in file instead of the customary line abreast,

many Germans simply turned and fled. By midday, almost all the British objectives had been taken at minimal cost, except at Flesquières in the center. There, 51st Division's deliberate disregard of the new battle tactics meant that its tanks drew ahead of their supporting infantry. Heavy losses ensued as a result; one German NCO, named Krüger, was credited with knocking-out eight tanks single-handed, before being killed as he manned a field gun. It was incidents of this kind that led the Germans to underrate the tank.

Degeneration into stalemate
This hitch proved critical, since the gap into which the cavalry were to pour failed to materialize as a result, while it also gave the Germans time to deploy the newly-arrived veteran 164th Division. This plugged the gap in their defences. The fighting bogged down, as it proved impossible for the British to sustain their early impetus, with the result that Bourlon Ridge remained in German hands, despite many valiant assaults. Many tanks had now been destroyed, while the supporting infantry was tiring. Then on 29 November the Germans counter-attacked in strength – substantial reinforcements having arrived by road and rail. Using hurricane bombardments, and skilled infantry infiltration tactics (avoiding strongpoints) supported by low-flying aircraft, the Germans made good progress on the flanks, but were eventually held. The battle petered out on 5 December when the British fell back to a new line between Flesquières and Gonnelieu.

Cambrai, therefore, did not live up to its initial promise – it was the only battle in the First World War that was marked by the ringing of church bells at home in Britain in celebration of what was thought to be a clear-cut victory, at least in its initial stages. One of the problems was that the enormous losses at Third Ypres had drained the British army in France of its reserves, so there simply were not the men available to support and exploit the initial success. Nevertheless, the battle held enormous importance for the future. It had shown that the stalemate of positional trench warfare could be broken and that the tank would be a key weapon in the future. A new age of armored warfare had been inaugurated.

CAPORETTO
FIRST WORLD WAR, ITALIAN FRONT
⌐24 October 1917 to 12 November 1917⌐

A catastrophic defeat inflicted on the Italian Second and Third Armies by the Austrian 14th Army, reinforced by seven crack German divisions. In the rout that followed the Austro-German attack, the Italian forces fell back from the line of the River Isonzo to the Piave. The defeat almost put Italy out of the war.

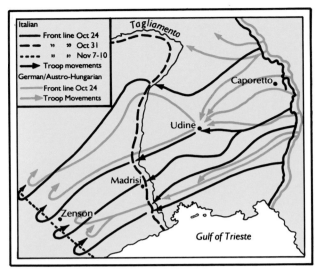

CAPORETTO *The speed of the Austro-German advance was facilitated by special infiltration tactics.*

Onslaught at Caporetto

By the autumn of 1917, both the Italian and Austrian forces on the line of the Isonzo had fought themselves to a standstill. The Italian commander-in-chief, General Count Luigi Cadorna, was aware that the Germans would come to the aid of the Austrians and that they would launch an offensive. Consequently, he had ordered the Italian Second and Third armies to set up a defence in depth, but General Capello commander of the Second Army, neither understood nor implemented the orders.

At 0200 on 24 October 1917, a whirlwind barrage fell on the Italian positions. High explosive and gas shells from over 3,000 guns, as well as mortars, tore great holes in the Italian lines. Behind the barrage, the German divisions of the 14th Army (commanded by General Otto von Bülow), using the tactics of rapid penetration that had been developed during the siege of Riga on the Eastern Front, streamed through the Italian positions, and fell upon the disorganized defenders. The chaos extended the whole length of the Isonzo front, but was at its worst in the Second Army's area, where, finding themselves assailed by German rather than by Austrian troops, panic set in among the Italians. Flight quickly became rout.

Supported by the Austrian 10th Army on the right, and the Austrian Fifth Army on the left, 14th Army raced forward. By 27 October they were in Udine, Cadorna's former headquarters. Attempts were made by the beaten Second Army to make a stand – notably on the Tagliamento on 31 October – but the Austro-German advance swept onwards. Not until 12 November did the Austro-German forces begin to run out of steam; Cadorna was then able to stabilize his battered front on the Piave.

Caporetto was one of the most dramatic battles of the war. At its end, the Italians had lost almost 70 miles of territory, 40,000 killed and wounded, 275,000

prisoners, 2,500 guns, and enormous quantities of war material. Austro-German losses were about 20,000. When these figures are added to Italian losses of 157,000 killed and wounded in the previous 11 battles of the Isonzo, it can be seen why the disaster at Caporetto meant that the Italians were no longer capable of taking the offensive unaided; French and British reinforcements had to be rushed to the stricken front accordingly. For their part, the Central Powers had reaped the benefit of surprise and intelligent tactics. Though numerically inferior overall (35 divisions to the Italian 41), von Bülow was able to concentrate his force at the critical point. He also used élite mountain troops to spearhead his advance. One such unit was led by the young Erwin Rommel, who won the *Pour la Merite* – imperial Germany's highest gallantry award – for his outstanding skill and courage.

GALLIPOLI
FIRST WORLD WAR, TURKEY
19 February 1915–9 January 1916

A combined operation launched by British, Commonwealth and French naval and land forces designed to knock Turkey out of the war, and open a supply route to Russia. Though the operation was brilliant in conception, it failed, largely due to bad planning and through growing political opposition to it in Britain.

As the First World War degenerated into stalement on the Western Front, two schools of thought arose in Britain – each with its own plan for ending the war. The "Westerners" believed that France was the decisive theater of war; the "Easterners", on the other hand, argued the futility of sending more and more men to die a useless death in Flanders and pressed for the adoption of an alternate strategy. They believed that knocking Turkey, Germany's weakest ally, out of the war would totally change the military and political situations; it would also open up a supply route to Russia, so enabling the western Allies to ship vitally-needed supplies of arms and munitions to Tsar Nicholas II's hard-pressed armies on the Eastern Front.

Winston S. Churchill, then First Lord of the Admiralty, was the scheme's chief supporter. The plan, as it eventually emerged, was for a Franco-British fleet to destroy the defences of the Dardanelles, while supporting troops secured the Gallipoli peninsula. This would be followed by a combined naval and military advance on Constantinople (Istanbul), Turkey's capital, whose fall would trigger a Turkish surrender.

Muddle and delay

From the outset, however, secrecy was lost. A premature naval bombardment in 1914 alerted the

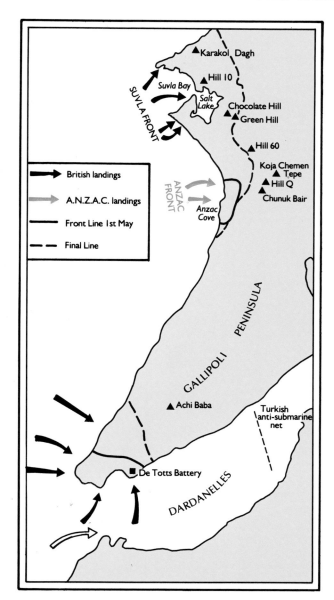

GALLIPOLI *The ingenuity of the campaign's concept was sabotaged by poor planning and indecisive leadership.*

Turks to the weakness of their Gallipoli defences and they strengthened them accordingly. In spite of this, a renewed naval bombardment in February and March 1915 came close to success; Admiral de Robeck's failure to realize this was a fatal error. Rather than pressing his attack home, forcing the Dardenelles regardless of loss, de Robeck now concluded that naval might alone would be insufficient to break through the Turkish defences. This meant that a major landing now had to be planned in order to support the fleet, rather than the minor mopping-up operations that it had originally been thought would be all that was necessary.

Quick action was obviously essential, since the element of surprise had now been totally lost. Though land forces were hastily assembled on the island of Lemnos during February and March, it was soon discovered that many of the ships carrying them had been wrongly loaded. The result was that the entire force had to transfer to Alexandria in Egypt, so forcing a further month's delay.

The landings take place
Finally, on 25 April 1915, a force of 78,000 Australian, New Zealand (ANZAC) and British troops under General Ian Hamilton made two daylight landings on the Gallipoli peninsula – the British at Cape Helles and the ANZACS at Ari Burnu, on the western side of the peninsula. A French division mounted a diversionary attack on the Asiatic side. From the outset, things started to go wrong. The two main landings were too widely separated to afford mutual support, while, both at Ari Burnu and Cape Helles, the ANZACS and British failed to capture the commanding heights above the beaches, which alone would have made their beachheads tenable. Command blunders and indecision were to blame for this – not the troops on the ground, who, in both cases, came within an ace of reaching their objectives.

"Those dammned Dardanelles"
Prompt Turkish reaction and failure in British command had an inevitable result. Rather than breaking through the defences and advancing swiftly up the peninsula, both the British and the ANZACS remained pinned down in their beachheads and the familiar stalemate of trench warfare developed.

For almost a year, the Allied troops clung to their shell-swept positions. Hamilton attempted a further landing at Suvla Bay on 6–8 August, but, though this was initially unopposed, the incompetence of its elderly commander Lieutenant-General Sir Frederick Stopford, gave the Turks time to bring up reinforcements. Attempts to break out failed, particularly the attack on the ridges above the bay launched by Stopford's replacement, Major-General de Lisle, on 21 August. In these, Hamilton was additionally hampered by the withdrawal of his main naval support, due to losses to submarines and the Turkish minefields laid in the straits.

In Britain, opposition to the venture, always vocal, grew with each new failure. In the Admiralty itself, the First Sea Lord, Sir John Fisher, threatened resignation, proclaiming that "those dammned Dardanelles" would prove the graveyard of the new navy he had created. Eventually, in October 1915, Hamilton was relieved of his command; his successor, Sir Charles Munro, recommended evacuation. In a masterpiece of planning, Suvla Bay and Anzac Cove were evacuated on 20 December and Cape Helles January 1916.

Failure at Gallipoli cost the Allies 252,000 casualties; Turkish losses were 251,000, including 20,000 troops who died of disease. The operation remains a tantalizing one, since success at Gallipoli might well have changed the entire course of the war, as its proponents had claimed before its launch.

JUTLAND
FIRST WORLD WAR, NORTH SEA
31 May 1916–1 June 1916

The only major surface action between the main battle fleets of Britain and Imperial Germany in the First World War; in terms of the numbers of ships at sea (250), it is the largest single fleet action that has ever been fought. Both sides had high hopes of the battle – the British, in particular, expecting victory – but the results were inconclusive. The German High Seas Fleet sank more tonnage than the British Grand Fleet, but the former was never to see action again.

In May 1916, the British Grand Fleet (Admiral Sir John Jellicoe), based at Scapa Flow, the Moray Firth, and Rosyth, numbered 28 battleships, nine battlecruisers, eight armored cruisers, 26 light cruisers, 78 destroyers, one minelayer, and one seaplane carrier. The Imperial High Seas Fleet (Admiral Reinhard Scheer) based at Wilhelmshaven, numbered 16 modern battleships, five

battlecruisers, six pre-dreadnought battleships, 11 light cruisers, and 61 destroyers. Despite the numerical advantage the British possessed, the balance between the two great fleets was more even than it might have appeared. In general, the German dreadnoughts and battle cruisers had more effective protective armor than their British counterparts, and their guns, though sometimes lighter, were harder-hitting and the explosives used to charge their shells were more effective.

The battle cruiser action

Forewarned by intercepted wireless traffic that the Germans intended a sortie, Jellicoe put to sea at 2030 on 30 May 1916; at 0230 the following day, Scheer sailed from Wilhelmshaven. Both fleets were preceded by their battlecruiser squadrons – the Germans under Admiral Franz von Hipper, and the British under Admiral Sir David Beatty. At 1531 on 31 May, these two forces sighted each other and immediately engaged at a range of 16,500 yards. Much to the surprise of the British, the superb German gunnery quickly took effect; Beatty's flagship *Lion* took several hits, while in a few minutes her consorts, *Indefatigable* and *Queen Mary*, were sunk. Beatty's pithy comment – "There seems to be something wrong with our damned ships today" – summed up the situation.

Beatty soon had other things to worry about. At 1642, he sighted the main German fleet, and turned to lead them on to Jellicoe's guns. For an hour he ran north, pounded by Scheer's battlecruisers, who in turn came under fire both from Beatty and from four supporting superdreadnoughts under Admiral Hugh Evans-Thomas.

The battle fleets clash

Shortly after 1800, Beatty sighted Jellicoe's battleships and turned to form a line in front of Jellicoe, who also turned to form a line, hoping to swing behind Scheer and cut him off from his base. At 1830, when the main fleets finally engaged, Jellicoe's manoeuvre had paid him full dividends; he was in the advantageous position of having crossed Scheer's "T", thus allowing the whole weight of his broadside to be directed against the German van. Within minutes every ship was engaged, and a furious exchange of fire took place. Hipper's flagship *Lutzow* was put out of action, and the British lost three cruisers.

Scheer was now in difficulties. His plan had been based on cutting off and destroying the British battle-cruisers, but he was now confronted by the entire Grand Fleet and taking severe punishment. At 1835, he reversed course and in a few minutes took his ships out of range. Jellicoe continued south, still hoping to cut Scheer off. Scheer turned back towards the British again (1855), but the move again exposed his fleet to the whole British broadside. Ordering his battle cruisers to cover his withdrawal and his destroyers to launch a torpedo attack, Scheer executed another about turn.

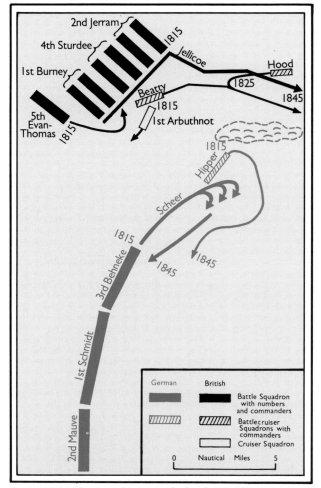

JUTLAND *The crucial point in the battle. As Jellicoe crosses the "T", Scheer orders a rapid "battle turn" away.*

Jellicoe, too, took evasive action to avoid the torpedo attack, turning away from the Germans. By the time the British line had reformed, Scheer had disappeared into the gathering dusk.

There followed a confused night action, in which the Germans showed superior night-fighting skills, and Scheer managed to break through Jellicoe's supporting squadrons, steaming straight for his base. At first light, the British broke off the action and returned to port.

At Jutland the British lost three battlecruisers, three cruisers, eight destroyers and 6,784 lives. The Germans lost one pre-dreadnought battleship, one battlecruiser, four light cruisers, five destroyers and 3,039 men. Both sides claimed the victory, but it was the British who had driven the Germans back to port.

KUT AL-AMARA
FIRST WORLD WAR, MESOPOTAMIA
September 1915–April 1916

An attempted advance on Turkish-held Baghdad by a detachment of the Indian Army's expeditionary Force to Mesopotamia. The campaign was misjudged and culminated in capitulation at Kut al-Amara.

Major-General Charles Townshend, with a reinforced division of 11,000 men, 28 guns, and a river boat flotilla, set out from Amara (captured in June 1915) that September to advance on Kut al-Amara, 300 miles up river. Much of this force had to be deployed to protect his tenuous line of communication.

At Kut, Townshend encountered Nur-ud-Din Pasha with 10,000 men. He attacked the strong Turkish position, driving the Turks back towards Ctesiphon, but this initial success was to prove his undoing. Despite his plea that his numbers and resupply capacity were inadequate, an obdurate High Command ordered Townshend to continue his drive on Baghdad. Obeying this order, Townshend attempted to dislodge the Turkish forces dug in at Ctesiphon on 22 November 1915, but after four days of intensive fighting, he was obliged to disengage, having incurred heavy casualties. He fell back on Kut, where, on 7 December, he was enveloped and besieged by the Turks.

Kut under siege
For five months, from December 1915 to April 1916, Townshend held out at Kut. Four Turkish divisions, under an elderly, but competent, German general, Count Kolmar von der Goltz, beat off four separate attempts at relief, and a last-ditch attempt to drop supplies by air failed. With this failure, Townshend's position became critical, and, faced with starvation, he finally surrendered on 29 April 1916. Over 2,000 British troops and 6,000 Indians went into captivity.

The relief attempts had cost 21,000 casualties. After an advance of great speed, and a creditable initial victory at Kut, Townshend had displayed a fatal lack of caution at Ctesiphon, and made an equally fatal overestimation of his strength once he was besieged.

THE MARNE
FIRST WORLD WAR, WESTERN FRONT
5–10 September 1914

A five-day battle in September 1914 that marked the turn of German fortunes in their invasion of Belgium and France. The German armies on the Western Front, 60% of Germany's mobilized strength, numbered nearly two million, less the casualties already incurred in the opening battles of the war. French forces numbered 1,300,000, plus the British Expeditionary Force of 100,000, and divisions of the Belgian army.

The Marne was a battle the Germans might never have had to fight, had they adhered to their original battle plan. Devised by the pre-war chief of the German General Staff, Count von Schlieffen, this had called for the encirclement of all the French armies, and Paris itself, by a vast sweeping move by 90% of Germany's mobilized forces, attacking through Belgium and Holland. But Schlieffen's successor, Helmuth von Moltke, substantially altered the plan. He diverted troops to the Eastern Front to hold off the Russians, he refused to violate Dutch neutrality, and he weakened the right wing of Schlieffen's attacking force by transferring troops to strengthen the left. Schlieffen's vision of a great enveloping, flanking movement, therefore, never materialized.

Nonetheless the progress of the German right wing in Belgium and France in 1914 was very swift –

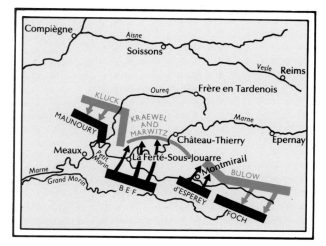

THE MARNE *The Schlieffen Plan's final breakdown came with the BEF's advance into the gap between two German armies.*

particularly that of von Klück's First Army. During August, while the French First and Second Armies spent their strength in fruitless attacks on the German defences in Lorraine, the German First, Second and Third Armies swept through Belgium and northern France. Heroic delaying actions by the Belgians, the BEF and the French Fifth Army did little more than slow von Klück's impetuous thrust, and by 30 August he found himself well ahead of the German Second Army on his left, with no apparent enemy threat to his front or his flanks. He therefore shifted his axis of advance to the south-east to support von Bülow's Second Army, and to roll up, as he saw it, the French Fifth Army.

This, however, proved to be the final and fatal modification of the Schlieffen Plan. The French supreme commander, Marshal Joseph Joffre, recovering from the near disaster of his Lorraine offensive, quickly divined the Germans' true intentions, and also saw the fatal nature of von Klück's change of direction, of which he learned by air reconnaissance. Also, as the French armies fell back towards Paris, it became easier for contact to be maintained between Joffre's headquarters and his army commanders; on the other hand as the German armies advanced, communication between them and von Moltke's headquarters, never good, became worse and worse.

Joffre acts

Joffre's reaction to what appeared to be an appalling predicament, with the German armies storming down on Paris, and his own offensive strangled, was masterly. He boldly drew units from his right flank to create two new armies – the Ninth Army (Foch), which was deployed to strengthen the French center, and the Sixth Army (Maunoury), which was deployed near Paris. Here, it threatened the right flank of the German First Army – at the very moment that von Klück, turning south and east across the Marne, most exposed this flank to counter-attack. Sensing that the Germans were now overextended, Joffre, despite the exhausted state of his own armies and the BEF, ordered a general counter-attack on 4 September. The French Sixth Army was ordered to take von Klück's First Army in flank; the BEF was to advance in the direction of Montmirail; and the French Fifth and Ninth Armies were to attack the German Second Army.

On 5 September, the French Sixth Army accordingly attacked the German First Army. Only vigorous action by the German corps commander on the right – General von Gronau – prevented von Klück's envelopment, but the latter still failed to appreciate the seriousness of the threat, and he continued his pursuit of the BEF and the French Fifth Army. Not until 7 September, when most of his army was to the south of the Marne, did he realize his true predicament. He quickly withdrew north of the river, and turned to repel the French Sixth Army, compelling General Galliéni, the governor of Paris, to take

desperate defensive measures – including the commandeering of 600 Paris taxis – to get French reserves to the battlefield. By this time, however, the other Allied formations had rallied, which meant that von Klück's left wing was now open to attack by the advancing BEF. His tactics had also widened the gap between him and von Bülow's Second Army, and this gap was now forced wider by the BEF.

The decision to retreat

On 8 September von Moltke, badly out of touch with his army commanders, and worried by the alarming and incomplete reports he was receiving from the battle front, sent a staff officer on a tour of inspection. This officer, Colonel Hentsch, arrived at von Bülow's Second Army headquarters at a moment when the army was under vigorous attack by the French Fifth Army. Hentsch was also aware of von Klück's critical position. He approved von Bülow's decision to retreat, and on 9 September he used von Moltke's authority to order von Klück to retreat as well. On 10 September, von Moltke confirmed this with an order for a general withdrawal to a line between Noyon and Verdun.

A large-scale tactical victory was not achieved on the Marne because the Allied forces were too exhausted to follow up and destroy the retreating Germans. But the battle's strategic importance was very great. German intentions in the west had been foiled. The surprise and shock element of their assault on France had been vitiated and then lost. It was not to be regained until 1918.

The Marne was not only the most decisive European battle since Waterloo; it was also Europe's biggest and most costly battle to date. The Allied losses in killed and wounded were 250,000; the Germans' were somewhat greater. In the three weeks since the outbreak of war, each side had lost nearly 500,000 men, killed, wounded or captured, the casualties including a high proportion of officers. Losses on this scale had never been seen before, and were an augury of the future.

MEGIDDO
FIRST WORLD WAR, PALESTINE
19–21 September 1918

The culminating battle of the Palestine campaign between British and Commonwealth troops under General Sir Edmund Allenby, and Turkish forces of the Ottoman Empire under the German general, Liman von Sanders. A meticulously-planned and stunning victory for the British and Commonwealth forces involved, the battle also marks the last use of massed cavalry in warfare.

Following Allenby's capture of Jerusalem in December

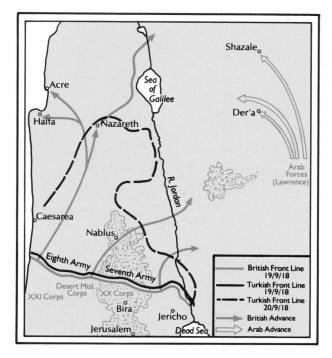

MEGIDDO *A masterpiece of deception, surprise and pursuit and the swansong of cavalry as a decisive factor in warfare.*

1917, the Turkish forces regrouped on a well-fortified line between Jaffa on the Mediterranean and the Jordan valley, a total of 36,000 men and 350 guns being deployed. Allenby faced them with 57,000 infantry, 12,000 cavalry (to a large extent armed like mounted infantry), and 540 guns. His plan was to persuade von Sanders that the British attack would fall inland, on the Turkish left; to this end an elaborate deception plan was put in train. Complete air superiority was also achieved.

The Turks deceived
On 19 September Allenby's blow fell on von Sanders' right, along the coastal plain. An intense artillery bombardment paved the way for the British XXI Corps to force a gap along the coast, through which Allenby then poured his cavalry. At the same time, British aircraft brought activity in the Turkish rear to a standstill. Both cavalry and infantry exploited the coastal breach, and by dawn on 20 September the Turkish Eighth Army had been destroyed, while the Seventh was reeling back towards the Jordan valley, where its retreating ranks were swollen by the Turkish Fourth Army. Von Sanders himself narrowly escaped capture at Nazareth. Allenby ordered all-out pursuit, the RAF bombing the routed Turkish columns while irregular Arab forces cut the main railway line at Deraa. Allenby entered Damascus on 1 October, and his forces entered Beirut on 2 October. Aleppo fell on 15 October, and Turkey sued for peace on 30 October.

Allenby's Palestine campaign, and Megiddo in particular, won him his place as one of Britain's greatest generals. At Megiddo he achieved surprise, shock, overwhelming victory and relentless pursuit. In just under a month he advanced 360 miles, destroyed three Turkish armies, and took 76,000 prisoners and over 300 guns at a cost of only 853 dead, 4,482 wounded, and 385 missing.

THE SOMME
FIRST WORLD WAR, WESTERN FRONT
24 June 1916–18 November 1916

A joint offensive by 14 British and eight French divisions operating on each bank of the River Somme, launched with the intention of breaking through the German lines and operating in open country. The offensive was the first in which Britain's "New Army", raised and organized by the legendary Lord Kitchener, took part. It was a costly failure.

The Somme was undoubtedly the biggest battle on the Western Front to date and preparations for it were suitably massive. The British, on whom the brunt of the fighting was to fall, believed that this would be "the big push" to end the war and laid their plans accordingly. On 24 June 1915, a seven-day barrage was begun, during which over 1,500,000 shells were fired at the German positions. Such was the fury of the bombardment that the guns could be heard across the Channel, but even this stupendous barrage was insufficient to destroy the Germans' deep dugouts – nor did it cut the barbed wire protecting their positions.

Over the top
At 0728 hours on 1 July 1916, the infantry of the British Fourth Army (Rawlinson), the British Third Army (Allenby), and the French Sixth Army (Fayolle), climbed out of their trenches and advanced into No Man's Land, confidently expecting to find all German resistance to have been obliterated. To the north of the river, however, the advance immediately snarled, as the British, advancing in line abreast, encountered carefully-sited, German machine guns behind undamaged belts of barbed wire. By the end of the day 56,000 British and Empire soldiers were casualties, 19,000 of them dead, and no significant gains had been made. South of the river, the French had fared slightly better, but were equally unable to break the German defence.

Despite the losses of the first day, however, the British armies continued to launch smaller-scale, but still costly, attacks from July to September, gradually gaining ground from the Germans. A night attack, launched on 13 July, did succeed in denting the German line, but only temporarily. The British commander-in-chief General Sir Douglas Haig,

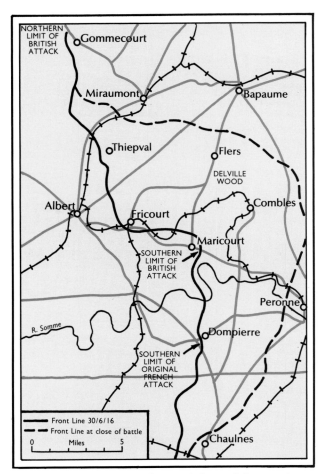

THE SOMME *The "big push" to end the war led to an advance of six miles at a cost of 615,000 Allied casualties.*

TANNENBERG
FIRST WORLD WAR, EAST PRUSSIA
20–31 August 1914

A ten-day battle between the Russian and German armies at the outbreak of war in 1914, culminating in total defeat for the numerically-superior Russians. Though the halting of the so-called "Russian steamroller" proved a disaster for tsarist Russia, the Russian offensive helped to save the situation on the Western Front by forcing the Germans to divert troops to reinforce the east at a critical moment.

Following the strategic plan devised before the war by Graf von Schlieffen, Germany's eastern frontier in 1914 was guarded only by the Eighth Army, under General Max von Prittwitz. He faced two Russian armies – the First, under General Pavel Rennenkampf, and the Second, led by General Alexander Samsonov – who, even before Russian mobilization had been completed, took the offensive into East Prussia advancing to the north and south of the Masurian lakes.

The "Russian steamroller"

As events were to prove, the Russian advance, though gallant, was premature and ill-planned. From the outset, the two armies were too widely separated to support each other in the event of a German counter-attack. However, this fact was not immediately apparent to von Prittwitz, who lost his nerve as a result of Samsonov's lumbering advance on his right rear while he was unsuccessfully trying to fend off Rennenkampf in the north. On 20 August, he was relieved of his command for suggesting withdrawing

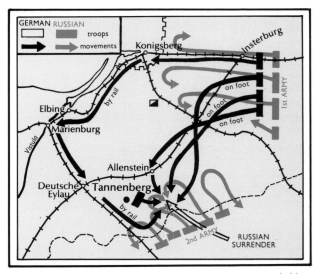

TANNENBERG *While Rennenkampf's First Army was held by a single division, Ludendorff moved to crush Samsonov.*

ordered another major attack on 15 September, when 12 British divisions attacked on a 10–mile front preceded by the first tanks to be seen in battle. These revolutionary machines, the brainchildren of Winston Churchill and Colonel Ernest Swinton, were eventually to change the face of war, but here, though they achieved surprise, they were still too unreliable and slow to achieve a decisive breakthrough (some broke down, while others became stuck in the all-pervasive mud). Haig renewed his assaults in October and November, but the fall rains were turning the ground into a quagmire, and movement gradually came to a halt.

By 19 November, therefore, the British had gained a strip of land about 20 miles long and six miles deep – none of it of strategic importance – for a cost of over 400,000 killed, wounded and missing. The French had lost 200,000, while German losses are estimated as being over 600,000. The battle had destroyed a large part of the "New Armies" – the armies raised by voluntary enlistment – but it had also cost the old German army a huge proportion of its junior officers and experienced NCOs. These were losses it was never able to make good.

from East Prussia to hold the line of the Vistula. At that moment, it looked as if the Russian offensive might well be crowned with success, but von Prittwitz's successors had other plans.

Von Prittwitz was replaced by the redoubtable duo of Paul von Hindenburg and Eric von Ludendorff. Adapting a plan that had already been drawn up by Colonel Max Hoffman, von Prittwitz's chief of operations, Ludendorff ordered his forces to concentrate against Samsonov in the south, leaving only a single cavalry division to screen Rennenkampf in the north.

Twin Russian disasters

So matters stood when, on 24 August, the over-confident Samsonov, advancing without reconnaissance or benefit of a cavalry screen, blundered into the German XX Corps, which was entrenched at Orlau-Frankenau. The Russians were so badly mauled that, on the following day, they were forced to pause to regroup, while the German corps retired in good order to Tannenberg. The battle proper began the following day.

One key factor in Ludendorff's success at Tannenberg was his ability to read Samsonov's wireless messages detailing his dispositions and intentions, since, incredibly, these were transmitted in plain language and not in code. In any event, the Russian commanders were slow to appreciate the full peril of the Second Army's position and, by the evening of 29 August, the Germans had succeeded in surrounding the bulk of its forces. The Russian troops, panic-stricken and disorganized, were slaughtered as they attempted to break out of the trap. Samsonov committed suicide that evening, leaving his army leaderless; by 31 August, the Russians had lost 125,000 men and 500 guns. The Second Army had ceased to exist.

After Tannenberg

The Germans were then able to turn and attack Rennenkampf's First Army in the battle of the Masurian Lakes (9–14 September 1914). A second German attempt at a double envelopment was foiled on this occasion by an unexpectedly vigorous Russian counter-attack and Rennenkampf managed to withdraw. However, the action cost the Russians a further 125,000 men and 150 guns; German losses in both actions were about 20,000 men.

Tannenberg was one of the most complete victories in history. The myth of the invincible "Russian steamroller" was shattered and Tsar Nicholas II's troops never fully recovered their confidence as a result of this devastating blow. Unpreparedness, rash use of wireless and general incompetence in the field – particularly in reconnaissance – were all contributing factors in the Russian disaster. To these must be added brilliant German staffwork and aggressive battlefield leadership, particularly by General von Francois, the commander of I Corps.

However, even before Tannenberg was fought, the

Russian offensive had had a decisive effect. Von Moltke, the German commander-in-chief, on receiving news of von Prittwitz's failure, had hastily transferred German troops from the Western Front to save the situation in the east. Ironically, these did not arrive in time to fight at Tannenberg; their absence, however, was to play a key role in the halting of the German drive on Paris, which put an end to Germany's hopes of a quick victory.

VERDUN
FIRST WORLD WAR, WESTERN FRONT
February 1916–December 1916

A battle planned by General Erich von Falkenhayn (chief of the German General Staff) deliberately as a campaign of attrition to "bleed France white" and so knock the French out of the war. There was no other strategic objective. Falkenhayn calculated that holding Verdun – though, in fact, the fortress-city was of little strategic significance – was so important to French national pride, that it would be defended regardless of cost. He was not to be disappointed.

Verdun lay in a salient of the southern sector of the French line, bisected by the River Meuse. In February 1916 the area was lightly garrisoned, being largely used to rest troops transferred from more active sectors of the front. This quiet was to be abruptly shattered. During the first weeks of February 1916 the German Fifth Army (commanded by Crown Prince Wilhelm) concentrated 1,400 guns on an eight-mile front on the right bank of the Meuse – a superiority of 221 batteries over the 65 of the French. On 21 February, this mass of artillery launched the greatest bombardment yet

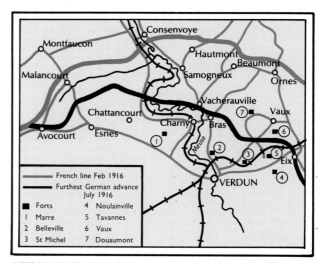

VERDUN The French fortress system here broke the "hopes of imperial Germany" according to President Poincaré.

witnessed in the war. Along the whole of the eight-mile front, entire sections of the French front line simply disintegrated under the weight of high explosive hurled at it by the German gunners.

The following day, the German infantry moved up to attack, again supported by their artillery – this time, firing gas and smoke shells, as well as solid high explosive. The French defenders, though thin on the ground, resisted valiantly, but they were driven back and the Germans seemed close to a break through. Over the next few days, many key positions were lost, including the vital Fort Douaumont.

Had one of Hitler's generals been in command, the French line might well have been broken, but the calculating von Falkenhayn stuck to his plan, so throwing away the chance of winning a great victory. Indeed, the French commander-in-chief, Joffre, reacted as Falkenhayn had hoped, rushing reinforcements to the stricken front. On 26 February, resolved to hold Verdun at all costs, he despatched General Henri Philippe Pétain to assume command of the French Second Army. The latter arrived at a moment when the Germans had achieved their first objectives, and so enjoyed a breathing space in which to reorganize his artillery and tackle his supply problems. These were formidable. The rail links to Verdun were exposed to German artillery, and became to all intents and purposes unusable. Pétain's only remaining link with the French rear was a 40-mile-long minor road to Bar-le-Duc. Over this he organized a constant stream of lorries, with permanent repair gangs to make good artillery damage. Throughout the battle lorries moved and out of the salient at regular intervals along what became known to the French as the *voie sacrée* (the "sacred way"), enabling Pétain to "rotate" his front-line units and formations, so ensuring their regular relief after comparatively short spells of front-line duty.

"They shall not pass"

On March 6, the Germans struck again and were halted only when Pétain ordered all-out counterattacks to recapture the lost ground. Throughout March, attack and counterattack followed in almost continuous succession and the casualty figures mounted. On April 9, the third German offensive struck both sides of the salient – the moment that the cautious Pétain was promoted, to be succeeded at Verdun by General Robert Nivelle, who was placed in operational command. German attacks on the west of the salient were held by May 29, but, in the east, German assaults continued against Fort Vaux and Thiaumont Farm. Fort Vaux fell on June 9, and Thiaumont on June 23. In late June and early July the German attack on the west of the salient was renewed, and the French line came close to breaking. Pétain advised withdrawal to a line west of the Meuse, but Joffre overruled him. Verdun could — and would — be held, and the Germans would be driven back.

The turning point of the battle, however, had been

reached, and, from July 11 onwards, the Germans were increasingly thrown on the defensive as divisions were shipped from the west to meet the Brusilov offensive in eastern Europe and transferred to deal with the British offensive on the *Somme*. With the collapse of his strategy, Falkenhayn was relieved of his command; his successors, Hindenburg and Ludendorff, immediately decided that the Germans should take up a defensive posture on the Western Front.

The French counter-offensive

The French forces at Verdun, now commanded by Nivelle and General Charles Mangin, went over to the offensive in October 1916, using new tactics, devised by Nivelle, an artillery specialist. Advancing behind a creeping barrage they retook Forts Douaumont and Vaux in November, and regained about two miles of the ground lost between February and July. Verdun was saved – but at a terrible cost.

The battle of Verdun lasted ten months. It was a battle that had been launched with the intention of causing high casualties, and this it achieved, even if the outcome was not the one that Falkenhayn had hoped for when he planned the campaign. The French losses totalled 542,000; the Germans lost 434,000. The battle also established Pétain's military reputation as a master of the defensive, while his catchphrase *"Ils ne passeront pas!"* ("They shall not pass!") made him a national figure. What also impressed the French was the way in which their fortifications – notably Forts Douaumont and Vaux – had held up entire divisions, a fact that directly led to the decision to build the Maginot Line (*see* battle of *France*) in the 1930s.

THIRD YPRES
FIRST WORLD WAR
WESTERN FRONT
July 1917–November 1917

Otherwise known as the Battle of Passchendaele, the Third Battle of Ypres was launched by Sir Douglas Haig, supreme commander of the British army in France, to take pressure off the French armies (still suffering the effects of the mutinies that had broken out in their ranks earlier in the year), and to try to break through the German lines between the North Sea and the River Lysre.

Passchendaele was the biggest offensive the British had launched on the Western Front to date and months of meticulous preparation went into it. As early as June 1917, the British Second Army (General Sir Herbert Plumer) had detonated a series of massive mines under the German positions on Messines Ridge, and attacked under cover of the devastation brought about by their simultaneous explosion. The ridge was

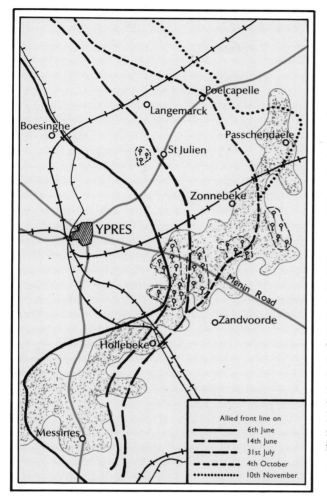

THIRD YPRES *Haig's initial objective was Ostend. After three months, the British had advanced five miles.*

Allied front line on
———	6th June
– – –	14th June
— — —	31st July
—·—·—	4th October
··········	10th November

was unwilling to give up his master plan. Instead, he now turned to Plumer, giving him command of the sector. With his usual care and thoroughness, Plumer devised a series of limited attacks, launched on narrow fronts. These piecemeal methods enabled him to nibble away at the German line, until the British eventually took the Passchendaele ridge which for so long had dominated their positions in the Ypres salient.

As October wore on, however, the autumn rain continued to soak the ground, making further attacks futile in the eyes of many. Haig, though, refused to abandon the offensive until the beginning of November, on the specious grounds that it was necessary for the British to secure the best possible line to hold during the forthcoming winter.

When the Third Battle of Ypres officially ended on 10 November, the British had deepened their salient by about five miles, and had taken Passchendaele Ridge and village. These gains had cost almost 300,000 casualties, killed, wounded, and missing. German losses were about 260,000. Many historians have argued as to the wisdom of Haig's tactics, the consensus view being that he fatally underestimated the strength of the German forces confronting him, believing that a break-through was imminent long after many of the men on the spot had given up hope of achieving it. More importantly still, the distrust the appalling casualty figures aroused in the British Prime Minister David Lloyd George led him to starve Haig of front-line reinforcements, so leaving a weakened British army to face the German onslaught of March 1918.

MADRID
SPANISH CIVIL WAR
November 1936–March 1939

The 28–month siege of the Spanish capital by the rebel nationalists and the forces that Italy and Germany sent to their support. The city was defended by Republican forces, assisted by Soviet military advisers, and volunteers fighting in the celebrated International Brigade.

At the end of 1936, the Nationalists controlled the northern and western part of Spain. Madrid, still held by the Republicans, lay close to Nationalist territory, and obviously was a key target. Accordingly, four columns of rebel troops under General Emilio Mola converged on the city. (Mola's boast that he had a "Fifth Column" of sympathizers ready to rise inside the city gave the world a new political catchphrase).

The Republican government moved to Valencia, and the defence of the capital was entrusted to General José Miaja. Rebel troops, mainly Spanish and Moroccan regulars, fought their way into the suburbs backed by heavy aerial and artillery bombardment, but the

taken at the cost of 17,000 casualties; German losses were 25,000.

Encouraged by this, Haig pressed on with his plan for the main attack, and on 31 July, the British Fifth Army (General Hubert Gough) attacked the German Fourth Army (General Sixt von Arnim) following an intense three-day bombardment. But things soon started to go wrong. The ground selected was low-lying, with a high water table, which meant that the heavy artillery bombardment had turned it into a quagmire, over which movement was agonisingly slow and difficult. The bombardment had also alerted the Germans, whose defence was well organized. After some early gains, Fifth Army literally bogged down in no man's land; conditions were so bad that some of its troops literally drowned in the mud.

"In Flanders' Fields"
By the end of August, Gough had shot his bolt. His attack had cost nearly 35,000 casualties and his gains could be measured in yards. Heavy unseasonal rain worsened the conditions on the battlefield, but Haig

Republican defenders, who were mainly untrained volunteers, held the rebel attacks for nearly four months. From February to March 1937, there was a brief respite for the defenders, during which period Soviet training of the Republican militias, and "volunteer" reinforcements did much to strengthen the overall position.

Battle at Guadalajara

The next Nationalist move came on 8 March, when two Italian "volunteer" divisions – regular Italian forces sent by Mussolini to fight for the rebels – attempted to break through the Republican lines at Guadalajara, and so isolate Madrid from the rest of Republican Spain. They were routed by Soviet dive bombers and tanks. On 18 March, largely as a result of this repulse, Republican forces were able to rout the Italians at Brihuega, capturing much war material and removing the immediate military threat to Madrid. However, the bombing of Madrid by German and Italian planes continued. It was now the turn of the Republicans to attack, and, between 6 July and 25 July, an offensive was launched from the city to raise the siege. After some initial success, the Republican break-out attempt

was driven back by General Jose Varela, commander of the investing forces. The siege continued, while both sides sought a decision in other war zones.

The fall of Madrid

Indeed, it was on these other war fronts that the fate of Madrid – and of the Spanish Republicans – was decided. In January 1939, the Nationalists captured Barcelona, routing the city's 20,000 Republican defenders. Resistance to the rebels now continued only in Madrid and Valencia. On 26 March Franco launched a fresh offensive against Madrid, and two days later the city surrendered.

The siege of Madrid held an important lesson for the great powers, which they failed to learn. Although subjected to intense bombing with heavy civilian loss of life, Madrid did not capitulate, nor fall easily to ground attack. The widely-held theory that terror bombing would initiate rapid collapse had been disproved, but few observers were inclined to take heed of this evidence.

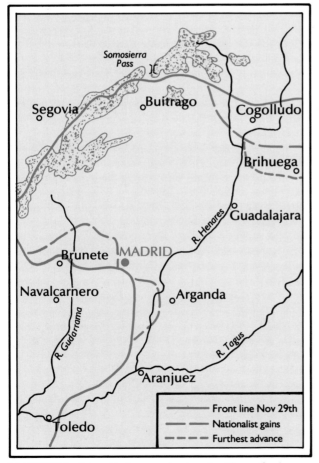

MADRID *Spain's capital was under siege for 18 months. In spite of bombing and shelling, morale remained high.*

THE MANNERHEIM LINE
RUSSO–FINNISH WAR
November 1939–March 1940

An attempt by the USSR to consolidate her influence in the Baltic and secure the approaches to Leningrad by invading Finland. Soviet forces, though far outnumbering the Finns, were decisively rebuffed at first; in the long run, it was Finland's exhaustion and a determination to win regardless of cost that led to Soviet victory.

The first invasion

War between the USSR and Finland began on 30 November 1939, when without warning or a formal declaration of war, Soviet planes bombed Helsinki and Viipuri. The same day, five Russian armies of nearly a million men attacked Finland from the east and southeast, and across the Gulf of Finland. They were opposed by 300,000 Finns, of whom 80 per cent were reservists. The world expected a swift Russian victory – as did the Soviet leadership itself – but the Finns held firm, despite the odds against them. All the seaborne attacks in the Gulf were repelled, while the main Russian attack against the Mannerheim Line across the Karelian Isthmus came to costly grief among the complexities of the cleverly-designed Finnish field fortifications. Elsewhere Russian troops pressed on into the forest and lake wilderness of central Finland, ill-equipped to stand the sub-zero temperatures and, being unequipped with skis, unable to move easily in the thick snow. The Finns, all ski-trained and clad for low

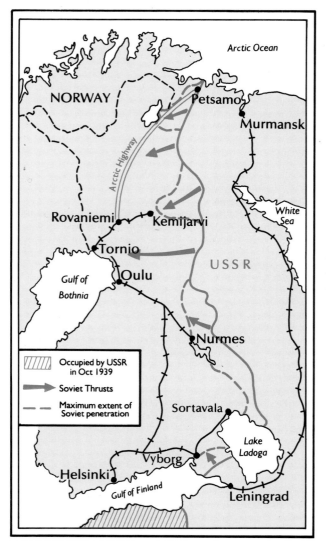

strength against the Mannerheim Line and smash through it, regardless of cost. The armies – the Seventh and 13th – were strengthened to over 35 divisions for the purpose. Starting in February, these troops set in motion a series of non-stop attacks against the Finnish defences – four or five being launched a day, covered by heavy artillery bombardments and air attacks. Again and again, the Finns repulsed the human waves of Russian attackers, but, on 13 February, the Russians achieved a breakthrough. Gradually the Finns were pushed back to Viipuri by sheer weight of numbers. Their armies exhausted and without hope of foreign help, the Finns capitulated on 12 March 1940.

Much of the credit for the magnificent Finnish performance must go to Marshal Baron Carl von Mannerheim, the architect of the Finnish army, and of its defences. The Soviet performance was lamentable – one of the reasons for this was Stalin's pre-war purges of the Soviet army's most able officers – and the cost appalling. Nearly 200,000 Russians had been killed, and 1,600 tanks and 684 aircraft had been lost. Finnish losses were 24, 923 killed and 61 aircraft.

MANNERHEIM LINE *It took 54 Soviet divisions to finally break through the Finnish Mannerheim Line defences in 1940.*

temperatures, were able to harass them mercilessly.

The next major clash was the battle of Suomussalmi. In this, the Russian 163 Division was attacked at the village of Suomussalmi in eastern Finland by the Finnish 9th Division on 11 December. The Russians were quickly cut off in the rear; attempts at relief by the motorized 44th Division were also ambushed. The Finnish attacked in earnest from 27 to 30 December and the 163rd was annihilated. The Finns then turned their attention to the 44th, cutting it into smaller groups, which could be mopped up in detail. By the end of the battle, the Finns had destroyed two Russian divisions for the loss of 900 killed. Elsewhere Russians met with similar reverses.

The Russians regroup

The Russians now paused for thought and came up with a new plan. Crack troops were rushed to the front, the Soviet intention now being to concentrate their

EL ALAMEIN
SECOND WORLD WAR, WESTERN DESERT
23 October–4 November 1942

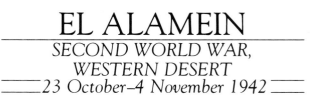

The decisive battle of the "Desert War" in North Africa between the German and Italian expeditionary forces on one side, and the British and Commonwealth 8th Army on the other.

The spring and summer of 1942 was Britain's darkest hour in North Africa. Between January and July, the 8th Army was driven back from El Agheila in Cyrenaica to El Alamein by General Erwin Rommel's combined German and Italian forces, who stood poised to smash through the final British defences and reach Cairo and the Suez Canal. Though the British commander, General Claude Auchinleck, had made a stand at Gazala, and again at Mersah Matruh, Rommel's brilliant leadership, using his 88–mm guns in skilful co-ordination with his infantry, tanks and aircraft, forced the British further and further back. By July, however, Rommel was dangerously overstretched, while British strength was gradually increasing as their naval position in the Mediterranean improved. When Rommel came up against the prepared British positions at Alam Halfa, south of El Alamein, he lacked the strength to break through them. However, the importance of this was not fully recognized at the time. The following month, Auchinleck and his subordinate Ritchie were both relieved of their commands by the British Prime Minister Winston Churchill, and replaced by General Alexander and Lieutenant-General

Montgomery, though, in hindsight, many historians believe that Auchinleck's defensive action at Alam Halfa sowed the seeds for ultimate victory. A further attack by Rommel on Alam Halfa in September, repulsed by the British forces, expended his last offensive strength, and German commitments in Russia, together with Allied naval success in the Mediterranean, crippled his chances of effective resupply.

"Hit Rommel for six"

During September and October, Montgomery, in command of Eighth Army, carefully laid his plans. By October he had 150,000 men ready for action in seven infantry and three armoured divisions, plus a further seven armoured brigades. This gave him a total tank strength of 1,114. Rommel could muster 96,000 men, of whom only 50,000 were German. He had eight infantry and four armoured divisions, but only 600 tanks.

The two armies faced each other sandwiched between the sea to the north and the Qattra Depression to the south. Flanking movements were impossible, as the depression was impassable to vehicles. Montgomery's plan was to force a gap in Rommel's lines, hold off the German armour while he eliminated the German infantry, and then to unleash his own tanks on Rommel's numerically inferior force. The RAF had by this time achieved almost total air superiority over the German and Italian air forces.

At 2140 hours on 23 October, 1,000 British guns

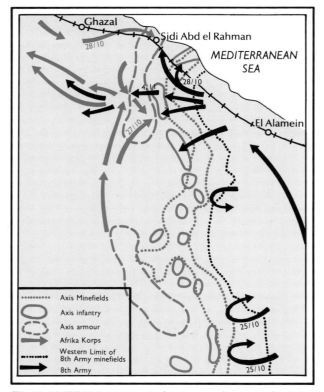

EL ALAMEIN *Montgomery's slogging match against the Axis armies eventually led to a breakthrough in the north.*

began a barrage along a six-mile front stretching from the sea inland. Twenty minutes later – there was a full moon – the British XXX Corps fell upon the Axis left, opening two corridors through the formidable minefields in front of the German positions, while, to the south, a diversionary attack was mounted near the Qattra Depression. At 0200 hours the next morning, the British X Armoured Corps advanced through the swept passages, but a counter-attack by the German 15th Panzer Division put paid to their progress, while the attack in the south similarly failed to make much headway.

On 25 October Rommel, who had been on leave in Germany, flew back to his command (his temporary replacement, General Stumme, had died of a heart attack during the battle), and the next day Montgomery suspended activity in the south, throwing all his weight into the coastal area. For a week, an armoured battle raged, in which the Axis armour, threatened from the air and decisively outnumbered, suffered heavily. Shortages of fuel, replacements, and ammunition further weakened Rommel's position. The 9th Australian Infantry Division came within an ace of pinning down Rommel's 164th Infantry Division, and, to extricate his infantry, Rommel had to commit his last reserves, retiring three miles west on 1 November. Montgomery regrouped and renewed his attempts to break through the Axis front. On 2 November the 2nd New Zealand Division attacked behind a rolling barrage, and cleared a corridor for the British armour.

By the end of that day, only 35 German tanks remained in action, and Rommel, having exhausted his fuel and ammunition, had no option but to withdraw. He had reckoned without his *Führer*, who ordered him to hold on for another pointless 48 hours at all costs. Under further attack from Montgomery, Rommel disregarded Hitler's orders, and managed to extricate the Afrika Korps from the battle, abandoning his Italian allies in the process. The Axis position promptly collapsed, but, because Montgomery failed to follow up his success hard enough, the Afrika Korps – or what was left of it – managed to escape. Rommel had lost 59,000 men killed, wounded, or captured, 500 tanks, 400 guns, and a vast amount of miscellaneous vehicles and material. Montgomery had lost 13,000 killed wounded or missing, and 432 tanks.

Both from the viewpoint of morale and in its effect, El Alamein was the turning point of Britain's war. Montgomery's victory not only saved Egypt and the Suez Canal; it marked the first serious reverse outside Russia for the *Wehrmacht*. If Montgomery can be criticised for failing to pursue and destroy Rommel – to which he could well have argued that Rommel's fate was sealed in any case by the Anglo-American invasion of Algeria four days later – he had no alternative, to a frontal attack, given his position. The skill with which he rang the changes against Rommel's front and kept up a constant pressure on the enemy justify the fame that this battle won him.

THE ARDENNES
SECOND WORLD WAR, BELGIUM
15 December 1944–7 February 1945

Hitler's last offensive in the west in the winter of 1944 led to the largest pitched battle in the USA's history, 600,000 US troops being involved. The action is sometimes called the Battle of the Bulge, from the salient the *Wehrmacht* carved in the Allied front as the Germans strove to reach the Belgian port of Antwerp.

By the winter of 1944, the end of the war seemed in sight as far as the Allied leadership was concerned. Poised for their assault across the Rhine, the Allied commanders completely discounted any further German attempt to launch an offensive. However, they reckoned without two factors – the *Wehrmacht's* astonishing powers of recovery and Hitler. He was determined to attack with his last reserves, his aim being to drive a steel wedge between the American and British armies, separate them and push on to Antwerp. He therefore assembled in Army Group B (Field-Marshal Model) the Sixth SS Panzer Army (General Sepp Dietrich), the Fifth Panzer Army (General Hasso von Manteuffel, and the Seventh Army (General Erich Brandenberger) – a total of 24 divisions, ten of them armoured – in conditions of strictest secrecy.

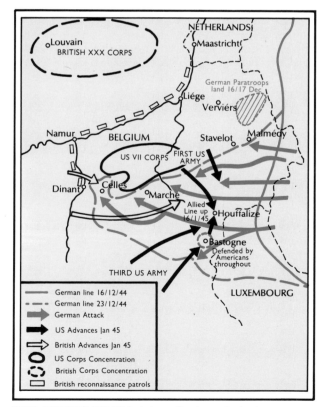

THE ARDENNES *Hitler's last offensive took the Americans by surprise but was eventually halted short of the Meuse.*

Attacking through the Ardennes at dawn on 16 December, in thick snow and concealed by heavy cloud, which neutralized Allied air power, at the outset the German forces secured complete surprise. The US forces opposing them were thrown into grave confusion and a gap opened between the US First Army (General Courtney Hodges) and the US Third Army (General George Patton). By 24 December, the Germans had punched a huge triangular salient in the Allied line, with its apex at Dinant, and the US 101st Airborne and 10th Armored divisions were surrounded at Bastogne. Such was the gravity of the situation that supreme commander General Dwight Eisenhower, transferred command of all troops north of the salient to General Sir Bernard Montgomery, with orders to close the gap at all costs. With their fuel running out, Allied resistance stiffening, and the skies clearing, the German offensive had, however, run out of steam.

Beating back the "Bulge"

The Allied counter-thrusts were two-pronged – Hodges' First Army advancing from the north and Patton's Third Army moving northwards from the south. Both started to close in on the salient on 26 December. By 2 January 1945 Bastogne was relieved, and on 8 January Hitler authorized his troops to withdraw from the point of the salient, preparatory to assembling his *Panzer* divisions for transfer east to meet the expected Russian winter offensive. By 7 February, 1945, the salient had been eliminated.

Hitler's last offensive had cost him 100,000 killed, wounded and missing; US losses were 81,000, of which 19,000 were killed. Above all, the Germans had lost irreplaceable armour and aircraft, which, as Hitler's generals had foreseen, made it impossible for them to halt the next Soviet offensive – an offensive that was to take the Russians to *Berlin*.

ARNHEM
SECOND WORLD WAR, HOLLAND
17 September 1944–26 September 1944

An ambitious plan devised by Field-Marshal Sir Bernard Montgomery to drop three airborne divisions in and around the town of Arnhem to secure key bridges across the Rhine intact so that the Allied armour could advance speedily through Holland into the Ruhr and northern Germany. Montgomery hoped that the plan – codenamed *Market Garden* – would help to end the war in 1944, but it foundered on unexpectedly strong German resistance.

When Montgomery came to draw up his plan for the airborne contingents involved in *Market Garden*, the objectives he gave them were multiple. They included the capture of the canal crossings at Wilhelmina and

Veghel by the US 101 Airborne Division; the capture of the bridge over the Maas at Grave and the bridge over the Rhine at Nijmegen by the US 82 Airborne Division; and the capture of the Arnhem bridge over the Rhine by the British 1st Airborne Division. The airborne operation was to be supported by an advance by XXX Corps of the British Second Army, which was to be co-ordinated with the drops. The plan seemed reasonably straightforward, but success depended on three key factors – the weather, the strength of German opposition, and the speed at which XXX Corps could advance to provide the necessary support.

The airborne assault
On 17 September 1944, 2,000 aircraft and gliders carrying 19,000 troops took off from bases in England to launch the airborne part of *Market Garden*. The drops enjoyed mixed success. The 101 Airborne Division gained the two canal crossings, while the 82nd captured the bridge at Grave, but, it encountered unexpectedly heavy resistance after this and so was unable to advance on Nijmegen. For its part, the British 1st Airborne Division had ground to make up, since it was dropped some miles short of its Arnhem objectives. (This decision was taken in defiance of airborne

doctrine, and in spite of the misgivings of the divisional commander, Major-General Robert Urquhart because it was feared that anti-aircraft batteries might be stationed around the bridge itself.

The battle stalls
While the components of the 1st Airborne Division were thus struggling to reach their main objective, the armoured spearhead of XXX Corps began its advance up the "corridor" towards Arnhem, linking up with the US 101 Airborne Division on the afternoon of 18 September. By this time, however, Urquhart's men were in trouble in Arnhem itself. The lightly-armed paratroops had expected to be facing only second-line troops; instead, they found themselves confronted by the crack II SS Panzer Corps.

Only one Allied battalion (2nd Battalion, Parachute Regiment) reached the bridge. By heroic exertions, the paratroops took it, but were immediately cut off by prompt German reaction, while the rest of the division was encircled near its dropping zone. Behind them, the Germans now completely blocked any further advance by XXX Corps, though a joint Anglo-American attack took the Nijmegen bridge on 20 September.

Bad weather compounded the paratroopers' problem, since it prevented reinforcements or supplies reaching them. Nevertheless, the men of 1st Airborne fought on with their backs to the lower Rhine near Osterbreek. On 21 September an attempt to reinforce them was made by dropping the Polish Parachute Brigade on the south bank near Driel, but the Poles met immediate opposition, and were badly mauled. A gallant attempt at relief by the leading units of XXX Corps was likewise repelled. Of the 9,000 men dropped at Arnhem, 2,200 were evacuated across the river on the night of 25/26 September, leaving nearly 7,000 killed, wounded or captured behind them.

The stand at Arnhem (the operation is still the largest airborne operation ever mounted) is one of the epics of the Second World War. Their heroic failure was largely attributable to faulty intelligence and the presence of II SS Panzer Corps.

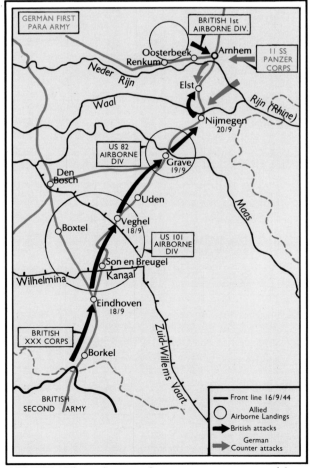

ARNHEM *This ambitious airborne operation encountered far heavier opposition than Montgomery had anticipated.*

BATTLE OF THE ATLANTIC
SECOND WORLD WAR, ATLANTIC OCEAN
1939–1945

The struggle between the German *Kriegsmarine* and Allied naval and air forces for command of the Atlantic shipping lanes. The struggle reached its peak in 1941 and 1942, during which the Nazi submarine fleet came close to severing the Allies' vital trans-Atlantic supply line.

The surface raiders

In 1939, Germany had a surface fleet of four battleships (two obsolete and the *Bismarck* and *Tirpitz* in the process of completion), three "pocket" battleships, four heavy cruisers, and six light cruisers, plus supporting vessels. The German admirals saw clearly that no fleet action could be risked against the vastly superior British fleet of 18 battleships, 10 aircraft carriers, 15 heavy cruisers, and 62 light cruisers – indeed the German naval programme was based on a date for war of 1943. However, they also realized that Britain was dependent on imported food and war material, and that their fast, modern "pocket" battleships and cruisers were ideally suited to commerce raiding. The "pocket" battleship *Graf Spee* was the first of these, until, after an inconclusive action with a British cruiser force, she was scuttled on Hitler's orders in Montevideo harbour in late 1939.

Like all surface ships in the Second World War, the German big-gun vessels were vulnerable to air and undersea attack, so, after the failure of the *Bismarck's* attempt to break out into the North Atlantic, the Germans decided that it was preferable to keep their fleet in being in their Norwegian and French Atlantic coast bases. This policy persisted until the end of 1943 and paid considerable dividends. The very existence of the threat heavily influenced Allied naval dispositions in the Atlantic theatre of war – particularly as far as the Arctic convoys to Russia were concerned. These were highly vulnerable to German ships and aircraft operating from Norway.

The submarine offensive

The main German effort at sea thus depended on the U-boat arm, though E-boats (fast motor-torpedo boats) were effective weapons in the English Channel and the North Sea. Germany started the war with 98 submarines, as against the British total of 70. Within a few hours of the declaration of war, they had claimed their first victim, with the sinking of the passenger liner

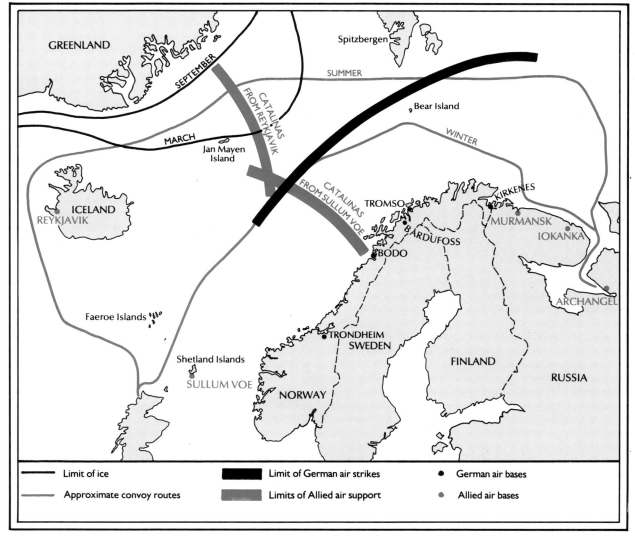

BATTLE OF THE ATLANTIC *The German Kriegsmarine and Luftwaffe co-operated to good effect in the war against merchant shipping, particularly when it came to attacks on the vital supply routes to the Soviet ports of Archangel and Murmansk.*

Athenia at the cost of 112 lives. Two weeks later, U-29 sank the aircraft carrier HMS *Courageous* and the British immediately reintroduced convoys for their merchant marine.

Despite this, British merchant losses mounted; by August 1940, 2.5 million tons of shipping had been sunk. The following month, the pressure eased slightly, when, under the terms of the "Lend-Lease" agreement, the USA supplied Britain with 50 elderly destroyers for convoy escort duty.

The "wolf packs" in action

Admiral Karl Doenitz, commander of the U-boat arm, was alive to the situation, however. Rather than deploying Germany's growing U-boat strength singly, as had been the custom, he organized the so-called "wolf-packs" operating as an effective striking force over the sea approaches to Britain. By June 1941 – in what U-boat commanders termed "the happy time" – over 5 million tons of shipping had been lost, and British yards had been able to replace only 800,000 tons of it. The threat the U-boats posed to Britain's survival was intensified by German long-range bombers, operating beyond the range of British fighter cover. The introduction of escort carriers was eventually to counter both these threats, but too few were available in 1941 to turn the scales.

In December 1941, the USA entered the war and the field of action for the U-boats widened accordingly. In January 1942 a total of 64 U-boats, with supply back-up, were despatched to ambush shipping off the US coast. The US Navy was not yet experienced in anti-submarine operations, and the toll in shipping was high — 80 ships being sunk between January and April 1942. As US countermeasures improved, however, the U-boats were forced further afield to the Caribbean. In the second half of the year, though the U-boat campaign intensified, so did Allied countermeasures; by December, 85 U-boats had been sunk, and US ship-building was beginning to keep up with the losses.

The battle's turning point

At the time, however, it seemed as if the U-boat menace was uncontrollable. In January 1943 the daily number of U-boats in operation averaged 116. By March, 108 Allied ships had been lost and only 15 U-boats destroyed and, as a result, Britain's food supplies were reduced to a three-month safety margin. During the first week in May, Convoy ONS2–42 (Commander Peter Gretton) fought a running battle with 51 U-boats, sinking five for the loss of 13 of 42 merchantmen.

In the same month, RAF Coastal Command (Air Vice-Marshal Sir John Slessor) mounted a combined air-sea offensive against the U-boats, and, in June, the US Navy organized "hunter-killer" groups of escort carriers and destroyers. Both airplanes and ships were also now equipped with radar, which meant that the hunter turned rapidly into the hunted. By the end of the year,

German U-boat losses outstripped the ability of her shipyards to replace them, while new Allied shipbuilding exceeded Allied losses by six million tons. The lease of bases in the Azores from Portugal completed Allied air cover of the Atlantic. In spite of the introduction of the schnorkel "breathing" apparatus (allowing U-boats to use their diesel engines underwater and therefore to remain submerged for much longer than previously), the Allies were able to ship over a million US soldiers and 1.9 million tons of war material across the Atlantic between January and June 1944 almost without loss: from June onwards, as the Allies overran the French U-boat pens, the Germans were forced back on their Baltic and Norwegian bases.

Doenitz was not beaten yet, however. In November 1944 he adopted a new tactic, operating his submarines in shallower water, where Allied sonar devices were less effective, and shipping losses again mounted as a result. In early 1945 the Germans were still producing an extraordinary total of 27 U-boats per month, some of a revolutionary new design, and they were still able to sink over 250,000 tons of Allied shipping. But in April/May 1945 a massive "sweep" of the north Atlantic by the US Navy eliminated this last U-boat threat, though the arm kept fighting until literally the last hours of the war.

Of almost 1,200 U-boats deployed by Germany in the Second World War, 781 were sunk by the Allies, with the loss of 32,000 German sailors. Over 2,500 Allied and neutral vessels had been sunk, with 50,000 Allied casualties. These dry figures disguise one of the most prolonged and intensive struggles in naval history; in terms of shipping destroyed, the campaign was infinitely the most costly of all time.

BERLIN
SECOND WORLD WAR, GERMANY
15 April–2 May 1945

The climactic battle of the war on the Eastern Front. It culminated in the suicide of the German leader, Adolph Hitler, and the fall of Berlin to the Russians.

Across the Oder

By April 1945 the Russian armies, grouped in the 2nd Belorussian front (Rokossovski), the 1st Belorussian Front (Zhukov), and the 1st Ukrainian Front (Koniev), were established on the Oder, only 40 miles from Berlin, and poised for the final drive on the German capital. Between them and the city, lay almost 1,000,000 German soldiers in Army Group Vistula (Heinrici) and Army Group Centre (Schörner), occupying defensive positions on the west bank of the Oder. For the final offensive against Berlin, Zhukov took command of both the 1st Belorussian and 1st

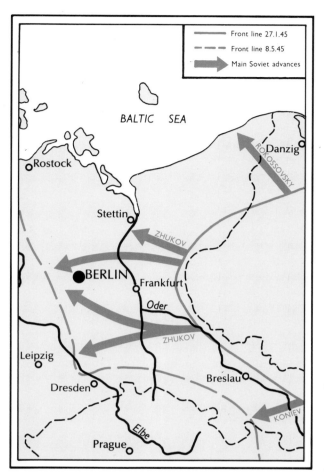

BERLIN *In the last great battle in the west, Stalin orchestrated a race to Berlin between Zhukov and Koniev.*

Ukrainian Fronts, a total of 2,500,000 men. While Rokossovski was to occupy all east Prussia up to the Elbe, Zhukov was to attack Berlin itself.

On 16 April over 20,000 Russian cannon and rocket batteries – one gun to every few feet of front – opened fire in a barrage of unprecedented violence against the hand-pressed defenders of Army Group Vistula. This move, however, had been anticipated by the gifted Heinrici who employed a tactic that had served him well in Russia. He moved the main German defences back to a second line, thus "false fronting" their assailants. The ensuing Russian attacks were bitterly contested; by 18 April, only two small bridgeheads had been forced across the river. The Soviet supremacy – and Zhukov's determination – proved irresistible, however, and by 20 April, the Russians had smashed through the German resistance, and the Russian armour was racing forward. By 25 April, Berlin was surrounded.

Berlin burns

All that now remained of the once mighty *Wehrmacht* were isolated pockets of resistance, of which the Berlin garrison consisted of a mere 30,000 men, supported by teenagers from the Hitler Youth and the scrapings of the *Volkssturm* (Home Guard). At the time of encirclement the city contained some 2,000,000 civilians – orders for evacuation were never given.

As the troops of Zhukov's two fronts closed in on the defenders, every street and house was tenaciously defended, but, by 28 April the leading Russian columns were only a mile apart in the centre of the city; they met on 2 May in the Tiergarten. In a fitting finale to their epic struggle, Russian troops hoisted the red flag over the remains of Hitler's Chancellory.

Hitler's himself did not live to see the final defeat. Having ordered phantom armies to the relief of his battered capital, he eventually despaired and, in a final gesture reminiscent of Brunnhilde's immolation in Richard Wagner's *Gotterdämerung*, committed suicide on 30 April, having ordered his body to be burnt, along with that of his long-time mistress, Eva Braun, whom he had married as Russian shells rocked his bunker. The fall of the city marked the utter defeat of the Germany he had created. Destruction and loss of life were on a huge scale. In the last three months of the war, Germany is reckoned to have lost – on the Eastern Front alone – 1,000,000 killed, 6,000 aircraft. 12,000 tanks and 23,000 guns.

BATTLE OF BRITAIN
SECOND WORLD WAR, SOUTHERN AND EASTERN ENGLAND AND THE CHANNEL
August 1940–October 1940

The conflict between the RAF and the *Luftwaffe* to establish air superiority over the English Channel, which it was essential for Hitler to achieve in order to launch an invasion of Britain, and equally vital for the British to resist.

Following Britain's refusal to make peace with Nazi Germany in the summer of 1940, Hitler responded by ordering the activation of Operation *Sealion*, his plan for the invasion of Britain. He faced an immediate problem — Britain's surface naval superiority over the German *Kriegsmarine* – therefore decided to use the *Luftwaffe* to defeat the RAF, and then having established air supremacy, to neutralize the Royal Navy in the invasion area. Both tasks were ones that Goering assured him the *Luftwaffe* could perform.

German air power was at its peak, with 900 fighters and 1,300 bombers assembled at airfields in France, Belgium, Holland and Norway. Against this, RAF Fighter Command (Air Marshal Sir Hugh Dowding) could oppose 650 fighters, organized in 52 squadrons.

The *Luftwaffe* intended to lure the RAF fighters into combat by attacking selected British targets and forcing the RAF to defend them; this tactic relied on achieving local superiority on each sortie. Aided by radar, however, it was Fighter Command that found it possible to concentrate superior forces at the scene of battle. Thus the Luftwaffe's huge onslaught (almost 1,500 sorties on 8 August – the first day of the battle – rising to 1,700 per day on 15 August) was confronted by the RAF in unexpected strength throughout the 500–mile battle zone.

Attacking the airfields

Reacting to the unexpected strength of the RAF, Goering now switched his attack to Figher Command's bases. Bomber formations, protected by heavy fighter cover, hammered the airfields and communication centres of southern and eastern England. 450 British fighter planes were destroyed, and 103 pilots killed. British fighter strength was almost overwhelmed, when Hitler and Goering again switched their tactics. This was a fatal mistake.

Target London

Hitler had given strict orders that London was to be avoided, but a stray *Luftwaffe* bomber accidentally unloaded its bombs over the capital. The British response was immediate — on 24 August RAF Bomber Command was ordered to Berlin. The attack enraged Hitler, who promptly ordered the *Luftwaffe* to concentrate its attacks on London, so providing the airfields and communication of Fighter Command with an invaluable respite. Moreover, the *Luftwaffe* was now operating in a single definable zone.

On 15 September 1940, over 1,000 German bombers, escorted by 700 fighters, bombed London in continuous waves, but at the cost of 56 planes lost. On the same day, RAF Bomber Command attacked and

destroyed nearly 200 invasion barges in the Channel ports, effectively wrecking Hitler's invasion plan. London was raided heavily again on 10 October, but two days later Hitler cancelled Operation *Sealion*. Daylight operations were now becoming too much of a burden for the *Luftwaffe* to support; by the end of October, German aircraft losses had reached 1,733 and all realistic hope of gaining air superiority had failed. British losses were 915 aircraft of all types, but production under Lord Beaverbrook was rapidly replacing these. The *Luftwaffe* now switched to a nighttime blitz in an attempt to bomb Britain into submission, but, despite the damage they inflicted, its tactical bombers were ill-equipped for this role.

The battle of Britain ensured that Britain would remain unconquered, and that Hitler could never rest secure in control of his conquests on the European mainland. The British owed their victory to the technical advantage of radar, which allowed them to track German formations and concentrate against them; to a highly efficient ground control system; to the Germans' blunder in switching the focus of their attack from the airfields to London; to the superiority of the RAF's Hurricanes and Spitfires over the German Messerschmitts; and to the fact that Dowding understood exactly what issues were at stake in the battle he was fighting – and ensured Fighter Command did the same – while Goering failed to do so.

CORREGIDOR
SECOND WORLD WAR, PHILIPPINES
7 January 1942–6 May 1942

The defence of the Bataan peninsula and Corregidor island by US and Philippino forces against the invading Japanese 14th Army. Though the combined Allied forces put up a stout resistance, Japanese military strength was at the height of its power, and eventually forced a capitulation.

By 7 January 1941, the invasion of the Philippines was going well for the Japanese. They had forced the forces under General Douglas MacArthur into the Bataan peninsula of Luzon, and had established total air superiority, and almost complete naval superiority. MacArthur's main defence lines lay across the massif of Mount Natib, with I Corps (Wainwright) on the left, and II Corps (Parker) on the right. The inland flanks of each corps were exposed, since it was judged impossible to defend the gap of jungly and mountainous terrain between the two positions.

"I shall return"

Frontal attacks by the Japanese on the 9 and 11 January were repulsed, but a move to outflank II Corps on 22

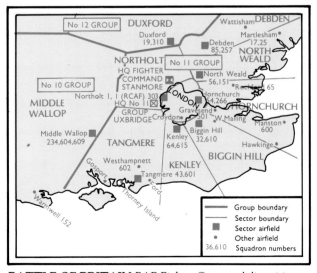

BATTLE OF BRITAIN *RAF Fighter Command dispositions in 1940. The Luftwaffe failed to destroy the vital sector stations.*

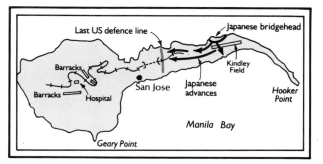

CORREGIDOR *Corregidor was the last Philippine strong-point to hold out against the Japanese.*

January forced both units to pull back to MacArthur's "reserve battle position" half-way down the peninsula, the move being completed by 26 January. Stout US defence, as well as disease and battle losses, held the Japanese here for two months.

Attempts to resupply MacArthur by sea failed, however; practically the only boat to get through the Japanese naval blockade was the one which evacuated MacArthur himself on 11 March to take up the command of all Allied forces in the south Pacific. Leaving his troops with the pledge "I shall return", MacArthur ordered General Jonathan Wainwright to take command in Bataan.

The Japanese breakthrough

Bold words were not enough to stop the Japanese, who, reinforced by a fresh division, attacked again on 3 April 1942, following a five-hour air and artillery bombardment. In six days of bitter fighting, they forced the US forces back to the tip of Bataan, where they surrendered on 9 April. The survivors were forced to make the 90-mile "Death March" into captivity.

The Japanese now turned their attention to the island of Corregidor, which had supported the forces on Bataan with its heavy artillery throughout the final stages of the campaign. The island itself now came under Japanese bombardment; this quickly had an effect, since, with the exception of the "concrete battleship", Fort Drum, Corregidor's gun emplacements were vulnerable to both bombing and plunging artillery fire. On 5 May the Japanese landed on the tip of the island; despite enormous losses (some 4,000), they overran the garrison by the end of the following day.

CRETE
SECOND WORLD WAR, MEDITERRANEAN
20 May 1941–31 May 1941

The invasion of Crete was the first great airborne assault to be launched in the history of war. After their successful attack on Greece, the next logical step for

the Germans to take was to mount an invasion of Crete; the island was important to them as an air base from which to strike at the Suez Canal. For their part, the British planned to use Crete for the same purposes against the Balkans and central Europe.

In May 1941, Crete was garrisoned by the 15,000 British and Commonwealth troops who had been evacuated there from the Greek mainland, plus a further 12,000 reinforcements hurriedly rushed there from Egypt. Two under-strength Greek divisions – 14,000 men in all – 35 aircraft, and nine tanks completed the forces available for the defence of the island. They were commanded by Major-General Bernard Freyberg VC.

Freyberg was given little time to prepare, and what preparations he could make were severely hampered by German air raids mounted from Greece. This was a foretaste of the strategy the Germans were to employ to take the island. Since they lacked naval control of the area, the decision was taken to rely on airborne assault. The German XI Airborne Corps (General Kurt Student) consisting of about 23,000 men equipped for both parachute and glider landings, was given the task by the German High Command.

The invasion begins

After heavy preparatory bombing to soften up the defences, the German 7th Parachute Division made landings at the three main airfields on northern Crete on 20 May 1941. The defenders of the 4th, 5th and 10th New Zealand Brigades took a heavy toll of the German parachutists, but once again were hampered by constant German air attack, and the lack of wireless and other vital facilities. Despite the massive casualties

CRETE *The Luftwaffe's dive bombers took a heavy toll of British warships during the battle for Crete.*

his first wave had taken. Student continued to send in reinforcements – more troops arriving by air on 21 and 22 May. Sheer determination and total air superiority enabled the German airborne forces to force back the British, Commonwealth and Greek defenders, and, on 28 May, Freyberg was forced to withdraw his forces to the south coast, ready for evacuation. During 29/30 May, he maintained a bridgehead around Sfakia, from which he succeeded in embarking 15,000 of his troops. More than 11,000, however, were left behind and forced to surrender.

By daring, disregard of casualties, and through command of the air, Student's forces had wrested the island of Crete from numerically superior forces – which enjoyed naval superiority – in just 11 days. Total British ground casualties were 17,325, including those the Germans captured; over 2,000 ships were lost. German losses were 7,000 killed — one third of the attacking force. The 7th Airborne Division was virtually wiped out, and the Germans never again attempted an airborne operation of Crete's scale.

D-DAY TO THE SEINE
SECOND WORLD WAR, FRANCE
6 June 1944–20 August 1944

D-Day was the greatest amphibious operation in history. Its planning, which had been begun by the British almost as soon as they had been thrown off the continent at Dunkirk in 1940, involved far more than the landings themselves. It also involved a massive build-up of the invading forces on the beachheads – here, the specially-developed artificial harbours played an important part – and the break-out of the Allied armies from their Normandy beachheads, to decisively defeat the German forces in north-western France.

The Allied plan to invade occupied Europe in 1944, code-named *Overlord*, was meticulously planned in near-perfect secrecy. A gigantic cross-Channel

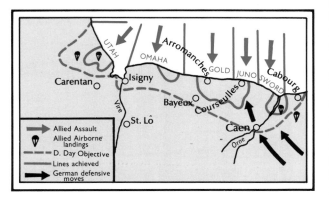

D-DAY *The Germans were deceived by Allied deception plans and surprised by the sheer weight of the invasion.*

amphibious attack, involving a total of nearly 3 million men, was put under the overall control of General Dwight D. Eisenhower. The plan was to land on five main beaches on the Normandy coast, preceding these landings with airborne landings to secure the flanks of the bridgehead. The US First Army (General Omar Bradley) was to land on *Utah* and *Omaha* beaches, separated by the Carentan Estuary. The British Second Army (General Miles Dempsey), which also contained the 3rd Canadian Infantry Division, was to land on *Juno*, *Sword*, and *Gold*. Immediate overall command of these two armies was in the hands of General Sir Bernard Montgomery. The total combatant strength of the invasion force was 45 divisions, with a combined strength of nearly a million men. A further million served in the vast logistical tail needed to support the combatants in action. The landing forces were supported by massive naval and air formations, which, again, had another million men serving in them. The invasion fleet was commanded by Admiral Sir Bertram Ramsay, and the tactical air forces by Air Marshal Sir Trafford Leigh-Mallory.

Facing the Allied invasion was the German Western High Command (Field-Marshal Karl von Rundstedt) with 10 Panzer, 17 infantry, and 31 coast defence divisions. This total looked impressive on paper, but in the actual invasion area, only parts of Army Group B (Field-Marshal Erwin Rommel) were concentrated. These consisted of three Panzer, two infantry, four coast defence divisions, and the garrison of Cherbourg. The remainder of Rommel's forces were stationed further to the east – this disposition had been insisted on by Hitler against Rommel's wishes, as the Führer had been persuaded by a comprehensive Allied deception programme that the real blow would fall in the Pas de Calais and that any landing elsewhere would be a feint. The Allies also enjoyed total air superiority, while the German naval forces were reduced to torpedo boats and submarines.

The longest day
Boldly taking advantage of a "window" in otherwise unfavourable weather, Eisenhower ordered his invasion forces into the assault at dawn on 6 June 1944. Over 9,000 aircraft flew sorties against targets on and behind the beaches, dropping some 10,000 tons of explosive to soften up the Germans and interrupt their communications. At 0200, the airborne divisions were dropped on their targets, while 4,000 transports and 600 warships convoyed the main assault force across the channel. At 0630 the first waves went ashore. By nightfall, though the planned objectives had not, in fact, been reached, five divisions had been landed; only on *Omaha* had the Allies failed to secure a comfortable foothold. Here, the US 1st Infantry Division had run into the veteran German 352 Division, and, deprived of their amphibious armour by heavy seas, had been unable to make such headway.

Rommel now faced a situation he had long feared.

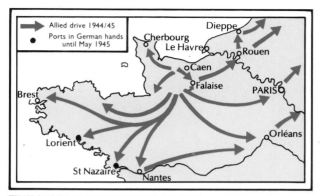

THE NORMANDY BREAK-OUT *Four Allied armies closed in on the Falaise Gap and then pursued Army Group B.*

He had a low opinion of the coastal defences of Hitler's vaunted *Festung Europa* (Fortress Europe) and had argued fervently that, given Allied air supremacy, every available German unit had to be at the tide line ready to drive the Allies into the sea. However, he was denied the opportunity to put his plan into operation by Hitler who, even after receiving news of the invasion, was still reluctant to release the reserves held further to the east. Thus, in spite of the loss of one of their artificial harbours to bad weather on 19 June, the Allies were able to increase their forces rapidly, until by the end of July a million men, 150,000 vehicles and a million tons of supplies were ashore. Nonetheless, progress on the ground was slow in the face of stubborn German resistance. An additional blow to Allied hopes came when Cherbourg (captured on 27 June) was found to be too badly damaged to use as a port.

The Allied break-out

Slowly, the Allied position improved. While the US First Army cleared the Contentin peninsula and drove south to St Lo, Montgomery launched a series of costly attacks around Caen, which did not fall until 13 July. These assaults compelled Rommel to commit his armour to the Caen sector at the expense of the overall balance of the German front.

Meanwhile, Hitler was demanding action. After his blunt advice to "make peace, you fools," von Rundstedt was relieved of his command and replaced by Field-Marshal Gunther von Klüge in July; Rommel was severely wounded by an Allied aircraft. On 25 July, however, the Allied break-out finally began, when Bradley's First Army launched operation *Cobra* west of St Lo. Attacking behind a massive aerial bombardment, the US VII, VIII and XIX Corps broke through the German defences, and, against heavy opposition reached Avranches by 31 July. The Allied forces were now expanded and reorganized as the US 12th Army Group (Bradley) and the British 21st Army Group (Montgomery). The US Third Army (General George Patton) poured through the gap opened at Avranches. German counterattacks were destroyed on their start lines by Allied aircraft, and the enveloping Allied armies closed in on the German forces in the Falaise-Argentan pocket.

Slowness and misunderstanding allowed disorganized elements of the German Seventh and Fifth Panzer armies to escape eastwards, but, by the time the gap was closed on 20 August, 50,000 Germans had been captured, and 10,000 killed. Von Kluge, who had been relieved of his command and replaced by Field-Marshal Model, had already extricated much of Army Group B; the retreating Germans were across the Seine and heading east by the time the US XV Corps crossed the river north-west of Paris on 20 August.

Since 6 June 1944, the Allies had put over 2 million men into Europe. They had comprehensively defeated the German Seventh and 15th Armies, throwing them back in rout into a retreat that ended only on their own borders. This had been achieved at a cost of 40,000 dead, 165,000 wounded, and 20,000 missing. The Germans had lost over 500,000 dead, wounded and missing from their forces in the field, and another 200,000 from their coast defence divisions, though their command structure and discipline remained intact (even though some of the key German generals in France had been involved in the abortive July bomb plot against Hitler). France had been liberated, and Hitler's dream of a *Festung Europa* was finally shattered.

DIEPPE
SECOND WORLD WAR, FRANCE
19 August 1942

A landing by British and Canadian forces at Dieppe. The aims of the raid were to destroy port installations, assess German defensive capabilities to aid the D-Day planners, and to give Allied officers and men experience of amphibious warfare.

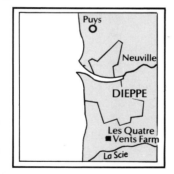

Dieppe was selected as the site for the raid because it was within range of fighter cover from Britain. The troops chosen for the job were the 2nd Canadian Division (Major-General J.H. Roberts), with 3 Commando and 4 Commando providing the flank forces that were to silence the coastal batteries to the east and west of the town. The total landing forces amounted to just over 6,000 men, transported in nine landing ships escorted by eight destroyers.

At dawn the batteries were to be silenced; 30 minutes later the main force was to land on the sea front of the town. All German positions were to be destroyed before the force was evacuated.

Disaster at Dieppe

From the start, the Dieppe raid was dogged by failure. To the east of the town, 3 Commando found itself unable to silence the "Goebbels" battery at Berneval, while the Royal Regiment of Canada, detailed to knock out the "Rommel" battery at Puys, was put ashore late, lost the advantage of surprise and was pinned down as soon as it landed. To the west, however, 4 Commando reached its objectives and was re-embarked safely.

At Dieppe itself, the main landings met intense resistance from the German defenders and the troops taking part in them were pinned down on the beach. Armoured support might have saved the situation, but the few tanks of the 14 Canadian Tank Regiment that did manage to scale the sea wall were then halted by carefully-positioned anti-tank obstacles. The attackers held their positions for three hours under very heavy fire, but, at 1100 the withdrawal began. By 1300, the survivors were on their way back to England.

Though a failure, the Dieppe raid proved invaluable to the Allies in the lessons it taught. The planning inadequacies and faulty intelligence that caused the Allied failure were remedied on D-Day. The cost of the lesson was extremely high, however. Of 5,000 men put ashore, 3,350 were casualties. Naval losses were one destroyer and over 30 landing craft. German losses were about 600.

BATTLE OF FRANCE
SECOND WORLD WAR, FRANCE
10 May 1940–25 June 1940

The triumphant *Blitzkrieg* (lightening campaign) launched against the Low Countries and France by 123 German divisions (2.5 million men) in May 1940. By 25 June, Holland, Belgium and France had surrendered, while the British Expeditionary Force had been evacuated from Dunkirk, leaving Hitler master of the European continent.

The German forces were organized into three army groups, under the overall command of Hitler, with General Wilhelm Keitel as his chief of staff. The Allied forces numbered more than 2 million men in 137 divisions – 20 Belgian, 13 British, one Polish, and 103 French. Of the French divisions, 13 were fortress divisions, incapable of movement outside the Maginot Line, the chain of fortifications the French had built along the Franco-German frontier.

Tanks were to be a key factor in the coming battle, together with air support. Contrary to popular belief, the Allied tank forces outnumbered the German *Panzers* by 3,609 to 2,574, but this superiority was vitiated by the Allied practice of scattering their

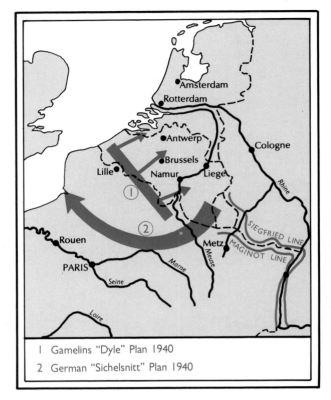

THE BREAKTHROUGH *The Allies expected a replay of 1914, but the Sichelschnitt struck through the Ardennes.*

I Gamelins "Dyle" Plan 1940
2 German "Sichelsnitt" Plan 1940

armour piecemeal among their conventional divisions. By contrast, the German armour was massed in 10 *Panzer* divisions – and it was these that achieved the decisive breakthrough. In the air, the *Luftwaffe* was definitely superior, fielding 3,500 modern aircraft against 290 British and 1,400 French machines of varying degrees of obsolescence.

Battle in Flanders

The attack began on 10 May 1940, when the Germans launched a surprise attack on neutral Holland and Belgium. After a pre-dawn raid on the Dutch and Belgian airfields, paratroops were dropped to paralyze the rear areas of the Dutch and Belgian armies, while another elite force captured the vital Belgian strongpoint of Fort Eben Emael, which controlled a key river crossing. The attacks were supported by the terror bombing of civilians. It seemed to many observers that the Schlieffen Plan, with which Germany had gone to war in 1914, was being replayed, but that this time it was being carried through with utter ruthlessness, without the distraction of Russian involvement. Certainly, General Maurice Gamelin, the Allied commander-in-chief, had no doubt of the *Wehrmacht's* intentions. As German troops pressed on into Flanders, he flung his best motorized forces – the British Expeditionary Force and the French Seventh Army – across the Franco-German border to take up position along the River Dyle.

Surprise in the Ardennes'

These attacks, however, were not the main German *Schwerpunkt* (thrust). They were designed to concentrate the Allies' attention on the northern frontier. Meanwhile, almost unnoticed, elements of Army Group A – with the majority of Hitler's *Panzer* divisions – were making their way through the heavily wooded Ardennes towards the Stenne Gap. The Ardennes, though a traditional invasion route, was disregarded by the French High Command on this occasion, since they believed that the area was totally unsuited to armoured operations. Accordingly, it was defended by weak units of the French First and Ninth Armies – and it was on these that the full armoured might of the *Wehrmacht* was to fall.

By 14 May, Panzer Group Kleist had forced the crossing of the River Meuse and opened up a 50-mile gap in the Allied front. Thrown into confusion by the German thrust, French resistance collapsed and the German *Panzers*, supported by Stuka dive-bombers, swept along the valley of the Somme, opening a corridor that was eventually to lead to the Channel coast. The purpose of this encircling move was obvious — to cut off the British, French and Belgian divisions in the northern sector of the front from the remainder of the French army to the south.

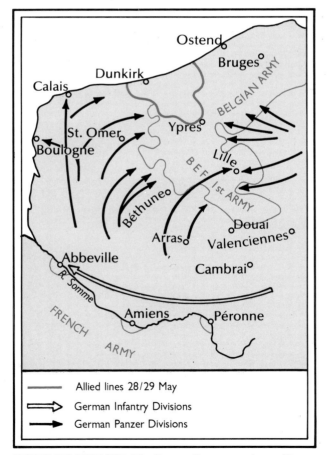

DRIVE TO THE SEA *The German Panzer corridor swiftly reached the sea, so cutting off the northern Allied armies.*

Gamelin seems to have been totally paralyzed by the weight and audacity of the German attack, and demoralized by the failure of the French troops to hold it. Already, "by a series of unbelievable mistakes that will be punished," as the French premier, Paul Reynaud, proclaimed to the Chamber of Deputies, the Ninth Army had failed to blow up the crucial bridges in its sector; now, when asked by the newly-appointed British Prime Minister, Winston Churchill, where was his "mass of manoeuvre", so that a counter-attack could be launched, he tersely replied *"aucune"* (there no longer is one). Nevertheless, he attempted to deploy reserves to plug the gap, but they were completely routed, only three armoured counterattacks by Brigadier-General Charles de Gaulle enjoying any success (17–19 May). On that day, Gamelin was relieved of command and replaced by General Maxime Weygand. On 21 May a pincer movement by the French from the south and the British from the north attempted to cut the German corridor, but in vain. By 20 May the German armour had reached the Channel at Noyelles. By 25 May, the Germans were at Boulogne, and three days later, at Calais.

The "miracle" of Dunkirk

The situation was now as follows. The Dutch and Belgian armies had surrendered, and the British Expeditionary Force (Gort), together with the French First Army, were now isolated from the remaining Allied forces, surrounded by the armoured divisions of Army Groups A and B. The infantry of Army Group A held the line of the Somme and the Aisne with bridgeheads at Peronne and Amiens. The situation was critical, but, on 26 May an ill-judged order to halt from Hitler stopped the German *Panzers* in their tank tracks. This allowed the British, now pinned with their backs to the sea at Dunkirk, to organize evacuation of their army, plus a large part of First Army.

It was not until 28 May that German pressure was renewed. Three British divisions, holding defensive positions in some depth, checked the German attack, while 850 assorted naval and civilian vessels embarked the remaining troops from the harbour and beaches. In eight days (28 May–4 June inclusive) 338,226 troops (including 120,000 French) were evacuated. The operation was made possible by the intervention of home-based RAF units, who destroyed 179 German aircraft over the beaches for a loss of 29. On the morning of 5 June the Germans overwhelmed the remnants of the French First Army, which had screened the final embarkation.

The conquest of France

The respite Dunkirk provided was of little use to Weygand in the south, however. He attempted to organize a defensive line along the Somme, and then the Aisne, but half of France's available strength had already vanished, while his efforts were hampered by the *Luftwaffe*'s bombardment of railways and roads.

For their part, the German armies regrouped quickly. On 5 June, Army Group B, led by Kleist's *Panzers* swarmed across the Somme, and broke through the French Tenth Army (Altmeyer) to reach the Seine west of Paris by 9 June. The following day, Army Group A broke through the French forces east of the city. The government fled south, the capital being declared an open city on 13 June, the Germans marching in the next day.

The French armies continued to disintegrate as the German columns poured south, west and east. On 17 June, Reynaud resigned, to be replaced by the senile Marshal Pétain, who on 22 June, accepted the German surrender terms. The only military success enjoyed by the French in this overwhelming debâcle was the vigorous repulse by six French divisions of an invasion launched by 31 Italian divisions after Mussolini, anxious for a cheap victory, had finally declared war.

The German execution of their plans for the invasion of France was meticulous, ruthless and brilliant. They had correctly judged the tactical potential of the new motorized armour. Though the *Wehrmacht* as a whole was numerically roughly equal to the Allies, it was the key eight per cent of their forces concentrated in their armoured divisions that caused the disruption and collapse of the Allied front. Where the Allies met the Germans on equal terms, or where they concentrated their armour, as in the BEF's counter-attack at Arras on 21 May, they fought effectively as well as bravely.

Nor should the importance of Dunkirk be underestimated. Though, as Churchill aptly remarked, "Wars are not won by evacuations," by rescuing the bulk of the BEF from France, the British were able to rebuild their armies and so continue the war.

GAZALA–BIR HACHEIM

SECOND WORLD WAR, WESTERN DESERT
28 May 1942–13 June 1942

A key battle in the drive launched against the British Eighth Army by Rommel's Afrika Korps in the summer of 1942. Rommel's success in breaking Eighth Army's front led to the surrender of the fortress of Tobruk, while Eighth Army itself was forced back across the Egyptian frontier to take up position at *El Alamein*.

In January 1942, British naval losses in the Mediterranean theatre and Axis bombing of Malta meant that Rommel's supplies could be built up faster than those of Eighth Army (the British were being forced to sail their supply convoys via the Cape, rather than directly through the Mediterranean). On 21

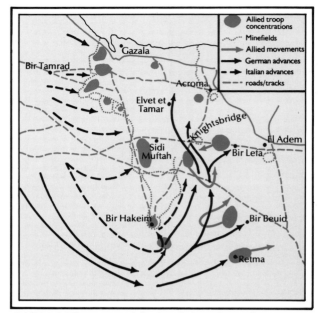

GAZALA *The turning of the Gazala Line. Rommel sweeps around Bir-Hacheim, while Cruwell pins down the defences.*

January, therefore, Rommel was able to take the offensive against Eighth Army's position at El Agheila.

The British forces, dispersed and unprepared, were forced back beyond Benghazi, losing large quantities of war material in the process, but by 4 February, General Claude Auchinleck, in overall command, had been able to halt the retreat at Gazala. There, the British established a strong defensive position in depth between Gazala on the coast and Bir Hacheim 40 miles inland.

The Axis thrust
On 26 May, the Axis forces attacked the British positions. British strength was 125,000 men, 740 tanks, and 320 aircraft, with an additional Free French division holding the left flank. Rommel's combined German and Italian forces numbered 113,000 with 570 tanks and 500 aircraft. Though inferior in number, the German tanks had greater hitting power than their British counterparts.

Rommel decided to attack in the south, hoping to envelop the desert (left) flank of the British position and roll it up towards the sea. Though the Free French repulsed the Italian attacks on Bir Hacheim, Rommel's armour succeeded in turning the British flank – a move that enabled them to engage the British armoured forces from the rear at a crossroads code-named *Knightsbridge*. Auchinleck's defensive lines had been successfully turned.

Battle in the "Cauldron"
By now, Rommel was running short of petrol. Accordingly, he halted his drive north, and concentrated his armour in a defensive laager behind the British lines in an area known as the "Cauldron" (May 30). After four day's desperate fighting, Italian

infantry broke through the British minefields to join up with Rommel's forces. A British counterattack on 5/6 June was beaten off, and, on 10/11 June, the French, after a magnificent defence, were compelled to abandon Bir Hacheim. On the same day, Rommel's resupplied and rested armour broke out from the "Cauldron", thrusting south and east to threaten the rear of the whole British position. Eighth Army was compelled to disengage and retreat all the way back to the Egyptian frontier.

In this battle, Rommel displayed all the qualities of leadership that had won him the nickname of the "Desert Fox". This success was also a tribute to the superiority of his tanks, and of the 88mm AA gun, which his forces used with devastating effect as an anti-tank weapon. But, though his tactics had paid off, he had squandered the last of his offensive capability, as events at El Alamein were to show.

GUADALCANAL
SECOND WORLD WAR, SOLOMON ISLANDS
7 *August 1942–9 February 1943*

A six-month battle to establish and maintain the US 1st Marine Division's bridgehead on Guadalcanal, to prevent its use by the Japanese as an air base and to secure a foothold on the south-west perimeter of the Japanese conquests.

On 7 August 1942, a hastily-assembled task force, under Rear-Admiral Richmond K. Turner, landed the first waves of the 19,000 men of the US 1st Marine Division (Major General Alexander A. Vandergrift) on Guadalcanal. The operation was supported by Admiral Frank J. Fletcher's three-carrier task force; Fletcher himself was in overall command of the operation. In spite of the haste in which the landing had been planned and the inexperience of the troops involved, 1st Division achieved surprise and landed unopposed, though smaller landings on neighbouring islands met with fierce opposition.

By 8 August, all the landings had been completed. On Guadalcanal itself, the marines captured the vital Henderson Field, the airstrip the Japanese were constructing, but, during the night, a naval action fought in Ironbottom Sound (adjacent to the landings) forced the transports to withdraw, leaving the marines unsupported and scantily equipped. Between 9 and 18 August, it was as much as they could do to strengthen their perimeter around Henderson Field, facing a constant Japanese bombardment as they did so.

The Japanese response
On 18 August, the first Japanese reinforcements landed at Taivu, 20 miles east of Henderson Field. These consisted of one regiment under Colonel Ichiki. On 20 August the marines received their first aircraft, and, over the next two days, they destroyed Ichiki's force by a brilliantly-executed encircling movement. The battle for Guadalcanal was by no means over, however. Between 20 August and 12 September, nightly dashes by Japanese destroyers kept up a steady flow of reinforcements (by day the Americans enjoyed superiority at sea), and, by 12 September, the Japanese were strong enough to launch an attack in divisional strength.

For two days the battle of Bloody Ridge raged, until the Japanese were forced to withdraw with heavy losses. Fighting continued at sea and in the air as each side built up its strength. By the middle of October, the marines numbered over 23,000, while the Japanese 17th Army (Major-General Haruyoshi Hyakutake) had 20,000 men under command.

The crunch came on 23 October when the Japanese launched intensive attacks against the marine

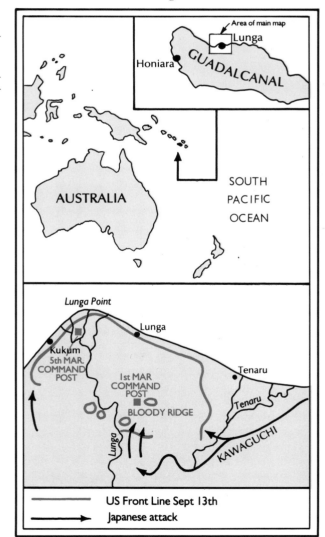

GUADALCANAL *In savage fighting, US forces gradually expanded their perimeter to force back and defeat the Japanese.*

perimeter. The fighting was severe, but the Japanese wrecked their chances of success by launching their attacks piecemeal. These failed with heavy losses, and, during November and December, the marines were able to expand and consolidate their perimeter once again. On 9 December the hard-pressed marines were relieved by fresh troops under General Alexander Patch; in January, by which time US strength had increased to 58,000 men, Patch was able to launch an offensive to drive the Japanese out of the island. The Japanese, though weakened by disease and near-starving, fought ferociously, but in four weeks they were driven back to the north-western tip of Guadalcanal (Cape Esperance), where a daring operation by the Japanese navy extricated almost 13,000 of them from the US trap (1–7 February).

Guadalcanal was the first major Allied land victory over the Japanese; in the six-month campaign Japan lost 25,000 men, 600 planes and 24 ships. American losses were 1,500 dead, 4,800 wounded, and 24 ships.

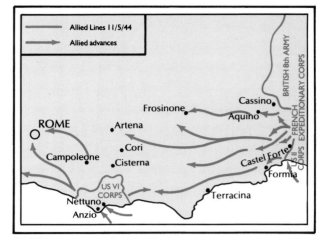

GUSTAV LINE *Allied break-through attempts centred on Cassino, while the Anzio bridgehead stubbornly held out.*

THE GUSTAV LINE
SECOND WORLD WAR, ITALIAN FRONT
January 1944–May 1944

Attack by the Allied 15 Army Group (General Sir Harold Alexander) on the Gustav Line, the name given to the strong German defensive positions in the mountains south of Rome, manned by the German Army Group C (Field-Marshal Albert Kesselring). The most costly action in the campaign was the attempt to storm Monte Cassino; at Anzio, where Allied amphibious forces were landed in an attempt to turn the defences, prompt German reaction nearly succeeded in driving the Allies into the sea.

Cassino and the Rapido
By the beginning of 1944 the Allied drive up the "toe" of Italy towards Rome had stalled. Now, British Eighth Army (General Oliver Leese) and the US Fifth Army (General Mark Clark) faced the German 10th Army (General Heinrich von Vietinghoff) across the rivers Rapido and Garigliano. Behind these natural obstacles, the Germans had constructed immensely strong defensive positions, incorporating gun pits blasted out of rock, concrete bunkers, machine gun emplacements, barbed wire, and minefields. It was dominated in the northern sector by Monte Cassino.

To break the threatened stalemate, Alexander planned a frontal attack on the Gustav Line, supported by a seaborne landing at Anzio, behind the German defences. On 17 January 1944, the Brish X Corps won a bridgehead across the Garigliano, but the US II Corps was repulsed with great loss when it attempted to do the same on the Rapido, as was the French

Expeditionary Corps. Though no significant gains were made, the action did have a bonus. German reserves were drawn to the Rapido front, and Kesselring's attention was distracted from the impending amphibious landings at Anzio.

The Anzio landings
On 22 January 1944, some 50,000 Anglo-American troops comprising VI Corps (Major General John P. Lucas) made an unopposed landing at Anzio, establishing a beachhead seven miles deep. Though the landings took the Germans completely by surprise – Allied scouts reaching the suburbs of Rome – the over-cautious Lucas failed to make good his advantage, while Kesselring, on the other hand, reacted all too quickly. He extemporized a 14th Army (General Hans Mackensen) out of the scanty reserves he had available, which quickly attacked the Allied beachhead (16–29 February). The demoralized Lucas was replaced by Major-General Lucius K. Truscott, but, from February to May 1944, the Anzio beachhead was under siege.

Alexander now had little choice but to mount an intensive air interdiction campaign – Operation *Strangle* – to literally blast the Germans out of their mountain positions. This followed further unsuccessful attempts to break the Gustav Line by frontal attack, notably the attempt by the New Zealand Corps to take Monte Cassino after it had been bombed to rubble.

On 11 May, having regrouped 15 Army group, Alexander finally won success when he launched a surprise attack between Monte Cassino and the sea. The Allies broke through the German lines, with Cassino at last falling to the Poles (17/18 May). At Anzio, VI Corps attacked inland (23 May), and contact was made between the two forces two days later.

Though the Gustav Line had been breached, the Germans were not driven back in rout, however. Skilful rearguard actions delayed the Allied thrust towards Rome long enough for the bulk of the German forces to retire in reasonable order.

IMPHAL/KOHIMA
SECOND WORLD WAR, INDIA
March 1944– September 1944

The twin sieges of Imphal and Kohima by the Japanese 15th Army (Lieutenant-General Renya Mutaguchi) marked the apogee of Japan's attempted invasion of India in the Second World War. Their defence and relief by the British IV Corps (General Geoffrey Scoones) and XXXIII Corps (General Montagu Stopford) of 14th Army (General William Slim) was the turning point in the British resistance; the next move was to move from defence to attack and launch the reconquest of Burma.

The Battle for India
Ordered north in March 1944 to deny the Manipur/Assam area to the British as a base for a Burmese counteroffensive and, if possible, to cut the Assam railway, Mutaguchi moved in great strength at brilliant speed. British outposts holding the Chin Hills were driven back or surrounded; by 5 April, the Japanese 33rd and 15th Divisions had cut off IV Corps at Imphal, while the Japanese 31st Division had isolated a smaller detatchment at Kohima, 60 miles to the north.

Things were not as black as they seemed for the British, for Slim, although surprised by the speed of the attack, had been expecting such a Japanese move, and had drawn up plans to counter it. Immediately an airlift was launched to supply the beleaguered garrisons, while Stopford's XXXIII Corps began an advance to relieve Kohima. Slim also flew in reinforcements to Imphal, until the strength of the garrison rose to more than 100,000.

Intense fighting was almost continuous around both perimeters, and Kohima almost fell several times. The Japanese, however, were constantly harassed by US and British air power, and on 20 April XXXIII Corps broke through and relieved Kohima. Outnumbered and short of supplies, the Japanese fought with ferocious tenacity, and Stopford's subsequent progress toward Imphal was slow. The British, however, had time on their side, since the Japanese had been counting on the capture of British supplies to keep them in action, while the onset of the monsoon period compounded their difficulties. As Japanese fighting strength continued to be seriously eroded by disease and hunger, Stopford's advance gained momentum; on 22 June 1944, IV Corps and XXXIII Corps at last linked up.

Half-starving, and having incurred huge losses, the remnants of 15th Army fell back to the Chindwin. Although attacked from the air and pursued by British troops, the Japanese did not lose their discipline or battleworthiness. Since April 1944, 15th Army had lost 65,000 dead (against British losses of 13,000), 250 guns, and most of its tanks and transport.

KURSK
SECOND WORLD WAR, EASTERN FRONT
14 July–23 August 1943

The greatest tank battle ever fought and the last major offensive launched by the *Wehrmacht* on the Eastern Front. It involved 2,000,000 men, 6,000 tanks, and 4,000 aircraft. The battle was planned by the German High Command to cut off the Soviet forces in the Kursk salient, the twin thrusts of the necessary pincer movement coming from Army Group Centre (von Kluge) in the north, and Army Group South (von Manstein) in the south.

The German attacks
After the *Wehrmacht*'s debâcle at *Stalingrad*, Hitler ordered a new offensive at Kursk to regain the initiative

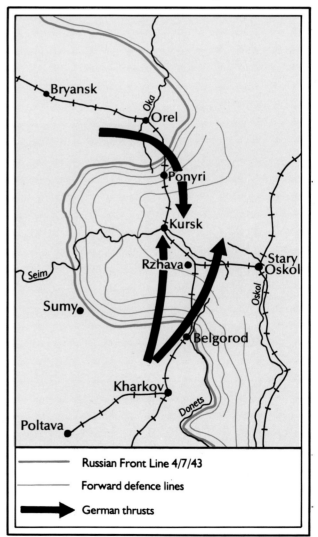

KURSK *Hitler's last great eastern offensive aimed at pinching out a huge salient, defended in depth.*

on the Eastern Front, but his forces started at a disadvantage. The Russians were aware of the weakness of the salient, and had been at pains to reinforce it. Two Fronts, the Central Front (General Konstantin Rokossovski) and the Voronezh Front (General Nicholas Vatutin), occupied the area and had constructed eight concentric lines of defence. In addition to this the Russians knew the details of Operation *Citadel* (the codename for the German attack) from intelligence sources.

Hitler was not to be deterred, however, and on 5 July 1943 the offensive opened, though delayed by a spoiling bombardment that hit the forward areas as the German troops were assembling. Results were unimpressive in the north, where Ninth Army gained only six miles at the cost of 25,000 killed, 200 tanks and 200 aircraft; by 10 July all Army Group Centre's reserves had been committed with no further gains. In the south, things were slightly better, as Manstein had managed to drive a wedge 25 miles into the Russian salient at the cost of 10,000 men and 350 tanks. Vatutin, however, reinforced his front and halted Manstein's.

The Soviet counter-blow

On 12 July, the Russian Fronts counterattacked, and by 20 July, all their formations were advancing. Three days later, the 23rd the Germans were back at their start lines, and, by 5 August, the Russians had made substantial gains on each side of the salient.

Defeat now turned to rout. By 11 August, Soviet forces were converging on Kharkov in the south; by 23 August, the Orel salient in the north had been eliminated. Soviet military superiority alone did not account for this result; on 12 July, as the Russian counteroffensive was launched, Hitler had ordered his generals to abandon *Citadel* and rush forces to the west, where the Allies had launched their invasion of Sicily.

The fighting around Orel, Kursk, and Kharkov during July and August 1942 was on a vast scale and the costs were equally high. The Germans lost 70,000 killed and wounded, 3,000 tanks, 1,000 guns, 5,000 motor vehicles, and 1,400 planes; Soviet losses are not known, but were probably slightly less. However, they could make these good, while the Germans could not recover.

SIEGE OF LENINGRAD
SECOND WORLD WAR, EASTERN FRONT
September 1941–January 1944

An epic 900-day siege of Russia's second city by the German *Wehrmacht*. It was one of the most costly actions of the war, particularly as far as the civilian inhabitants of Leningrad were concerned; it is estimated that 1,500,000 Leningraders died during the course of the siege.

On 1 September 1941, Leningrad came under bombardment, as Army Group North closed in on the city. By 15 September, when the Germans took Schlüsselberg on Lake Lagoda, so cutting Leningrad off from the rest of Russia, it was clear that its citizens faced the grim alternatives of continued resistance, or capitulation. They chose the former, though it was calculated that, even with strict rationing, the city's remaining food stocks could only last a further month. All sorts of expedients were pressed into service to try to make food stretch further, but it was not until December that an "ice road" could be opened across Lake Lagoda to bring supplies into the starving city. This link was tenuous at the best; on Christmas Day 1941 alone, 3,500 Leningraders died of starvation.

Leningrad under siege

Within the Leningrad enclave, the Leningrad Front (under General Leonid Govorov from 1942) could muster the battered remnants of 42nd Army, plus the 55th Army and units of the Baltic Fleet. All these forces were well under strength. They were opposed by the German 18th Army, containing some of Hitler's best divisions. Despite this, Leningrad held on. The Germans failed to storm the city, or to establish a second siege line around it, which could well have proved fatal.

Hitler was not cast down by this failure, however. Having failed to take Leningrad in their initial thrust, the Germans were quite content to let starvation do its work for them. The *Führer* summed up the German view when he said: "Leningrad's hands are in the air. No one can save it. It falls sooner or later. Leningrad is doomed to die of famine." The Germans relied on this, plus constant artillery and air bombardment, to bring the city to its knees.

The city of death

By all logical calculation, Hitler was correct in this view. As the Russian winter reached its peak, the city was thrown on its own dwindling resources; food, fuel and ammunition were all lacking. At the height of the siege, the death toll from disease, hunger and cold – discounting fighting casualties – was to reach 20,000 a day. But patriotism, discipline and hatred of the German invaders somehow kept the Leningraders fighting, in the hopes that the siege would eventually be lifted and the city relieved.

The first relief operations that were attempted failed. In August 1942, for instance, the Leningrad and Volkhov Fronts simultaneously attempted to sever the German-held corridor on the left bank of the Neva, but the offensive was unsuccessful. In January 1943, however, the Soviets scored their first positive success, when they managed to open a thin corridor south of Lake Lagoda. For the remainder of that year, this remained Leningrad's only link with the outside world, but the trickle of supplies that passed along it meant the difference between survival and capitulation.

Lifting the siege

Not until January 1944 was the siege fully lifted. As part of the general Russian winter offensive, the Leningrad Front and the Volkhov Front (General Kirill Meretskov in command) fell upon the 18th Army (now commanded by Colonel-General Georg Lindemann). Lindemann attempted to hold his ground, but the Soviet pressure was such that he was compelled to withdraw to avoid encirclement. By the end of the month, Leningrad had finally been relieved. The railway links with Moscow were re-opened and the Germans driven ·50 miles back from the city.

LEYTE GULF
SECOND WORLD WAR, PHILIPPINE ISLANDS
23 October–25 October 1944

A four-phase naval action in defence of the US reconquest of the Philippines; its successful conclusion finally destroyed Japan as a naval power.

On 20 October 1944, the US Sixth Army began its landings on Leyte Island, with the US Seventh Fleet (Admiral Thomas Kinkaid) in direct support and the US Third Fleet (Admiral William Halsey) further off. Between them, the two fleets consisted of 12 battleships, 32 carriers – it is worth noticing how, by this stage of the war, the traditional battleship preponderance had been reversed – plus 29 cruisers and 104 destroyers.

The Japanese, recognizing that US success in the Philippines would cut Japan off from her sole remaining sources of raw materials, were prepared to risk everything to defend their Philippine conquests. Their *Sho* (victory) plan called for an attack by the entire Japanese fleet on the US landings. Four Japanese groups were to sail from different locations. Between them, the groups numbered nine battleships (two of them the new superbattleships), four carriers, 20 cruisers, and 31 destroyers. Thus, the balance of numbers favoured the Americans. Moreover to the 1,000 planes the US carriers could field, the Japanese could put only 116 into the sky. Their hope was that shore-based planes would make this difference good.

The Sibuyan Sea

The countdown to battle started on 23 October 1944, when scouting US submarines located the Japanese Centre Force of five battleships, 12 cruisers and 15 destroyers under Admiral Tokeo Kurita and sank two cruisers. Kurita was then attacked by planes from Task Force (TF) 38 (Admiral Mark Mitscher), part of Third Fleet. The superbattleship *Musashi* was sunk after two day's constant attack, while TF38 lost a light carrier (*Princeton*) to land-based planes. Kurita made as if to withdraw, but turned under cover of darkness and resumed his westerly course.

Meanwhile, warned of the approach of the Japanese Force C (Admiral Nishimura; with two battleships, one cruiser and four destroyers), Kinkaid ordered his Gun Support Group (Rear-Admiral J.B. Oldendorff with six battleships, eight cruisers and 26 destroyers) to intercept the Japanese before they could close for action. Moving at night up the Surigao Strait, Nishimura was attacked by US PT boats, and then steamed straight into Oldendorff's waiting forces. The resulting action was conclusive, all but one destroyer of Force C being sunk. A supporting Japanese squadron of three cruisers and four destroyers did manage to make its escape, however, at the cost of a further cruiser sunk.

San Bernadino

Believing Kurita to be out of the fight, Halsey now sailed north to engage the Japanese Carrier Decoy Force (Admiral Ozawa, with four carriers, two

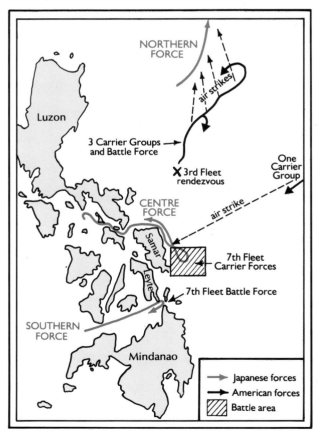

LEYTE GULF *The decisive phase on 25 October saw the destruction of Nishimura's command and Ozawa's carriers.*

battleships, four cruisers and eight destroyers). Kurita, debouching unopposed on 25 October from the San Bernadino Strait, was therefore able to take US Escort Carrier Group (Rear-Admiral Clifton Sprague with six carriers and seven destroyers) by surprise. Sprague's planes were armed for land operations only, while his destroyers had only 5-inch guns as their armament. Facing him were Kurita's four remaining battleships and their attendant cruisers. Despite his inferiority, Sprague fought a masterly running action, losing the carrier *Gambier Bay* and three destroyers. By 0930, the Japanese were coming under attack by planes from other carriers, and, learning of Force C's debâcle, Kurita finally withdrew once and for all.

The same day, Halsey's northward dash was rewarded at 0220, when Mitscher's TF 38 located Ozawa's force. At 0845 Mitscher launched the first of four strikes that were to continue until 1740. By nightfall, the four Japanese carriers were sunk, together with five other ships.

Leyte Gulf destroyed the Japanese imperial navy as an effective fighting force. They lost four carriers, three battleships, ten cruisers, 11 destroyers and a submarine outright, while almost all their surviving ships were damaged. Some 500 planes and 10,500 men were lost. American losses were three carriers, three destroyers, 200 planes and about 2,800 men.

MALTA
SECOND WORLD WAR, MEDITERRANEAN
1940–1943

Lying only 60 miles from Sicily, Malta was a vital base for British aircraft and ships in the Mediterranean theatre of war. Aptly dubbed the "unsinkable aircraft carrier", the island enabled the British to dominate the sea lanes of the central Mediterranean; in particular, it threatened the Axis supply routes from Italy and Greece to their forces fighting in North Africa.

Malta's importance was not lost on the Axis powers. Immediately on declaring war Mussolini ordered the Italian air force to launch bombing raids on the islands on 11 June 1940 – the first of thousands. By December 1941 the *Luftwaffe* had joined in the attack, since British aircraft were taking a heavy toll of the Afrika Korps' supplies (in October, 63 per cent of Rommel's supply ships had been sunk).

The German blitz
Their shipping losses provoked the Germans into launching a blitz of Malta in an attempt to neutralize it, Axis aircraft from Sicily bombing the island day and night from December 1941 to April 1942. In the face of this onslaught, British losses mounted, and German

supplies in North Africa were built up. Seeking to secure his supply line once and for all, Rommel flew to Germany to persuade Hitler to capture Malta by direct assault – a plan also supported by the Italian supreme command in Rome. Two airborne divisions were earmarked for this, but the plan was eventually cancelled against the wishes of Kesselring, the overall German commander in the Mediterranean. The air attacks, however, continued, reaching a peak in April 1942. British attempts to resupply Malta by convoy were immensely costly, but enough food got through to keep the population alive, and enough aircraft to keep the defence active. Some 350 Spitfires, were flown in from carriers, and, with these reinforcements, Malta was able to continue to take its toll of Axis aircraft and shipping.

The tide started to turn in the summer of 1942, when as Rommel drove towards Egypt – thus totally over-extending his communications – the Malta garrison again reduced his supplies to a trickle. His defeat, and the Allied landings in North Africa, took the pressure off the island, and, with the Allied invasion of Sicily in June 1943, the siege ended.

The failure to reduce Malta was the Axis powers' biggest single blunder in the Mediterranean theatre of war. The high cost the British paid for Malta – one carrier, several cruisers and destroyers, hundreds of aircraft, thousands of fighting men, and almost 1,500 civilian Maltese dead – probably saved the Allied position in the region.

MIDWAY
SECOND WORLD WAR, PACIFIC
4 June–6June 1942

A two-day naval battle in the central Pacific that culminated in a crushing American victory over the Japanese. It was the second, and greatest, carrier battle in history, and ranks as one of the decisive naval battles of all time. It checked the Japanese advance across the Pacific, destroyed their fleet carrier forces, and gave the strategic initiative in the Pacific to the Americans.

During the first week of May, 1942, the Japanese and American fleets had clashed in the Coral Sea. In this, the first carrier battle of the Pacific war, the Japanese lost more aircraft than the Americans, while, the Americans lost more ships than the Japanese. In particular, the US carrier *Lexington* was sunk, and the carrier *Yorktown* severely damaged. The Japanese commander-in-chief, Admiral Yamamoto, wrongly concluded that the *Yorktown* had also been destroyed and, on top of this, also mistakenly believed that the two remaining US carriers – *Hornet* and *Enterprise* – had remained in the Coral Sea area after the battle.

Yamamoto concluded therefore that a Japanese

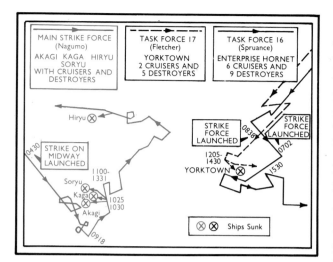

MIDWAY *The conflict between the two carrier forces ended with the loss of four Japanese carriers and Yorktown.*

advance across the mid-Pacific to capture the strategically important island Midway could not be opposed by an American carrier force, and accordingly, in June, he devised plans to attack and occupy Midway. The scheme was a complex one, involving all available Japanese ships – 165 in all – deployed in five groups with separate objectives as follows:
1. A northern force under Vice-Admiral Hosogaya, consisting of two light carriers, seven cruisers, and 12 destroyers, was to sail from the northern Japanese port of Ominata to mount diversionary raids on the Aleutian Islands.
2. The Midway occupation force under Vice-Admiral Kondon was to sail from the Marianas to occupy Midway. It consisted of the Second Fleet, plus occupation and support forces – in all one light carrier, two battleships, two seaplane carriers, seven cruisers, 25 destroyers, and 12 transports carrying 51,000 troops.
3. The main force, under Yamamoto himself, consisting of one light cruiser, seven battleships, four cruisers, and 12 destroyers, was to sail from Kure to cover the attack on Midway.
4. A screen of 18 submarines was to be deployed between Midway and Pearl Harbour to give warning of, and to intercept, any American force putting to sea.
5. The first carrier striking force, under Vice-Admiral Nagumo, consisting of the carriers *Kaga*, *Akagi*, *Soryu*, and *Hiryu*, carrying 250 aircraft, was to sail with Yamamoto from Kure and provide air cover for the attacking force.

These forces were so dispersed that only the third and fifth elements (the fleet carriers and Yamamoto's main force) could provide each other with mutual support. From the point of view of the Americans, who had accurate wireless intelligence of Japanese intentions (the Americans had been reading Japanese wireless traffic since before the war), there was one overwhelmingly important target – Nagumo's four fleet carriers.

Admiral Nimitz, Commander-in-Chief of the American Pacific Fleet, had the three fleet carriers, *Hornet*, *Enterprise*, and *Yorktown* at his disposal to meet this threat. *Hornet* and *Enterprise*, contrary to Yamamoto's appreciation, had returned to Pearl Harbour from the Coral Sea, and *Yorktown* had been refitted with remarkable speed. Between them, the three carriers could carry about 250 aircraft, while a further 109 were based on the airstrip on Midway.

The American ships put to sea in the last week of May, before the Japanese submarine screen was in position. Nimitz divided this force into two groups:
1. Task Force 17 under Rear-Admiral Fletcher – *Yorktown*, two cruisers and six destroyers.
2. Task Force 16 under Rear-Admiral Spruance – *Enterprise*, *Hornet*, six cruisers, and nine destroyers. Fletcher was given overall command.

Between 3 and 7 June, 1942, Hosogaya's northern force made its diversionary attacks on the Aleutians. Had Nimitz not known these to be a ruse, they might have had the intended effect of drawing off American forces to the area. As it was, though the Japanese captured two islands, he failed to take the bait. During 3 June, Yamamoto's main force and Nagumo's carrier striking force approached Midway.

The first phase: 0300 to 0700 hours 4 June 1942
Believing there to be no American ships in the area – least of all a carrier – Nagumo launched his first air strike at 0430 hours on 4 June. It was aimed at the land defences of Midway, and Nagumo had calculated that only one strike would be needed. For that reason the second wave of aircraft on Nagumo's carrier was armed to meet naval contingencies – that is, armed with torpedoes and armour-piercing bombs.

At the same time the first wave of American aircraft took off from Midway to attack Nagumo's carriers, and to intercept the Japanese bombers. The American aircraft were outclassed, the majority being shot down, but they pressed their attack so hard that the commander of the Japanese airstrike signalled to Nagumo that a second strike on Midway would be needed after all.

The second phase: 0700–1700 hours
Nagumo received this message at 0700, and accordingly started to rearm his reserve aircraft with incendiary and fragmentation bombs – more than an hour's work. At 0728, while this was in progress, Nagumo was handed a message from a spotter plane reporting the presence of ten American ships to the north-east at a range of 200 miles. If this force contained no carrier (and the message gave no clue as to its composition) it posed no immediate threat to the Japanese. This feeling was reinforced at 0758, when Nagumo received a second misleading message, identifying the American ships as five cruisers and five destroyers. At the same time his force came under attack by the American planes from Midway. The attack did no damage, but, confident that

he did not face a carrier threat, Nagumo sent up every fighter plane he had available to intercept the Midway bombers.

At 0820 hours, however, Nagumo at last received accurate intelligence – "enemy force accompanied by what appears to be a carrier." This news came at the worst possible moment for the Japanese commander. The rearming of his reserve aircraft for land targets was almost complete. His Zero fighters needed refuelling after beating off the American bomber attack, and at 0830 his first wave of bombers returning from Midway was due to be recovered. His dilemma was insoluble. He decided to recover his Midway aircraft before launching an attack on the American ships, and at 0918 hours he altered course by 90 degrees to the east to meet the new threat. This was not long in materializing. At 0752 hours the first American carrier strike had been launched from *Enterprise* and *Hornet* (*Yorktown*, some miles to the north-east, did not launch her main strike until 0900 hours). Both strikes consisted of a combination of Dauntless dive bombers, Devastator torpedo bombers, and Wildcat fighters.

Nagumo's change of course made the American dive bombers overshoot, and so fail to locate the Japanese. At 0930, however, the torpedo bombers found Nagumo's force and attacked. Lacking fighter cover, they were exposed to the fire of the Japanese cruiser cordon and to interception by the protective umbrella of Zero fighters. Almost all the attacking aircraft were shot down without scoring a single hit.

Nagumo, witnessing the destruction of the attacking planes, believed that victory was within his grasp, and so continued to rearm his reserve strike. At 1025 this was nearly complete, the decks of all four Japanese carriers being crowded with aircraft – some refuelling, some rearming, and some ready for launch. At this moment, however, the American dive bombers finally located Nagumo's force, and attacked. Within five minutes *Kaga*, *Akagi*, and *Soryu* had been sunk. Only *Hiryu*, cruising separately, was undamaged, and so able to launch counter strikes against the US task forces. Between 1200 and 1430, planes from *Hiryu* hit the luckless *Yorktown*, which was abandoned at 1500 hours when Fletcher transferred his flag to a cruiser. But strikes from *Enterprise* continued to hit *Hiryu*, and by 1700 hours she was damaged beyond repair. She was scuttled on 5 June; *Yorktown* was sunk by a Japanese submarine the following day, while she was under tow.

The final stages
Yamamoto, appalled by the disaster that had befallen Nagumo's carriers, made resolute attempts to bring the Americans to battle with his still greatly superior surface fleet. Throughout 5 and 6 June, Spruance, to whom Fletcher had delegated command after *Yorktown* had been damaged, pursued the Japanese by day, and avoided possible traps by night. Finally, with fuel running low, he abandoned the pursuit, and turned back to Pearl Harbor.

American losses at Midway consisted of the *Yorktown*, her escort destroyer, 132 planes, and 307 men. The Japanese lost four fleet carriers, one heavy cruiser, 275 planes, and 3,500 men. In one day – in effect, in five minutes – the Japanese had lost their fleet carrier force, and with it the naval command of the Pacific Ocean. American tactics were faultless, but the deciding factor in their favour was the comprehensive and accurate intelligence they had received of Japanese intentions. Japanese intelligence, on the other hand, was faulty throughout the Midway operation – from Yamamoto's initial miscalculation of American strength and dispositions to Nagumo's failure to recognize the nature of the force confronting him.

MOSCOW
SECOND WORLD WAR, EASTERN FRONT
October 1941–December 1941

What Hitler had intended as the climax of Operation *Barbarossa* turned into his *Wehrmacht*'s first major defeat. Having out-run their supplies and being ill-prepared for the Russian winter, the German *Panzers* bogged down within sight of the gates of the Soviet capital; a powerful winter counter-offensive by the Russians then forced them into retreat.

The road to Moscow
Following their successful drive against the Ukranian city of Kiev, the Germans regrouped for the postponed attack on Moscow at the end of September 1941. The *Wehrmacht*'s key striking force – Army Group Centre (Field Marshal Fedor von Bock) – was reinforced, its armour being divided between three *Panzer* groups – the Second Panzer Army (Panzergruppe Guderian) in the south: the Fourth *Panzergruppe* (General Erich Hoeppner) in the centre; and the Third *Panzergruppe* (General Herman Hoth) in the north. Opposing them were the Russian West and Bryansk Fronts. The Germans enjoyed a 2:1 superiority on the ground, and a 3:1 superiority in the air.

On 30 September, Guderian attacked towards Bryansk, and on 2 October Hoeppner and Hoth drove towards Vyazma. By 7 October more than 650,000 Russians had been cut off and captured, and, three days later German units were within 50 miles of the Russian capital. However, the autumn rains and fuel shortages were already starting to slow down the advance.

Outside the capital
As soon as the ground froze enough to allow rapid movement, the Germans launched another assault. Army Group Centre was now commanded by Field-Marshal Gunther von Kluge, while the Russian armies were under the overall command of Marshal Semën

Timoshenko. Marshal Georgi Zhukov was in command of the Russian forces directly in front of Moscow, strongly reinforced with fresh Mongolian divisions brought from the Soviet armies in the east.

Russian resistance was now more determined and effective than any the Germans had previously encountered, yet, despite this, northern elements of Army Group Centre came within 25 miles of the city, with advance patrols entering the suburbs and getting within sight of the Kremlin. In the south, however, Guderian's attack was turned back 70 miles short of Moscow. As the temperature dropped to -40°F, the Germans, unequipped for winter warfare, began to suffer casualties from frostbite and exposure. On 5 December the Germans pulled back and went over to the defensive.

Driving back the Wehrmacht

Reinforced with 100 new divisions, three Russian Fronts now launched massive offensives against the over-extended German forces. A week's fighting brought them dramatic successes, and by the New Year, the city had been saved. Further, more ambitious, attacks in January 1942, ordered personally by Stalin, also enjoyed success, but used up Russian reserves and were blunted by German counterattacks. By April, the Soviet forces had come to a standstill, and the Germans had been pushed back on all fronts.

Operation *Barborossa* had been fatally aborted. There were two main reasons for this. First its launch had been delayed by a crucial month, due to German intervention in Yugoslavia, and second, Hitler had fatally weakened its thrust by changing objectives when he had victory in his grasp. Had Hitler not diverted forces from the central front to the Ukraine, and, instead, concentrated on capturing the Soviet capital earlier in the campaign, the fall of the city might well have led to a Soviet surrender, or to a fatal weakening of the power of the ruling Communist dictatorship.

OKINAWA
SECOND WORLD WAR, RYUKYU ISLANDS, JAPAN
1 April 1945–21 June 1945

The only invasion of the Japanese homeland by the Allies, the capture of Okinawa was a grim warning of what the invasion of the Japanese mainland might cost. The operation, codenamed *Iceberg*, was undertaken as a final preliminary to the invasion of Japan itself.

The build-up to the invasion of Okinawa started a month before the actual landings, when US and British carrier groups attacked Japanese air bases on Formosa and other islands. In turn, they became the targets of *kamikaze* (suicide aircraft) attacks, but of 196 such

OKINAWA *The battle lasted nearly three months. The main Japanese defences were in the south on the Shuri Line.*

missions launched, 169 were shot down before reaching a target. From 23 March Okinawa itself was intensively bombarded, and small adjacent islands were captured to serve as anchorages and bases.

Iceberg is launched

On 1 April 1945, Operation *Iceberg* was launched. The US 10th Army (General Simon Buckner) successfully landed two marine and two infantry divisions on the south-western coast of Okinawa. The invasion forces faced fanatical opposition from the island's garrison of 130,000 Japanese of the 32nd Army under Lieutenant-General Mitsuru Ushijima. The marines were luckier than their companions; turning north, they had cleared the greater part of the island by 20 April. In the south, however, the two infantry divisions ran up against the formidable Machinato defence system on 4 April; here the Japanese had constructed defensive positions in great depth in mountainous terrain.

To destroy the American beachhead, the Japanese mounted a simultaneous air and sea suicide attack. The superbattleship *Yamato*, fuelled only for a one-way trip, was to attack the American landing forces. At the same time a massive *kamikaze* air strike was to attack the same targets. On 7 April, nearly 700 Japanese planes fell upon the beachhead, 383 being destroyed at a cost of five US ships sunk. On the same day US carrier planes found the *Yamato* and sunk her.

The Shuri lines

On 24 April, Buckner's forces pierced the Machinato Line, but were again brought to a standstill by a further defensive zone, the Shuri Line. While Buckner redeployed his forces to cope with this, nine further *kamikaze* air attacks were launched against the US naval forces, while, between 2 and 4 May, Ushijima delivered a counterattack against Buckner's eastern (left) flank. This incautious action, which was repulsed with great loss, revealed the Japanese artillery dispositions to Buckner's staff. Between 11 and 31 May Buckner broke through the Shuri defences, and forced the Japanese to retire into the southermost tip of Okinawa. Here between 1 and 22 June, a massive enveloping operation, with supporting amphibious landings at the extreme south of the island, finally overcame last-ditch resistance. Both generals died – Buckner was killed by shellfire, while Ushijima committed *hari-kari* (ritual suicide).

The Okinawa campaign saw the destruction of the last remnants of Japanese air and sea power. Their ground losses were also colossal – 107,500 of their troops fell. For the first time, however, large numbers (7,400) of Japanese surrendered, rather than fighting to the last man. The 10th Army losses were 7,374 killed and 32,056 wounded. The US Navy lost 5,000 killed 4,600 wounded, 36 ships and 763 planes, while the Japanese lost over 4,000 aircraft.

PEARL HARBOR
SECOND WORLD WAR, HAWAIIAN ISLANDS
7 December 1941

A surprise carrier aircraft attack on the main base of the US Pacific Fleet by the Japanese Imperial Navy in the hope of eliminating US naval power in the Pacific.

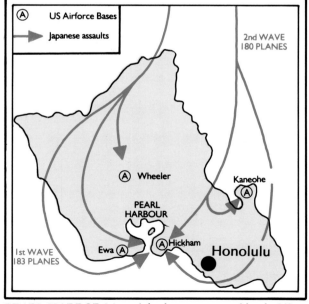

PEARL HARBOR *Most of the damage sustained by the US Pacific Fleet occurred in the first five minutes of the attack.*

In November 1941, the Japanese enjoyed a heavy preponderance of naval power in the Pacific – 11 battleships and battlecruisers (including the largest battleship ever built, the *Yamato*, with 18–in guns), 11 carriers, 18 heavy cruisers, 23 light cruisers, 129 destroyers, and 67 submarines. Against this, the Americans fielded 9 battleships, three carriers, 13 heavy cruisers, 11 light cruisers, 80 destroyers, and 56 submarines. The Japanese were well aware that they could not match the USA's potential industrial strength, and so pinned their hopes on launching a knock-out blow.

Having broken the Japanese naval wireless codes, US planners were aware of Japan's warlike intentions and of the location of most Japanese naval units. The Japanese, though unaware that their codes were being read by the Americans, were nonetheless conscious that the intensity of their radio traffic was being monitored.

The Japanese sail
The force detailed to attack Pearl Harbor, therefore, sailed in strict radio silence, while other units simulated its normal radio traffic. This force, the First Air Fleet under Vice Admiral Chuichi Nagumo, included six carriers, supported by battleships, heavy cruisers, and midget submarines. The submarines were to lie in wait in ambush off the exits from Pearl Harbor, while the carrier aircraft attacked the US Pacific Fleet at its anchorage. The fleet sailed on 26 November 1941; by 6 December, it was within striking distance of the US base.

On Sunday 7 December, the US forces at Pearl Harbor were on a peacetime footing. Aircraft were undispersed, no special reconnaissance flights were mounted, and the fleet lay lined up at anchor, totally unprepared for attack. Nagumo's first strike of 360 planes therefore was faced with a completely unprepared target. Three of the eight US battleships in the harbour were sunk immediately, one capsized and the remainder were seriously damaged. Of 231 US Army planes, 65 were destroyed outright and many others damaged, while, out of 250 Marine Corps planes, 196 were destroyed. Three light cruisers and three destroyers were also sunk. US dead numbered 3,226, and wounded 1,272. The Japanese withdrew at 0945, having lost 29 aircraft.

Nagumo's attacks on Pearl Harbor were well-planned and executed, but he failed in his main objective, since the three vital US carriers were not in harbour. He subsequently failed to launch a further strike, which might have located these ships, and certainly could have completely destroyed the US battleships and shore installations at Pearl Harbor itself. The reason why no third strike was launched was that Nagumo thought that its cost in aircraft would be prohibitive; however, the failure of either Japanese strike to attack the vast oil storage bunkers was another major error, since their destruction would have put the Pacific Fleet out of action for months.

PLOESTI AND PEENEMUNDE
SECOND WORLD WAR, RUMANIA AND GERMANY
August 1943

Two raids by US and British bombers – Ploesti by day and Peenemunde by night – that exemplified the difficulties and hazards of the strategic bombing campaign.

Ploesti by daylight

By 1943, Allied bombing techniques had greatly improved. Accurate target finding, using radar, had been perfected by both RAF Bomber Command, and the US 8th Air Force. The US B24 Liberator bomber, with a potential range of 2,850 miles, greatly increased the Allies striking ability, which meant that the oil fields around Ploesti in Rumania – these provided Hitler with the bulk of his oil – could now be bombed from Allied bases in North Africa.

On 1 August, 178 B24s of the US 8th and 9th Air Forces took off from bases in Libya, each plane carrying more than 4,000lbs of high explosive bombs. Under the command of Brigadier General Uzal G. Ent, the formation flew high over the mountains of the Balkans, and crossed the Danube. There it dropped to a level of 500 feet, in preparation for a low-level attack on the vast complex of oil refineries at Ploesti. However, here fate took a hand. Part of the force became separated from the main body and lost its way, alerting the German and Rumanian defences by flying over Bucharest. Proceeding to Ploesti, this group encountered intense anti-aircraft fire and was forced to seek out targets of convenience, bombing the heavy smoke rising from the burning refineries. The main force eventually found the target and nonetheless delivered its low-level attack, even though Ploesti was by this time shrouded in smoke.

The raid caused extensive fires, but prompt action by the defenders soon got the refineries back into production. US losses were 54 bombers and 532 men. The 1,000–mile penetration was the longest raid yet attempted.

Peenemunde by night

Aerial reconnaissance and other intelligence sources had revealed Peenemunde as the test site and experimental installation for the German V weapons – the VI "Flying Bomb" and the V2 rocket. Accordingly, on 17 August 1943, RAF Bomber Command mounted a 597–strong raid on the site. In bright moonlight, 40 of the attacking planes were shot down – even though the bulk of the German night fighters had been diverted to Berlin. The raid did not halt production of the V2 rocket, but considerably delayed it.

SEVASTOPOL
SECOND WORLD WAR, EASTERN FRONT
April 1944–May 1944

The isolation of the German 17th Army in the Crimea, followed by the successful recapture of this area of southern Russia by the Russians.

Retreat into the Crimea

The German 17th Army, on the extreme right of the German battle line in Russia, had led a chequered existence since the onset of the successful Russian counteroffensives in 1942. In 1943, it had found itself trapped south of the Don, but it withdrew successfully over the Kerch Straits into the Crimea during September and October. In December, however, it was cut off once again, when the Russian 4th Ukrainian Front (General F.I. Tolbukhin) drove Army Group A back over the River Dniepr.

On 8 April 1944, Tolbukhin attacked across the Perekop Isthmus. At first, the Germans managed to contain the attack, but, three days later, the Russian Independent Coastal Army crossed the Kerch Straits. The outflanked Germans were forced to fall back on Sevastopol itself.

Tolbukhin now faced an undefeated and intact German army behind strong fortifications. Using his superiority in artillery to batter the defences, he launched a two-day assault that cleared the city by 9 May. Most of the German army were evacuated by sea.

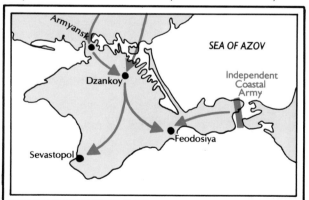

SEVASTOPOL *The Russian offensive south of the Pripet Marshes early in 1944 isolated an entire German army.*

SINGAPORE
SECOND WORLD WAR, MALAYA
February 1942

The most humiliating defeat of British history, culminating in the surrender of the largest British-led

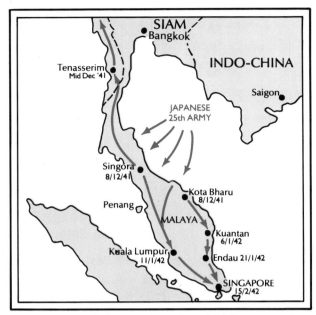

SINGAPORE *The Japanese drove through Malaya to attack Singapore from its virtually defenceless landward side.*

force ever to lay down its arms and the loss of the great naval base of Singapore, which had been intended to be the lynchpin of the British empire in the Far East.

The collapse of Malaya

The Second World War became a truly global conflict as far as the British were concerned on 8 December, when the Japanese 25th Army (General Tomoyuki Yamashita) landed in Malaya and Thailand. At the same time the Japanese 11th Air Fleet bombed Singapore, the first of many such air raids. The British were totally unprepared for the Japanese offensive, and defeat followed defeat, as Yamashita rapidly overran the Malayan Peninsula. Air superiority was non-existent from the start, while the sinking of the British battleship *Prince of Wales* and battlecruiser *Repulse* by Japanese bombers as they steamed in a desperate attempt to sink the Japanese invasion force meant that command of the sea vanished as well. By 31 January, the British commander in Malaya, General Arthur Percival, had evacuated the mainland and concentrated his forces on the island of Singapore.

The fall of Singapore

Literally millions of pounds had been lavished on Singapore, but the guns in its vaunted defences pointed towards the sea – not towards the land. After a protracted air bombardment, Yamashita's forces began to cross the Johore Strait on 8 February. Using armoured barges, and covered by intense machine gun fire, the Japanese drove deep into the defences of the Australian troops opposing them. By 11 February, Yamashita had occupied almost half the island up to a line from Jurong to Nee Soon, and Percival had drawn into a defensive perimeter around Singapore itself. Food

and ammunition were low, and Singapore was repeatedly devastated by air attack. On 14 February the last British ships managed to leave the port and on the following day Percival agreed to surrender unconditionally. Nearly 80,000 British, Australian and Indian troops laid down their arms. British casualties throughout the campaign had been 138,700, many of them prisoners. The Japanese had lost 9,824.

This comprehensive defeat of a numerically superior force was a great testimony to Yamashita's planning and tactical ability. With one shining exception (the Argyll and Sutherland Highlanders) no British units had been trained to fight in the jungle, and the command were woefully ignorant of the terrain over which they had to fight. In extenuation of Percival, it must be said that the Japanese enjoyed almost complete air superiority. Had the British had a substantial air presence in Malaya, Yamashita's force might never have got ashore. Nor was it Percival's fault that Singapore's formidable naval defences were in fixed emplacements, capable of firing only out to sea.

STALINGRAD
SECOND WORLD WAR, EASTERN FRONT
November 1942 to January 1943

The attempted German capture of the city of Stalingrad on the Volga in south Russia marked the turning point of the war on the Eastern Front. Determined Soviet resistance and eventual counter-attack led to the destruction of the crack German Sixth Army and the surrender of its remnants.

The drive to the Volga

Undeterred by the huge losses his armies had suffered in the east (approximately one million by the spring of 1942), Hitler planned a major summer offensive. Making good his losses with troops of doubtful quality from his eastern European allies and a reinforced Italian Expeditionary Corps, he launched a two-prong attack in the south in June 1942, with the twin aims of seizing the Caucasian oil fields, and capturing the city of Stalingrad, in spite of his generals' warnings that the German forces were not strong enough to take both objectives. Stalingrad, a city of 500,000 inhabitants, extending along 18 miles of the west bank of the Volga, was an important industrial target, producing a quarter of the USSR's vehicles. But the fact that it was named after Joseph Stalin, the Soviet dictator, though an irrational factor, was to have an incalculable bearing on the outcome of the battle.

German successes between June and August 1942 – highlights of these being the capture of *Sevastapol* and the fall of Rostov – encouraged Hitler to overrule his generals. The Fourth Panzer Army, originally switched

STALINGRAD *The Soviet counter-offensive, Operation Uranus, successfully trapped von Paulus' 6th Army in the city.*

from the Stalingrad front to support the Caucasus campaign, was redirected to support the German Sixth Army (General Friedrich von Paulus) in its drive on Stalingrad (1 August). Hitler's forces were now inadequate in every sector, being too far apart to support each other, or even to hold their ground. To compound his errors, Hitler ordered the Eleventh Army (von Manstein), his only reserve in the south, to the Leningrad front.

Nonetheless Sixth Army succeeded in reaching the Volga (23 August), north of Stalingrad. But the opportunity to take the city unopposed had passed, as time had been gained to organize its defence.

The German assault

The Caucasus offensive now ground to a halt, as Hitler concentrated all his resources on capturing Stalingrad, reinforcing the attackers with troops that should have been protecting their extended flanks. In very costly street fighting, the Sixth Army made slow progress against the Russian 62nd Army (Marshal Vasili Chuikov), but reached the Volga in the city centre by 12 October. Much of the fighting was at punishingly close quarters, since Chuikov had rightly appreciated that to close with an enemy superior in air power and artillery would rob him of much of his advantage.

Still determined to reduce Stalingrad Hitler ordered the unconquered area to be bombed and shelled into rubble. The result was to create a condition favourable to the defence. By 18 November, though the German Sixth Army had reached the river in the city's industrial zone in the north, substantial areas on the west bank still remained in 62 Army's hands.

The Russian counterattacks

By the onset of the Russian winter, therefore, Hitler had achieved neither of his 1942 objectives, and had placed his armies in untenable positions, separated by large gaps, with tenuous supply lines and feeble, extended flanks. The Russians now moved into the counter-offensive. Timed to coincide with the arrival of winter and the Allied landings in North Africa, the Russian South West Front (Vatutin), Don Front (Rokossovski) and Stalingrad Front (Yeremenko), launched massive, well-planned attacks to the north and south of Stalingrad on 19 and 20 November 1942. Within four days, the two attacks had met, isolating General Paulus's force of 270,000 men. At this point such a large force could probably have fought its way out of the encirclement, but Hitler unwisely believed the pledges of *Luffwaffe* supreme commander Herman Goering, who undertook to supply the beleaguered garrison by air — a promise the *Luffwaffe* never came close to fulfilling.

On 24 November, therefore Paulus was ordered to hold fast, taking up a "hedgehog" position, and await relief. A relieving force, under Field Marshal Erich von Manstein, launched a counter-offensive, which got within 30 miles of Stalingrad (19 December), where Manstein on his own authority ordered Paulus to break out. Paulus, however, refused to do this unless he had direct permission from Hitler, and Manstein was forced to withdraw to save his own command. As the main German armies withdrew to the west under constant and massive Russian pressure, Sixth Army was left to hold an ever-closing ring.

Short of ammunition, nearly starving, and without winter clothing, the position of Paulus's troops quickly became untenable. On 8 January he rejected an ultimatum from Rokossovski, and the Russians began an all-out assault on the remaining German positions. Paulus was ordered by Hitler to fight to the last man. By 25 January 1943 the last German airfield within the "hedgehog" at Gumrak had been overrun, and on 31 January the bulk of Sixth Army laid down its arms. The last German resistance ceased on 2 February.

The extent of the German collapse was colossal. Of the original 270,000 Germans in Stalingrad, about 34,000 had been evacuated by air. Over 100,000 had been killed. The remainder – including Paulus and 24 other generals – marched off to a captivity from which fewer than 6,000 were to return, while the war material lost to the Germans amounted to six months' production, including 500 transport aircraft shot down.

Psychologically, the defeat was an overwheming disaster, both for the generals who had seen their plans and armies frittered away by Hitler's unrealistic orders, and for the ordinary soldiers, who lost their belief in the invincibility of the armies in which they served. By a combination of vacillation and obstinacy Hitler had blunted his superiority in the east, at a time when, buoyed up by Allied aid, the Russians were gaining strength, confidence, and courage.

CHAPTER EIGHT
Modern Warfare

Since 1945, the nature of war has significantly changed. With the memory of total war – and of atomic attack in particular – fresh in mind, many people have come to feel that an unrestricted use of force to gain political advantage cannot be contemplated in any circumstances short of desperation; although the resultant trend towards war-prevention rather than war-fighting has affected only a proportion of the countries that make up the modern world, it has been enough to create a discernible downgrading of war as an instrument of policy. Fear of the consequences of war, reinforced by the growing effectiveness of nuclear weapons, has affected the policies of the two major superpowers (the USA and the USSR), this, in turn, has dictated the scope and impact of war in key areas of the globe.

This, however, does not mean that war has disappeared from the scene; indeed, this is far from the case. Since 1945, it is estimated that more than 150 wars have taken place, leading to more deaths than those in both world wars put together, and affecting the lives of millions of people. What has changed, however, is the fact that none of these conflicts can be described as a total war, affecting the world as a whole and threatening the future of mankind. Certain areas of the globe, such as Europe and North America, have been free from the scourge of war for over 40 years – a virtually unique situation – while, elsewhere, the political actions of the superpowers have ensured that local wars have not escalated into full-scale global conflicts.

Even when the superpowers themselves have become involved, as in Korea (1950–53) or Vietnam (1965–73), deliberate policies of restraint have helped to prevent a spread of violence on to the world stage. In short, since 1945 a "lid" seems to

THE NUCLEAR AGE *The ICBMs of the super-powers have imposed their own nuclear balance on modern war, with the development of theories of deterrence.*

have been placed firmly on top of state-engendered violence, keeping it contained so as to avoid the need to resort to nuclear weapons as a means of resolving political differences. There is no guarantee that this will last – as nuclear capability spreads, the existing restraints on the use of such weapons are being weakened – but, so far at least, the world has been spared the experience of nuclear war.

The concept of deterrence
The "lid" is kept in place by means of deterrence, created and sustained through fear of the consequences of a nuclear exchange, and the realization that five of the world's most powerful countries (the USA, USSR, Britain, France and China) have access to weapons of guaranteed

destructive capability, which can be delivered with accuracy to targets anywhere on the globe. It is this fact that preserves a precarious peace at the highest level. It is a peace that is constantly under threat, particularly from the development of new technology, or the more mundane problems of human miscalculation or error, but, so long as it survives, the rival superpower blocs are likely to consciously avoid an escalation to an unsurvivable all-out conflict. Indeed, in an historically familiar reaction to the impact of new weapons, an initial response to the dawning of the nuclear age was a widespread belief that war had disappeared entirely as a political option.

That this has not been the case is shown quite clearly by the number of wars that have taken place beneath the nuclear "lid", but this does not alter the fundamental way in which strategy has changed at the highest levels of world politics. What has happened is that nuclear-capable countries have searched for ways to use force beneath the nuclear threshold, and it is this fact more than any other that has affected warfare in the modern age. In the USA, for instance, the immediate post-war belief that possession of an atomic capability meant an end to conventional war was undermined by events in Korea. As soon as South Korea had been invaded by the Communist north in June 1950, the Americans faced a situation that demanded the use of military force in South Korea's support. Their response was to use that force within strict parameters: the war was restricted to the Korean peninsula, with no attempt to spread it elsewhere, even after Chinese intervention in October 1950; the size of the forces committed to the campaign was deliberately controlled; targets, particularly in terms of airpower, were carefully chosen to prevent the

escalate the level of violence, if the Pact continued in its aggression. Thus, for example, if Communist forces attacked using purely conventional weapons (a likely scenario, as the Pact would have no desire to commit nuclear suicide), NATO would defend its territory using similar weapons, while threatening a controlled nuclear response if the attack persisted. This would force the Communists to make what is termed a "cost-gain calculation" – that is to say, if they felt that what they were aiming for did not merit the losses they would inevitably suffer in a nuclear exchange, they would be deterred from continuing the war. If they persisted, and NATO was forced to use nuclear weapons at a battlefield level, the same pattern of defence and deterrence would be followed at the various stages of escalation, leading eventually, but not inevitably, to an all-out nuclear exchange. Even if this occurred, each side at least would have been given ample opportunity to assess its policies, and to consider the consequences of its actions at every stage.

Such an elaborate response to the threat of war may enhance the chances of survival; in recent years, however, it has led to fears within NATO that it is too passive a policy, since it might allow the Warsaw Pact to pursue limited aims in the full knowledge that the west will not respond effectively. If, for example, a conventional move was made and the Communists then agreed to halt rather than face a nuclear war, they would still have gained territorial or political advantages, particularly if, as many European members of NATO fear, the USA proved unwilling to make nuclear threats that might lead to a strategic exchange between the superpowers. As a result, a new emphasis is becoming apparent within NATO, based on the likely impact of ET (Emerging Technology) at a conventional level. The Ameri-

sort of civilian damage that might provoke a more global response from North Korea's Communist supporters; the weapons used were restricted, with no deployment of atomic bombs nor, indeed, of heavy bombers, against the enemy homeland. What emerged, in the USA at least, was a belief that if war could be limited through conscious and deliberate restraint, it would still be possible to fight beneath the nuclear level, avoiding escalation and keeping the "lid" in place.

Limited war

Theories of limited war were refined by American intellectuals such as Robert Osgood and Robert Mc-Namara in the late 1950s and early 1960s, citing the example of Korea as a pattern of response. Their views were boosted by a growing general realization in the USA that, with the development of intercontinental weapons by the USSR, any recourse to nuclear war would be suicidal. This was reflected in the evolution of such strategies as "Graduated Response" (1964) and, in the context of the North Atlantic Treaty Organization (NATO), "Flexible Response" (1967), in which a new emphasis on conventional (non-nuclear) forces emerged. Within NATO, this led to policies aimed specifically at establishing the ability of western states to meet and absorb an attack from the Soviet-controlled Warsaw Pact at whatever level it emerged, although this does not mean that deterrence was ignored or undermined. At every stage in the ensuing conflict, NATO would threaten to

cans, in particular, are convinced that new conventional weapons, if used carefully, could give NATO the ability to fight – and win – a non-nuclear war, plugging the gap at the lower levels of the military ladder and deterring the Communists from even contemplating a limited engagement.

Since August 1982, when the doctrine of Airland Battle was enshrined in Field Manual (FM) 100–5, American strategists have been arguing that technology, in fact, can be used as a "force multiplier" – in other words, that the enhanced accuracy and impact of new conventional weapons will compensate for any NATO shortages of men or equipment by destroying vast numbers of an attacking enemy force. Although this idea has not received full backing from the US Congress or the European states chiefly affected by it, the notion is a pointer to the future. If this is correct, the "lid" of nuclear deterrence would remain in place, but the nature of conflict beneath it would change, reintroducing a level of violence which has not been seen since 1945 in the superpower context.

Non-nuclear war

Further evidence of the increased level of conventional violence may be found in those wars that have taken place without direct superpower involvement. In the Middle East, for example, the long drawn out conflict between Israel and its Arab neighbours – a conflict that has led to full-scale conventional wars in 1948, 1956, 1967, 1973 and 1982 – has seen the level and sophistication of violence steadily increase and the true nature of non-nuclear war emerge. In October 1973, for instance, when Israel was taken by surprise by a concerted attack from both Egypt and Syria, the impact of technology on the modern battlefield became particularly apparent. Earlier Israeli advantages of airpower and armour – which, when used together in a *Blitzkrieg*-style assault, had led to a series of stunning Israeli victories in the Six-Day War of June 1967 – were now countered.

Wars of attrition

Not all armed forces have access to high technology, however, and in their cases the fighting may still degenerate into long drawn out attritional engagements, reminiscent of the trench deadlock of the First World War. Since September 1980, for example, Iran and Iraq have been locked in a seemingly endless conventional war, the full horrors of which are rarely appreciated. When the Iraqis opened the fighting, many commentators felt that they would quickly defeat Iranian forces weakened by the fall of the Shah and the religion-motivated purges of the Ayatollah Khomeini. Since then, however, Iran has not only survived but has even managed to regain the initiative, chiefly through a willingness to make enormous sacrifices. Iraq may still retain an edge in terms of the technology at its disposal (although that is being undermined by a shortage of money to purchase the necessary equipment from the outside world), but the sheer weight of Iranian numbers has meant that the gains of 1980–81 have now been lost and that Iranian troops are operating inside Iraqi territory, threatening Baghdad. In desperation, the Iraqis have come to depend on massive firepower (described as a "moving wall of fire") to prevent breakthroughs, and this inevitably increases the cost in both human and material terms. Although precise

KOREAN CONFLICT *Korea was the scene of the first open armed clash between Communist east and the west.*

figures are impossible to cite, most commentators agree that the Iran-Iraq War may have cost over a million men to date, with many more injured or held as prisoners of war. The absence of high technology may condemn the two countries to attritional rather than short, sharp engagements, but the psychological strains must be enormous.

From attrition to decision

This example seems to confirm that, regardless of the duration of modern wars, conventional battle is becoming increasingly violent, producing death, destruction and human suffering on a scale virtually equal to that of a small-scale nuclear strike. Indeed, wars outside the Middle East – in Indochina/Vietnam (1945–75), Nigeria (1967–70) and between India and Pakistan (1965 and 1971) – would seem to reinforce this view, particularly when civilian casualties are taken into account. But, at the same time, it is clearly possible to fight a decisive campaign that does not automatically result in high casualties, or degenerate into costly attrition. The Israelis showed this in 1967 with their swift campaigns to defeat the Arabs while the British achieved a similar result against the Argentinians in 1982.

VIETNAM WAR *In the long-drawn-out Vietnam War, a technologically backward people took on the might of the USA and won through to victory. Despite its military superiority (far left), the USA failed to win the "hearts and minds" of the people it was supporting, as the guerrilla threat showed (left).*

Guerrilla conflict

Thus, although the advent of nuclear weapons may have prevented total war on a global scale, limited conventional wars are both possible and – contrary to the evidence of Korea, Vietnam or the Gulf – winnable, always provided that the forces involved are well trained and the aims of the campaign precisely laid down. There is more to it than that, though, for in the Falklands the British were fortunate in the fact that they had a straightforward military task to fulfil against an enemy using predictable tactics. In both Vietnam and, since 1979, in Afghanistan, both of the superpowers involved experienced something far more complex – a "mix" of conventional and guerrilla actions – making the evolution and implementation of an effective response extremely difficult. Although guerrilla warfare as such is as old as the hills – indeed, it could be described as the lowest common denominator of war, open to anyone who is prepared to use organized force – its adoption as part of the process of revolution and its association since 1945 with politically motivated "liberation struggles" represents one of the most important changes to the spectrum of war in modern times. To a certain extent,

this is a natural result of the nuclear "lid", which has forced countries or dissident groups to avoid all-out war as a means of achieving their aims, but it is actually far more significant that the types of struggle experienced in vast areas of the world (particularly those in which colonial empires were opposed) have lent themselves to such low levels of violence simply because nothing more sophisticated is possible for the people concerned.

The military response

Terrorist threats inevitably affect the nature of modern war, forcing conventional armies to respond to situations outside their normal experience. Since 1945, as guerrilla and terrorist attacks have grown in scale, few armies have proved capable of responding to them effectively, showing a marked preference for conventional military campaigns, which have little relevance to the essentially political nature of the aggressors. Thus, in Indochina between 1945 and 1954, the French used firepower and mobile forces to conduct a campaign designed to trap and destroy the *Viet Minh* guerrillas in open battle, doing little to deal with political subversion, or the covert nature of guerrilla attack. The lack of tangible victories that resulted led French political leaders seriously to question the costs of the war, so that, when conventional battle was experienced at *Dien Bien Phu*, the already weakened French army was unable to achieve victory.

A very similar pattern of events affected the Americans in Vietnam after 1965, for, although they fared well in main-force battles against the North Vietnamese Army (NVA), chiefly in the valleys close to the demilitarized zone on the northern borders of South Vietnam, they did less well in the villages of the interior, where *Viet Cong* guerrillas protected bases of political subversion. In the end, as American domestic opinion turned against a continuance of what seemed to be an unwinnable war, US forces had to be withdrawn, leaving the NVA to achieve conventional victory in 1975. The fact that in the "Village War" the Americans used tactics and technology more suited to the "Main Force War", conducting large scale "search and destroy" missions under the umbrella of massive firepower, merely reinforced their lack of appreciation of the essentially political nature of counter-insurgency (COIN).

Other regular armies have been able to evolve more effective COIN techniques, but complete success against politically inspired guerrillas has proved extremely elusive.

ACTION MAN *Technology and the modern infantryman are equal partners in the warfare of today, as this picture from the Falklands War shows.*

Guerrillas and terrorists

THE FACE OF TERROR *Members of the PLO (Palestine·Liberation Organization) pose in Lebanon during the civil war.*

Guerrilla warfare is nothing new. Throughout recorded history, small groups of fighters have used ambushes and hit-and-run attacks to wear down and demoralize superior enemy forces. Over a long campaign in difficult, hostile terrain, such techniques could be effective, but in purely military terms, they could never achieve total victory.

Mao and guerrilla warfare
This began to change in the 1930s, when the Chinese Communist leader Mao Tse-tung exploited the advantages of guerrilla warfare as an integral part of revolution. Mao's aim throughout was to gain political power, overthrowing the Nationalist government of Chiang Kai-shek and replacing it with a Communist one. He based his "theory" of revolution on three key factors – time, space and will – arguing that if he sacrificed space (territory) to gain time, he could use that time to affect the will of the predominantly peasant people of China, persuading them to support the Communist cause. As a first move, Mao set up "safe bases" in remote rural areas, using education and social care as weapons to gain peasant support free from the interference of government forces, which, quite understandably, would know little (and care even less) about events taking place far from the center of power in the state. Eventually, these safe bases would house a Communist-run infrastructure of local government, with the people looking to Mao, or his fellow leaders, for such things as education, medicine and justice.

But there was clearly a limit to government unawareness and, as soon as the existence of a rival hierarchy became apparent, moves would be made to destroy the bases. Mao therefore had to provide them with protection, and it was here that he turned naturally to guerrilla techniques. Although the peasants lacked military skill, organization and weapons, they enjoyed two priceless advantages – knowledge of local terrain (which, in remote locations, was likely to be inhospitable to incoming government forces) and support from the local people. Using these advantages, government troops could be drawn into hostile areas, where they would be susceptible to ambush and forced to spread out thinly to defend lengthy lines of communications and supply. Even if they tried to pursue the guerrillas, the latter would merely melt into the surrounding countryside, taking up their normal everyday lives, indistinguishable from the broad mass of the people.

Meanwhile, new safe bases would be established in regions left unguarded by government actions, and, as these bases produced their own guerrillas, an "ink-blot" effect would ensue, with each new group acting like ink on blotting paper – appearing and then spreading inexorably. After a time, government forces would be spread so thinly that they would be unable to cope with the problem, leaving vast areas to be occupied by the revolutionaries and facing steady demoralization under the relentless pressure of hit-and-run attacks. In the end, the guerrilla forces would be stronger than those of the government and, backed by the peasants, would sweep the enemy aside, exposing the center of power in the state and allowing the Communists to take over. The revolution would then be complete.

A blueprint for revolution
There is no doubt that this pattern worked in China between 1927 and 1949 – indeed, it is tempting to regard Mao's theory of revolution as little more than a retrospective description of events between those years – and, inevitably, it became something of a blueprint for similar revolutions elsewhere. But it could never be slavishly followed; even in the Vietnam conflict (1945–75), where Ho Chi Minh's revolution clearly owed much to Mao's example, intimidation, rather than persuasion, of the peasants became the norm. Elsewhere, fundamental changes had to be made to

GUERRILLA TACTICS *Classical guerrilla tactics, based on the teachings of Mao Tse tung, have been adopted to meet changing circumstances over the years since they were first employed by Mao in China. One of the key factors has been the ever-increasing backing given to guerrilla groups by major powers; the PLO infantryman (left) is armed with the latest in Soviet weaponry, supplied initially to a Soviet client state in the Arab bloc. It is an open question, too, whether the Viet Cong would have achieved success in South Vietnam without the support provided by regular troops from the north and Soviet and Chinese arms; here (below), a NVA platoon leader demonstrates how to use an "S" hook to hold open a path through a barbed wire entanglement.*

allow for differences in geography, terrain, peasant opinion and government response. In Malaya (1948–60), for example, the Communists could only operate among a small proportion of the population, leaving the majority of Malays both willing and able to help the British to evolve successful methods of counter-insurgency, based on a mixture of political and military responses. In Cuba (1956–59), Fidel Castro lacked the space in which to set up "safe bases"; he achieved victory over Fulgencio Batista by organizing mobile columns of guerrillas to act as a focus for the wide-ranging discontent within Cuban society.

This latter point was taken one stage further by Ernesto "Che" Guevara, who believed that all a revolutionary leader needed to do was to appear in a repressed society for all the malcontents to flock to him as a *foco* (focal point), creating a momentum for change that would be literally unstoppable. However, as events were to prove, this failed in Bolivia in 1967, by which time rural-based revolution was rapidly becoming obsolete. As the peasants in many countries moved to the cities, so the center of gravity in revolutionary

terms shifted to the slums they inevitably occupied. Attempts by the revolutionaries to match this with a shift to urban guerrilla warfare effectively altered Mao's original theory out of all recognition.

But the threat to established governments remained, based increasingly upon intimidation through the tactics of terror. Designed to make people afraid to oppose the revolutionaries, techniques such as assassination, kidnap, bombing and hijack can have a significant impact, particularly in a liberal democratic society where the response to the threat may involve suspending or undermining the basic freedoms of movement, speech and association upon which the society is structured; however, terrorism on its own has yet to win a campaign. Since the late 1960s, some groups, particularly the Palestine Liberation Organisation (PLO), have taken their campaigns on to the international stage; the west in particular has had to respond to a spate of such attacks. They can be countered, chiefly through policies of multilateral co-operation and selective counter-strikes, but the threat remains. It is an integral part of modern warfare.

Air mobility

One of the most important tactical developments in warfare since 1945 has been the introduction and refinement of the helicopter. Early examples, such as the German Focke Achgelis Fa-223 and American Sikorsky R-4B Hoverfly, saw limited service in the closing stages of the Second World War, and their potential was quickly recognized. Unlike fixed-wing aircraft, helicopters did not require elaborate landing strips, making do with cleared areas of ground close to front-line units, which meant that they could deliver supplies or personnel with unprecedented speed and precision. At the same time, they could be used as observation platforms and close liaison links, providing ground commanders with a unique overview of military operations.

These early designs suffered from certain limitations, however, arising chiefly from their poor power-to-weight ratio. Engines were simply not powerful enough to lift much more than the weight of the helicopter itself. This limited load-carrying, while speed and ceiling both remained low, leaving the machine vulnerable to ground fire. Thus, when the Americans deployed helicopters like the Bell OH-13 and Sikorsky H-19 in Korea (1950–53), they used them for little more than casualty evacuation, or the rescue of downed pilots.

It was not until the mid-1950s, when the French Sud-Aviation and Turbomeca companies introduced turboshaft propulsion, that a breakthrough occurred. Performance figures improved dramatically, allowing battlefield roles to be perfected, and stability in flight opened up the possibility of mounting machine guns or grenade launchers on board the helicopters, transforming them from utility to assault machines.

The helicopter revolution

This new potential was soon exploited. On 6 November 1956, Britain's 45 Commando, Royal Marines, became the first unit to be helilifted into battle, arriving in Port Said aboard Westland Whirlwinds as part of the Anglo-French invasion of Egypt. At much the same time, both the British and the French were using helicopters in counter-insurgency (COIN) operations in various parts of the world. In Malaya (1948–60), Whirlwinds and Dragonflies were used to transport parties of British troops over areas of difficult jungle terrain, landing them deep in insurgent territory to take on guerrillas on their own ground; in Algeria (194–62), the French used similar techniques, particularly during the wide-ranging sweeps through the Ouarsenis mountains in 1959. The process was taken one stage further in Borneo (1963–66), where helicopters played a key role in the confrontation between Britain and Indonesia: here, special forces patrols were inserted covertly to set up

CASUALTY CLEARANCE *Casualties being evacuated from Dien Bien Phu. This was one of the helicopter's first roles in war.*

observation "hides" astride likely infiltration routes close to the border, alerting more powerful heliborne units whenever a threat materialised. Meanwhile, transport helicopters such as the twin-rotor Westland Belvedere, capable of carrying more than 5000kg of stores (half of them underslung), kept isolated border outposts supplied and reinforced. It was an effective "package" of response, which soon became a regular feature of COIN and conventional techniques: in both Northern Ireland (post-1969) and the Falklands (1982), helicopters have played key roles, providing flexibility and mobility which would have been impossible by other means.

The helicopter in Vietnam

This is only one aspect of helicopter operations, for the Americans took the development process still further, evolving what became known as "airmobility". This they used effectively in Vietnam (1965–73). The concept had its origins in studies carried out by Lieutenant-General Hamilton Howze in the early 1960s, when he considered the problems associated with the movement of troops across a confused and "broken" battlefield in Europe. Helicopters clearly had a part to play, but, if unprotected, they would quickly fall victim to enemy fire; if, however, they were provided with a strong support team of armed helicopters and fixed-wing aircraft, capable of destroying ground forces preparatory to an assault landing, they could be given at least a degree of protection. Despite initial opposition, Howze persuaded

"AIRMOBILITY" IN ACTION *Helicopters play a vital part in today's military operations. Here, US supply helicopters return to their base to refuel (left) during the Vietnam War, AH-1 Huey Cobra gunships are seen on patrol (above) and a Soviet Hind E attack helicopter shows off its paces (top). It was in Vietnam that the US developed the concept of "airmobility" to take full advantage of helicopter potential.*

the Pentagon to authorize trials, and a special unit – the 11th Air Assault Division (Test) – was raised. It was out of this that the Americans formed the 1st Cavalry Division (Airmobile) for commitment to Vietnam in 1965.

Airmobile tactics gradually evolved out of the experience of combat, based upon "teams" of specialized helicopter platoons, color-coded for ease of reference. The "white" team, equipped with OH-6 Cayuse light observation helicopters, was responsible for locating enemy forces and marking out a suitable landing zone (LZ), while the "red" team, flying gunships such as the AH-lG Huey Cobra (after 1967), "prepped" the area with suppressive fire and called in the "blue" team. Equipped with UH-lD Iroquois helicopters, the latter provided lift capacity, delivering soldiers to take and consolidate the LZ. A fire-base could then be set up, with CH-47 Chinook heavy-lift helicopters delivering 105mm artillery pieces; thereafter, all supply, reinforcement and casualty evacuation missions would be carried out by "chopper". If the enemy reacted, gunships and fixed-wing aircraft would be available to provide close fire support. Such a combination of mobility and firepower worked remarkably well and became an accepted part of American tactical doctrine;

today, the role is carried out by the 101st Airmobile Division, committed to play a central part in the Rapid Deployment Joint Task Force.

Since Vietnam, helicopter fire power has been further improved, particularly in terms of anti-tank weapons. The ability of helicopters to act as platforms for precision-guided missiles was recognized in the 1960s, but it is only recently – in the Falklands and in Lebanon (1982) – that they have been deployed with any success. Machines such as the HOT-armed Westland/Aerospatiale Gazelle, or the Hellfire-armed AH-64 Apache now have the ability to hover behind hills or woods, popping up to loose off their missiles at incoming enemy armor.

As "fire-and-forget" munitions become available, enabling the helicopter pilot to appear in the open for less time than it will take for the enemy to react, the chances of success are high. However, as both superpowers are currently working to produce interceptor helicopters, designed to seek out and destroy enemy machines in aerial combat, the advantage may be short-lived.

The Nuclear Revolution

At 0815 on 6 August 1945, the Japanese city of Hiroshima was devastated by a single, earth-shattering explosion. In less than a second, more than 78,000 people were killed by a combination of heat and blast, while the survivors received invisible doses of radiation which, in many cases, were to eat away at their bodies for years. As a mushroom-cloud of dust and debris rose above the ruins, the American B-29 Superfortress "Enola Gay" turned to begin the long journey back to its base at Tinian in the Mariana Islands, having carried out the first atomic attack in history. A new and terrifying era of warfare had begun.

The Hiroshima bomb, nicknamed "Little Boy", was the culmination of experiments carried out by Allied scientists on the Manhattan Project. It was based upon the theory, put forward by the German chemist Otto Hahn in 1938, that, if the atoms of a heavy element such as uranium were bombarded with neutrons, they would split to create a chain reaction and an enormous burst of energy, estimated to be the equivalent of 20,000 tons of TNT (trinitrotoluene). First tested at Alamogordo in the New Mexico desert on 16 July 1945, the "fission" process was triggered by one of two methods: over Hiroshima, two subcritical pieces of Uranium 235 were fired towards one another using conventional explosions, whereas over Nagasaki three days later an outer casing of TNT was "imploded" onto the fissile material, in this instance Plutonium 239. The results were the same.

Atomic weapons may not have been used in anger since August 1945, but their development has continued ever since. As early as 1949, the USSR test-exploded an atomic device; by 1954, both superpowers had gone one stage further, producing thermonuclear (or hydrogen) bombs, created by fusing together the hydrogen nuclei of deuterium and tritium under the enormous pressure of a fission explosion. This releases a tremendous burst of helium, and the resultant explosion of energy equals that of millions of tons of TNT (megatons). It is estimated that a one-megaton device alone would produce a searing flash of light, capable of blinding anyone looking toward it from a distance of 100 miles, followed by fierce heat and blast which would destroy brick buildings within a radius of 3¾ miles; in 1963, the Soviets tested an H-bomb with an estimated yield (explosive impact) of 58 megatons.

MAD and the nuclear balance

Possession of such weapons inevitably affects a country's attitude to war, shifting the emphasis away from the business of fighting towards the prevention of conflict. This is achieved through deterrence – a concept defined as "the ability to prevent aggression by

THE ULTIMATE DETERRENT *The awesome fireball that followed the explosion of a US hydrogen bomb at Bikini in 1956. The picture was taken 50 miles from the test site.*

persuading a potential enemy that the gains to be had by undertaking a particular course of action are outweighed by the losses he will suffer if he persists" (in other words, "you hit me, and I can – and will – hit you back harder"). This has become a central feature of the superpower relationship during the post-1945 period. At first, as the Americans had an effective monopoly of intercontinental delivery systems, this was a somewhat one-sided arrangement, but, since the achievement of a rough parity between the two sides in the mid-1960s, it has evolved into a situation known as Mutual Assured Destruction (MAD). Now, both superpowers have the ability to hit targets in the other's homeland.

MAD works so long as this balance exists. It is based on the calculation that if one side was to carry out a pre-emptive "first strike" against the nuclear forces of its rival, the latter would be able to absorb the attack and still have sufficient weapons with which to carry out a devastating retaliatory "second strike". In such circumstances, it would take a particularly irrational leader to initiate a nuclear war.

The balance, however, is under threat. Both sides depend for survival upon a "mix" of nuclear delivery systems – bombers, Intercontinental Ballistic Missiles (ICBMs) and Submarine Launched Ballistic Missiles (SLBMs) – which ensure that, if a first strike takes

ON LAND AND SEA *A Tomahawk gound-launched cruise missile launcher (left) deploys for action, while (above) the ICBM-carrying USS Michigan is seen under way. The two superpowers currently rely on a "mix" of delivery systems to ensure that they both possess an effective second-strike capability.*

Protection from attack

In much the same way, if either side could protect its homeland (and ICBMs) from a first strike, it would gain a major advantage. Mobile ICBMs, such as the Soviet SS-24 or the projected US Midgetman, would make it impossible for a first strike to destroy any part of the enemy's arsenal without extending the attack's scope considerably; however, it would be even more significant if one side developed a defensive system, designed to destroy incoming missiles before they reached their targets. On 23 March 1983, President Reagan announced the USA's intention of developing just such a system when he put forward his Strategic Defense Initiative (SDI, popularly known as "Star Wars"). "Star Wars" depends on a network of space-based satellites, which it is argued, could monitor a Soviet missile launch and trigger special "killer satellites", armed with lasers, charged-particle beams or hypervelocity "rail guns" to destroy the missiles or their warheads in flight. Reagan's aim is to make the idea of a nuclear attack unthinkable – if the USA was secure and its arsenal untouched, it would retain an enor mous second-strike capability – but the plan is opposed. The technology is as yet unproven and, as many Europeans fear, a stalemate at strategic level would enhance the temptation to fight at theater or battlefield levels, using smaller but equally devastating nuclear forces on European soil. The nuclear debate is thus likely to go on for some time.

place, it will not leave the recipient totally disarmed. If, for example, the Soviets were to initiate the war, they would logically aim to knock out the USA's land-based ICBMs, which they could "see" and so target accurately. This would be a devastating blow, but the USA's bombers (in the air from the moment of alert, and so impossible to target) and nuclear-armed sub-marines (equally invulnerable in the deep-ocean areas of the world) would survive to carry out the retaliatory strike. If, however, the submarines could be tracked, they, too, could be taken out in the first strike, leaving the USA with insufficient strength to retaliate effectively. As both sides are actively engaged in ASW (anti-submarine warfare) research, which aims specifically to track such weapons platforms, the whole basis of MAD could thus be undermined.

ALGIERS
ALGERIAN WAR
January 1957 – October 1957

A counter-terrorist action by French parachute units in Algiers, characterized by ruthless operations in the Muslim areas, particularly the Casbah. The terrorists were successfully rooted out, but the political costs, both in France and Algeria, were high, forcing many to question the value of continuing the war.

By mid-1956 the Algerian nationalists – members of the *Front de Libération Nationale* (FLN) – had begun to shift the emphasis of their war against the French away from the rural areas, where the French army was enjoying some success, into Algeria's cities. The FLN's aim was to relieve the pressure on their rural operations by forcing the French to redeploy their forces, but the urban campaigns soon built up a momentum of their own, particularly in Algiers. In June 1956, European settlers (known as *colons* or, more graphically, *pieds noirs*) were gunned down in the streets, leading to a reaction against the Muslim population that quickly threatened to get out of hand. Bomb attacks on *pied noir* cafés were followed by reprisal attacks on Muslim

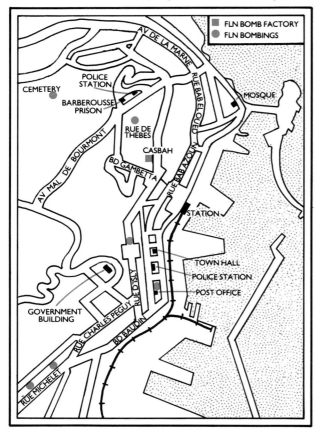

ALGIERS *The chief French aim was to penetrate and control the Casbah and locate the main FLN bomb factory.*

areas and, as law and order broke down, the civilian administration turned to the army for help. On 7 January 1957, Robert Lacoste, Governor-General of Algeria, authorized General Jacques Massu to impose control over the city of Algiers, using the four battalions of his 10th Parachute Division.

Massu takes over
Massu was ordered to root out the FLN, and was given a free hand as to the measures to adopt to do so. Dividing the city into four areas, he assigned a battalion to each of them, and began a policy of ruthless control. Constant foot patrols and checkpoints curtailed the movement of FLN bombing teams, while Colonel Marcel Bigeard's 3rd Colonial Parachute Regiment moved into the Casbah – a rabbit-warren of narrow streets in the centre of the city, used by the terrorists as a base. An attempted general strike on 28/29 January was forcibly broken and, as house-to-house searches intensified, the FLN's leadership was forced to go into hiding.

Though the level of violence dropped dramatically, Massu recognized that the lull was likely to be only temporary. What his troops needed was reliable information to enable them to arrest the FLN leaders and break up the organization's infrastructure. Using police files as their starting point, Bigeard and his officers – many of whom were veterans of the war in Indochina (1945–54) and fully aware of the various "phases" of modern revolution – gradually built up an accurate picture, rounding up thousands of Muslim suspects and subjecting them to often brutal interrogation. The results were impressive; by March, as the city fell quiet, the paratroops were withdrawn.

A new twist of terror
This was a premature move, for the hard-core FLN leadership, under Saadi Yacef, was still at large, supported by bombing teams that were prepared to resume the offensive. Co-ordinated by Ali Amara (known as "Ali la Pointe"), they struck on 3 June, when bombs were planted in lamp standards throughout the *pied noir* areas; six days later, in a new twist of terror, a popular nightspot (the Casino) was rocked by a devastating explosion, which left nine young *colons* dead and 85 seriously injured.

Massu was immediately recalled – this time under orders to stop at nothing to end the attacks. He concentrated on the Casbah, allowing Bigeard and his men virtual *carte blanche*. Muslims loyal to the French were infiltrated into the area, day and night patrols were mounted, and house-to-house searches and interrogations of suspects were revived. On 26 August, two of Yacef's bombing-team leaders, "Mourad" and "Kamel", were killed by a patrol; a month later, Yacef himself was captured. By then, a very detailed intelligence picture had emerged, enabling the French to concentrate on specific personalities. In early October, "Ali la Pointe" was cornered in his hideout;

when he blew himself up rather than face interrogation, the battle effectively came to an end.

In purely military terms, this was a major triumph, but politically it spelt disaster for the French. As it became clear that many interrogations had involved the use of torture, support for army actions declined signficantly, both in France itself and among the Muslim Algerians. By 1958, when General de Gaulle returned to power (partly as a result of army pressure), he was quick to realize that political compromise was the only solution. Four years later, amid great bitterness and recrimination, Algeria gained its independence.

CEDAR FALLS/JUNCTION CITY

VIETNAM WAR
January 1967 – May 1967

American and South Vietnamese multi-divisional search-and-destroy sweeps to the north of Saigon, in the so-called "Iron Triangle" and War Zone C. Designed to put an end to *Viet Cong* control of village areas, the operations involved the use of a mixture of heavy firepower and airmobility; however, despite some initial success, they failed to prevent the insurgents returning to the region.

As the size of US forces in South Vietnam increased in 1966, the Americans concentrated much of their

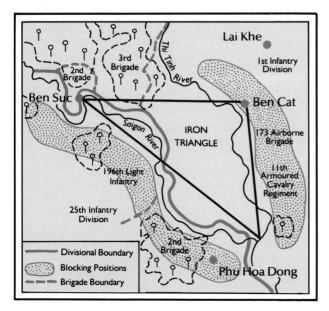

CEDAR FALLS *The intention was to block Viet Cong movement out of the Iron Triangle and destroy their bases inside it.*

attention on War Zone C, situated to the north of Saigon. An area of jungle, paddies and cultivated forest, it had long been a center of *Viet Cong* (VC) activity, into which the Army of the Republic of (South) Vietnam (ARVN) dared not move for fear of ambush. Close to "safe bases" in Cambodia yet extending to just north of Saigon, the zone posed a threat that the Americans could not ignore.

Into action in the "Iron Triangle"
Initially, the aim was to mount large-scale "search-and-destroy" missions in the north of the zone, close to the Cambodian border, but it soon became clear that the main threat came from further south, in the "Iron Triangle" close to Saigon. On 8 January 1967, therefore, a multi-divisional operation, codenamed *Cedar Falls*, began in the "Iron Triangle", designed to clear the area of VC, remove its civilian population and create a "free-fire zone," which could be attacked at will. The triangle itself followed the lines of the Saigon and Tri Tinh rivers, with a third "side" running between the villages of Ben Cat and Ben Suc. Although covering only a limited area of ground, more than 15,000 US and ARVN troops, with massive artillery and air support, were deployed, the plan being to secure the sides of the triangle before moving in to conduct detailed search-and-destroy operations. Any VC in the area would be forced to fight or, if they tried to escape, destroyed by the blocking units.

The line of the Saigon river was secured by elements of the 25th Infantry Division, deployed in strength from the Ho Bo Woods in the north to the village of Phu Hoa Dong in the south. At the same time, the 1st Infantry Division took the line from Ben Cat to Ben Suc, leaving the villages themselves to be captured by the 11th Armored Cavalry Regiment and a heliborne battalion of the 26th Infantry Regiment respectively. The 11th Cavalry then moved through the Triangle, cutting it in two and preparing the way for search-and-destroy operations. These continued until 26 January, by which time an estimated 750 VC had been killed and 280 captured, along with large amounts of equipment and enemy documents. The villages were destroyed, the population forcibly removed to more secure areas and the forests liberally sprayed with chemical defoliants.

Within days, however, reports of a VC return were being received, reinforcing the need for similar clearing operations further north, deep inside War Zone C. A similar pattern of blocking moves therefore began in early February, when US and ARVN units seized the villages of Lo Go and Xom Giua in the west (Operation *Gadsden*) and created firebases in the east (Operation *Tuscon*). The scene was set for *Junction City*.

Launching Junction City
This operation, involving over 25,000 troops, was divided into three phases. Phase One (22 February–17 March) concentrated on the north-west area of the

zone, when a paradrop by the 173rd Airborne Brigade seized a base around Kotum. The 2nd Brigade, 25th Infantry Division, and the 11th Cavalry then moved north, along Route 4 to link up, effectively splitting the zone and allowing clearing operations to begin towards the forces already established in the west. This was followed up in Phase Two (18 March–15 April) with operations further east, around Minh Thanh, while Phase Three (16 April–14 May) cleared the southern area. In all cases, whenever clashes with VC units occurred, the Americans were able to inflict enormous casualties, but the zone was never entirely secured. Although a total of 2,700 VC dead were claimed and significant captures of arms, equipment and documents reported, the Allies could not afford to garrison the region in strength. As US troops were withdrawn in late May, the VC returned. It was a pattern which was to be repeated throughout the war.

CHINESE FARM
YOM KIPPUR WAR
15 October – 18 October 1973

Israeli counter-attack on the Sinai Front during the Yom Kippur War, in which armored and infantry units fought to breach the Egyptian defences and cross the Suez Canal. The success of the operation, achieved after heavy fighting, ensured that Israel ended the war with a significant military advantage over its Arab adversaries.

The defeat of the Syrian attack on the *Golan Heights*, apparent by 10 October 1973, allowed the Israelis to concentrate on the Sinai front, where Egyptian forces, having crossed the Suez Canal four days earlier, had dug in behind a defensive shield of anti-tank and anti-aircraft missiles. An Israeli counter-attack on 8/9 October had met with disaster as tanks, unprotected by mechanized infantry and denied close air support, fell victim to AT-3 Sagger ATGWs (anti-tank guided weapons), but the Israeli commanders in Sinai – in particular, Major-General Ariel Sharon – were still pressing for action. Victory on the Golan, coupled with the introduction of "all-arms" combat teams and the development of revised air tactics, prepared the way for a more effective countermove, although it was not until 14 October, after Egyptian armor had been heavily defeated in central Sinai, that the Israelis felt confident of success.

Outflanking the Egyptians
The counter-attack aimed to exploit the interface between the Egyptian Second and Third Armies on the east bank of the Canal around Deversoir, to the north of the Great Bitter Lake. In general terms, the plan was for Sharon, closely supported by paratroops (fighting as

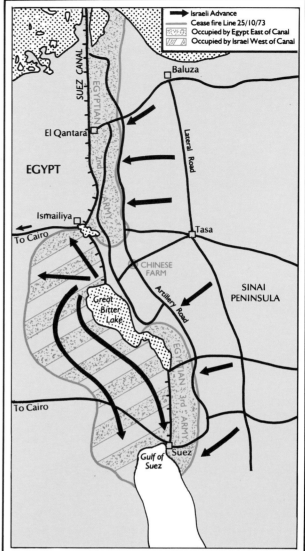

CHINESE FARM *Israeli success opened the way for the crossing of the canal and encirclement of the Egyptian Army.*

infantry) and with Major-General Avraham Adan's armoured division in reserve, to drive west towards a prepared crossing-point on the canal. Using pontoons, rafts and a prefabricated "roller" bridge, part of Sharon's force was to establish a bridgehead on the canal's western bank, opening the way for Adan's division to move across, advancing north and south to threaten Cairo and the Egyptian Third Army around Port Suez. A supplementary aim would be to destroy static SAM (surface-to-air missile) sites, creating gaps in the Egyptian anti-aircraft "umbrella" that would allow the Israeli Air Force to fly close-support missions. Eventually, as the Egyptians were outflanked and their rear areas threatened, they would be forced to sue for peace on Israeli terms. At 1600 on 15 October, one of Sharon's brigades, with paratroop in support, accordingly attacked southwestwards towards Lakekon (on the Great Bitter Lake) and reached the Lexicon road. Turning north, the Israelis neared the bridging site, and then fanned out, aiming to push Egyptian forces out of mortar and Sagger range. At the same time, one of Adan's brigades moved in from the east to divert Egyptian attention and open up the Akavish-Tirtur Road, along which the bridging equipment would have to pass.

All went well until 2120, when Sharon's men suddenly found themselves in the middle of a huge Egyptian concentration, with tanks and Saggers well dug-in around Chinese Farm. The subsequent fighting took place in the dark among a myriad of broad irrigation ditches; it quickly degenerated into an attritional slogging match, although part of the Israeli attacking force managed to cross the canal to establish a small, highly vulnerable bridgehead on the west bank. By 0630 on 16 November, the first tanks had been ferried across, probing deep into Egyptian territory, but with the east bank still insecure and no bridge yet in place, Israeli prospects looked uncertain at best.

The same day, Adan committed part of his force (which should have been kept back for exploitation) to the bitter fighting around Chinese Farm, but it was not until early the following morning that the Israelis gained the upper hand. As paratroops advanced to clear the area to the north, Egyptian units began to pull back, but the breakthrough was still not complete, as later Adan had to deal with a potentially dangerous Egyptian counter-attack from the south.

It was not until 0515 on 18 November that Adan was able to ferry forces across the canal. Once on the other side, his armor advanced south towards Port Suez, threatening the rear of the Egyptian Third Army and opening up the air corridor, as the Israelis had planned. By 24 October, with Third Army encircled, Cairo under threat and the superpowers expressing concern about possible escalation, a ceasefire was imposed. The Israelis had achieved a remarkable victory.

DIEN BIEN PHU
FIRST INDOCHINA WAR
November 1953 – May 1954

The final battle of the First Indochina War (1946–54), marking French defeat at the hands of *Viet Minh* regular and guerrilla forces. Some 16,000 French troops were besieged for 55 days in a fortified "air-land base" at Dien Bien Phu by up to 60,000 *Viet Minh*, who used artillery and infantry to win a crushing victory.

At 10.35 on 20 November 1953, the skies above Dien Bien Phu, a small village close to the Laotian border in the French colony of Tonkin, were filled with the

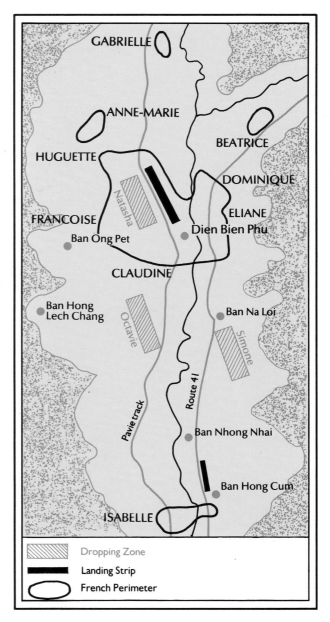

DIEN BIEN PHU *On paper, the French position looked strong, but they ignored the menace of the surrounding hills.*

silken canopies of an airborne assault force. French paratroopers of Airborne Battle Groups I and II consolidated their drop-zones, dealt with local opposition and set up a rudimentary base; by the end of the day, Operation *Castor* was complete.

Dien Bien Phu had been chosen for attack because of its position astride a main communication route into northern Laos. In the previous April, Vo Nguyen Giap, commander of the Communist *Viet Minh*, had pushed units into Laos, forcing the French to deploy part of their strategic reserve from the Red River Delta (around Hanoi) on to the Plain of Jars. There, they had set up "hedgehog" positions to stem the *Viet Minh* advance. Operation *Castor* was intended to force Giap to pull back into Tonkin by threatening his supply lines.

Unfortunately, there were different views about the long-term purpose of the operation within the French High Command. The commander of the northern region, Major-General René Cogny, regarded Dien Bien Phu as no more than a "mooring point" – a base from which local T'ai tribesmen, loyal to the French, could attack *Viet Minh* positions; the French commander-in-chief in Indochina, Lieutenant-General Henri Navarre, saw it as a magnet that would irresistibly attract the *Viet Minh*, tempting Giap to fight a set-piece battle he could never hope to win.

A trap for the Viet Minh
Cogny's plan was undermined in December, when T'ai groups failed to break through from their threatened capital, Lai Chau, in Operation *Pollux*. From then on, Navarre's strategy prevailed. Dien Bien Phu, a heart-shaped valley, surrounded by thickly wooded hills, – was quickly fortified. The main defensive position, established around an airstrip – had no land supply route – essential, as the valley close to the village of Dien Bien Phu, consisted of a number of fortified posts, reputedly named after the mistresses of the garrison commander, Colonel Christian de Castries. In the center, close to a command bunker, were strongpoints "Huguette", "Claudine", "Elaine" and "Dominique", with more isolated posts to the northwest ("Anne-Marie"), northeast ("Beatrice") and north ("Gabrielle"). A short distance south, was strongpoint "Isabelle", protecting an auxiliary airstrip.

No attempt was made to fortify the surrounding hills, partly because of supply problems but mainly because the French underestimated the abilities of their enemy. Although they realised that five *Viet Minh* divisions were converging on the valley, they regarded this as amply justifying Navarre's plan. They refused to believe that Giap could concentrate sufficient strength (especially in artillery) to overwhelm their "air-land base" and its crack garrison.

The battle begins
Giap's plan was to isolate and destroy the outlying strongpoints, preparatory to an all-out assault on the main French positions. He began to put this into effect on 11 March, with probing attacks against "Gabrielle", followed two days later by a full-scale assault on all three isolated posts in the north. After bitter fighting, "Beatrice" fell, leaving the French with no choice but to abandon "Gabrielle", which was now effectively outflanked. This enabled Giap to concentrate against "Anne-Marie". When this fell on 17/18 March, the vital airstrip, now under mortar and small-arms fire, had to be closed. Thereafter, all resupply and reinforcement had to be carried out by paradrop and, as *Viet Minh* anti-aircraft guns opened up, even this became precarious. "Forlorn hope" paratroops battalions were still arriving at Dien Bien Phu as late as 2 May, but, as supplies fell into enemy hands and

casualty evacuation ceased, conditions inside the besieged base rapidly deteriorated.

But Giap did not have it all his own way. On 30 March, a major *Viet Minh* assault on "Dominique" failed to break through, and when this pattern was repeated against "Huguette" (1 April), "Elaine" and "Isabelle" (3 April), he was forced to pause to recuperate. By then, the French had pulled back to a new defensive zone just under a mile in diameter, and Giap decided that, instead of conducting "human wave" assaults, he would lay siege in traditional fashion. Between 5 April and 1 May, therefore, *Viet Minh* engineers constructed elaborate trenches, gradually digging towards the French lines under a covering barrage of 105mm artillery fire. On 1 May, *Viet Minh* infantry rose from these trenches to carry out their final assault. The monsoon, which delivers a staggering downpour of rain on Dien Bien Phu each year, had begun in late April and the defenders, waterlogged, weakened and (in many cases) demoralized, fought a hopeless battle. On 7 May, de Castries and 11,000 of his men surrendered, followed 24 hours later by the garrison at "Isabelle".

French casualties during the 55-day siege totalled 7,184, and when those taken prisoner were added, this represented a crushing defeat, made all the worse by the fact that the cream of the French forces had been destroyed by a "peasant army". By comparison, Giap lost an estimated 23,000 dead and wounded, but was left in possession of the battleground against an enemy who had run out of strategic options. With their reserve destroyed, the French could only accept peace terms, negotiated at Geneva in July, which dismantled their Indochinese empire. Vietnam was split along the 17th parallel, with the Communists in the North and non-Communists in the South.

ENTEBBE
ISRAELI RAID IN UGANDA
3–4 July 1976

Israeli airborne mission to rescue hijack hostage victims at Entebbe in Uganda. Organized in considerable haste and mounted at extreme range, the operation was a major success, setting a pattern for subsequent rescue missions by western states facing the threat of international terrorism.

At precisely 1210 on Sunday, 27 June 1976, Air France Flight 139, *en route* from Tel Aviv to Paris with 12 crew and 256 passengers on board, was hijacked over the Mediterranean. The four terrorists – two from the West German Baader-Meinhof Gang and two from the Popular Front for the Liberation of Palestine (PLO) – ordered the pilot to divert to Benghazi in Libya, where the plane was refuelled. After more than six hours on the ground, it took off for Entebbe in Uganda – a deliberately long haul, designed to place the hostages beyond the range of any rescue attempt – where it landed at 0315 the following day. The hostages, more than 100 of whom were Israeli citizens, were herded into the old terminal building, where more Palestinian gunmen were waiting. On 29 June, Uganda Radio broadcast the demands: the hostages would be released in exchange for 53 convicted terrorists, held in gaols in Israel, West Germany, Kenya, France and Switzerland.

Imprisoned at Entebbe

From the start, it was the Israelis who faced the greatest pressure, and this was made worse when, on 30 June, the non-Jewish hostages were suddenly released. However, the government of Yitzhak Rabin had no intention of surrendering to the terrorists' demands. An outline rescue plan was presented to the Israeli cabinet on 1 July, even though the problems were immense. Despite Israeli knowledge of Entebbe airport (they had helped to rebuild it during less troubled times) and invaluable intelligence provided by the released hostages, Entebbe was at the very extreme of the range of the C-130 Hercules transports available to the Israeli Air Force. In addition, any rescue flight would have to cross potentially hostile territory, increasing the chances of the Ugandans getting advance warning, while there could be no guarantee that, even if the force arrived safely, they could rescue the hostages before the terrorists could take action.

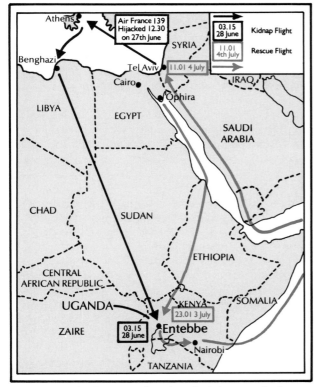

ENTEBBE *The daring Israeli raid marked the triumph of determination over distance and potential hostile activity.*

An audacious plan

Nevertheless, Major-General Dan Shomron, director of infantry and paratroops, remained confident that a carefully-timed assault would work and, in the absence of any viable alternative, Rabin agreed to let the operation go ahead. Shomron's plan was based upon surprise, using around 200 crack paratroops, divided into four groups each with a specific role to play. The C-130s would land in the dark, using a scheduled commercial airflight to Entebbe as cover. Group 1 would seize the runway, Group 2 would release the hostages from the old terminal building, Group 3 would seize the new terminal and Group 4 would secure the airport perimeter. Two Boeing 707s – one converted into a hospital plane and the other equipped as a communications centre – would accompany the force, but would not land.

The C-130s set off from Sharm el Sheikh, on the southern tip of Sinai, on the afternoon of 3 July, flying down the Red Sea before swinging south-west over Ethiopia to approach Entebbe. Worsening weather was a worry, but the skies cleared over the target, allowing the first transport to land at 2301 without alerting either the Ugandans or the crew of the unsuspecting commercial plane it followed. Group 1 of the paratroops disembarked and fanned out, allowing Group 2, under Lieutenant-Colonel Jonathan ("Yoni") Netanyahu, to drive towards the old terminal in a black Mercedes car similar to one used by the Ugandan dictator, Idi Amin.

The Ugandan sentries were not fooled, and Netanyahu was forced to abandon his disguise; however, his attack on the terminal was brilliantly successful. Shouting to the hostages to keep down, the paras identified and killed 13 terrorists before herding the hijack victims onto one of the waiting C-130s. As they did so, a sudden burst of gunfire killed Netanyahu, although this did not prevent the Hercules taking off at 2358 hours, bound for a refuelling stop in Nairobi. Meanwhile, the remaining paratroops destroyed a number of Ugandan MiG fighters on the ground to prevent pursuit.

THE GOLAN HEIGHTS
YOM KIPPUR WAR
6 October – 22 October 1973

Major encounter battle on the northern frontier of Israel during the Yom Kippur War (6–24 October 1973). Syrian mechanized infantry and armor attacked the Israeli defences in overwhelming numbers, only to be checked and eventually pushed back on to the Damascus plain. The battle involved some of the most concentrated conventional fighting of the modern age.

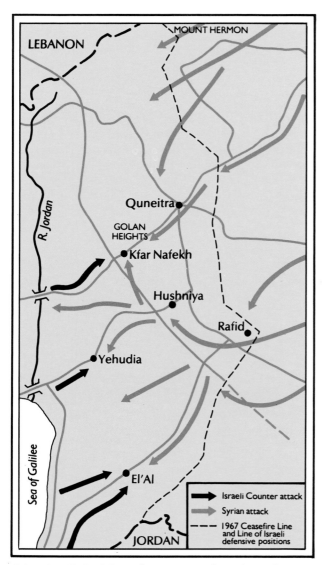

GOLAN HEIGHTS *Israeli counter-attacks to the south eventually blunted the Syrian thrusts into the Golan.*

At 1400 hours on Saturday, 6 October 1973, Israel was attacked simultaneously by Egyptian and Syrian forces. The Egyptian assault across the Suez Canal into Sinai was the more unexpected of the two thrusts, with its innovative use of high-pressure hoses to break through the banks of the canal preparatory to extremely rapid bridging operations, but Sinai could be used as a buffer to slow up the Egyptian advance, so giving time for the Israelis to call up their reserve formations. The same was not true on the Golan Heights, on Israel's northern border, where Syrian assaults posed immediate strategic problems. Occupied by Israeli forces during the Six-Day War (June 1967), the Golan was vital to the security of the Jewish state, affording views eastward onto the Damascus plain and denying the Syrians the opportunity to observe Israeli settlements in northern Galilee, but they did lack depth. If any enemy breakthrough occurred, Israel would be under threat.

The Golan defences

Since 1967, the Israelis had constructed a defence line against the Syrians, running from Mount Hermon in the north to the Jordanian border in the south. This was based on a series of 17 fortified posts, protected by an anti-tank ditch and elaborate minefields. Crossing-points on the ditch and gaps in the minefields acted as channels for any Syrian advance, creating "killing zones" in which Israeli artillery or airpower could be brought to bear. Finally, special ramps had been built at various points to enable defending tanks to go "hull down" and engage in long-range tank-to-tank gunnery duels.

All this was essential if Israel was to contain an attack for long enough to deploy her reserves, but, in October 1973, the line was inadequately held. The whole of Golan was defended by no more than 80 main battle tanks (MBTs), belonging to the 188th Barak Brigade, and, although Syrian preparations were sufficiently obvious for the Israelis to deploy the 7th Armoured Brigade on to the heights on 4 October, the new total of 170 MBTs was still pitifully low. By 6 October, the 7th Armoured was committed to the defence of the northern sector of the front, from Mount Hermon to a line running from the Benot Ya'akov Bridge on the Jordan river (the pre-1967 Israeli border), through Nafekh to Quneitra, while the Barak Brigade was further south, centered on Rafid. They faced more than 1,500 Syrian tanks, backed by 1,000 guns and three divisions of mechanized infantry.

The Syrian thrusts

The Syrian plan, based on Soviet tactical doctrine, was to use the infantry to probe forward, seeking out lines of least resistance for the armor to exploit; to begin with, it seemed to work. After a preliminary artillery bombardment lasting for 50 minutes, dense columns of Syrian armored personnel carriers (APCs), supported by their own organic armor, motored towards the Israeli defences, aiming to bridge the anti-tank ditch and open up gaps in the protective minefields. Syrian morale was high, and, although they suffered enormous casualties, particularly in those areas where the "killing zones" could be used, the momentum of an overwhelming advance began to build up. Israeli losses mounted, which meant they were too weak to prevent a Syrian advance down their right flank towards Quneitra.

Further south, the situation was even worse. The Barak Brigade was virtually destroyed, so opening the way for a major Syrian breakthrough. Here, the Syrian 1st Armoured Division outflanked the fortifications at Rafid and, in a two-pronged advance, moved north towards Nafekh and the Benot Ya'akov Bridge and south towards El Al. A link-up of Syrian forces at Nafekh, possible before the battle was 24 hours old, would have spelt disaster for the Israeli defenders. In the event, as the fighting continued through the night, introducing the concept (and nightmare) of the 24-

hour-a-day battle, it was only through a mixture of high professionalism and tactical skill that the Israelis could prevent a Syrian victory. The exhausted Israelis managed to hold a tenuous line just long enough for reserve divisions, under Major-Generals Dan Laner and Moshe Peled, to arrive late on 7 October. This, however, was not the turning point, for the Syrians were also able to feed in reinforcements, and they fuelled the fighting for the next two days and nights.

The Israeli recovery

By Tuesday 9 October, both sides were close to exhaustion. Indeed, in the northern sector, 7th Armored Brigade, reduced to a strength of only seven tanks, had begun to withdraw when, suddenly, they were joined by 13 Centurions, hastily gathered from rear-area workshops and led into battle by Lieutenant-Colonel Naty Yossi. These proved sufficient to halt the Syrians, who thought they were the first elements of a new Israeli brigade. This fortunate incident coincided with major Israeli countermoves further south, carried out by Laner and Peled, and the battle began to tilt away from the Arabs. In the south, as Israeli armor advanced on three axes, towards Nafekh, Yehudia and Ramat Magshimim, large parts of the Syrian 1st Armoured Division were caught in a trap around Hushniya and destroyed. By 10 October, the Syrians were in retreat, leaving 867 tanks on the field.

The Israelis followed up immediately, mounting a counter-attack along the Quneitra-Damascus road early on 11 October, supported on the left by elements of the refurbished 7th Armored Brigade. The fighting was hard as the Syrians fell back into familiar terrain, but, though the battle reached a new crisis when Iraqi and Jordanian armour intervened on the Arab side, at no time was an Israeli defeat on the cards. On 22 October, the Syrians accepted a United Nations ceasefire, having lost over 1,150 tanks and nearly 3,500 men. By comparison, the Israelis had lost 250 tanks (150 of which were recovered) and 772 soldiers.

GOOSE GREEN
FALKLANDS WAR
20 May – 29 May 1982

First major land engagement of the Falklands War (April–June 1982), in which a British paratroop battalion of about 450 men attacked and defeated an Argentinian garrison of over 1,200. At a cost of 17 dead and 35 wounded, the British established a moral ascendancy they were not to lose for the remainder of the war.

Late on 26 May 1982, the men of Britain's 2nd Battalion, The Parachute Regiment (2 Para) left their defensive positions in the Sussex mountains,

overlooking the beachhead at San Carlos on the west coast of East Falkland, and marched south towards the settlements of Darwin and Goose Green. Supported by a Royal Marines detachment equipped with Blowpipe SAMs (surface-to-air missiles), three 105mm light guns of 29 Commando Regiment, Royal Artillery, offshore naval gunfire provided by the frigate HMS *Arrow*, and a promise of Harrier airstrikes as required, the battalion's task was to engage and defeat an Argentinian garrison (estimated to comprise 500 men) on the narrow isthmus connecting the main part of East Falkland to its inhospitable southern region, known as Lafonia. This would shield the southern flank of a general British advance out of San Carlos toward the high ground around the capital, Port Stanley, and prevent Argentinian use of a small grass airstrip, ideal for Pucará ground-attack machines, at Goose Green.

The British attack

The attack was scheduled to begin early on 28 May, by which time 2 Para had occupied Camilla Creek House, north of the neck of the isthmus, and despatched C (Patrol) Company to secure projected start-lines between Camilla Creek in the west and Burntside House in the east. The battalion's commander,

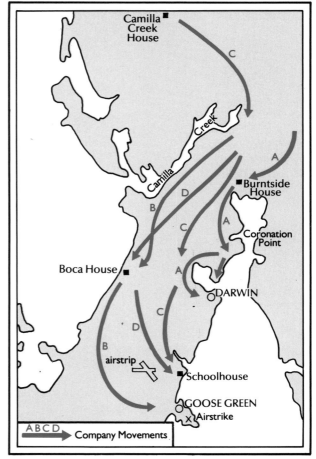

GOOSE GREEN *The British flank attack at Goose Green was an essential preliminary to the main drive on Port Stanley.*

Lieutenant-Colonel Herbert Jones ("Colonel H") had decided on a night attack, partly in an attempt to maintain secrecy but also to avoid Pucará strikes against his advancing troops.

The area into which the paratroops moved late on 27 May was low-lying scrubland, bisected by a single line of gorse. Muddy tracks radiated out from Darwin and Goose Green, but communications overall were virtually non-existent. In addition, the narrow isthmus had little natural cover, with only a thin spine of slightly higher ground running north-south down the center and a single prominent feature – Darwin Hill – to the west of Darwin settlement. Argentinian defenders were known to be established in positions on top of Darwin Hill and around the settlements, although clear information about numbers was not available. In fact, just after dusk on 27 May, the clatter of helicopters was clearly heard, bringing in Argentinian reinforcements from Port Stanley. It would not be an easy battle.

Jones' plan was for A Company to move down the east coast from Burntside House towards Darwin and Goose Green, with B Company advancing parallel to them along the west coast, towards Boca House, a ruined structure opposite Darwin, but shielded from it by the contours of the ground. Meanwhile, C Company, having secured the start-lines, was to march down the centre of the isthmus, shielding A Company and outflanking Darwin Hill, while D Company would be held back slightly, ready to reinforce as required. A series of precise objectives was laid down, the idea being that each would be seized before the next was approached. By dawn on 28 May, Jones hoped, sufficiently ground would have been secured to threaten Darwin and Goose Green.

The first stage

The assault enjoyed mixed success. A Company set out at 0630 hours on 28 May and, supported by the guns of 29 Commando Regiment and HMS *Arrow*, succeeded in taking Burntside House, whereupon B Company advanced towards Camilla Creek. Here the paratroops began to encounter resistance and were forced to clear dug-outs and trenches using well-tried infantry techniques. As automatic fire kept the defenders' heads down, special assault teams, armed with anti-tank rockets, grenades and phosphorus bombs, rushed forward to seize objectives. Some enemy positions were inevitably missed in the darkness, but D Company, following up behind, rooted out the remaining Argentinians, allowing B Company to push on toward Boca House. Unfortunately, the building proved to be well defended and, as *Arrow* had to pull back at dawn for fear of enemy air attack, the paratroops had to go to ground, unable to continue their advance. By then, A Company had also stalled, finding it impossible to move beyond the well dug-in Argentinian machine guns on Darwin Hill.

As dawn broke therefore, the situation did not look good. Both A and B Companies had effectively halted, while C and D Companies were experiencing great difficulty in finding ways to outflank the areas of fighting. In essence, the momentum of the attack had died away, leaving the British strung out on open ground, with little room for manoeuvre.

Death of "Colonel H"

It was at this point that Colonel Jones, accompanied by his TAC HQ, moved forward to join A Company on the lower slopes of Darwin Hill. At 1330 hours, in an exceptional display of personal bravery (for which he was to be awarded a posthumous Victoria Cross), Jones was killed leading an attack on a machine-gun position. His sacrifice galvanized his men into action. Running up the hill, they cleared the enemy trenches one by one with grenades, automatic weapons and anti-tank rockets. At much the same time, the Support Company (equipped with Milan anti-tank missiles) arrived to help B Company and, as D Company discovered a route around Boca House to the west, beneath a small cliff, the Argentinians in the west were also prised out of their positions. By 1515 hours, the vital breakthrough had been made.

Major Chris Keeble, who had assumed command on the death of Jones, immediately modified the plan of attack, ordering B Company to push south and then east to outflank Goose Green, while C and D Companies continued down the spine of the isthums towards an isolated schoolhouse to the north of the settlement. A Company remained to clear Darwin.

As dusk fell, the balance of the battle shifted firmly in favour of the British. Overnight, the British positions were consolidated and, early on 29 May, Keeble contacted the Argentinians in Goose Green to negotiate their surrender. When they finally agreed terms at 1450 hours, the paratroops were shocked to see a total of 1,200 enemy troops march out to lay down their arms. It was a remarkable victory.

HSUCHOW
CHINESE CIVIL WAR
6 November 1948 – 10 January 1949

The turning-point in the Chinese Civil War (1945–49), in which Chiang Kai-shek's Nationalists were defeated in a series of pitched battles around the city of Hsuchow by Communist forces loyal to Mao Tse-tung. In the aftermath, the Communists were able to consolidate their gains in central China, preparatory to launching their final campaigns south of the Yangtze river.

By late 1948, the long Chinese Civil War had reached crisis point. Chiang Kai-shek's Nationalist forces had lost control of the key northern region of Manchuria, and were pulling back to new positions south of the

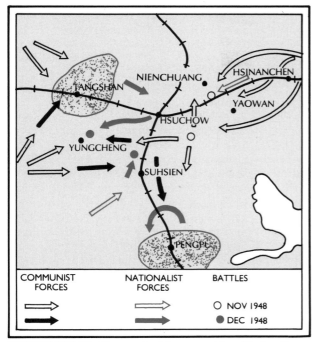

HSUCHOW *The Communist drive trapped four Nationalist army groups, which were forced to surrender.*

Great Wall of China. The next natural line of defence was the Huai river, but Chiang, intent upon retaining his hold on as much territory as possible, chose to make his stand further north, around the city of Hsuchow in the province of Anhwei. This was not a sound military decision. Although Hsuchow itself was defensible, the surrounding countryside was open and relatively featureless – ideal for the sort of wide encircling moves favored by the Communists.

On paper, the two forces appeared to be evenly matched. As the battle-lines were drawn, both sides committed about 500,000 men, organized into a number of armies or army groups, to the campaign. The Nationalist 2nd Army Group (12 divisions) was situated to the west of Hsuchow under Ch'iu Ch'ing-ch'uan, while Huang Po-t'ao's 7th Army Group (10 divisions) protected the Lunghai railway to the east. Troops of the Nationalist Armored Corps were stationed in the city itself, and within marching distance were units of the 6th, 8th, 12th, 13th and 16th Army Groups (a further 29 divisions). In addition, the Nationalists enjoyed air supremacy. Against them, the Communists fielded Liu Po-ch'eng's Central Plains Field Army (to the west) and Ch'en Yi's East China Field Army (to the east), comprising hardened fighters who enjoyed local peasant support and high morale. The scene was set for a major pitched battle that would help to decide the future of China.

Deciding China's fate

Fighting began on 6 November 1948, as Communist forces seized towns close to Hsuchow, driving a wedge deep into Chiang's 8th Army Group, which promptly

withdrew to the safety of the Huai river. Two days later, four Nationalist divisions surrendered *en masse* to the north of the city, enabling Ch'en Yi's East China Field Army to advance through the gap to sever communications between the 7th Army Group and its supporters in Hsuchow. Huang Po-t'ao, desperate to protect his forces, withdrew isolated garrisons from positions along the Lunghai railway to the east, so cutting himself off from the sea and allowing the Communists to move into the evacuated area. Simultaneously, Liu Po-ch'eng sent elements of his Central Plains Field Army south-east to take Suhsien on the Tsin-po railway, isolating Hsuchow from reinforcements in the south. By mid-November, the city was encircled and four Nationalist army groups (the 2nd, 7th, 13th and 16th) were effectively cut-off from outside support.

Chiang responded by ordering his 12th Army Group under Huang Wei to attack towards the city from the south-east at the same time as a breakout from Hsuchow took place, but personal rivalries among the Nationalist generals prevented co-ordination. The 7th Army Group was destroyed as it tried to escape, losing an estimated 87,000 men and, as the communists massed 250,000 soldiers between Hsuchow and Suhsien, the counter-attack by 12th Army Group quickly ground to a halt. The remainder of the Hsuchow garrison tried to break out between 28 November and 15 December, but were similarly destroyed in confused and bitter fighting to the south of the city.

The Nationalist collapse

By then, Huang Wei had been forced to surrender, along with the bulk of 12th Army Group. As the Communists launched a final offensive into Hsuchow on 6 January 1949, the Nationalists collapsed; four days later, the campaign was over. More than 550,000 Nationalist troops were lost, weakening Chiang's attempts to create a new defensive line on the Yangtze river. The loss of Hsuchow and its environs also opened the way to Communist seizure of Tientsin and Peking, left them in possession of the central China plain and gave them a military advantage they were not to lose in the final engagements of the war.

IMJIN

KOREAN WAR
22 April – 25 April 1957

An epic stand by a British infantry brigade to protect crossings over the Imjin river in Korea, delaying the Chinese Communist advance toward Seoul, the South Korean capital, and enabling United Nations forces to create a new defensive line further south. One of the British battalions (1st Glosters) was wiped out, having fought for three days against overwhelming odds.

Chinese intervention in the Korean War on the side of the North Koreans in late 1950 produced a series of offensives and counter-offensives that were still taking place the following April. United Nations (UN) forces, having pulled back to the south of the 38th parallel, had mounted counter-attacks in January, which had sent the Communists reeling north to the Imjin river, but a renewed Chinese assault was quickly planned. In its path, guarding the Imjin, stood the British 29th Brigade, comprising battalions of the Gloucestershire Regiment (Glosters), Royal Northumberland Fusiliers (RNF) and Royal Ulster Rifles (RUR), with a Belgian battalion under temporary command. The Belgians held positions to the north of the river, while the Glosters and RNF occupied the high ground to the south and west, with the RUR placed centrally in reserve. The defence of the river was crucial; if the Chinese crossed the Imjin, and especially if they secured the valley between the positions held by the forward British battalions, the road to Seoul would lie open.

First indications of the Chinese advance came at 0945 on 22 April, when an RNF patrol made contact with enemy units just north of the river. Battle patrols were sent out to gauge the size of the Chinese force, but were obliged to pull back, as it became clear that this was a major attack, involving the entire 63rd Army. Elements of the RUR were despatched to reinforce RNF companies on Hill 257, only to be hastily recalled as a greater threat emerged in front of the Glosters on the left. In fact, Chinese units had already infiltrated the British line, probing along the right flank to take Hill 398, behind the RNF, and between the RNF and Glosters.

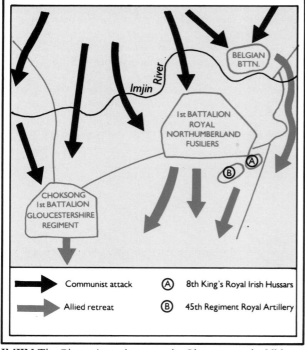

IMJIN *The Glosters' stand against the Chinese won the UN forces the vital time they needed to regroup.*

"The glorious Glosters"

As dusk fell, the Glosters were already facing encirclement, although they gave no indication of withdrawing. A Company, slightly isolated on the left, fought a tough battle throughout the night, only pulling back to the main battalion position around Hill 235 (soon to be renamed Gloster Hill) – held by C Company and Battalion HQ – when dawn revealed the enormous strength of Chinese opposition. Only one officer and 53 men of A Company succeeded in breaking out, joining survivors of D Company, which had also spent the night opposing large Chinese forces, in this case to the north of Gloster Hill. B Company took the opportunity to extricate itself from isolated positions to the east, fighting through to take Hill 314, slightly further south. By midday, the surviving members of the battalion were occupying a much tighter perimeter, ready for the inevitable onslaught. To make matters worse, Chinese forces suddenly appeared behind the British positions, severing the only remaining land route to the south.

The fighting was particularly hard during the night of 23/24 April, when two Chinese divisions threw themselves against the Glosters' positions. B Company could not remain on Hill 314 indefinitely and, just before dawn, it was ordered to pull back to Gloster Hill, where the British prepared to make a final stand. Elsewhere, the Belgians and RNF had been forced to withdraw.

Throughout 24 April, the Glosters, low on ammunition and reduced to 50 per cent battalion strength, were completely isolated, with no hope of relief. At dawn the following day, after a night of fierce hand-to-hand combat, their commanding officer, Colonel James Carne (who was to receive a Victoria Cross for his part in the battle) ordered the remnants of his units to break out independently. Only 39 men managed to reach safety; the Glosters had ceased to exist.

Their sacrifice was not in vain. The delays they imposed enabled UN forces to create a new defensive line on the Han river, protecting Seoul. Though the Communists pushed forward, their offensive failed to gather the necessary momentum to achieve a quick victory; instead, they were forced to fight set-piece battles around every defensive feature. The war was about to degenerate into an attritional slogging match.

INCHON
KOREAN WAR
15 September 1950

Strategically audacious amphibious landing in the early stages of the Korean War (1950–53), in which US Marines launched an attack on the port of Inchon, close to Seoul, the occupied capital of South Korea.

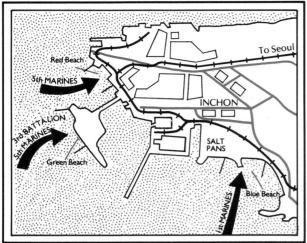

INCHON *MacArthur's spectacular amphibious left hook led to the recapture of Seoul and Communist retreat from Pusan.*

Their success severed the North Korean lines of communication and supply, forcing the Communists to withdraw into their own country, north of the 38th parallel.

By September 1950, United Nations (UN) forces in Korea were in trouble. North Korean's invasion of the south (25 June 1950) had caught the defenders unprepared, forcing them back to Pusan, in the south-eastern corner of the peninsula, and a Communist victory seemed assured. American units, hastily despatched from garrison duties in Japan, had managed to throw a defensive ring around Pusan and various UN member nations had agreed to send military assistance. However, unless additional pressure could be brought to bear on the North Korean, forcing them to withdraw, the chances of non-Communist survival were slim.

Desperate times call for desperate remedies, and the UN commander, General Douglas MacArthur, was equal to the task. As early as 29 June, he had realized that the North Koreans were in danger of outstripping their lines of supply, most of which flowed through the city of Seoul, close to the pre-war frontier on the 38th parallel. To the west of Seoul lay the port of Inchon and, in a remarkable display of strategic perception, MacArthur planned an amphibious landing – a "left-hook" designed to outflank the North Koreans at Pusan and sever their supply chain – as a matter of priority. By 4 July he had driven his staff to prepare a plan for an operation (codenamed *Bluehearts*) in which the 1st US Cavalry Division from Japan would seize Inchon, preparatory to a swift advance on Seoul.

Planning the landing

Bluehearts was originally scheduled for 22 July, when the tides at Inchon would be most favorable, but it proved impossible to prepare such a complex operation in the short time available. The plan accordingly was cancelled on 10 July, although the idea remained, to be revived in August under the new codename of *Chromite*. By then, the Americans had begun to recover from the initial shock of the North Korean attack, and although a general shortage of troops, caused by successive cutbacks since the end of the Second World War, was still being experienced, reservists had been called up and the 1st Marine Division – the natural formation for an amphibious landing – made ready. Detailed planning, carried out by the Joint Strategic Plans and Operations Group (JSPOG) of MacArthur's Far Eastern Command HQ in Tokyo, began on 12 August.

The problems were immense. As one of the JSPOG staff officers pointed out: "We drew up a list of every conceivable natural and geographic handicap and Inchon had 'em all". The harbor itself was approached by a long narrow seaway called Flying Fish Channel, which twisted and turned in such a way that large ships could not sail close to the shore, and the rise and fall of the tide meant that any landing at high tide would leave assault vessels stranded on mudflats as the waters receded. Any supporting warships (essential if off-shore artillery support was to cover the landing) would have to remain a considerable distance from the landing area, while their need to drop anchor against the current would leave them vulnerable to enemy fire from shore-based artillery – particularly from that known to have been captured by the Communists on the small island of Wolmi-do in the center of the harbor.

Even if these problems could be resolved, Inchon was by no means a natural choice for amphibious attack, since it lacked beaches – at least in the conventional sense. Instead of gently sloping areas of firm sand, the port was surrounded by rocky sea walls, designed to halt the encroaching mud, so any assault would have to begin with the nightmare task of scaling enemy defences, presumably under fire. If Wolmi-do was not seized first, this problem would be even worse, as batteries located on the island would enfilade beaches closer to the port. Finally, preliminary reconnaissance was difficult, as it was feared that paying too much attention to Inchon would alert the North Koreans to the likelihood of attack. In the event, South Korean agents were infiltrated into the area and, on 1 September, a US naval lieutenant conducted a one-man reconnaissance mission, gathering information about tides, enemy dispositions and defences, although this was widely felt to be insufficient for such an important operation.

From doubt to success

Such a comprehensive list of potential shortcomings inevitably led to doubts about the viability of *Chromite*; without MacArthur's strength of personality – manifested most clearly at a major planning conference at Tokyo on 23 August, attended by representatives of the Joint Chiefs of Staff – it is unlikely that it would have gone ahead. By early September, however, a detailed plan had been approved and the go-ahead given for 15 September, when the tides would be high.

In broad terms, Battalion Landing Team 3 of the 5th Marines (BLT 3/5) was to land on Green Beach on Wolmi-do early in the morning, seizing the island as a preliminary to further landings on the evening tide, directly into Inchon. The remainder of the 5th Marines were assigned Red Beach to the north, while the 1st Marines were to attack Blue Beach to the south. Having seized the port, both regiments, backed by the 7th US Infantry Division, were to move east and north, threatening the approach to Seoul.

The landing force left Japan on 5 September and, despite a tropical storm, made good progress; five days later, a sustained air and naval bombardment of Inchon began, designed to destroy North Korean defensive positions. At 0633 hours on 15 September, BLT 3/5 stormed ashore on Wolmi-do, clearing the island with unexpected ease. Although the marines were effectively cut off by the tide for most of the day, no North Korean counter-attack materialized and, at 1730 hours, the assaults went in on Red and Blue Beaches simultaneously. The sea walls were scaled and, by midnight, the landing's initial objectives had been secured – all for the loss of 20 Marines killed and 176 wounded or missing.

Communist defences hardened considerably as the Americans approached Seoul, and hard fighting ensued. By 27 September, however, the South Korean capital had been liberated and the North Koreans, in danger of being cut off, had begun to pull back from Pusan. Despite the odds, *Chromite* had been a brilliant success.

INDONESIAN–BRITISH CONFRONTATION
SARAWAK AND NORTH BORNEO
April 1963 – August 1966

An "undeclared war" between Britain and Indonesia over the political future of Sarawak and North Borneo. Indonesian guerrillas and regular forces mounted raids across the jungle border from Kalimantan, only to be met and turned back by British and Commonwealth troops in some of the least hospitable terrain in the world.

Between April 1963 and August 1966, British and Commonwealth troops fought what was almost a secret war against Indonesian infiltrators in Borneo. As the British colonies of Sarawak and North Borneo (Sabah) moved towards independence and federation with Malaya, scheduled for September 1963, the Indonesian leader, General Kusno Sosro Sukarno, made it clear that he was intent upon gaining control of the whole of Borneo. To achieve this, he used "volunteers", drawn

in large measure from the Indonesian Communist Party and backed by regular Indonesian troops, to mount raids across the length of the border from Kalimantan into British territory. As the "confrontation" developed, the Indonesian regulars assumed a more active role, even to the extent of carrying out raids into Malaya in 1965, but were contained by British and Commonwealth forces using a mixture of jungle skills and helicopter mobility. It was a strange, undeclared war.

Indonesian infiltration
The first signs of trouble occurred as early as December 1962, when the military wing of the Brunei People's Party tried to overthrow the ruling sultan. Brunei, a small, oil-rich state on the northern coast of Borneo, was a British protectorate and British troops were accordingly rushed from Singapore to support the regime. After their commitment, the situation was controlled, but Sukarno's support of the People's Party indicated that there was further trouble to come. This started in April 1963, when a small group of Sukarno's "volunteers" attacked a police post near the border village of Tebedu in Sarawak. Though little damage was done, Indonesian intentions were clear and the British, under the command of Major-General Walter Walker, were forced to take appropriate defensive measures.

In the dense jungle of the border regions, this was no easy task. The immensely long border posed obvious problems in its own right, for the British had only a limited number of troops available and so found it impossible to guard every potential infiltration route. Even if there had been more troops on the spot, the task was formidable. They faced hostile, largely unmapped terrain, ideal for the guerrilla-style ambush and hit-and-run tactics adopted by the enemy. In such

SARAWAK AND NORTH BORNEO *The confrontation with Indonesia's infiltrators took place along the jungle frontier.*

circumstances, helicopters came into their own, for, if
routes could not be blocked on the ground, small
groups of soldiers could be lifted into surveillance
positions; if they reported enemy activity,
reinforcements could then be rushed to their aid from a
centrally-located base.

The Special Air Service (SAS) Regiment, with
recent jungle experience in Malaya, was ideally suited
for the role of surveillance, but, as the confrontation
progressed, other troops – particularly the Gurkhas –
proved just as effective. Their jungle skills, tactical
flexibility and the deliberate policy they adopted of
making friends with local tribes on the border, offering
them aid and protection under the title "hearts and
minds", succeeded in blunting the Indonesian assaults,
sending Sukarno's men reeling back across the frontier
on a number of occasions. By early 1964, the initiative
was firmly with the British.

Climax of the confrontation

Sukarno responded by deploying regular troops close to
the border and authorizing their use in cross-border
attacks. Indonesian military outposts were pushed
further forward, so cutting down the advance warning
available to the British, who had little choice but to
allow selected pre-emptive raids to be launched into
Indonesian territory in response. Carried out under the
codename *Claret*, these were highly secret affairs,
carefully controlled and deliberately restricted to areas
reasonably close to the border. Small groups of SAS, or
similarly-trained troops, were sent into the jungle to
observe Indonesian bases and, if necessary, prevent
incursions. It took time, but by mid-1965 the
Indonesians had been forced to pull back, easing the
pressure on the border areas. By then, Sukarno had
come under political attack at home; in September
1965 his position was weakened as the Indonesian army
took over effective power.

In August 1966, Indonesian's new leader, General T
N J Suharto, ended the fighting and accepted the status
quo. The confrontation had cost the lives of over 2,000
Indonesians and 59 British and Commonwealth
servicemen, but the expansionist policies of Sukarno
had been checked and the Federation of Malaysia
allowed to emerge.

JERUSALEM
SIX–DAY WAR
5 June 1967 – 7 June 1967

An action that was part of the Israeli seizure of the
West Bank from Jordan during the Six-Day War. The
capture of the Old City of Jerusalem involved heavy
fighting in built-up areas. Success gave the Israelis
access to the Wailing Wall, and helped to improve the
security of Israel itself.

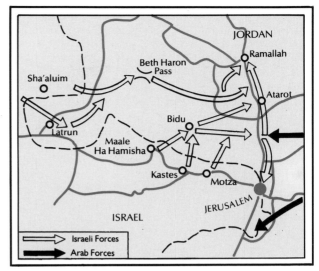

JERUSALEM *Having secured their northern flank against the
Jordanians, the Israelis launched their drive on the city.*

During the Six-Day War of June 1967, Israel fought and
defeated three of her Arab neighbors in turn. By the
end of the conflict, a "buffer" zone had been created
between Israel and Egypt in Sinai, the threat from the
Jordanian positions in Judea and Samaria (the West
Bank) had been eliminated, and the Syrians had been
pushed back off the *Golan Heights*. But, through Israel
captured an impressive amount of Arab territory, none
of her gains was more symbolic and important to
Judaism than the Old City of Jerusalem.

War on the West Bank

The war against Jordan began on 5 June 1967. The
campaign was not one that the Israelis sought, since,
concentrating on the threat from Egypt, they had
hoped that King Hussein would not join with the other
Arab powers. However, when he ignored reassurances
from Tel Aviv, and ordered his air force and artillery to
engage targets in the thin coastal strip of Israel
bordering the West Bank, the response was immediate.
Israeli aircraft bombed Jordanian airfields and units of
Uzi Narkiss' Central Command advanced towards
Nablus in the north and Jerusalem in the center.

The Israeli intention was to force the Jordanians to
withdraw out of artillery range of Tel Aviv, and to
forge a link with the Jewish enclaves in Jerusalem,
which were under threat from enemy attacks around
the city, as well as from the high ground to the north of
the Tel Aviv-Jerusalem road. Indeed, as soon as the
fighting began, soldiers of the Jordanian Arab Legion
had tried to put pressure on the Jewish enclaves, only
to be pushed back by the Israeli 16th Brigade, which
then had gone on to sever the main road south.

Narkiss began his offensive late on 5 June, sending
Colonel Uzi Ben Ari's 10th Mechanized Brigade along
the Tel Aviv-Jerusalem road with orders to seize the
vital high ground to the north. Ben Ari was
outstandingly successful, first driving along the road and

then suddenly turning off it to attack the Jordanian positions head-on. By midnight, after hours of fierce fighting, his troops had captured Radar Hill, Abdul Aziz and Beit Iksa, the heights that controlled the roads to the west and north of Jerusalem.

With the 16th Brigade to the south and the Israeli Air Force creating havoc on roads to the east, Jerusalem was effectively cut off. This enabled Colonel Mordechai Gur's 55th Parachute Brigade to advance towards the city.

Battle in Jerusalem

Gur's men faced a difficult task. The Jordanians had spent much of the time since 1948 fortifying the approaches to the Old City, creating an elaborate defensive system. Moreover, the garrison – comprising the 27th Infantry Brigade of the Arab Legion, under Brigadier Ata Ali – was familiar with the terrain. But the Israeli paratroops were tough and, when the battle for the city began on 6 June, they slowly inched forward, clearing each position in turn. By dawn, they controlled most of the Sheikh Jarrach district, had captured Ammunition Hill and pushed down as far as the Rockefeller Museum, facing the northern sector of the Old City Wall. Meanwhile, Ben Ari had continued his spoiling attacks further north, while the Israeli Air Force had stopped Jordanian reinforcements moving up.

The decision to enter the Old City was taken early on 7 June, although its capture was seen as being of secondary importance compared to the capture of the high ground to the east – the Augusta Victoria Hill and the Mount of Olives. Gur's forces set out at 0830, but it was to be another hour before any of them entered the Old City. By then, contact had been made with the 16th Brigade to the south, sealing off all the Jordanian approaches. At 1000, the Wailing Wall was reached and, as the Israelis mopped up remaining snipers, the Old City fell.

KHE SANH
VIETNAM WAR
21 January – 7 April 1968

Siege of a US combat base in the province of Quang Tri, in northern South Vietnam, in which about 6,000 US Marines and South Vietnamese Rangers held out for 77 days against an estimated 20,000 North Vietnamese regulars. Khe Sanh survived by making full use of American airmobility and firepower.

By January 1969, US forces in Vietnam seemed to be enjoying some success in preventing the fall of the south to the Communists. Their strategy, introduced with the commitment of combat units to South Vietnam in 1965, hinged on the ability to block any infiltration of the south by regular troops of the North

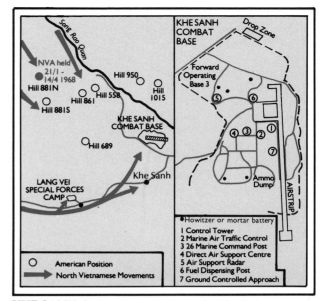

KHE SANH *Communist attempts to take Khe Sanh were defeated in both the north and along Route 9 in the south.*

Vietnamese Army (NVA), leaving the Army of the Republic of (South) Vietnam (ARVN) to deal with *Viet Cong* (VC) activity in the villages of the interior. Since 1965, the distinction between "main-force" and "village" operations had blurred, with US units taking a more active role in the latter, but the deployment of forces astride likely infiltration routes, especially in the northern provinces, remained a priority.

"A cascade of shells and bombs"

The northern provinces constituted Corps Tactical Zone (CTZ) 1. Since 1965, this had been a primary concern of the US Marine Corps. Backed by Special Forces ("Green Berets") and, on occasion, by army units, the marines had fought a series of set-piece conventional battles against the NVA and had constructed a line of defended "combat bases" to block any sudden enemy moves. As early as October 1966, a marine battalion had occupied the small plateau overlooking Khe Sanh, which, with its Special Forces outpost at Lang Vei, constituted the westernmost anchor of this line, close to the Laotian border and dominating Route 9, the main road to the coast. By late 1967, after a period of relative quiet, intelligence reports began to indicate that NVA were staging a build-up. Khe Sanh was reinforced and a massive aerial bombardment – Operation *Niagara* – was planned, using fighters, fighter-bombers and even B-52 heavy bombers to create a "cascade of shells and bombs" in the path of any NVA advance.

Khe Sanh was held by all three battalions of the 26th Marines, commanded by Colonel David E. Lownds.

He had substantial artillery support and, from late January 1968, the 1st Battalion, 9th Marines, as well as the ARVN's 37th Rangers, under his command – a total of approximately 6,000 men. Opposing them were between 15,000 and 20,000 regulars of the NVA, drawn from the 304th, 320th, 324B and 325C Divisions, who began to close in on Khe Sanh sometime in mid-January. Fully aware of the fate that had befallen the French at *Dien Bien Phu* (1953–54), Lownds concentrated the bulk of his infantry on top of the hills that surrounded the position, being determined to prevent a close siege of Khe Sanh and its vital airstrip. Thus, although the base itself was strongly defended by mortars and 105mm artillery pieces, most of the fighting was planned to take place a short distance to the north, around a series of hills – 881 South, 881 North, 861, 558 and 950.

The assault begins
The first indication of NVA presence came on 20 January 1968, when elements of the 3rd Battalion, 26th Marines, tried to push forward from 881 South on to a neighbouring hill, 881 North, only to encounter stiff enemy resistance. Falling back to 881 South, the marines dug in; within less than 24 hours, they were to be surrounded and dependent for resupply upon a fleet of helicopters, flown at great risk from bases further east. At the same time, early on 21 January, an NVA assault on Hill 861 was beaten off, while the main base came under sustained bombardment from 122mm rockets. The siege had begun; for the next 76 days, Khe Sanh was to be under practically constant artillery or rocket fire, earning the dubious distinction of being "the most bombed place on earth".

General William C. Westmoreland, head of the US Military Assistance Command, Vietnam (MACV), decided to fight for Khe Sanh, not just because of its strategic position alongside Route 9, but also to show the South Vietnamese the importance the USA attached to giving them support. This response was particularly significant after the events of 31 January, when NVA and VC units assaulted a host of targets throughout the country in the *Tet Offensive*. As soon as Lownds came under attack at Khe Sanh, Westmoreland initiated *Niagara*, creating a protective ring of airpower around the embattled base, and ordered the 1st Cavalry Division (Airmobile) to conduct helicopter support missions. As NVA assaults intensified, conditions inside the base steadily worsened. The marines were forced underground to escape enemy fire and, as aerial resupply developed, losses among the C-130 transport aircraft and CH-46 helicopters supplying the base rose alarmingly.

The height of the siege
While American attention was riveted on the Tet Offensive, the NVA took the opportunity of mounting renewed attacks on Khe Sanh – this time along Route 9 from the west. On 6 February, the isolated base at Lang Vei, held by nearly 500 locally-raised troops under Special Forces command, was overwhelmed by NVA forces using Soviet-supplied PT-76 tanks (the first time

such weapons had been deployed in the south), while Khe Sanh itself came under yet greater artillery attack. This reached a peak on 23 February, when 1,307 shells hit the base; by then, the airstrip had been effectively closed to fixed-wing aircraft, leaving the defenders dependent upon parachute drops or extremely quick "in-out" helicopter missions. Six days later, as a major NVA attack was launched from the east, toward a part of the perimeter held by the 37th Rangers, the danger of defeat reached its height. Fortunately, the attack was held.

American efforts to relieve Khe Sanh, codenamed Operation *Pegasus*, had been planned for some time, but it was not until 1 April that they could be initiated. Centered upon the airmobility of the 1st Cavalry Division, *Pegasus* involved a co-ordinated series of attacks designed to hammer the NVA against the anvil of Khe Sanh. A "firebase" was established to the east, from which US artillery pounded NVA positions and, as elements of the besieged garrison mounted assaults towards Hill 471, the 1st Marines advanced to the southeast along Route 9. A link-up was achieved on 7 April, so raising the siege.

KHORRAMSHAHR
GULF WAR
⁻22 September 1980 – 31 October 1980⁻

The opening battle in the drawn-out Gulf War between Iran and Iraq, in which Iraqui troops, attacking across the Shatt al-Arab waterway, fought to gain control of Iranian oil refineries and centers of population. Despite the eventual capture of Khorramshahr, the campaign soon degenerated into stalemate.

The origins of the current conflict between Iran and Iraq are centuries old, as the border between the two states marks a religious and ethnic boundary that has traditionally led to friction. Although both countries follow the Muslim religion, they adhere to different sects within it, reflecting a dispute which goes back to the 7th century AD and the death of Muhammed. The Iranians, followers of the fundamentalist Shi'ite sect, opposed the more secular Sunnis of Iraq; the additional ethnic divide between Arab Iraq and Aryan Iran also meant that peace was unlikely to be the norm.

There was more to it than this, however. Territorial disputes, particularly over rights of passage along the Shatt al-Arab waterway at the head of the Arabian (Persian) Gulf, gave an added impetus to the rivalry between the two powers and, on paper at least, provided the excuse for war in 1980. Traditionally, the border had run along the east bank of the waterway, giving Iraq complete control of it, but the Iranians refused to accept this. They called for a revised line to be drawn along the center, with full rights of passage for Iranian ships moving up the Shatt al-Arab to the oil refineries at Abadan and Khorramshahr. An agreement had been hammered out at Algiers in March 1975, by which Iranian claims were upheld in exchange for a withdrawal of their support from the Kurds (a separatist group in northern Iraq who had been fighting a guerrilla war against the regime since 1972), but the chances of this actually ending the dispute were slim. The overthrow of the Shah of Iran in early 1979 by religious fundamentalists under the Ayatollah Khomeini merely made the problem worse, since the Sunni rulers of Iraq recognized the threat to their authority that would arise if the new ideas should spread to the substantial Shi'ite minority under Iraqui rule.

The outbreak of conflict

By early 1980, therefore, Saddam Hussein, the leader of Iraq, had cause for considerable concern. The Aytollah, a sworn enemy, had already announced his intention to "export" his revolution to neighboring states, Iranian forces were still occupying bases on the Shatt al-Arab in defiance of the Algiers agreement, and signs of renewed Kurdish activity within Iraq were apparent. At the same time, the temptation to mount a surprise attack against the Iranian armed forces, which had been weakened by the purges that accompanied the Ayatollah's revolution, must have been overwhelming. The advantage which the Shah had always enjoyed through his purchase of western military equipment

had been undermined by the Ayatollah's declared opposition to the west; although the Iraqi armed forces, dependent upon inferior Soviet-supplied weapons, were theoretically at a disadvantage, this could be countered if they secured surprise. On 17 September, therefore, the Iraqis formally abrogated the Algiers agreement and, five days later, attacked Iran.

Battle in the Gulf

Iraqi forces, supported by air strikes launched deep into Iran, crossed the border in three main areas. In the north, a single division had seized the region around Qasr-e-Shirin and Naft-e-Shah by 25 September, while in the center, opposite Baghdad, another division (probably of mountain infantry) attacked Mehran. These, however, were essentially diversionary actions. The main assault, involving up to seven divisions of armor and mechanized infantry, concentrated on the southern sector, crossing the Shatt al-Arab and advancing across relatively open ground towards the towns of Susangerd, Ahvaz, Khorramshahr and Abadan.

The aims of the attack were to clear the east bank of the waterway and destroy the Iranian oil refineries, but it soon became clear that Saddam Hussein had underestimated his enemy. Deploying Chieftain tanks purchased from Britain under the Shah, Iranian troops created pockets of resistance amid sand-dunes, canals and ruined buildings. These blunted the Iraqi assault, forcing Saddam Hussein to commit more and more of his ground forces to the attack. Khorramshahr finally fell on 13 October 1980, but the Iraqis could advance no further as the Iranians recovered.

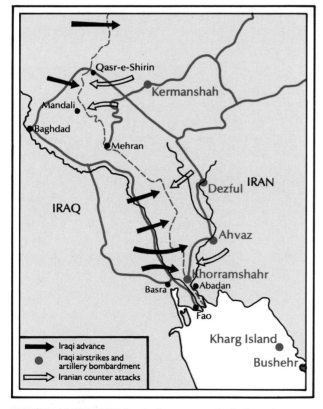

KHORRAMSHAHR *Iraq's thrusts towards the key oil refineries were eventually halted by determined Iranian resistance.*

MALAYA
BRITISH vs INSURGENTS
June 1948 – July 1960

An extremely effective counter-insurgency (COIN) campaign, fought by the British against Communist revolutionaries in Malaya. Characterized by a strongly co-ordinated politico-military response, the campaign became a model for future COIN operations.

Between June 1948 and July 1960, the British and Malayan authorities fought a protracted campaign against the threat of Communist subversion. The Malayan Communist Party (MCP), founded in 1927, drew the bulk of its support from the Chinese population, many of whom, by the late 1940s, were living in squatter camps close to the jungle fringes. With promises of social reform and political domination once the British colonial authorities had been overthrown, the MCP established subversive roots through trades unions, schools and youth movements, creating "safe bases" in remote rural areas, on the Maoist model. Between 1942 and 1945, they helped to organize resistance to Japanese rule, gaining experience in guerrilla warfare and stockpiling captured arms. By 1948, with significant support among a minority ethnic group (although, notably, not among the indigenous Malays), and an infrastructure of "safe bases" and a "passive wing" (the *Min Yuen*) established throughout Malaya, the insurgents were ready to take the offensive. This began in June, with hit-and-run attacks on isolated rubber plantations, carried out by the newly formed Malayan Races' Liberation Army (MRLA).

The campaign begins
The British reacted by declaring a State of Emergency, which gave extra powers to the colonial authorities. However, the insurgents, exploiting the element of surprise, retained the initiative, mounting ever more ambitious attacks, which threatened to undermine British credibility in the eyes of the Malayan population. By 1950, the number of incidents had risen alarmingly (as had the numbers of insurgents, which had increased to an estimated 10,000); when the High Commissioner, Sir Henry Gurney, was assassinated by a guerrilla gang in October 1951, the British position appeared distinctly weak. It began to look as if Communist victory was on the cards.

MALAYA *British counter-insurgency success in the towns gradually drove the Communists deep into the jungle.*

This proved to be an unnecessarily gloomy picture, however, for a number of policies had been initiated during these early years that were to act as a basis for eventual counter-insurgency success. The police – essential for the gathering of grass-roots intelligence – had been reformed, army patrols had been inserted into remote jungle areas to take on the guerrillas at their own game and, most significantly of all, Lieutenant-General Sir Harold Briggs had been acting for 18 months as Director of Operations. His realization that the problem was essentially political, rather than military, and his "Plan" for countering subversion, starting in the populated areas and moving out to split the insurgents from their supporters, were the keys to victory. On Briggs' instigation, the civil authorities, the police and the army were closely integrated, intelligence collation was centralized and a policy aimed at winning the "hearts and minds" of the people – particularly the Chinese squatters – introduced.

The Templer years
Briggs retired in late 1951, to be succeeded as Director of Operations by General Sir Gerald Templer, who also held the post of High Commissioner. This unique combination of civil and military power allowed him to put the Briggs Plan into full effect. By 1954, when Templer left Malaya, the guerrillas were on the defensive, forced to fend for themselves in jungle areas as their squatter support vanished and a British-instituted policy of food control denied them supplies.

At the same time, Briggs' civil-military infrastructure was operating well, building up a clear picture of Communist organization and deployment. This enabled the security forces to mount more effective operations deep into the jungle, rooting out the guerrillas and freeing vast areas of Malaya from subversive influence. A British promise of independence by 1957, which was duly implemented, ensured that the ordinary people had something for which to fight. In 1955, Chin Peng, the MRLA leader, requested an armistice, but this was refused; by 1960, he and less than 500 demoralized supporters had retreated to the Thai border. The campaign was over and, for once, the existing government had won against insurgents. It was a significant victory.

MIRBAT
WAR IN OMAN
19 July 1972

A fierce engagement between British members of the Special Air Service (SAS) Regiment and up to 250 insurgents in Dhofar, the western province of Oman. Victory for the SAS marked a turning-point in the war, forcing the rebels on to the defensive and preparing the way for counter-insurgency success.

At 0530 on 19 July 1972, Captain Mike Kealy, commander of an eight-man SAS team in the village of Mirbat, eastern Dhofar, was woken by the sound of gunfire. Rushing outside, he quickly realized that his position was under attack from a strong rebel force – members of the Marxist-dominated Popular Front for the Liberation of Oman and the Arabian Gulf (PFLOAG), dedicated to the overthrow of the pro-Western ruler of Oman, Sultan Qaboos bin Said. The firing was concentrated against a small outpost, the Jebel Ali, north of Kealy's fortified headquarters, where eight members of the locally-raised Oman Gendarmerie were acting as perimeter guards; however, it was obvious that Mirbat itself, with its SAS detachment and small garrison of *firqat* (tribesman loyal to the sultan) was the real target for the insurgents.

Such an open attack by the rebels was unusual; organized as a revolutionary force by activists from the neighbouring state of South Yemen, the PFLOAG had concentrated hitherto on subversion among the tribes of the *jebel* (the mountainous hinterland of Dhofar). Although they had enjoyed some success in the late 1960s, the process of insurgency had been halted in recent months. When Qaboos seized power from his father in July 1970, he had called on the British for aid and initiated politico-military reforms, which had acted as a firm basis for counter-insurgency success. Civil-military co-ordination, pro-government propaganda, effective intelligence gathering and a careful policy of "hearts and minds" among the *jebali* tribesman had

been combined with offensive military action in the mountains to reassert government control.

British aid was confined to a number of seconded or contract officers, appropriate equipment and about 50 men of the SAS, widely recognized as experts in the difficult art of counter-insurgency. By 1972, deep inroads had been made into PFLOAG positions on the eastern *jebel*, preparatory to the undertaking of clearing operations further west. If the attack on Mirbat succeeded, much of that work would be undermined, implying to the *jebali* tribes that the Sultan's Armed Forces (SAF) were incapable of defeating the rebels.

The consequences of failure

Kealy was aware of the consequences of failure, but this did little to reassure him as he stared through the drizzle and mist of the early monsoon on 19 July. The rebels, estimated to number 250, and armed with AK-47 Kalashnikov automatic rifles, mortars and heavy machine guns, had chosen the time of their attack well – early in the morning, when mists would curtail air support – and were opposed by a tiny force of gendarmarie, *firqat* and SAS. The SAS, however, were occupying strong defensive positions and were equipped with machine guns, a mortar and a single 25-pounder field gun, situated close to the fort on the outer perimeter. One of the SAS men, had already rushed to man the 25-pounder, while other members of the detachment laid down covering fire, concentrating on the barbed-wire defences through which the rebels had to pass. By 0700, when a slight lull set in, it was apparent that the first crisis was over.

Kealy, though, was still in grave danger. Urgent radio messages had alerted other SAF units, but the mist made air support unlikely and, as contact with the 25-pounder gun pit broke down, things began to look bad. Kealy and Trooper Tobin rushed forward to the gun pit to investigate, just in time to go through a renewed rebel attack. Two of the SAS men (Labalaba and Tobin) were killed as the enemy penetrated the barbed-wire defences, only to be met by bursts of concentrated machine-gun fire. Just at that moment, the delayed air support arrived, when Strikemaster jets broke through the mist and, at great risk to the pilots, screamed into action. The rebels broke and fled.

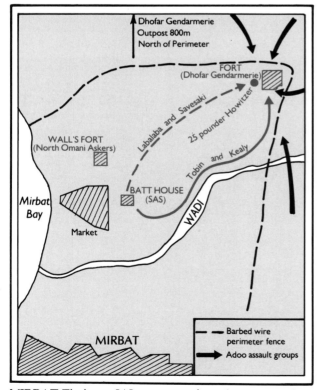

MIRBAT *The key to SAS success was the swift reaction to the attack launched on the fort by the PFOAG assault groups.*

EAST PAKISTAN
INDO-PAKISTAN WAR
⎯4 December 1971–16 December 1971⎯

Indian attack on East Pakistan, designed to overwhelm Pakistani defending forces in a multi-pronged advance, using armor, infantry and airpower. Despite the difficult terrain, the Indian victory was achieved remarkably quickly; it led to the creation of the independent state of Bangladesh.

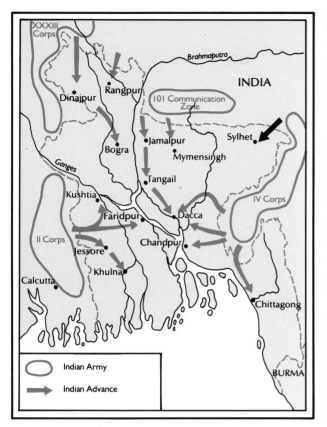

EAST PAKISTAN *The Indian eastern drive, which took the Pakistanis by surprise, culminated in the fall of Dacca.*

When the British withdrew from India in 1947, they left behind a sub-continent deeply divided along religious lines and ripe for future conflict. Hindu India and Muslim Pakistan clashed almost immediately over disputed border areas, particularly in the north-western province of Kashmir, and the antagonism between them did not cool down over the succeeding years. In 1965, a full-scale war broke out between the two countries, producing no outright winner; further crises and confrontations were inevitable.

A divided continent

Trouble was not confined to the inter-state level, for Pakistan was subject to enormous internal pressures as well. By 1970, these had led to a virtual civil war. At independence in 1947, the country had been split into two parts, separated by a vast tract of Indian territory, and, despite the unifying religious factor of religion, West and East Pakistan had enjoyed an unequal relationship since partition. Although the east contained more people and contributed more to the economy than the west, it was the latter that dictated policy, viewing the east as little more than a convenient source of wealth.

Political reaction in the east was inevitable, manifesting itself in Sheikh Mujibur Rahman's Awami League, which won the East Pakistani elections of

December 1970. Pakistan's western-based rulers responded by ordering the army to clamp down on Awami League supporters – a decision that led to widespread unrest (brutally suppressed) throughout East Pakistan. As refugees fled across the border, the Indian authorities, recognizing an opportunity to weaken their rivals, organized anti-Pakistan guerrilla groups known as *Mukti Bahini*.

East Pakistan was ideal guerrilla country. Split by the waters of three great rivers – the Ganga, Brahmaputra and Meghna – the terrain was broken and difficult to control using regular forces, particularly as the latter had also to protect the state against possible Indian attack. As *Mukti Bahini* raids intensified during the monsoon period (June–September 1971), the Pakistani Eastern Command, consisting of about 60,000 regular troops and 18,000 paramilitary supporters, faced an impossible task, particularly as the Indians used the period to build up their border forces to a strength of 250,000 by December 1971.

Pakistan attacks

In the event, the war began in the west, where Pakistani forces mounted an abortive pre-emptive air strike on 3 December 1971. This was followed by ground attacks into Kashmir and Rajasthan, but these were contained easily by the Indian defenders. The Pakistani move rebounded quickly on its initiators, since it provided India with the excuse it needed for action; on 4 December, a series of co-ordinated Indian assaults into East Pakistan began. The plan was to advance simultaneously from the west, north-west and east, crossing river obstacles and infiltrating Pakistani border positions in a "lightning" campaign designed to disrupt defences and capture key ground. It turned out to be a devastating success.

The Indian blitzkrieg

In the west, the Indian II Corps, under Lieutenant-General T L Raina, crossed the border and advanced on Jessore in an enveloping move designed to avoid a pitched battle in unfavorable terrain; by 7 December, Jessore was in Indian hands. Although this success was not exploited to the full, the Pakistani 9th Division dissolved under the Indian pressure. Further north, the Indian XXXIII Corps, under Lieutenant-General M L Thapan, using Soviet-supplied T55 and PT76 tanks, made steady progress towards Rangpur and Dinajpur, splitting the Pakistani 16th Division in two and pushing south to Bogra.

However, it was in the east – a thrust that caught the Pakistanis by surprise – that the most spectacular advances were made. Here, the Indian IV Corps, under Lieutenant-General Sagat Singh, attacked towards Sylhet, Ashunganj and Chittagong, forcing the Pakistani 39th Divison back towards Dacca. Indian parachute drops disrupted the enemy withdrawal, and, as yet more forces advanced from the north, Dacca, now under attack from all sides, fell.

PANJSHER VALLEY
SOVIET INVASION OF AFGHANISTAN
May 1982 – September 1982

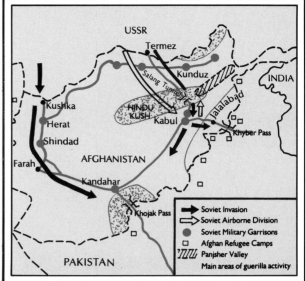

A sustained Soviet offensive against the *Mujahidin* guerrillas in Afghanistan, aimed at clearing the Panjsher Valley, to the north of Kabul, and so secure the Soviet line of communication with southern Russia. Characterized by new Russian tactics, the offensive enjoyed some success, but failed to end the fighting.

When the Soviets invaded Afghanistan in December 1979, seizing Kabul and setting up their own puppet president, they undoubtedly expected the campaign to be a short one, their first intention being to leave the Afghan army to deal with opposition from the mass of the population. This, however, proved not to be the case. Guerrilla groups, known collectively as *Mujahidin* resented both the intervention and the continued imposition of Communism, and used their knowledge of the terrain and their popular backing to create substantial pockets of resistance. Soviet and Afghan supply columns were ambushed, lines of communication severed and hit-and-run attacks mounted within the major towns. The Soviets, unprepared for anything other than full-scale conventional war, failed to respond effectively; by early 1982 they controlled little beyond their fortified bases in the towns.

The Mujahidin threat

A major threat was posed by *Mujahidin* groups in the Panjsher Valley, a fertile area surrounded by the mountains of the Hindu Kush, only a relatively short distance from Kabul. The population of the valley (estimated at 100,000 peasants) was firmly behind the guerrillas, who were led by a young engineer called Mahsoud Ahmad Shah. He had proved to be one of the most successful *Mujahidin* leaders, mounting a series of attacks on Soviet and Afghan columns as they wound their way along the main road between Kabul and the Soviet border. Refusing to accept the authority of the puppet regime in Kabul, Mahsoud effectively ruled the Panjsher area.

For both strategic and political reasons, therefore, an offensive into the valley became a Soviet priority. Their previous tactics of calling up Mil Mi-24 Hind D helicopter gunships to strafe guerrilla positions clearly had proved ineffective – the *Mujahidin* merely hid in caves in the mountains – while small-scale attacks, using tanks or armored personnel carriers, which were tied to existing roads, had proved extremely susceptible to ambush, particularly at night. Something far more sustained was obviously needed.

Accordingly, in May 1982, 12,000 Soviet and Afghan troops, closely supported by armor and helicopter gunships, swept out of Kabul towards the

PANJSHER VALLEY *Conventional tactics, though initially successful, failed against determined guerrilla activity.*

Panjsher Valley, intent upon a major campaign to pacify the area once and for all. Mahsoud, realizing that he was outnumbered and outgunned, withdrew the bulk of his guerrillas deeper into the valley, leaving small forces to harass and ambush the invaders. Armed with nothing more lethal than bolt-action rifles, mortars and a few anti-tank rockets, however, there was little that could be done to stop the Soviet advance, particularly as it was obvious that new tactics were being used.

As the armor pressed into the valley, following the road, helicopter gunships concentrated on likely ambush sites and deposited small groups of heavily armed men on the high ground to search out the guerrillas. Other helicopters landed entire companies of soldiers at strategic points in advance of the main ground forces' advance and, as self-propelled guns and rocket launchers arrived, the aim of the offensive became clear. Massive bombardments were directed at the surrounding hill-tops while each village in the valley was razed, forcing the population to surrender or flee. As Mahsoud watched from the mountains, his "liberated state" was systematically destroyed.

The Soviets did not have it all their own way, however. Guerrilla attacks continued at every opportunity, and, although it is impossible to give precise figures, an estimated 3,000 Soviet and Afghan troops were killed or wounded in the offensive, which lasted until September. By then, the Soviets had made it clear that they were intent upon a policy of ruthless suppression, using overwhelming force to destroy guerrilla bases and disperse the people. There is no doubt that this had a stunning effect on the *Mujahidin*, but with Mahsoud and the majority of his fighters still at large, the Soviet advantage was short-lived.

238

"PEACE FOR GALILEE"

ISRAELI INVASION OF LEBANON
6 June 1982 – 25 June 1982

The Israeli invasion of southern Lebanon, designed to destroy the Palestine Liberation Organization (PLO) to the south of Beirut, so preventing further attacks on Israeli settlements in northern Galilee. Although successful, the operation committed Israeli forces to a lengthy siege of Beirut they could ill afford.

Late on the evening of 3 June 1982, the Israeli ambassador to London, Sholomo Argov, was gunned down by terrorists as he left a reception at the Dorchester Hotel. Although he survived, the attack fitted into a pattern of renewed activity by the Palestine Liberation Organization (PLO), which caused the Israeli government grave concern. The Israelis ordered retaliatory air strikes against Palestinian refugee camps in southern Lebanon, only for the PLO to respond by launching a series of artillery and rocket attacks on Israeli settlements in northern Galilee. On 5 June, the Israeli Prime Minister, Menachem Begin, authorised a limited invasion of southern Lebanon – Operation *Peace for Galilee* – a scheme designed to push the PLO out of range of the border.

"Peace for Galillee" begins
The invasion began at 1100 on 6 June 1982 when three columns of Israeli armor and mechanized infantry, supported by air power, crossed the Lebanese border, aiming to isolate Palestinian positions and to prevent any interference from Syrian forces, committed to the Beqa'a Valley since 1976. The main attack took place along the coast, where a force of 22,000 men and 220 tanks thrust north to by-pass the Palestinian camps at Tyre, Sidon and Damour (leaving them to be destroyed by follow-up infantry) and threaten the southern approaches to Beirut. Amphibious landings ahead of the column aided the operation, which, in line with traditional Israeli strategy, aimed for a short, sharp conflict, occupying territory and inflicting maximum damage before the superpowers stepped in to prevent its escalation. Meanwhile, in the center, a second column of 18,000 men and 220 tanks crossed the border from Metalla in a two-pronged advance to seize the vital cross-roads at Nabitiya, occupy the Arnoun Heights (including the Palestinian fortress at Beaufort Castle) and, eventually, link up with the coastal force to the south of Beirut. Finally, a much stronger column, consisting of 38,000 men and 800 tanks (including some of the new, Israeli-produced Merkavas) concentrated on the east, moving to the area of Lake Qaraoun to "plug" the Beqa'a Valley and so prevent the Syrians from taking action to support the Palestinians.

From the start, it was obvious that this was far more than just a limited attack, and during the first few days, the Israelis enjoyed remarkable success. On 6 June, the coastal column advanced beyond Tyre and, despite hard fighting whenever the Israelis entered Palestinian camps, the PLO were contained, or forced to withdraw. By 12 June, the column was within striking distance of Beirut, having effectively destroyed or captured all the Palestinian positions to the south. Meanwhile, the central force had taken Beaufort Castle – this Palestinian stronghold was captured on 6 June by the Golani Brigade after six hours of hand-to-hand combat – seized Nabitiya, and linked up with the coastal column at Zaharani.

This move threatened to outflank the Syrians from the west, but it was the actions further to the east that were more dramatic. As the Israeli column pushed through Hasbaiya and the Syrians responded by reinforcing their SAM (surface-to-air missile) batteries, the Israelis carried out one of the most successful air strikes on record. On 9 June, having located SAM sites and monitored their radars with remotely piloted vehicles (RPVs), a series of air attacks destroyed 19 batteries, as well as the 22 Syrian fighters that tried to intervene. By 11 June, the Syrians had lost 70 aircraft

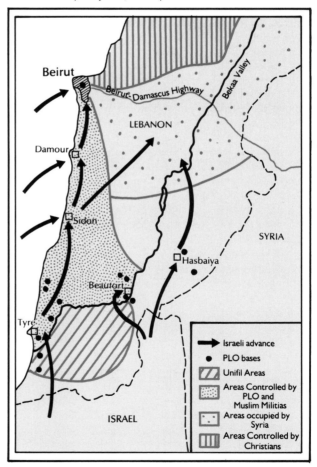

"PEACE FOR GALILEE" *The Israelis planned a Blitzkrieg-style assault to crush the PLO before the Syrians could intervene.*

in the area, with no Israeli casualties. When this was combined with a number of tank clashes to the south of Lake Qaraoun, in which Syrian T62s and T72s were destroyed by the Merkavas, the Arabs had little choice but to fall back, negotiating a ceasefire on 12 June.

The ceasefire freed the Israelis to concentrate against Beirut, where they were drawn into urban battles they had not foreseen. The superpowers, diverted by events in the South Atlantic, did not rush to organize a general ceasefire, and it was not until 25 June that one came into operation. By then, despite the success of *Peace for Galilee*, the Israelis were committed to a siege of Beirut they could not afford.

PORT STANLEY
FALKLANDS WAR
11 June 1982 – 14 June 1982

The final British offensive in the Falklands War, launched to liberate Port Stanley, the capital of the islands, and force an Argentinian surrender. In wintry conditions over rocky terrain, British units gradually closed in on the town; the defenders soon ran out of resolve and military options, negotiating a ceasefire on 14 June 1982.

The British breakout from the San Carlos beachhead, achieved in late May 1982, was dominated by the action of 2nd Battalion, The Parachute Regiment (2 Para) at *Goose Green*, but this was only one part of the process. At the same time, 3 Para and No 45 Commando (Royal Marines) thrust eastwards across the barren interior of East Falkland to close in on the main Argentinian positions around Port Stanley. The ranking Argentinian, General Mario Menendez, convinced that San Carlos was a feint and that British reinforcements would mount a direct amphibious assault on the capital, had kept nearly all his forces (about 10,000 strong) in defensive location in or immediately behind the ring of mountains protecting Port Stanley to the north and west. His plan was to force the British to fight attritional battles in the worsening winter conditions – battles that would be so costly that a negotiated settlement would have to be sought by the government in London.

"Yomping" to Port Stanley
Menendez, however, had reckoned without the speed of the British advance. By 31 May, 3 Para and 45 Commando had covered a great deal of ground without encountering any opposition, and had already established themselves close to the high ground in the northern sector. More significantly, elements of the SAS and 42 Commando had been lifted by helicopter to occupy the summit of Mount Kent, a short distance from Port Stanley.

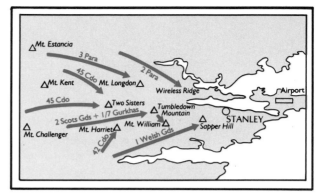

PORT STANLEY *British success at Port Stanley depended on breaking through the Argentinian positions in the mountains.*

By 5 June, the remainder of 42 Commando had moved on to Mount Challenger and British reinforcements, consisting of the whole of 5th Infantry Brigade (2nd Battalion Scots Guards, 1st Battalion Welsh Guards and 1st Battalion 7th Gurkha Rifles), with 2 Para in attendance, had opened up the southern route through Fitzroy and Bluff Cove. The latter move was not without its problems – on 8 June, 51 servicemen (including 33 Welsh Guards) were killed when the *Sir Galahad* was bombed by the Argentinians at Fitzroy – but, by 11 June, an arc of British forces had been created, poised to assault the main enemy positions. They were supported by five batteries of artillery, each with six 105mm guns, laboriously helilifted into position, along with enough ammunition to allow each gun to fire 1,200 rounds.

The British assault
Major-General Jeremy Moore, commander of the British land forces, envisaged a two-phase assault, which would seize the hills to the east of Mount Kent, and gradually push the Argentinians back towards Port Stanley. On the night of 11/12 June, 42 Commando began the offensive by marching silently around Mount Harriet, approaching the defenders from the east. The marines managed to get nearly to the summit before the enemy realized what was happening, so, although the final burst of fighting was hard, the hill was taken with minimum casualties. At the same time, 45 Commando seized Two Sisters, slightly to the north. Here, the fighting was more bitter, but it was 3 Para, even further north on Mount Longdon, who undoubtedly faced the worst combat of the night. Losing the advantage of surprise early on in their attack, when one of their men stepped on a mine, they went through a nightmare close-quarter battle, which was only resolved in their favor at dawn at a cost of 23 dead (including Sergeant Ian McKay, awarded a Victoria Cross for his bravery in tackling a machine-gun nest).

Moore had intended to follow this up immediately, but the need to bring up more supplies delayed him until 13/14 June. The Scots Guards were the first to move out, approaching Tumbledown Mountain, to the east of Two Sisters, as quietly as possible to avoid detection. As at Longdon, however, the Argentinians realized the British intention, and the Scots Guards soon found themselves involved in firefights. These lasted throughout the night and cost them nine dead.

As Left Flank Company reached the summit, however, 2 Para cleared Wireless Ridge to the north after an attack given massive fire support, and Port Stanley lay exposed. As 1/7th Gurkhas took Mount William and the Welsh Guards (supported by men of 40 Commando) seized Sapper Hill, both to the south of Stanley, the Argentinians broke and fled. By 2100 on 14 June, Menendez had surrendered.

PUSAN
KOREAN WAR
1 August 1950 – 8 September 1950

A series of desperate defensive actions, fought by US and South Korean forces to prevent the fall of Pusan, the last remaining pocket of South Korean territory, to the North Koreans. Success at Pusan was an essential prerequisite to General MacArthur's amphibious landing at *Inchon*.

As far as the Communists were concerned, the Korean War was intended to be short, the North Korean People's Army (NKPA) being given two months in which to seize the whole of South Korea. It came very close to success. The initial invasion across the 38th parallel on 25 June 1950 caught the Republic of Korea (ROK) Army by surprise, and the NKPA was allowed to sweep through Seoul towards the southern tip of the peninsula with remarkable speed. By late July, the remnants of the ROK Army, together with hastily-deployed US reinforcements, had been pushed almost to Pusan, in the extreme south-east; if Pusan fell, South Korea would cease to exist.

Lieutenant-General Walton Walker, commander of the US Eighth Army in Korea (EUSAK), had managed to prepare a rudimentary defensive line earlier in July, and on 1 August he ordered all Allied formations to fall back across the Naktong river, destroying its bridges behind them, to make a last desperate stand. The pocket into which they withdrew was a small one, but it did have the advantage of short lines of communication, enabling Walker to shift units quickly from one danger-spot to another. He could also count on supplies, reinforcements and air support. By comparison, the NKPA was overstretched.

Last stand at Pusan
The Communists, however, had no intention of allowing their enemy breathing space to recover, and made the most of their existing momentum to smash

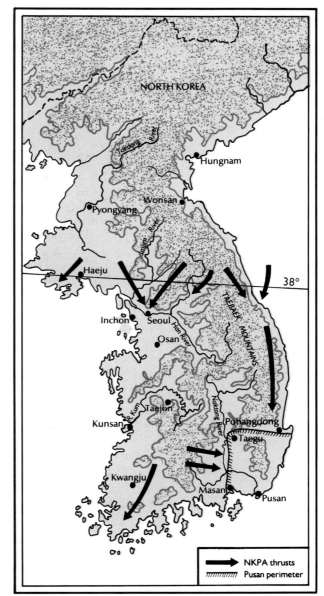

PUSAN *The NKPA drive southwards was halted at Pusan, where UN forces held their perimeter against all attacks.*

into the perimeter from all directions. On 5/6 August, the NKPA 4th Division crossed the Naktong in the west, where the river made a wide sweeping curve, and advanced into the area known as the Naktong bulge, which was thinly held by men of the US 24th Infantry Division. As NKPA units found and exploited gaps in the Allied line, Walker committed the newly-arrived US Marines. The fighting was hard, but the line held; by 18 August, the NKPA had been forced to pull back.

Meanwhile, however, a much more serious attack had developed further to the north, where five NKPA divisions, backed by Soviet-supplied T34 tanks, were concentrated against Taegu, the site of EUSAK HQ on the main road to Pusan. Between 5 and 8 August, the NKPA 1st and 13th Divisions crossed the Naktong and, by 15 August, were poised to advance on Taegu from the north, backed by the 15th Division, which had seized the high ground to the north-west. In both cases, ROK units had been unable to prevent the advance, but the same had not been true when the NKPA 3rd and 10th Divisions attacked from the west. They had been met by troops of the US 1st Cavalry Division as they tried to cross the Naktong on the night of 8/9 August and, under strong artillery fire, the Communists were decimated. A second assault on 11/12 August was more successful but, as Walker fed additional troops into the sector, the Allied line was consolidated – at one point through bitter tank-to-tank engagements, fought at close range by T34s and US M26s.

By then, however, the danger had shifted to the north-west, where NKPA attacks against the ROK 3rd Division broke through at Pohang-dong, forcing the allies to retreat by 17 August. US reinforcements managed to plug the gap, and by 21 August a lull had set in. This, however, was merely a prelude to renewed attacks, beginning on 31 August, against Masan (in the south-west) and the Naktong bulge. Yongsan fell to the NKPA and, as Taegu came under renewed threat, Walker was forced to evacuate his headquarters.

Fighting broke out all around the perimeter. For a time, it seems as if the Communists would break through, but skilful redeployments by Walker, backed by air and artillery strikes, held the key sectors of the line. By 8 September, it was obvious that the back of the NKPA offensive had been broken.

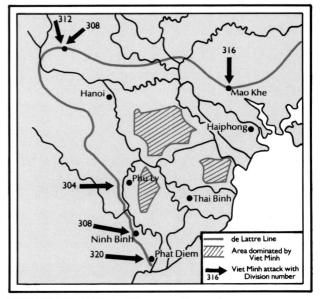

RED RIVER DELTA *Effective artillery and air support enabled the French to hold the Viet Minh on the de Lattre Line.*

RED RIVER DELTA
INDOCHINA WAR
13 January 1951 – 18 June 1951

A series of attacks launched by the *Viet Minh* against French positions around Hanoi and Haiphong during the First Indochina War (1945–1954). The *Viet Minh* divisions tried to break through the French defences, only to be pinned down and destroyed by specially designated mobile reserves.

By late 1950, General Vo Nguyen Giap, commander of the Communist *Viet Minh* forces in Indochina, was confident of victory over the French. Earlier in the year, he had mounted successful assaults on isolated French garrisons at Cao Bang and Lang Son, in the north-east of Tonkin, which had forced the enemy into a disastrous retreat to the Red River Delta, where defensive positions (known as the De Lattre Line after the French commander, General Jean de Lattre de Tassigny), were still being constructed. As he massed his divisions to the north of Hanoi, Giap could be forgiven for presuming that one more concerted push would end the war.

But de Lattre was not going to give in. Taking advantage of the temporary lull, he bolstered his defences by deploying loyal Vietnamese units in front-line positions, leaving the bulk of his French forces – including paratroops, Foreign Legionnaires and marines, backed by armour and airpower – to act as a mobile reserve, ready to spring into action at a moment's notice. Operating on internal lines of communication in an area relatively well served by roads, rivers and airstrips, the French would enjoy the advantages of speed and flexibility, bringing to bear the air and artillery firepower that they had been lacking in the Cao Bang-Lang Son battles.

Giap's offensive
Giap's offensive began on 13 January 1951, when the 308th and 312th *Viet Minh* Divisions appeared in front of Vinh Yen, to the north-west of Hanoi, close to the Red River. The village was defended by infantry in forward positions; as they fell back before the pressure of more than 20,000 Communist troops, another French defeat seemed likely. De Lattre, however, had two mobile groups available to support his hard-pressed infantry. Though one was caught and virtually destroyed in Vinh Yen on 14 January, the other managed to plug the gap, delaying the *Viet Minh* advance for 24 crucial hours.

During that time, de Lattre organized a massive airlift of other French units from all over the delta region, concentrating his forces in and around the threatened village. On 16 January, when Giap's men swept out of the jungle in a frontal assault, they were decimated. Caught in the open by French forces in Vinh Yen and hit repeatedly with napalm and bombs from the air, they withdrew to the safety of the mountains, having suffered an estimated 6,000 casualties for no appreciable gain.

The French hold

Success at Vinh Yen confirmed de Lattre's belief in "trip-wire" defences backed by mobile reserves, but it did little to deter Giap. During the night of 23/24 March, he carried out a second attack – this time at Mao Khe, a short distance to the north of Haiphong, using exactly the same "human-wave" tactics. At first, he came close to success – by 26 March the 316th *Viet Minh* Division seemed poised for victory – but, as at Vinh Yen, he was frustrated by superior French firepower, this time from gunboats on the Do Bac river.

It was hardly surprising that Giap decided to alter his battle plans. Ordering the 312th Division to mount diversionary attacks in the north-west, he moved the 304th and 308th south to join the 320th Division on the Day River. Once concentrated, they carried out a more subtle assault on the De Lattre Line, aiming to by-pass the French positions at Ninh Binh, Phu Ly and Phat Diem, and drive across the southern tip of the Red River Delta, leaving the enemy flank exposed. The attacks began on 29 May, but the French reacted swiftly, moving up eight mobile groups and two parachute units to blunt the assault. By 18 June, Giap was preparing to revert to guerrilla warfare.

ROLLING THUNDER/ LINEBACKER
VIETNAM WAR
March 1965 – December 1972

Attacks on targets in North Vietnam, carried out by US aircraft during the period of the USA's involvement in Vietnam (1965–1973). Initially confined to interdiction missions during *Rolling Thunder* (1965–1968), the bombing escalated in 1972 under the codename *Linebacker*, culminating in B-52 raids on Hanoi, the North Vietnamese capital, and Haiphong, the country's main port.

On 2 March 1965, US aircraft hit ammunition dumps at Xom Bong, north of the DMZ (demilitarized zone) in Vietnam, in the first of a series of raids codenamed *Rolling Thunder*. Designed to impede North Vietnamese infiltration of the south and to bring home to Hanoi the cost of its continued support of *Viet Cong* aggression, *Rolling Thunder* was to continue, with occasional "pauses", until 1 November 1968, when it was halted in response to North Vietnam's agreement to begin peace talks in Paris.

From the start, the *Rolling Thunder* raids were closely controlled, with restrictions imposed on the targets to be hit and the types of aircraft to be employed. In an effort to avoid direct Soviet or Chinese involvement in the war, certain areas of North Vietnam, including the centres of population around Hanoi and a "buffer zone" close to the Chinese border, were designated "sanctuaries", into which no raids could be mounted. At the same time, targets were confined to those which would disrupt, but not destroy, North Vietnamese society. This, in turn, limited aircraft that could be used, placing the burden upon "tactical" machines.

A limited offensive

Because of these restrictions, *Rolling Thunder* encountered a number of practical problems. The existence of "sanctuaries" allowed the North Vietnamese Air Force (NVAF), which was equipped with Soviet-supplied MiG fighters, to operate from secure bases; when this was coupled with the emergence of an effective air-defence system, including SAMs (surface-to-air missiles) and anti-aircraft guns, American losses began to mount. By the end of 1966, 455 US aircraft had been shot down over the north, and, although the NVAF was largely destroyed by F-4s in early 1967, the costs of the campaign were always high.

Similarly, despite the undoubted power of the attacking aircraft, few targets were completely destroyed, partly because the North Vietnamese were adept at repairing the damage, but also because the weapons used lacked pinpoint accuracy. In addition, any losses the north suffered could be replaced quickly by the Soviets or Chinese.

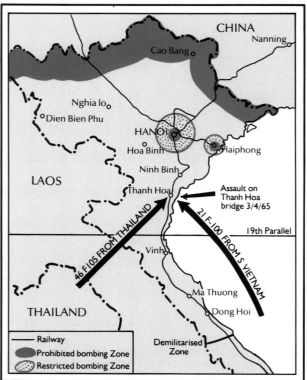

"ROLLING THUNDER" *Only restricted bombing was allowed around Hanoi and Haiphong.*

Renewing the offensive

The bombing halt imposed in November 1968 as a gesture towards the Paris talks remained in force until 8 May 1972, when, in response to North Vietnam's invasion of the south, President Richard M. Nixon authorized a resumption of the raids, under the codename *Linebacker*. This was a much more powerful campaign, with fewer target restrictions and less concern about possible escalation. North Vietnamese ports were mined to prevent resupply from outside sources, while a variety of targets were precision-bombed, using laser- or TV-guided "smart" bombs.

By late July, the peace talks had been resumed – but not for long. On 13 December, the North Vietnamese delegation walked out and Nixon, weary of prevarication, ordered a short, sharp air campaign (*Linebacker II*) to force the issue. For 11 days – 18 December-29 December, with a "pause" on Christmas Day – US airpower was allowed free rein over the North, with virtually no restrictions imposed on its use, while for the first time, B-52s were authorized to hit the Hanoi-Haiphong area. The results were impressive, though 26 aircraft (including 15 B-52s) were shot down. An estimated 80 per cent of the north's electrical power production was destroyed, its railway systems were devastated and the NVAF was wiped out. By the end of the year, the Paris peace talks had resumed and, on 15 January 1973, in anticipation of an agreement, all bombing was stopped.

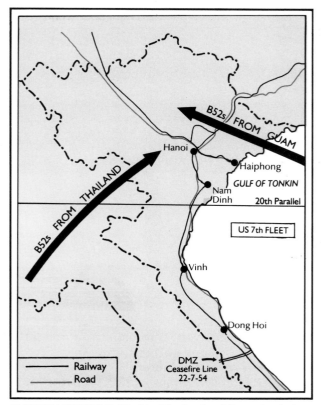

"LINEBACKER" *B-52s from Thailand and Guam bombed Hanoi, while the 7th Fleet mined the Gulf of Tonkin.*

SAIGON
VIETNAM WAR
April 1975

The final offensive by the North Vietnamese to seize control of the south, culminating in the capture of the capital, Saigon. Beginning with limited attacks in the Central Highlands, the North Vietnamese quickly realized how weak their enemy had become, and so mounted additional assaults, which led to the fall of Saigon and the end of South Vietnam's independence.

As US forces pulled out of Vietnam in 1973, the continued security of South Vietnam seemed to have been assured. The Paris peace agreement of 27 January had imposed a ceasefire on both sides, to be monitored by an International Commission; South Vietnam's armed forces had been trained by the US before the withdrawal; and assurance of economic and military aid (the latter in the form of weapons, rather than US units) had been given by the USA. Moreover, the record of the Army of the Republic of (South) Vietnam (ARVN) in blunting the North Vietnamese "Easter Invasion" of 1972 suggested that any future aggression would be unlikely to succeed.

Decline and fall

During the next two years, however, the balance of advantage shifted in favour of the north. The Saigon government, led by President Nguyen Van Thieu, was riddled with corruption and firm in its belief that American B-52s would always be on hand to guarantee the defence of the South. This was unlikely to be the case. Political events in Washington ensured that aid packages for South Vietnam were drastically cut and, once President Richard M. Nixon had been forced to resign over the Watergate scandal (August 1974), any idea of offering more substantial help disappeared. This left the South Vietnamese armed forces high and dry, denied the technology, spare parts and money needed to maintain their defensive capabilities. Thus, although the ARVN contained 1.1 million men in early 1975, they were short of essential hardware and tied to a tactical doctrine, inherited from the Americans, which they could not carry out.

By comparison, the North Vietnamese had used the ceasefire to prepare for the next round of the conflict. The Ho Chi Minh trail, free from US air interdiction, was improved, with new tracks pushed deep into the Central Highlands and into "War Zone C", to the north of Saigon; new weapons and equipment were delivered by the USSR; and the size of the North Vietnamese Army (NVA) was increased. By 1975, it consisted of no less than 19 divisions, of which 12 were already south of the 17th parallel, occupying areas taken in 1972. Indeed, since the ceasefire, the NVA had maintained a constant attritional pressure,

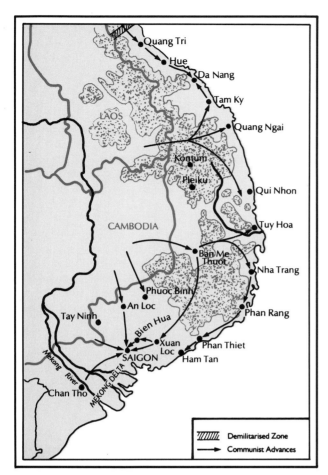

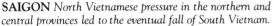

SAIGON *North Vietnamese pressure in the northern and central provinces led to the eventual fall of South Vietnam.*

particularly in the northern provinces of South Vietnam, close to the DMZ (demilitarised zone). ARVN morale was steadily drained by endless skirmishing and casualties, and a "top heavy" deployment of forces had occurred, with most of Thieu's units in the northern provinces, leaving the rest of the country sparsely defended.

The final offensive
It was this particular weakness that the north exploited in 1975, initiating a number of relatively minor attacks that were designed to seize key areas in preparation for a full-scale assault the following year. These attacks began in January 1975 in Phuoc Long province, to the north of Saigon, and even the NVA was surprised by the ease with which victory was achieved. This suggested that the time was ripe for a more general offensive; in early March, therefore, NVA units moved into Darlac province in the Central Highlands, with the twin aims of capturing the ARVN base at Ban Me Thuot and of advancing to the coast, so splitting South Vietnam into two. Thinly defended by a single ARVN regiment, Ban Me Thuot fell on 12 March.

Thieu responded in panic, ordering a redeployment

of forces from the northern provinces (to prevent them being cut off) and withdrawing units in the Central Highlands to the coast. Both moves created chaos. In the north, the redeployment caused demoralization; in the Central Highlands, the withdrawal turned into a rout, as ill-disciplined forces pulled back along Route 7B. By 1 April, Hue and Danang had fallen, and the NVA had occupied most of the northern and central provinces. They immediately swung south, by-passing ARVN centres of resistance and closing in on Saigon. On 21 April, Thieu resigned in hopes that his successor, General Duong Van Minh, could negotiate a ceasefire, but the North Vietnamese were in no mood to compromise; on 30 April 1975, as the Americans conducted a chaotic evacuation of their nationals by helicopter from the grounds of the US embassy, Saigon fell. The Indochina Wars were over.

SINAI
SIX-DAY WAR
5 June 1967–9 June 1967

An Israeli attack against prepared Egyptian positions during the Six-Day War of June 1967. Carried out in the wake of air strikes that had totally wiped out the Egyptian Air Force, the attack was a stunning success, confirming the military skills of the Israelis and leaving them in full possession of Sinai as a "buffer" zone.

The genesis of the Six-Day War was the decision to attack Egypt taken by the Israeli cabinet on 4 June 1967 – this decision was based upon intelligence assessments warning them that they faced imminent invasion by the Egyptian forces massed in Sinai. Israel's aim was to occupy the whole of the area, so breaking the blockade imposed by President Gamal Abdel Nasser on the Strait of Tiran (Israel's only route to the Red Sea), and creating a "buffer" zone from the border to the Suez Canal, within which any future Egyptian threat could be absorbed. Pre-emptive air strikes against Egyptian airfields, carried out early on 5 June, helped to prepare the way – over 200 Egyptian aircraft were caught on the ground and destroyed, for the loss of only 19 Israeli machines – but with seven infantry divisions close to the border and two armoured divisions in central Sinai, ready to respond to any breakthrough, Nasser's ground units constituted a formidable barrier.

Striking into Sinai
Major-General Yeshayahu Gavish, commander of Israel's Southern Front, was responsible for the Sinai attack. On 5 June, he had three divisions available, commanded by Major-Generals Israel Tal, Avraham Yoffe and Ariel Sharon respectively. These forces fielded a total of 700 tanks (Centurions, Super Shermans, M-48s and AMX-13s), backed by

The defences crumble

Yoffe's success, in fact, unhinged the Egyptian defences, for on 6 June he was ordered by Gavish to despatch part of his armour westwards to take the eastern end of the Mitla Pass, close to the canal. In the event, only nine Centurions made the breakthrough (four of which were being towed, having run out of fuel), but their sudden appearance, blocking the Egyptian lines of communication, spread alarm and consternation among the Sinai defenders.

On 7 and 8 June, as all three Israeli divisions advanced steadily across the desert, many Egyptian units broke and fled, abandoning their equipment and streaming back towards the canal. There, they were met by Yoffe's Centurions and Israeli airpower, suffering substantial losses, which merely reinforced the panic. On 9 June, Nasser agreed to a ceasefire, accepting the loss of 15,000 troops.

SUEZ
ANGLO–FRENCH INVASION OF EGYPT
⌐5 November 1956 – 6 November 1956⌐

An Anglo-French invasion of Egypt, designed to seize control of the Suez Canal and reverse President Nasser's decision to nationalize the western-owned company that had controlled it. Carried out in the wake of an Israeli attack on Sinai, the invasion was militarily successful, but politically disastrous.

On 26 July 1956, President Gamal Abdel Nasser nationalized the Suez Canal Company, forcing future users of the waterway to pay tolls to the Egyptian government, rather than to an Anglo-French consortium based in Paris. In itself, this hardly merited a military response, but to Britain and France it was indicative of Nasser's wider aim of destroying western influence throughout the Middle East. Within 24 hours, Britain was preparing an expeditionary force to seize the canal unless Nasser backed down; three days later, France agreed to take part.

The practical problems were immense. By 1956, the British armed forces were overstretched, fighting counter-insurgency campaigns in Malaya, Kenya and Cyprus as well as contributing to the defence of western Europe and policing what remained of the empire. Many of the specialist troops needed for an attack on Egypt – particularly 3rd Commando and 16th Independent Parachute Brigades – were committed to more mundane duties, and the necessary equipment, such as landing craft and troop-carrying aircraft, was in short supply. The French were no better off, facing a war in Algeria which was absorbing a substantial part of their military man-power. In addition, the use of military force was strongly opposed by the superpowers

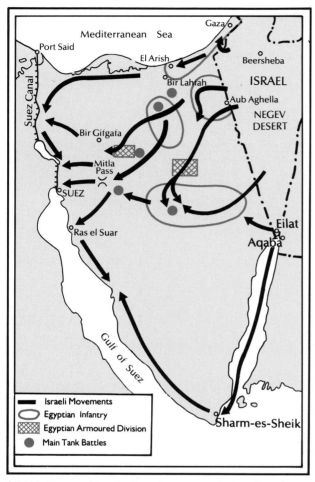

SINAI *After crushing the Egyptian armour, the Israelis took only four days to cross Sinai and reach the Suez Canal.*

Map legend:
- Israeli Movements
- Egyptian Infantry
- Egyptian Armoured Division
- Main Tank Battles

mechanized infantry, artillery and, once the pre-emptive air strikes had been carried out, supported by virtually unopposed airpower. The plan was to attack in the area between Nitzana and the Mediterranean, ignoring southern Sinai, and to concentrate on the seizure of the routes across the desert in the north (El Arish-Qantara) and centre (Abu Aweigila-Ismailia).

The assault began at 0800 on 5 June, when the leading units of Tal's division in the north advanced towards an Egyptian stronghold at Rafah, aiming to isolate the Gaza Strip and then move west, through El Arish, towards the Suez Canal. They encountered tough opposition, particularly around Khan Yunis, and as the tanks slowed under the impact of concentrated artillery fire, hopes of a swift breakthrough evaporated.

A major firefight ensued, in which Israeli close air support and superior gunnery skills gradually gained the day, but it was not until a tank battalion had advanced "regardless of cost" towards Rafah, supported by a parachute battalion which swung west through the desert, that the deadlock was broken. Even then, the advance to El Arish could only be carried out by a single Centurion unit, unrelieved until early on 6 June.

and the United Nations (UN), leading to a lack of clear political directives from the British and French governments, who were uncertain of the consequences of their intended action.

Confused planning

This uncertainty was reflected in the planning for Operation *Musketeer*. Although an expeditionary force was put together, its aims were confused. Initially, the intention was just to seize the canal but, as Nasser's popularity grew in hitherto pro-western Arab states, there was talk of securing his overthrow – an aim that would involve the capture of Alexandria and Cairo. By September, the French had begun to search for an alternative approach and, after contacts with the Israelis, a new plan was put forward. Finalized at a meeting in Paris (22 September–24 September) to which Britain sent representatives, this envisaged an Israeli attack on Sinai, which would pose a threat to the Suez Canal. This would allow Britain and France, as permanent members of the UN Security Council, to demand a ceasefire, which, it was presumed, Nasser would reject. This would trigger Anglo-French air attacks as a prelude to airborne and amphibious landings at Port Said.

The invasion is launched

The Israelis attacked on 29 October and, as expected, Nasser refused to stop fighting. Air strikes began 48 hours later, when Canberra and Valiant bombers hit

Egyptian airfields in the Nile Delta, and the expeditionary force, comprising 45,000 men, 12,000 vehicles and 100 warships, set sail from Malta. On 4 November, air and naval bombardments of Port Said took place; early the following morning, airborne forces landed on the outskirts of the town. To the west, 3rd Battalion, The Parachute Regiment (3 Para) seized Gamil airfield, while to the east, the French 2nd Colonial Parachute Regiment (2 RCP) captured Port Fuad. Both units dug in to await the amphibious assault by the main invasion force.

This began at 0430 on 6 November with tracked landing craft, carrying men of 40 and 42 Commando (Royal Marines), coming ashore. They were joined by 45 Commando, landed by helicopter, and by Centurion tanks of C Squadron, 6th Royal Tank Regiment. Together, they slowly cleared the town, linking up with 3 Para and 2 RCP (the latter now reinforced by Foreign Legion paratroops) by 1200. Delays occurred, as 2 Para, the chosen exploitation unit, had problems in disembarking from their transport ships in Port Said, but, by late evening they were in position ready to push south along the road to Ismailia.

Before this move could be made, however, a ceasefire was suddenly imposed. Under economic and diplomatic pressure, particularly from the USA, Britain and France could not afford to continue the operation, and, although 2 Para probed as far as El Cap, to the south of Port Said, that was the limit of their advance.

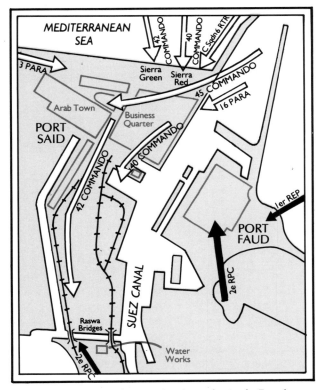

PORT SAID *After preliminary bombing, the Anglo-French assault combined sea-borne landings with paratroop drops.*

SUEZ
YOM KIPPUR WAR
═══6 October 1973 – 7 October 1973═══

The successful crossing of the Suez Canal by Egyptian forces at the beginning of the Yom Kippur War (6–24 October 1973) and subsequent assault on the Israeli positions on the east bank. The crossing, carried out using new techniques and Soviet-supplied equipment, was so swift that the Israelis, caught by surprise, were unable to mount an effective response.

In the years immediately following the Israeli seizure of *Sinai* (June 1967), the chances of Egypt launching a successful campaign to recover her lost territory seemed slim. Both sides of the Suez Canal – now the border between the two countries – were built up, so preventing conventional bridging operations at water level, while the Israelis constructed a system of elaborate fortifications (known as the Bar Lev Line after their Chief of Staff, General Chaim Bar Lev) to dominate Egyptian avenues of approach. Even if a crossing was achieved, the Israeli Air Force (IAF) was available to destroy ferry or bridging sites, while Sinai acted as a useful "buffer" zone, within which armoured attacks, counter-attacks could be contained without damage to Israel itself.

The Egyptians refused to be deterred, however, and searched for solutions to their problems. They found them through the Soviets, who were prepared to provide a range of equipment designed to achieve river crossings, even under heavy defensive fire. Motorized rafts, each able to carry eight main battle tanks, or an equivalent weight of stores, were supplied to Egypt, together with special PMP pontoon bridges, capable of being constructed in less than 30 minutes. At the same time, a sophisticated air-defence system was provided in an effort to negate the IAF; static SA-2 and SA-3 surface-to-air missile (SAMs) were deployed on the west bank, while mobile SA-6s and ZSU-23/4 cannon would accompany the assault force. This meant that IAF sorties would be met by a "brick wall" of defence. Finally, as a counter to the Israeli armour, which could be expected to attack any bridgeheads, Egyptian

infantry were equipped with RPG-7 and AT-3 Sagger anti-tank weapons and trained to move ahead of the main assault units to set up an effective barrier. By 1973, the odds had been evened considerably.

Across the Canal

In its final form, the Egyptian plan was to cross the Suez Canal at a number of points to north and south of the Great Bitter Lake, establishing bridgeheads that would by-pass or neutralize the Bar Lev positions and force the Israelis to fight the kind of attritional battles they could not afford. But problems remained, chiefly as to how best to create approach routes and exits at water level. On the west bank, this was solved by digging away at the sand until only a thin façade (facing the Israelis) remained; this could then be breached quickly by spearhead units. The problem of the east bank was much more difficult to solve, until an Egyptian engineer officer came up with the brilliant solution of using high-pressure hoses to literally blast a way through it.

The attack began at 1400 on 6 October 1973 – the Yom Kippur holiday in Israel. Over 2,000 artillery pieces, together with mortars, rockets and surface-to-surface missiles, bombarded Israeli positions, while Egyptian aircraft struck at targets further afield. Simultaneously, Egyptian commandos, armed with Sagger missiles, scrambled down to the canal, paddled across in rubber boats and then climbed up the Israeli bank before disappearing inland. A second wave followed, deploying to contain or destroy the Bar Lev fortifications, while the bridging operation began. Ferries were in use within an hour; once the hoses had been brought forward, the Egyptian pontoons began to appear. The Israeli defenders were stunned.

Not all the problems had been solved, however. In the south, where Major-General Abdel Muneim Wassel's Third Army was supposed to cross the Great Bitter Lake, Israeli defenders took a heavy toll of the Egyptians' amphibious tanks and helicopters, while attempts to use the hoses on soil, rather than sand, produced nothing but mud. In the north, however, Major-General Saad Mamoun's Second Army met with success. It would take time and hard fighting before the Israelis regained the initiative.

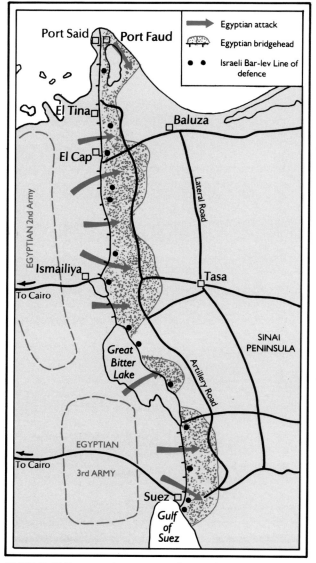

SUEZ *Bold Egyptian thrusts across the canal were intended to break through the Israeli Bar-Lev Line defences.*

TET OFFENSIVE
VIETNAM WAR
30 January 1968 – 25 February 1968

A co-ordinated series of attacks by the North Vietnamese Army and *Viet Cong* (VC) guerrillas against targets throughout South Vietnam. Although they failed to destroy the Saigon government, or to trigger a popular uprising, the attacks had far-reaching effects in the USA, where support for the war declined rapidly.

By mid-1967, the North Vietnamese were beginning to question the effectiveness of their strategy in the war against the south. The North Vietnamese Army (NVA) was finding it difficult to support *Viet Cong* (VC) actions in the villages, as their attempts to infiltrate units into the country were being increasingly blocked by US firepower and mobility. At the same time, however, it was apparent that public support for the war in the USA was on the decline, and that Vietnam was likely to become a major issue in the forthcoming US presidential elections. It was therefore tempting to presume that a concerted attack by NVA and VC units, threatening towns and villages throughout the south, might break the deadlock, forcing US troops away from their positions astride NVA infiltration routes and breaking the morale of politicians in both Saigon and Washington. A popular rising could then be engineered, forcing the USA to withdraw and opening the way for a Communist seizure of power.

It was decided that the attacks should coincide with Tet (the Vietnamese New Year) – a time when, traditionally, little fighting took place – but that they were to be preceded by diversionary operations. In December 1967, therefore, NVA units mounted cross-border incursions south of the DMZ (demilitarized zone) to draw Allied forces away from the towns, and on 21 January 1968 the siege of *Khe Sanh* began. The main Tet offensive was scheduled to start 10 days later, although some VC units in the Central Highlands pre-empted the time by 24 hours. This caused some Allied units to go on to the alert, but most were caught by surprise, when, on 31 January, an estimated 84,000 NVA and VC soldiers attacked five major cities, 36 provincial capitals, 64 district capitals and 50 villages simultaneously throughout the south. Many of the attackers infiltrated through the Allied defences disguised as Tet holidaymakers.

Tet in Saigon

In the early stages, the most dramatic events took place in Saigon, where up to 4,000 Communists seized control of key areas and a special 15-man suicide squad occupied part of the US embassy compound. The Allied response was swift and ruthless, rooting out the VC in operations characterized by a massive use of firepower. This inevitably caused widespread damage and civilian casualties, and, as television coverage of events in Saigon reached the USA, many people began seriously to question the value of US involvement, if it had to be fought with such little regard for the civilian population. The filming of a captured VC guerrilla, hands tightly bound, being shot in the street by a Saigon police chief did little to help.

It took until 5 February for Saigon to be cleared completely, but, by then, the majority of NVA/VC attacks elsewhere had been countered. The only exception was in Hue, the former imperial capital of Annam, where the Communists had infiltrated the Old City. US Marines, stationed at Phu Bai, had been

rushed to the city as soon as the attacks began, but by the time they mounted a counter-attack in early February, the VC were well-established in strong defensive positions. It was to take bitter fighting, involving both American and South Vietnamese troops, before the enemy could be finally ousted from the citadel in the centre of the Old City, where a red, blue and gold VC flag had fluttered provocatively since 31 January. The costs were high – the marines lost 142 killed and 857 wounded in a nightmare of urban battle – but by 25 February Hue had been liberated.

The north had clearly failed in its aim of destroying the Saigon regime and, having suffered an estimated 30,000 losses, the NVA and VC had been badly mauled, but the ramifications in the USA were dramatic. As President Lyndon B. Johnson announced his decision not to stand for re-election and began to search for a negotiated settlement, an atmosphere of war-weariness set in. In this respect, Tet was a turning-point in the fortunes of the Vietnam War.

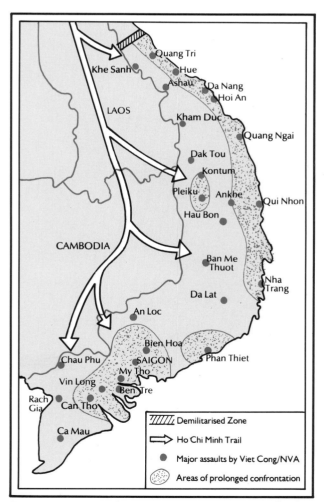

TET OFFENSIVE *This series of major assaults was fuelled by men and supplies moved south down the Ho Chi Minh Trail.*

Index

PICTURE INDEX FOR DICTIONARY
OF BATTLES